MAS   # 30.00

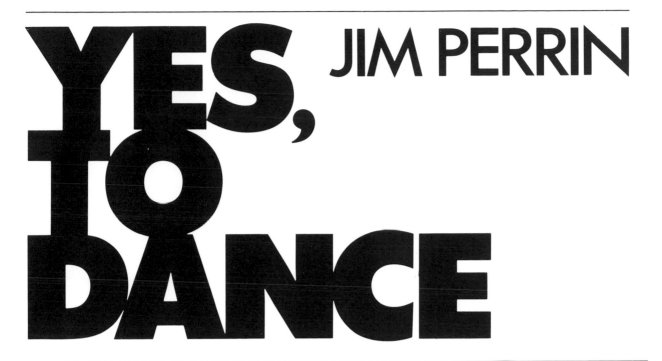

YES, TO DANCE

JIM PERRIN

Essays from Outside the Stockade

The Oxford Illustrated Press

For Sarah

'They had wanted to get to the top of that hill. But no-one of them could do it today.'

'And they felt sad, did they, because they couldn't do what they so wanted to do?' I commented.

'Yes,' Dibs sighed. 'They wanted to. And they tried. But they couldn't quite do it. But they did find their mountain. And they did climb it. Up. Up. Up. Quite a way! And for a while they **thought** *they would get to the top. And while they thought they could, they were happy.'*

'Just trying to get to the top of the hill made them happy?' I asked.

'Yes', Dibs said. 'It's like that with hills. Did you ever climb a hill?'

'Yes. And you, Dibs?' I asked.

'Yes. Once I did. I didn't quite get to the top of it,' he added wistfully. 'But I stood at the bottom of it and looked up. I think every child should have a hill all his own to climb. And I think every child should have one star in the sky that is all his own. And I think every child should have a tree that belongs to him. That's what I **think** *should be,' he added, and he looked at me and nodded with emphasis as he spoke.*

Virginia Axline, *Dibs: In Search of Self*

"In Japan for an international conference on religion, Campbell overheard another American delegate, a social philosopher from New York, say to a Shinto priest, 'We've been now to a good many ceremonies and have seen quite a few of your shrines. But I don't get your ideology. I don't get your theology.'

The Japanese paused as though in deep thought and then slowly shook his head.

'I think we don't have ideology,' he said. 'We don't have theology. We dance.' "

Bill Myers in *Joseph Campbell: The Power of Myth*

ISBN 1 85509 217 4

Published by The Oxford Illustrated Press, Haynes Publishing Group, Sparkford, Nr Yeovil, Somerset BA22 7JJ, England

Printed in England by: J. H. Haynes & Co Limited, Sparkford, Nr Yeovil, Somerset.

British Library Cataloguing in Publication Data:
Perrin, Jim
  Yes, to dance.
  1. Mountaineering
  I. Title
  796.522

ISBN 1-85509-217-4

Library of Congress Catalog Card Number:
90-83284

© 1990, Jim Perrin

All photographs by the author

CONTENTS

CONTENTS

Right: *"Yes, to dance beneath the diamond
sky With one hand waving free . . . "*

For permission to reprint articles, thanks to: Cameron MacNeish, Geo. Outram Magazines, *Climber & Hillwalker* and *Environment Now*; Bernard Newman and *Mountain* magazine; Sebastian Faulks, Robert Winder and *The Independent;* David Twiston-Davies, Hugh Montgomerie-Massingberd and *The Daily Telegraph;* Roger Alton, Christopher Driver and *The Guardian;* Bryn Havord and the North Wales Weekly News Group; John Barnie & *Planet;* Geoff Milburn and *The Climbers' Club Journal; High* magazine; the Royal Geographical Society; the Council for the Protection of Rural Wales; Ken Wilson and Diadem Books; Unwin Hyman & Co.; Thorson's Books. For giving their time and views so freely, thanks to the subjects of these articles. For friendship, support, and helpful critical comment, gratitude to Roger Alton, Al Alvarez, Jan Beatty, John Beatty, Martyn Berry, Gwenllian Bonner-Pritchard, Richard Bonner-Pritchard, Ginger Cain, Bill Condry, Ed Douglas, Jenny Fletcher, Kevin FitzGerald, Fay Godwin, Dave Gregory, Harry Griffin, Malcolm Griffith, Anthony Griffiths, Mike Harrison (to whom thanks also for his foreword), Bryn Havord, Sir Jack Longland, Cameron MacNeish, Gina MacNeish, Ian Mars, Julia Mars, Jean Paira-Pemberton, Doris Perrin, Tom Prentice, Martin Rigby, Medwen Roberts, David Rose, Barbara Sarre, Sue Shaw, Tony Shaw, Dermot Somers; to my editor at Oxford Illustrated Press, Jane Marshall, thanks for her good humour, patience and transcendent laughter; to William Perrin and Thomas Perrin, for humanising the monster; to the gilt-and-plaster Buddha in my room, for his calming presence; to Sarah Gregory, for the enlightenment she brings and her presence in my life; and finally, to everyone who's been to these points in their lives before and tried, in whatever way, to communicate what it's all about—thanks to you all.

Foreword by M. John Harrison

The first time I went climbing, it was with Jim Perrin. I don't mean that he appeared on the doorstep one day with his mother's clothesline over his shoulder and said, "Ay opp lad, we're off to t' crag." But in 1974 a friend bought me Ken Wilson's *Hard Rock*, and two pieces in that classic anthology made it impossible for me not to become a climber. One was by Al Alvarez; the other was Perrin's "Right Unconquerable: a Gritstone Paean":

"Hunching your body fearfully beneath the flake, reaching high and out one-handed, suddenly you go, swinging right up on to the flake on huge layback holds, hooked hands, the crack sometimes closing, occasioning little shuffles rightwards, awkward hand-changes, anxious moments, racing up the flake to where the top layer juts disturbingly, and all the time on your arms, moving fast. If you do the climb at all, you do it quickly. The top is rounded and frightening; you haul yourself over on flat hands in exultation. A race against failing strength and breath, fighting all the way, serious, yet an absolute joy in movement."

All the time on your arms, moving fast!

I was thirty years old and sick of sitting behind a desk. I signed up.

Some years later, bemused by the way climbers had wrong-footed themselves, perhaps a little jaded by the whole activity, I was to be awed and re-energised by the honesty of "Street Illegal", Perrin's infamous account of a cocaine-powered solo in the Cheddar Gorge. Climbing had entered a period of rapid change. The term "rock athlete" was gaining currency. It was no longer enough to climb on crags for personal reasons; from now on you would have to score goals to keep your self respect. You could already hear an eerie echo from the future: the boyz, boasting to one another any Wednesday afternoon at the Mile End Indoor wall . . .

"If you aren't leading E6, you aren't climbing." "If you're using your feet you aren't climbing."

To be climbing, it was no longer enough to be off the ground. In future, it wouldn't be enough to be yourself either: you would have to pretend to be Ben Moon.

"Street Illegal" made a powerful counter-argument to reductivism (not to say posturing) of this kind. Its values were shamanistic rather than sporting. Clearly Jim Perrin saw climbing as a kind of divine idiocy we condemn and revere in the same breath, because it speaks the raw speech of being alive, because out of sheer physicality it can bring back positive psychic goods.

The early Eighties were transitional. Now that we are on the other side of the cusp, and climbing has almost achieved the condition of organised sport, and its inter-nal literature is no longer even marginally interested in the experience itself (only in the tick-lists and score-sheets which can be made to quantify it), the essays collected in *Yes, to Dance* will be even more valuable to us. Jim's insistence on the differences between people—"Warrior Talent", "The Making of a Rebel", "Perception as Therapy"—as opposed to their similarities, compels us to remember how complex we are. His insistence that we always retrieve something worthwhile from the hills—"Touching the Void", "Playpower and the Cosmic Rascal"—focuses our attention not so much on our "adult toy" (Johnny Dawes' term) itself, as why we picked this one—rather than tennis—from the pile on offer. His often raw impatience and anger at the way the experience is limited for us—"Forbidden Land"—or the way we limit it for each other—"Better Out than In"—make this collection not just alive (as opposed to "lively") but powerfully engaged. I don't think Jim can be bothered with anything less than vital issues. As a result, everything he touches flares into high relief, even a book review. He just won't *let* things be banal . . .

Commerce abhors a vacuum. AU COEUR DE LA GRIMPE, goes the slogan of a French equipment manufacturer. Climbers continue to abdicate the heart of the climb, in pursuit of some notion of healthy, value-free athletics. Commercial interests fill it with brightly coloured items for us to buy, emptying it of the very things we originally sought there. Most climbing writers, even the younger ones, are content to be published as filler between one advertisement for pink friction boots and the next. Meanwhile other lobbies and vested interests multiply: physical educationists—and their insurance companies—want climbing to present itself as safe, character-building; the TV companies must have something a little snappier before really committing themselves; professionals need a proper, AAA sport, complete with rules and governing bodies; while governing bodies are, as ever, concerned to expand their areas of influence and take more power to themselves.

Curiously enough, given this climate of politics and abject consumerism, climbers and hillwalkers still often think of themselves as special; beyond the pale; having goals more valuable than those of everyday life.

But it's another edifice, perhaps, that Jim's subtitle refers to: the stockade of rehearsed controversies, dreary old oppositions and bad rhetoric which defends the interests of the climbing "village" against the individual experiences which might call its collective values into question. It's this fence Jim writes from outside, as a concerned, compassionate, moral, but above all individual human being.

When he and I finally got to climb together, in 1987, it was me who appeared on his doorstep with the clothesline. We went to Bwlch y Moch. I was so nervous to be on the crag with a hero of mine—and everything he represented—that I tried all day to fulfil the expectations I was sure he would have of me: the expectations of the village. So I fumbled, and made daft mistakes, and I hated every minute of it. When I admitted this, at the end of the day on the belay ledge of The Plum, Jim gave one of his gnomic, slew-eyed grins. (Odin, the Elder Edda tells us, bargained an eye for a drink at the well of wisdom.) He stared out across the estuary as if he was looking for something he knew was there but which was hard to locate in the clinging, greyish twilight.

"It's your climb, Mike," he advised me finally. "Why give a toss who climbed it yesterday?" And then: "Come on. I'll show you a boulder problem Peter Crew couldn't do, and I bet you can."

I think this is the message from outside the stockade. It isn't enough to be a villager. It's your climb. It's your walk. It's your hill. Take it back and enjoy it.

INTRODUCTION

Yes, to Dance by Jim Perrin

Most Sunday evenings of my youth, after a day's or weekend's climbing on Stanage or another of the Peak District's gritstone outcrops, with aching limbs and raw knuckles I stood on the Manchester platform at Hathersage station, waiting for the train, bantering with the Sheffield-bound climbers on the other side of the tracks before they entrained for their different destinations. It seems at times an apt image for these essays. We all view things from differing social, cultural and personal contexts; we are all on different sides of one set or another of divergent tracks. And the pieces collected in this volume are a form of banter or more or less friendly connection across that distance, and a way of making use of the moments—of opportunity, of attentiveness—when communication across the tracks is possible. They are selected from amongst a body of work produced in the main over the last five years (though a few items go back a little earlier) for a wide range of publications, from national daily newspapers through the outdoor press to small political reviews. Together they form a sequel to, and a development out of, my earlier collection of essays, *On and Off the Rocks* (Gollancz, 1986).

Like the essays in that volume, they chiefly concern themselves with a general response to our outdoor environment and matters which impinge upon it, often seizing on the particular activity of rock-climbing as an entry into their theme. If they restricted themselves to simple description or exposition of that sport, their range would be insufferably narrow. Rock-climbing is tangential to them; it is a pleasurable pastime, an obsession for some people, a point of connection or a symbolic dimension. The purpose of these essays lies elsewhere. They do not, I hope, ignore the potential even in climbing for the celebratory, but they set out to reflect widely differing personal preoccupations.

Many of them take personalities as their ostensible subject, and attempt to harness the intrinsic interest of the anecdotal to the exemplary. I have wanted to preserve all of them from the oblivion of the ephemera in which they were first published. Things born of effort and belief, and serving the end of dialogue, of letting others know how one person, in his vulnerability, prejudice, and occasional insight, might feel about condition, circumstance and chance meeting in his life, may help to broaden human understanding and thus deserve a better fate than that. Their commitment is to the "open word from a simple man", the "one single distinct word" which, in Brecht's poem on "The Anxieties of the Regime", causes the fortress of Tar the Assyrian to fall to dust. We can allow that to happen to most of the fortresses with which we—or the authorities which set themselves over us—surround ourselves, but the lesson is painful in the learning. In furtherance of that aim, let me tell you something of the process by which, in my case, this habit of writing, questioning, commenting has come about.

Essayists, whose form has fallen from fashion, unlike poets or novelists are seldom called upon for explanation, and can be thankful for that liberty. They hide, disclaim, as when Hazlitt, writing to his son, directs that we should ". . . not begin to quarrel with the world too soon: for, bad as it may be, it is the best we have to live in—here. If railing would have made it better, it would have been reformed long ago: but as this is not to be hoped for at present, the best way is to slide through it as contentedly and innocently as we may."

This wasn't the code he lived by, and nor do I. Every essayist—unless given over to the abject collusions of propagandism—quarrels with the world he or she inhabits, proposes new models, observes in protean subjectivity. As Abraham Maslow pleads, we should never adopt the pretence of being invisible and uninvolved spectators. That, after all, "means looking at something that is not you, not human, not personal, something independent of you the perceiver. You the observer are then really alien to it, uncomprehending and without sympathy or identification . . . peering, peeping, from a distance, from outside, not as one who has a right to be in the room being peeped into."

What point in entering that room, though, if we still wear the uniform of habituation? If we could but preserve that strangeness of normality, normality of strangeness, which is the province of uncorrupted childhood, how much more closely as human beings we would connect: " . . . the first step for a mind overwhelmed by the strangeness of things is to realize that this feeling of strangeness is shared with all men and that the entire human race suffers from the division between itself and the rest of the world."

Thus Camus, building up in *The Rebel* to his grand taunt that "Rebellion is the common ground on which every man bases his first values. I *rebel* therefore we *exist*". He is right, and the events of our century insist that the unconditional, impercipient Yes which an unquestioning desire to belong, to be acceptable, to be approved of by one's peers entails should no longer be an option. To be open to the strangeness of life necessitates a readiness to have the charge of strangeness levelled against oneself.

This text—*The Rebel*—I did not read until I was fifteen, by which time my grandmother and grandfather, who brought me up for most of the first years of my life and from whom (in retrospect and in the laying-down of a referential substratum as much as in that far-off present) I learned my first values, were dead.

They lived in a neat terraced house of shiny red brick with a sanded doorstep and a park at the bottom of the road—Mabfield Road, Fallowfield, Manchester—number 34. I was born there, in the front room upstairs at the end of March in the frozen winter of 1947. My grandparents were both in their seventies; a neighbour, out of kindness, brought round a bag of coal.

I hardly remember my parents being in that house, though I suppose at times they must have been. What I do recall is sitting on my grandfather's knee, listening to his stories:

My grandfather? He had a ballerina
Tattooed on his arm, faintly, in a green
The colour of copper with a patina
Of verdigris. There were books in that clean
Back room of his—a Bible, *Pilgrim's Progress*
(Though when, in a late year, television
Entered his house, my nan could not undress,
By his command, lest from their side the screen
Those watched watchers should see her nakedness).
This gaunt old man, blue-temple-veined and lean,
Stood, so he claimed, for no nonsense,
Fought in the Boer War, besieged Mafeking.
Death ran him a kind race, at the last forbore
(As he would have done) to boast itself victor.

Credulous though he may have been in the matter of television, from him I learned to read—from those same two volumes which, together with *Pear's Cyclopaedia* and a yearly copy of *Old Moore's Almanack* were the extent of his library—and by the age of three or four was stumbling through the Slough of Despond, Vanity Fair or the simpler passages from his favourite Books of Matthew, Exodus and Isaiah. His eccentric education of me was a boon which informs whatever I have become. I was intimidated by him, awed by him, hypnotised by him. But my grandmother I loved entirely:

Gertrude Charlesworth could charm warts, tell fortunes,
Palms and tea-leaves her magical domain.
To amuse me on afternoons of rain
She made predictions, sang them to old tunes,
Laughing and grave. On Fridays she baked bread.
For me, her grandson, the honeyed gold crust
Was her gift, came hot-dripping with her lust
For a better world than that which bowed her head
And judged her ignorant, who could not read
Words or write but was wise. It's her merit
Is the best part of all I inherit,
Her instinctive goodness is my best lead,
And to appease her spirit I have fled
Grim exiled corridors where she last bled.

These two old people connected me back, through their stories and reminiscences the memory of which outcrops frequently into my more abstract adult consciousness, to the culture, values and beliefs of the pre-urban world of farm labour in Cheshire and on the Welsh Border in which they had grown up. My parents, from the age of six, periodically took me away from their old-fashioned influence as they struggled to set up temporary homes: at number 34, Erskine Street, Hulme—a dark, cobbled street in the first of the Manchester slums to be cleared in the re-development of the fifties. I remember the smell of its crumbling brick, the damp rosettes on the wall, the smallness of the room my sister and I shared. I remember my cousin Glyn fighting with a bigger boy on the flat back of a burnt-out lorry on a bombed site at the end of the street, his face bloody; and myself jumping up, hanging on to the other boy's legs, being kicked in the mouth for interfering. (In the behaviour of small boys and its context, the world reflects; on our individual histories, the history of nations rebounds.)

Another place we lived briefly was Harrogate. Through ill-health—from lead in the paint—my father had retired from his trade as journeyman decorator, and taken a job as caretaker to an office block there. In the garden, he taught me cricket and rugby, taught me to box. Before the war he had played rugby league for Salford, had been a physical training instructor in the army, had been one of the first to arrive at the concentration camps. At St. Peter's Church primary school in Harrogate, a master called Bainbridge with a hard, red face beat me on the leg with a ruler in front of the class because my accent, when reading the Bible, was 'common'. It was a middle-class town.

In spring and early summer, there were frogs in the pond in Crimple Woods; I caught great crested newts, watched birds; the sharp, dry bracken at Birk Crag each autumn could cut your finger to the bone.

My parents could not afford the cost of living in Harrogate, and by the time I was ten we were back in Manchester. I went, unexpectedly, to grammar school and lost an eye. When I came back to school after a year mostly of operations and hospitals, my dear, kind, well-meaning headmaster, universally referred to as Sam Hughes, took me back into my form and introduced me: "Here's Perrin, boys, come back to school. His left eye's been removed, but which of you could tell the difference?"

My grandparents were in their eighties, and my mother had them moved to a council flat in Gorton, on a windy croft between the main road and the railway. Within the year they were dead. In pilgrimage, at the age of twelve I walked the twenty-or-so miles along the main road, the A34, to Congleton, whence they had come in the agricultural depression following the Great War, to visit my grandmother's sister. I had broken free of the town, and the soft, swelling green of the Cheshire landscape entranced and nurtured me. By Redesmere, sitting on the bank above the grey lap of its March waters, I first encountered the stillness and suspension, the "power of harmony and the deep power of joy" which is central to the mystical experience.

My uncle, Jack Charlesworth, a small farmer on Mow Cop, drove me to Macclesfield that night and put me on a train home. This day was the gate through which I danced out into a desire to remain amongst the normality of strangeness which hedges and borders the ways in which I've spent my life.

Why am I telling you this? Is it, in Blake's phrase, "To cast off the rotten rags of memory by inspiration"? Because this childhood *was* an inspiration to me, then and subsequently. Its *texture* was so rich. Even its negatives—rejection, isolation, insecurity, injury, difference—feed in to the tenuous, painful equilibrium of adult perception, and connect back to the human condition, the "feeling of strangeness . . . shared by all men". The difficulty which bars our way to that vital connection lies in disclosing, in admitting vulnerability and the desire to share and love and care in a society that, this last decade most stridently, has marched in a different step. But once the prisoner has escaped and found an individual rhythm, he or she, in gratitude or isolation, must keep on travelling.

I was just twelve when I walked to Congleton. There

"The more I see of humanity, the more I love my dog." (I think Frederick the Great said that . . .) Photo John Beatty

after, I left the city on every occasion I could, walked into Derbyshire and Wales, before my thirteenth birthday had climbed my first rocks. Books and rocks were the companions and teachers, the dancing masters of my childhood and youth. The first true rock climb I ever led, shortly before my thirteenth birthday, was the Slab Climb on Wimberry Rocks, in the Chew Valley above Greenfield. Its holds felt tiny, the risk immense, but in its course I came into possession of my body:

"What need have you to dread
The monstrous crying of wind?"

The discipline of the dance had begun to exert a hold which, thirty years on, not for a moment can I regret. Along with the discipline, and as significant, comes the companionship. Few children climb, and I was still a child. Fortunate in the agile physique inherited from my father, I trained to build up its strength. We lived by now in Albert Square, Manchester, where he was caretaker of an office block. In the darkness, after hours, seven floors up, I climbed up and down the underside of a fire escape each night and let my legs swing free a hundred feet above the paving stones. The physically enabling can become the mentally so; every weekend away, with companions older than myself, talking, arguing. Rock-climbing then was a fearful risk, a self-preserving, cautious disrespect whose devotees owned no authority. That attitude inculcated, supported and developed in all spheres through the arguments of friends, you learn thus the steps of the dancing mind, which circles empty boasts but helps and coaxes on the novice honesty.

Had I not discovered—and at the time, in the stage of its development, in the circumstances I did—the climb and its alienating Yes, the quest and solace of the dangerous lead, the systems and strictures of society which I have, or by which I have been, for much of my life disowned might more deeply have bothered me. As it is, after the climb and its many dimensions, if place, residual energy and circumstance allow, the instinct is to dance. Listen to Yeats:

"Sixty years old, man and boy,
And never once have I danced for joy."

To go for days without doing so, as sometimes I do,

Welsh right-of-way 1990—problems for William Perrin's generation.

feels tragedy enough. If we have no joy in our lives! A rainbow over slated city roofs; understanding contact with my sons; cartwheels along the sand; the release of having said what's right; the peace my sleeping lover brings, her soft-curled hair against my breast and thigh. For all his fine posturing, I would not have been Yeats for anything.

Why do I write? Not out of choice, but from the necessity to set out these resonant contexts that they should not be lost. My boy comes to me and tells me his experience. I listen, attentively, for he takes me to his realities, to contact with our fears and fantasies: more so than a thousand speakers of the jargon self-interest. Knowledge spanning generations unfolds patterns, helps towards wisdom. My father's father—dead years before my birth—witnessed (and his testimony came down to me) the Christmas Day truce of 1914, the football, the fraternisation between the lines. Then the officers ordered the men back into their trenches on pain of being shot. In our humanity, should we not all disown our officers and fraternise between the lines? The tendrils of connection bind me in to the conscience of a century which has seen trench-slaughter, the concentration camps, the atomic and conventional bombing of civilians, the principle of mutually assured destruction, desecration of the environment and the heedless, burgeoning obscenities of exploitation associated with international movement of capital. These activities of the—predominantly male—officer-class depend for their continuance on the ignorant, fearful complicity of those in the little worlds of credulous humanity I would like to think that I write in order to introduce even in the limited subject areas with which I deal—an appropriate scepticism, a different set of beliefs, a needful disrespect; in order to liberate those who choose to listen from various fears; particularly through disclosing my own fears, prejudices, delights. I can neither believe in nor accept any power other than that of communication, of voicing the word in which the spirit of honesty resides. Brecht's poem, "The Anxieties of the Regime", again says it best:

". . . the brownshirts themselves
Fear the man whose arm doesn't fly up
And are terrified of the man who
Wishes them a good morning.
The shrill voices of those who give orders
Are full of fear like the squeaking of
Piglets awaiting the butcher's knife, as their fat arses
Sweat with anxiety in their office chairs."

The solitary dance on rock which exorcises fear; the elaborate, ritualistic dance of loving partners—which exorcises loneliness and fear; the springing, quick-footed dance which keeps individual witness within the oppressions of social, political and peer-group expectations; in none of these does power overtly conquer and control; but it needs, controlled itself, to bear its own testimony, to attempt to understand.

Some things now are finer by far than in the time in which I grew up; grew out, in fact, of the questioning, the rebelliousness, the intelligent dialogue of that time. Best and most resonant of all is the balanced discourse and understanding between man and woman which the women's movement has brought about. In the macho world of rock-climbing at the time I performed well in that sport, this had no part. We were all—men and women—unreconstructed then, our values incompatible, or perverted by spurious needs. If that could corrupt the personal lives of generations, it can do so still. I have been wrong about many things in my time, no doubt am still so now, but in these following essays are some of the stances at which I have arrived, some of the dancing steps enacted along the way. I hope they are more than just essays about subjects connected with the outdoors. Through honest representation, exploration of context, even sometime confusion, they may assist others, as Gramsci wrote, to "turn and face violently things as they really are." To look, to question, to reject, to affirm, to bear witness—these are important to me. And to keep on, to understand, to celebrate, empower, support, avoid, taunt, laugh, delightedly to wheel about.

And to dance, yes, to dance . . . .

Which is, physically, symbolically, intellectually, the ultimate affirmation. And may even, here and there, in the minds of those who observe, go beyond mere mental grasp and make glad.

1: KEEPING COMPANY

On a Kerry cliff-top with friends from a civilised nation.

On the Rock with Joe Brown
Climber and Hillwalker, 1990

Joe Brown masticating.

Because my thoughts of late have been running on television programmes, I'll tell you about a visual image I have. It's of looking back along a narrow, dark tunnel of a cave. There are waves roaring through under my feet and I am clinging on to a slimy, rounded boulder in the blackness, blood trickling down my shins from grazes sustained in my haste to get through. Over my shoulder, behind me, against the light, methodically, rhythmically, arms akimbo, legs bridged out at right angles, a small figure scuttles after, a terrible efficiency in his movement. As he gets nearer, I see tombstone teeth bared in laughter . . .

No, it's not a nightmare, nor anything of the sort—though this particular experience could easily have become one. It's just a scene from an adventure with Joe Brown, and the salient point is the laughter, which is never far from his face.

At my age you shouldn't have heroes or heroines, so I try very hard to avoid letting anyone attain that status in my mind. But I have a sneaking suspicion that if I were forced to the point, if someone insisted that I regress, then I might grudgingly have to admit that this little silver-haired grin of a wrestler on his two bandy legs is as close as you could get. And it's not entirely because of his climbing.

I was thinking about this a few weeks ago whilst working on my Whillans book. It was a sunny after-

noon. I'd swivelled my chair away from my desk and was watching the tom-cats yowl about in the Liverpool back alley where I live. There was one which reminded me of John Barry—neat, pugnacious and preening itself; an elegant, languid specimen stretching in the sun on a shed roof was perfect for Martin Boysen, whilst a dirty-grey hustler with a shifty expression looked like a magazine editor I know.

What struck me, from these observations, was how far we rely on analogy as the starting point in our explorations of people. My take-off point with Whillans, for example, was a scurrilous hint Dennis Gray once gave me, which had me giggling for weeks at its cheeky appositeness:

"Of course, you do know Don's character changed totally on the day the first Andy Capp cartoon appeared . . ."

For Brown, no such comparisons—he is more perfectly of himself than anyone else I know, with a unique and individual presence which to me is both endearing and fascinating. More of this as we go on. There's some business—whether nostalgically or abreactively—to be got out of the way first.

No-one who was a young climber in Manchester at the end of the fifties and beginning of the sixties could help but be in awe of this man. I can remember the reverence with which what were supposed to be the scratches from his nailed boots on Blue Lights Crack and Freddie's Finale at Wimberry were pointed out to me. There was the aura which hung around his routes, the triumph and kudos which resulted from getting up even the easiest of them—his lines were the A-level Syllabus of my climbing youth. And I knew their author, saw him climbing on grit in his prime, often stayed weekends in the same hut—belonging to the Cromlech Club in Nant Peris—as he did. I bouldered with him, wrestled with him, made his tea, pinched his food, bantered with him, and he was even climbing nearby when I took my first big fall—90ft off The Fang (one of his then-quite-recent new routes) at Tremadog in the rain, as he more sensibly splashed up Striptease alongside.

He roped down to see if I was alright, chided me about the way I was tied on, put his arm round me and told me, "Never mind—it 'appens to the best of us". And the joke and the grin and the support were what I needed, because at home my father was dying terribly of cancer. Somehow Joe was lined in. There were the similarities of our poor Manchester Catholic upbringings. There was a picture in the old Cwm Idwal guide of Joe on Suicide Wall which I had shown to my father.

He'd said, "You'll never do that—you've only got one eye!" And though I did, it was not in time, for in his last weeks his body was rotting and his mind quite gone. These dark tunnels through which our lives sometimes lead are only lit by spontaneous and intuitive acts of kindness—an arm round your shoulder at the right time—which reveal more of a character's depth and attentiveness than any protestation.

I called in to see Joe the other day, at his home in Llanberis. He had just got a new video—a very old one actually, of himself climbing in the 1950s. Jack Longland was narrating it. There was a sequence of Joe climbing a route in, I think, Ilkley Quarry—a black-haired youth of twenty or so drifting with the most graceful and fluid economy up VS rock. It was breathtakingly beautiful, and the silver-haired 60-year-old grandfather on my right was regarding the image with a soft smile and an almost imperceptible shake of the head.

We chatted away, then looked back at the screen. There was the actual picture from the old Idwal guide, but animated now, the rope moving as the relaxed figure eased upwards on the grainy, grey film. I'd come to talk with Joe about his appearing in a series I was presenting for HTV. The frames edited themselves into my television state of mind. I had to do the route with him.

We made the arrangements. I heard on the grapevine that he'd been out practising the route. I was glued to my desk and the green screen, so muttered imprecations about what a competitive little bugger he still is and contented myself with a day's training on the Cyfrwy Arete (Route of the Year, 1888), trying not to worry too much about the disparity in standard between it and Suicide Wall. The last time I'd done the latter route had been twelve years ago, when I'd guided Roger Alton up it on a wet day. It had seemed quite hard and I was fit then. I thought of following Joe's example and going out for a rehearsal the night before we filmed it, but in the event was too tired or lazy or both. Also, the likelihood was that in that subtle way of his Joe would jockey for the lead, so all I needed to do was play the inept straight man role. Therefore the less competent I was, the better for television it would be, I argued.

"When did you first do Suicide Wall, Joe?"

We were walking up the Idwal path, Joe exulting in the tactic of a short-cut which had put us ahead of the producer and the film crew.

"I think it was in 1948 . . ."

(Joe claims to have a very bad memory, and always introduces an element of vagueness into his accounts. When I accuse him of having a selectively bad memory,

it's a charge he vigorously denies.)

". . . it was the same time as that early attempt on Cenotaph Corner when I dropped the peg-hammer on Wilf White's head. I'd been climbing for about a year at the time but I didn't find it too bad. I did it again after I came out of the army, which would be in about 1951. We'd been climbing in the Carnedds but were rained off—it was a terrible day—so we came back to the chapel where we were staying, brewed up, and I remember making some little slings out of line, cutting them up. They all blew off in the gale, and the only protection I had was when I clipped a downward-pointing peg. When Pete White, who was seconding, came up he fell off, swung across, and just the lateral tension pulled the peg out."

"What sort of status did the route have for you then?"

"It was the route to do. It was the hardest thing in Wales at the time."

People who dismiss Brown—and I have heard this actually said—as a cheating old has-been, should consider carefully that account, and consider it not on the strength of perhaps having made an ascent of Suicide Wall in their sticky rock-slippers with micro-nut protection on a sunny day, but relative to the plateau of climbing achievement in 1951. Contexts, which are the stuff of history, are so quickly forgotten. The only comment I'd make is that I've seen this man climbing in his prime, and know him to be one of the masters.

We started talking about climbing on wet rock, how it felt at times like climbing on very loose rock, how it changed your perception of apparently ordinary routes. I reminded him of his second ascent of East Gully Grooves Direct Start—thought at the time to be one of the two hardest pitches on Cloggy—on a day of torrential rain in the early sixties. He and John Cheesmond had arrived in the Cromlech hut, their black Gannex waterproofs streaming on to the floor and Cheesmond's eyes contra-rotating behind his glasses in delayed shock, to announce what they'd done and had been greeted with stony disbelief. Acts of provocation against people's received ideas were always Joe's stock-in-trade.

"I'll tell you a route to do in the rain . . ."

"Since you're making a point of it, I'll make sure I keep away from it, but what is it anyway?"

"It's that route of J.M. Edwards' on Gallt yr Ogof—Chalkren Stairs. And the hardest pitch is the crack right at the top. You'd think with it being a crack it would be alright. It's absolutely desperate."

"Harder than Pedestal or Chimney Route or Fallen

Suicide Wall: Al Hughes filming "echoes of that rock-mastery which was his".

The crux of Suicide Wall—old, bald heads forgetful of its sins.

Block Crack? They're all terminal when they're wet."

"No, they're not . . ."

The Brown denial! It's very rare to be in his company for more than a few minutes without being issued with a flat rebuttal of your views, a succinct rubbishing of what you've said, the whole point of which is to provoke you into arguing them out, defending them, coming out and playing with him in the province of words. He is as happily combative as anyone you'll ever meet. I let him get away with this one because he'd switched into conversational overdrive and was gabbing away about being a stunt man on *The Mission,* standing in for Jeremy Irons: "But he's twice your height, Joe . . ." "I know—they had to make sure there was never anyone else in the same frame."

"What's up with you today? You're rattling away as though you're on drugs or something."

"It's because I'm nervous. I'm always like this before I have to talk in front of cameras."

We'd reached the foot of the climb and I was chaffing him about having come out to practise it beforehand, suggesting that he was protecting his image. Dignity offended, he explained that he was simply adopting a professional attitude towards the job, asked how it would look if—having gone to all the trouble of getting a film-crew out—he failed to get up the route?

"Oh good!" I teased back. "That must mean that you're intending to lead it?"

He gave me a good-humoured look with a sly edge to it, as he always does when he's been detected in his manoeuvrings. Then he prepared himself for the climb.

In his preparations you get the first insight into his climbing. The organisation is meticulous. The full body harness goes on first. Then he considers his gear, assesses it against the route, distributes it carefully. You can almost hear the thought processes at work: 'I'll have this hand free on that move so I'll clip that on there . . .' Finally, the helmet is clamped on and carefully adjusted, and with a big smile that tells you this is why he's survived through 43 years as a climber, he's ready to go.

He's been telling me that the way to protect the first 20ft, which are the crux of Suicide Wall, is for the second to climb up, place a tape on a tiny spike at 20ft which would come off if simply used as a runner, and climb back down to belay on it. The second can then keep it on by tension and the leader can use it as a runner. The logic of this does not escape me, so whilst he's been getting ready I avoid the ploy by climbing up and pointing out to him a perfectly good place for an RP at shoulder level as you begin the crux moves. Detected, he gives me the sly look again, goes to inspect what I'm offering and looks very happy about it. Climbing with Joe requires that you have your wits about you.

The moves start from a sloping ledge a little way up the wall, which Joe stands on to give his boots a cursory wipe. At the bottom he's been castigating me for wearing a pair of Tao shoes without socks, asking me why I bother putting up with the cold and discomfort. I tell him they're neither but he doesn't believe me. He himself has pulled on a pair of thick socks and a dreadful old pair of something-or-others which look Chaplinesquely too big and which he protests are exceedingly comfortable. The first moves are delicate, on little friction holds and pockets and he asks me to guide his feet on to them. I tell him where they are. It's not entirely a tidy performance on his part, but then the perverse old bugger is climbing in the first cousins to a pair of galoshes. I needle him about it:

"Bit ragged, that, Joe—but I suppose it's not bad for a sixty-year-old . . ."

"I'm not sixty yet!"

He sounds hurt.

"Alright then—not bad for someone in his sixtieth year."

He continues up the pitch. Al Hughes, the cameraman, is filming us from the foot and from one side so the conversation on our radio-mikes is rather literal and informative: about Joe's early ascent, about the route's history, the top-roped ascents by Hicks and Kirkus, the first lead by Chris Preston in 1945.

Joe, meanwhile, is progressing steadily and I watch in rapt admiration the echoes of that rock-mastery which was his—the neatness of organisation, the innate rock-sense, the instinctive accommodation of bodily position to the features of the route, the ingenuity of the moves he creates, the relaxation and unfussiness of it all. It is a bleak, grey day now, with a spit of rain in the cold wind, but the forces of memory and continuing desire that are gathered here warm me through and through. When it's my turn to climb, I do it almost in a dream; my feet subtle in the pockets or caressed by the rough rock; the tiny flakes pricking at my finger-ends; thought, action and emotion in the sweetest coalescence. The route is a gradeless joy, a renewed acquaintance with whom to share experience, an entity and a piece of history. I feel so pleased to be doing it with this man who is himself—though he would never accept it as being thus—the great liberating chapter in climbing's history.

At the top we embrace and bash each other about in a friendly, fooling manner. I remember coming out of the top of a route in Pembroke the approach to which is what was described in the first paragraph, to find him with his feet down two rabbit-holes and with no belay, the rope running through his hands. Then he pulled me down on top of him and cuffed me severely. I remind him of it.

"That was because it was the loosest route I'd ever done, and you said it would be sound, you daft bugger!"

He gives me a few more sharp thumps to the shoulder to drive the point home, and then we abseil down to do the route once more, with Al Hughes filming from a rope to one side now. This time Joe is warmed up and move-perfect. Watching him, I remember a description I'd once read of Maria Callas giving a master-class at the end of her life, the sustained glories of her voice gone as she coaxed her students through—except that here and there, briefly, a ghost-echo of such rich splendour rose as to make every other sound seem utterly mundane. The analogy is near-perfect. Here he is, on what's no more than an E2, 5c route half as old as the century, but in the way he climbs it there are intimations, nuances, memories which, to anyone who witnessed its flowering, still speak of one of the glories.

At the top we talked—or rather Joe talked and occasionally I questioned or prompted—for half-an-hour, shivering in the cold gusts which were swirling around Idwal and quartering and patterning across the grey lake-waters. You'll hear it all in time. For now, there he is again, fixed firmly in my memory—this warm-hearted, brave, practical, funny little silver-haired grandfather on the sofa in front of his television, watching the perfection of decades before with a smile on his face as though he held the shell of that ability to his ear and it was softly whispering to him, "Ah, Joe, Joe, Joe— you were the nonpareil . . ."

A Vast Warrior Talent: Stevie Haston
Climber, 1987

Stevie Haston.

Here's an exercise for you. Go up to any climber operative to a high standard in North Wales and ask them who they respect most amongst the top performers on rock. They'll trot out a couple of names without thinking, by way of automatic responses: John Redhead, Johnny Dawes. They'll gesture towards the younger generation: Paul Pritchard, Trevor Hodgson. And then, with absolute predictability, they'll give you one of those amused, knowing looks which say, "But you and I both know the real name" and then they'll come out with it—a nod of the head, an unarguable finality:

"Stevie Haston!"

A shake of the head, an exhalation of breath, and we draw back from realms we don't even want to think about. Sight leads on South Stack's Yellow Wall, 6c moves with minimal protection on snappy dinks . . .

In Pete's Eats I await my fate. The rain falls on grey Llanberis streets which have been to climbers for twenty-five years a sort of home. Stevie's late, arrives hung over, depressed, moody as quicksilver in a weatherglass (watch what happens when the pressure gets high). We drink tea. He has just become thirty.

"I never expected to get there, you know . . ."

"Nor did anyone else, Stevie. Still, never mind—forty's worse. Your body's starting to fall apart at that age."

Sensing that this role of Job's comforter may bear

dangerous fruit later in the day, I hedge, argue consolations. He merely grimaces.

"It's too late to go to Anglesey."

He says it flatly, tone of voice in keeping with his general demeanour. I'm unsure whether to lament the lost adventure or feel relief.

"We'll go to Tremadog."

Ah, well—the mundane has its place alongside the marvellous. Another tea or two and we set off up to his house to collect his gear. Pinned to his wardrobe door is a newspaper cutting.

"Read that."

It's an obituary cut out of the *Daily Telegraph*. I start jawing on about the surprising quality of *Telegraph* obituaries these days, how much better they are than those in *The Times* or *The Independent*.

"Shut up and read it—it's background," he chides.

It's of an Edinburgh communist and union leader, name of Haston.

"My uncle!"

He chuckles at the irony of a good Scottish Marxist-Leninist developing the taste for fine food and wine mentioned in his death notice. In the car on the way round to Tremadog he fills out his own picture; father a physically tough and politically aware Scot settled in the East End, mother Maltese. Summers spent in native freedom with Catholic peasant relations on that island. The working-class kid winning his way to an exclusive London grammar school—and rebelling, eventually being expelled for thumping his headmaster. Then there was the climbing! Stir all the ingredients around and up rises the heady, sour-sweet scent of rebellion, alienation, of existential *angst:*

"This world, man, look at it! I climb because it makes me feel real."

You think about the nicknames, the role-playing, the masks behind which *someone* hides: Pengo, the Creature, the Wildebeeste. And next to you this extraordinary young man, falcon-featured, all clean vision and sad play whirling around a vortex, an immense warrior-talent skulking, half-amused, half-desirous of nothing beyond sensual ease, in a black pavilion where, among the banners, flutter suspicion and despair. He talks Alps:

"After that experience on the Eiger with Victor (Saunders) I got not to like climbing with someone else. I could do things by myself at least twice as fast. I did the Walker in a day, up and I'd have got down as well except a storm came in at the top. I soloed four EDs in four days, and going up late on the fifth day to do another, Roger Baxter-Jones gave me a lift. 'You can't

do that!' he told me, 'The seracs'll be coming down.' But I didn't care. I did it."

"And all the time there was one building up, cracking away, with RBJ's name on it?"

"Yeah—him, not me!"

He turns his right hand over, palm outspread, shakes his head gently. We arrive at the crag in a thin rain as Stevie castigates the bolt men, the sport-climbers.

"Red-point, French ethics, it's no good. It's just learning it, not feeling your way through. It's all body, no soul."

"Easy enough to learn a text, but could you have written the poem?"

"Just that."

Now we come to the choice of route and he's laughing.

"D'you know what I want to do?"

We've gone to the far end of Craig Bwlch y Moch, to beneath a nondescript Severe called Yogi. The wind squirts a fine spray of drizzle across our line of sight. I'm thinking it's all a bit bizarre, but the rules are that Stevie gets to choose.

"What?"

"That!"

He points out two thin, thin cracks just out of a grassy corner on a facet wall.

"There—it's a 20-ft route!"

I assume he's simply being mischievous, but no, he's serious.

"What is it?"

"It's a route of Andy Pollitt's and John Redhead's. It's called Sheer Resist. There's a block come out of it and I don't think it's been done since."

He's just been haranguing me about various members of the climbing community's obsession with grades and ticks, so I don't ask him how hard it is. Actually I don't need to—you can tell by looking. We scramble up the first arete of Yogi and across left to nestle on daisy ledges beneath the line. Mr Mischievous Haston's 20ft is a bit more than that—40ft perhaps. On gritstone it would definitely be a collector's piece, a hard little gem. But I'm in Wales with the man who does not collect, the chief exponent of the big adventure, wasted though he may be feeling today, I pinch myself to make sure I'm experiencing things right. Stevie uncoils a rope, I another, and they clot together amongst the vegetation and collapsing grass. He sets off.

Ten feet above me he turns to bridge, facing outwards, across the corner. Deliberately and conscientiously he cleans his boots, strips off his fibre-pile jacket, throws it down, and then considers things. Much giggling and quiet swearing ensues. He puts a Rock in behind a distinctly acoustic flake, moves out across the wall, gets his left hand on the side of the niche where the block came from, smears against the wall with the outside of his right toe, cants his left leg out for balance, unclips an RP from his rack, inserts it in the right hand crack, pulls the black rope through ("better not fall off on this rope—it's about ten years old"), clips it in, repeats the process with another RP slightly higher, then moves down and back across to his resting place in the corner, where he blows out vigorously and laughs down some comment about it all being a bit much.

"Oh, but Stevie, you're so *strong*. Good job, too, 'cause you'll be pulling me up this."

"Yeah, well watch me—the rock's a bit . . ."

Supply your own ending, I thought. Whichever way you looked at it, it certainly was *a bit* . . .

Off he went. He got back to the left-hand layback/outside-right-toe smear position. I took the ropes in. He warned me to pay attention, watch him and so on, which I was doing anyway, gimlet-eyed for clues. And then he leapt. Not for the crack. Nor for the parallel crack to the left. But for something invisible in the middle of the blank wall. Furthermore, it was such a perfectly controlled and timed leap that if I hadn't known, been watching, I could have just assumed it to be a controlled three-points-of-contact-and-all-that-outmoderie surge upwards. It wasn't. It was a powerdrive for some tiny, out-of-sight fingerhold off which he now hung, toes stabbing at dimples, as he brought his left hand up, stuck it in the right-hand crack, tugged and slapped across for the wider left-hand crack. He held himself in, his body lurching back right as he took the pressure off to adjust the finger-jam, then he jabbered off up with his feet skipping on to the fingerhold and both sets of digits now crammed in. Rest, of sorts, if you can call something that demands this outlay of power a rest. Nervous enquiries from below are answered with cautious, calm enthusiasm. Runners go in, Stevie thugs up, sharply-etched muscle-groups perfectly defined on his shoulder. Heavy breathing. A foot slips so he contorts his ankle round to a ridiculous angle to push it at the crack. The foot, as he moves, stays put. He's in the niche where the cracks converge now, reaching tenuously over the top before throwing up a heel

Sheer Resist—one of the sillier rock-climbs in Wales.

and jackhammering into a mantelshelf which takes him clear of the overhanging and into the horizontal world of grass and ease. A great, toothy grin and waggle of the head denote his temporary satisfaction, not with his performance or state of being, but at least with the present release. He belays, and takes up a previous strand of conversation:

"I really like going to the wall or being out bouldering with Johnny Dawes. It's sort of stimulating, inspiring, to see the way he uses his body to do the moves."

"The only person I've ever seen who was similar was Brown," I respond. "He was amazing to go bouldering with. Scored massively on cunning."

"Yeah—he's still amazing for an old bloke. He gave me this route on the secret crag in the Rivals—My Secret Garden I called it. It was really hard—loose and serious but he did it fine. I had to send him my chalk bag down the rope. He used it as well!"

My boots were clean. I'd taken out the first runners. I moved out on to the acoustic flake, the wall above pushing me off balance, and reached for the layback on the edge of the niche. To call it rounded would be an insult to your average curve. It was a 150-degree angle of rock against which you pressed your left hand. There was a tiny nodule of micah for the right hand which bit into the whorl of your middle finger. Both holds were at shoulder level. Neither made you confident to lean out and see what to do with your feet. Stevie's chalk glinted on the wall four feet above.

"What's that like and what d'you do with your feet?"

"It's good—just step up on your right and shove your left in the niche."

I look disbelieving, paw around ineffectually, whimper fatuous remarks about availability of the rescue services, ask what my right foot should be on.

"Just smear and jump—I've got you."

Lurching for the hold induces a very pleasant elevator sensation which doesn't feel wholly connected with my own exertions. Surprisingly, *the hold* turns out to be an excellent little incut which accommodates half the first joint of three fingers on my right hand. With my foot in the niche, it would be a very comfortable position if it were on a slab. But no such luck. Locking the elbow of my right arm I try to cram my fingers in the crack. No joy, but at one place two of them gain some purchase, sway me over leftwards, I grab for the next crack, let my weight on to the fingerlock and run a foot up on to the fingerhold. From here on it's just a harder version of Fingerlicker. These new-fangled ghecko-pads on my feet stick like glue. Stevie gives me a negative handicap, and in short order I belly flop over the top, arms shrieking for a halt.

"You're quite strong, aren't you? Not very strong, like me, but quite strong," he teases.

"Ah, time was . . ." I gasp, "That wasn't bad for a 20-ft route."

"Yeah, it's pretty good. It's all I could've managed today. I'm wasted."

We abseil down and drive round to go bouldering on the Isallt Quarry wall. Stevie bounces around. Mostly I just watch.

"You get to feel at times that you could do anything," he laughs.

"If you want to badly enough," I respond, half-convinced, arm muscles still shrieking lactic outrage.

The Limerick Climbing and Crochet Club
Climber and Hillwalker, 1989

The fact that such a body exists as the Limerick Climbing and Crochet Club was quite unknown to me until a few days ago. And now that I'm back in the prosaic realm of Thatcherland, I'm still half-inclined to dismiss it as a flight of fancy, a piece of whimsy. But no—last Sunday, barely into that dreadful night drive back across Ireland's mist-filled central plains, did not Dermot and Tony and I sit and drink tea in Mike Keyes' kitchen in Limerick? Did we not see the club logo of crossed ice-axe and crochet hook? And were we not given no explanation at all, beyond the broadest of smiles and a shrug that told us it was no matter to detain a rational mind, for the existence of such an organisation?

Let me tell you how it came about. We all have our ambitions, and some of them are easier to realise than others. One of mine was to climb Brandon Mountain. Brandon is not a hill, you should understand, it is a cult. There is a saint—Brendan, I think he's called; a latter day saint, only known by his initials, which are GWY, and a High Priest. The High Priest is Hamish Brown. Hamish is famous. He is a mountaineer, a Scot and a poet, any two of which categories might be deemed mutually exclusive but Hamish has worked up a subtle blend of all three. Apart from Brandon Mountain, he also worships an exceedingly beautiful canine companion called Storrum, photographs of whom have appeared in every issue of every outdoor magazine and every edition of every outdoor book for some decades past. I suspect that Hamish holds to Frederick the Great's creed,

Tony Shaw on the East Ridge of Brandon Mountain—one of the finest hill features in the British Isles.

that "the more I see of humanity, the more I love my dog". (If that's the case, then it's strange that he should be High Priest of a cult based in Ireland, where the inhabitants, after all, are recognisably human and in general rather more civilised than their Saxon counterparts across the Channel of St George.) Hamish also propounded the theory of colour pollution. I disagree with him in this, being all for the crowds wearing brightly coloured clothing—it makes them easier to observe and escape. Despite all appearances, this piece isn't about Hamish, who won't be mentioned again, it's about Ireland, about my wish to climb Brandon Mountain, and how it came to be realised.

Here are two facts—note them well, because they may well be the only ones you'll get. Brandon is on the Dingle Peninsula, famous for Sarah's Miles or some such, and it's an immense number of those on misty roads through the bog from Dublin. Fact two is that Sealink have a weekend excursion fare, Holyhead to Dun Laoghaire, of £99 for a car and four passengers. I was told, "Go, so long as you take The Dog"; Tony's wife said "Can you take Tony as well as The Dog?"; the Special Branch man in Holyhead asked why I was going; The Dog considered this to be rude and bit him. Tony looked concerned—if he'd laughed we'd have been arrested. In Dun Laoghaire the Customs Man wanted to know how old was the car and how old was The Dog and how much did we want for both or either. Dermot Somers, who was lurking round a corner of the shed as we drove out, leapt into the car like some character from a Liam O'Flaherty novel, and within three hours of landing on Irish soil we'd negotiated Dublin's one-way-system and were heading for Dingle.

Now the Irish are a great nation for racing and racing depends on handicaps. Dermot was our navigator. I won't spell it out but you'll see what I mean. Dermot refuses to countenance the use of a map, preferring to use his imagination. If you've ever seen an Irish map, you'll know this to be a reasonable attitude to take, so long as you have the directional instinct to remedy the deficiency. If you knew Dermot's mountaineering record—first Irishman up the North Face of the Eiger, the Freney Pillar, The Ramp on Aillidie and so on—you'd take the instinct as read, and as the finest present-day writer of climbing fiction, he's certainly got the imagination. But apparently even imagination and a directional instinct can't hope to read Dublin's one-way-system. Ever wondered about *Waiting for Godot*? For an explanation, you need look no further than Dublin's one-way-system. As to Dermot's reading of it, perhaps

I should claim some responsibility here, having distracted him with debate when he should have been on the look-out for turnings. When Dermot and I get together, at six-monthly intervals, we argue. On the boat, I took a bet with Tony: "Three minutes, and we'll be arguing, and it won't stop until we sail again!" I lost—we were at it in two! But at least it hadn't quite reached that hour by the time we arrived in Tralee.

The time passed easily enough, with both of us berating the deficiencies of our respective nations and praising the virtues of the other's. But it's a long way to Limerick and a longer one to Tralee, where we had an assignation with some Irish climbers in a pub the name of which escapes me, but I've an idea it was The Cabbage and Bucket. Anyway, the Guinness was cold and sour. We were warned not to drink it, but it was a part of what we'd come for, so drink it we did. The Dog stuck her snout into mine and took a lap or two from beneath the foam, then thought better of it, sneezed heartily, and took to licking her lips obsessively for the rest of the night. A showband was playing Dire Straits badly in the background. Mike Barry, his girlfriend Mags, and Pat, who are the climbing strength of Tralee, apologised for the drink and urged us to hurry it down so that we could get in another round or two before the pub shut. It was 2am. Mike gave Dermot directions for his home. We drove up and down the same road seven times before giving up and driving round to try another. It led back to the same place. We stopped at a house to ask the way and Mike opened the door. Dermot and I carried on arguing till 5am, discovering virtues in each other's political leaders which their loyal subjects had hitherto never suspected. Eventually we got to bed.

If you've never woken to a cold, clear autumn morning in the Irish countryside, you're missing one of life's pleasures. We drove along the shores of Tralee Bay, through Abhain an Scail with the Slieve Mish peaks all hazy and glowing above, and down the peninsula through a landscape of hills, sea and fuchsia hedges that's a million miles from the England to which economic reality forces too many of its own people to migrate. In the town of An Daingean we went into An Cafe Liteartha, where nothing was on that was on the menu in the room at the back of the bookshop, but they did you something or other of what you might like anyway, and from the speakers above my head came out as throaty-deep, warm and tuneful a voice as ever I'd heard, which belonged, so the woman behind the counter who cut the sandwiches with a great brown-handled

Brocken Spectre on Brandon (unique picture of the author with a halo).

blade told me, to Dolores Keane from Connemara, "One of the Keanes of Connemara, you know . . .!" Then we went to Brandon, by way of the Connar Pass.

Cameron, who edits this magazine and is an initiate of the cult, told me that you must climb Brandon from Faha, so we found our way to Faha. We did this by Dermot's usual tactic of quartering the terrain in the approximate area until the objective had made itself apparent. Looking at the map now that I bought later, the reasonableness of this tactic is made clear the road we took exists, but only on the ground. The map's cover actually gives you the best clue to the Irish attitude—it shows a car parked diagonally across a T-junction, its nose against the bank. The car is Italian. A young woman is carefully folding the map on its bonnet. There is frost on the ground. She is going to use the map to blank off the radiator grille. It is the best use to which it could be put.

Brandon Mountain is 3127ft high, and everyone who goes up it comes down to preach a gospel about the loveliest hill in the Celto-saxon Archipelago. I was sceptical, Dermot non-committal (never having seen the hill due to prevailing weather conditions on his previous sixty-three ascents), and Tony was already experiencing the sort of spiritual uplift he remembered from the Billy Graham prayer-meetings he'd attended in his youth. The Dog, whose shoulder height is ten inches, was practising standing jumps of four feet on the spot to pass the time as we made ready. It was mid-October and hot as high summer. A heat haze shimmered over the sea. There was a track marked by red and white poles but the ridge above beckoned. On the way to it you pass a shrine to Our Lady of the Mountains. Thunder rumbled away to the south and I crossed myself as devoutly as any lapsed Catholic might but put aside thoughts of making the ascent on my knees. For a mile the ridge ground its way uphill, haze blanking everything, nothing visible but the bulk of a dull whaleback. But as we climbed the mist

Dermot Somers emerges from the top of a route (the name of which does not bear repeating) at Dounshean.

cleared, the ridge narrowed, the view spread, and soon we were cantering along a crest like that of Stac Pollaidh with great drops and little pitches and perfect red sandstone, lovely corries beneath, the presence of the mountain to the left—as good a ridge, in fact, as any outside Skye and not the trace of a track along it.

Where it joined the main ridge of the mountain and we turned south for the summit, the sun was low, banks of mist were streaming over the route we'd taken, and the shadows of our three selves were stalking amongst them—Brocken spectres, glories, double and triple ones—more in an hour than I'd seen in a lifetime, huge and clear and active. We lay on top in the sunshine by the well beneath the cross and laughed and laughed. The way down was through the blackest cwm I've ever seen—black rock, black water, black peat, great ridges towering back into the mist and Dermot and I arguing furiously about choice and worth of lines upon them.

How do you end such a day? We chose to stay in a hostel, a converted piggery on Dingle Bay. Or rather Tony and Dermot did—The Dog and I had to sleep in a tent. In O'Flaherty's pub a man led a group of instrumentalists in playing traditional Irish music. He was a violent man, surely, for he played the tenor banjo like a machine gun and swung it round menacingly and suddenly at closing time as he sang The Soldier's Song. I saw Dermot hesitate before standing: "I was worried he might have the thing loaded," he explained. Normally, he'd not countenance standing for any of this nationalist sentimentality. Dermot's nothing if not astringent. Luckily for us a ray of cowardice gleamed through his scruples on this occasion.

Now as an afterthought, Tony and I had packed climbing boots, and Mike Barry was to turn up the next day to show us "his" cliff at Dounshean. Dermot was determined to show us the Kerry Gaeltacht in the morning. We drove round past huge slabs above a wrecked ship at Slea Head and argued about them: "Better prospect than anything left in Britain," I enthused. "Not worth doing just for the odd route they might give you," countered Dermot. We stopped for a pint at a jazzy, bleak alehouse with a German name and looked out across the sound to the Great Blasket, agreed heatedly that Tomas O'Crohan was a great man whilst Peig Sayers and Maurice O'Sullivan were nothing better than Ur–Thatcherites, had another session in An Cafe Lieartha, and got to Dounshean just as Mike's team arrived—Mike and Mags and Pat, that is.

A hundred yards, Dermot had assured us, but from the strand at Trabeg, not a glimmer of rock was in sight.

We ambled away through fields frisky with Friesian cattle, crossed a narrow neck of causeway guarded by ancient earthworks, and the views became interesting. Stacks, arches, cliffy coast. There was the awareness of space between us and the sea. The Dog crept anxiously to heel, and when I'd emptied it, bestowed herself in a rucksack, nose twitching in bewilderment at the strange intentions of mankind. You saw in her face how the myth about Lemmings grew up. Heedless of The Dog's disapproval we scrambled down to sea-level terraces. A wall of dark red rock, 150ft high and seamed with grooves hung over us. It was sandstone. At one end there was a fantastical free-standing flake curving up for a hundred feet. There was a dull mist, heavy cloud, a salty dampness in the air. It was dark enough to be evening. Mike and Pat, Dermot and Mags, roped up to climb. Tony and I exchanged glances and tagged along. Dermot was engaged on a slabby rib at the right, Mike had sidled down into a dark recess behind the flake, with deep water sluicing lazily in its base. The slow, graceful curve of a crack climbed out of it to the top of the crag. It was as good a line for its length as I'd ever seen.

Also, it was one of those lines the grade of which you'd be hard put to guess. You know the way it is when you're unacquainted with the rock, don't know how the holds run or what the friction's like. It could have been anything from Severe to easy Extreme. And since I'd never seen Mike climb before, his performance gave me no clue at all—he was competent and thoughtful about it, looked as if he was enjoying himself, but neither he nor Pat were saying a word about how hard it was. So I just sat at the bottom and watched and chatted to Pat, who's an Ulster Prod come down to the Free State because—as he told me—of his despair at the direction of the British government. Mike, meanwhile, had reached the top and Pat, who'd done the route before, gave me the end of one of the ropes and told me to be off up it. This made me suspicious. I wiped my boots, took a sly, small dip in my chalkbag, unaware of the local code but anticipating disapproval, and set to.

This climb is called The Giraffe because its line resembles the neck of that creature. It has all the power of presence of a great route. As you look up from each successive move, you wonder how hard the next one will be, but every move lands you at a perfect and usually unexpected hold. The crack is set in a shallow, discontinuous right-facing corner, never more than a foot deep. Horizontal stratification across it at intervals produces extraordinary sharp-edged pockets. You climb it almost entirely on holds—scarcely a jam in the whole length

of the route. Every move is about 4b or 4c, the rock is perfect and the situation magnificent. It would be a three-star classic anywhere in Britain. There's a perfect thread belay and a grass ledge at the top, where we sat and talked.

Mike's a short, strongly-built, dark-featured Kerryman with the fine quality of ingenuous enthusiasm that you encounter almost everywhere in Ireland and all too seldom in England these days. He runs a restaurant called The Skillet in Tralee, and a hostel—The Four Winds—in Killarney, and remains the most amenable product of the enterprise culture you'd ever hope to meet. To have a place like Kerry to explore, and just a few companions to explore it with, is a situation from the lost innocence of climbing. Up there on the clifftop, I almost envied him the freshness and relaxation of it all. But he was allowing no such dreaming idyll—once Pat was up, he handed me out the punishment for using chalk on *his* cliff—we were to abseil down behind the flake and climb a corner hidden in the blackness down there which revelled in the name of Stinky-Poo.

"How hard's that?" I asked

"Oh, it's harder than the last" was his only comment.

At the bottom, only 20ft of deep water and smooth, greeny-black rock separated us from the start of The Giraffe, but this line was evidently a different proposition. It looked like First Slip, but turned the other way and filled with slime. And it was steep and shadowed. Here and there the crack in the back opened out and you could take a rest from tenuous back-and-footing to jam for a move or two. The sloping holds were slick with salt, the pocketed and shattered crack painful to jam. It was a wonderful, old-fashioned, insecure struggle—like a modern throwback to the gully epoch at a meaty 5b. I grunted and sweated my way up, Mike, and Dermot as well by now, crouching in the blackness below, and emerged into a bright scatter of ribs below the ledge, where Pat, Mags and Tony were taking their ease. Soon we were all—Mike and Dermot included—bantering and chaffing away back at the sacks, with the cloud and mist around us not the least weight on our spirits on this obscure little crag of the uttermost West. The Dog sat on Mag's knee, turning her snout up imploringly to be kissed upon it. "Ingratiating cur," muttered Tony, half-fainting with jealousy.

We wandered back to Trabeg with the surf slapping far away beneath and oystercatchers piping away in pied formation across the sand. No good day's complete without an hour in the pub at its ending, and no pub's more complete than Dan Foley's at Abhain an Scail, where mine host is a magician and the Guinness likewise of magical quality. The hour was long over when Dermot and Tony and I tore ourselves away. How many things in life are as finely relaxing as a session in an Irish pub? We left for the long miles to Limerick and a further session at the house of Mike Keyes, of the aforementioned Climbing and Crochet Club: "No voice at all, but a great enthusiast," said Dermot, or maybe he said it about someone else, I don't remember for the stories were all so involved. They were going over the proceedings of the previous weekend's Federation of Mountain Clubs of Ireland's meet in a pub in Ballyvaughan on The Burren, where they'd played and sung for forty-eight continuous hours with not a nose set outside, for there wasn't a hill or crag to be found in the region anyway. I'd half forgotten that such spontaneous good-fellowship could exist, and only the memory of it and Dermot's singing kept us going through the mist-filled night-miles to Dun Laoghaire and home.

A Debate with Comrade Campbell
Climber, 1987

Comrade Campbell casting a cold eye on life.

Can comradeship produce harmony from chaos? Well, we'll see! This month's subject is the investigative journalist Duncan Campbell, a man whose name is synonymous with the Secret Society, whose liberty is still in jeopardy as the possibility of bringing charges against him for the programme he made for television on the

Zircon satellite remains open, and whose record of running hard along the boundaries of the Official Secrets Act stretches back ten years and more to events preceding the infamous ABC Trials of the 1970s. All this is of no account in a climbing magazine, you will quite properly say, but the fact is that *our* investigations have revealed the secret vice of Duncan Campbell—his leisure-time obsession with rock-climbing.

Anyone with half a mind for politics will know about the necessary balance between the ideal, the contingent and the pragmatic. When our meeting was arranged, the intention was a route on Great Gable. However, when the weekend came the clouds loured, the forecast for Cumbria gloomed, the steering on my car was suspect, there'd just been that dreadful crash on the M6, and pragmatism was forced into play. Duncan was on his way back from a media event in Finland, via Patterdale and a Red Rope trip from Liverpool. I was tied up in Pembroke, speaking to a conference about M.o.D. land tenure. Arrangements were hastily re-cast, and I collected him from a flat in Liverpool 8, where he was picking at an Indian takeway whilst carefully amputating the arguments of a young comrade at the knee.

The very first thing you notice about Duncan is a sort of satisfied incisiveness about his mind. In argument (and argument is the lifeblood of comradeship, spilling over into every sphere of its activity), he sits with lips pursed, eyes half-closed and head tilted slightly back, dexterously wielding his scalpel amongst the fatty flesh of words which overlays the bones of truth. Amongst the vodka, the whiskey and the cigarette haze, the ideas loomed and faded, all warmed by comradely affection. We set off for Wales at midnight in the rain, with a strict injunction from Comrade Campbell to obey the speed limits and keep open the windows to mask the smell of my car-bound, sleeping dogs. Routes for the morrow were canvassed, the recurrent theme being Cwm Silyn, where for Duncan a previous hailed-off failure had reinforced the desire to return. "Oh, Kirkus's! Outside Edge! Good!" I'd thought, the prospect of a relaxing day's climbing soothing my racing brain. We were neither of us in any state . . .!

Eight hours' sleep after days with none and the sun broke on my surfacing consciousness. Downstairs, Duncan was waiting at breakfast.

"Cwm Silyn still the thing, Duncan?"

"Do you have a guidebook?"

I brought him the guidebook, gobbled toast, scribbled a letter which had to be sent, grabbed gear and made for the car. The sun was high, the clouds had cleared from the hill, Wales was at her lovely best. On the way up to Maen Llwyd where the cars are parked, Duncan sketched in his background: born in Glasgow 35 years ago, brought up in Dundee, went to Oxford at the age of 17 and graduated with first-class honours in Physics three years later, then research at Brighton, a progress into socialism, investigative journalism, and his extraordinary and running battle with what he terms the "elective dictatorship" which he sees developing in this country, particularly over the last eight years.

We left the car on the moor and set off up the green track into Cwm Silyn, always one of my favourite places. White horses broke around the reefs running out from Anglesey into Caernarfon Bay, and Holyhead Mountain was obscured by a glimmering veil of heat. Duncan stormed off intently up the track.

"Didn't know you were into running, Duncan?"

"We've already wasted half the day," he replied, tersely.

He flogged up the scree, with me loafing along behind taking pictures. Streaks of water promised interest on Kirkus's Route. When we arrived at the foot of the crag, Duncan put down his sack, whilst I scrambled up a bit higher to a ledge at the start of Kirkus's and sat down, shirt soaked with sweat:

"Let's do this first, Duncan."

He came up to join me.

"Do you have the guidebook?"

"I *wrote* the bloody guidebook."

"Do you know where the route goes, then?"

"Somewhere, at some time along the route, a vague memory might emerge from the morass of rotting brain cells. Meanwhile, let's play it by instinct . . ."

This reply did not seem to please him. Perhaps he thought I was being sarcastic instead of giving an entirely straightforward account of my mental condition. Anyway, there was a distinct tension in the air as we roped up.

"Tell you what, Duncan, I'll lead the first pitch, which is the hardest, then if we swing leads all the way up that leaves the top pitch for you, which is the best."

He looked suspicious, I set off, and Tony Shaw, whom I'd told earlier by telephone of our plans for the day, arrived. I was enjoying myself in making variations around the first pitch's forked crack, where if you zig-zag around, above and below the normal route you can get some delightful slab moves at 5a or 5b on crisp little incuts and sideholds.

"Are you sure you know where you're going?"

"No idea, but it feels good."

Kirkus's Route, Cwm Silyn—Duncan kneels to pray.

The tremors issuing up the rope indicated that this was not an appropriately palliative response. I reached the first of those long, rising ledges on the Great Slab, tied on to a couple of nuts, sat down by a sweet-smelling juniper bush, chewed some grass and brought up Duncan.

"If you eat much more of that grass you'll become radioactive," he snapped.

"Ah, but then you'll know what makes me tick." I joked back.

We brought up Tony, who had tied on to a third rope. Duncan was surveying the pitch ahead in silence.

"Where now?" he asked.

I gestured vaguely at the slab ahead.

"Yes, but where?"

Concentration was demanded. Tony had arrived. We consulted. I argued for the left, Tony for the right alternative, which seemed politically apposite. Duncan appeared inclined to accept Tony's view, and believing in the wisdom to be derived from experience, I left him to it with a few caustic remarks about apostasy and the true gospel. Duncan having placed a runner, and keeping a careful eye on the movement of the rope, which was not moving, Tony and I then commenced to gossip, whistle and jolly about like childhood regressives on our expansive ledge. A stop was put to it!

"Look, do you two mind down there! You've failed to provide me with a clear description of where the route goes. I don't know how hard it is and I'm not confident at this standard as yet. And you insist on talking amongst yourselves. I'd be glad if you would pay total attention to what I'm doing."

Duncan, not to put to fine a point on it, was phased. I suggested he get back on the right path, the one to the left. He did so, full of scepticism and trepidation. My slapdash approach to things was obviously not much to his liking. And so our caravanserai progressed, a little icily by this time, and even obvious objective confirmation of being on route as we rose higher did not restore much good feeling. Duncan duly led the top pitch in suspicious dependence on the minutely particularised description I dredged up from the depths of memory, and I followed, hoping to restore the spirit of the day by grunts of enthusiasm about the exposed position, about the superb incut holds beneath the overlap, about the grainy texture of the white rock sucking at the soles of your feet, and the competence and courage of the leader. All to no avail. There was trouble brewing. The light of harmony was failing fast as that of day. We had been a long time on the route. I left Duncan and Tony and loped around the ridge to get a shot or two of the Great Slab in the last of the sun. When I re-joined them at the bottom of the crag, Tony was scuttling homewards and Duncan made meaningfully to sit down beside me.

"This is no way for a comrade to behave towards a comrade, comrade."

"How do you mean, Duncan?"

The catalogue of my vices and imperfections rolled out. I warmly agreed with him, applauded his perspicacity, and used it as a pretext to come back as a pair to climb Outside Edge the following day. This we did. I was up early in the morning. We left the house in good order. The early mist was dramatically clearing from the crag as we arrived. I raced Duncan up the screes, asked hordes of formal questions, remembered the guidebook, and offered not only to let Duncan lead every pitch but also to carry up a rucksack with all the gear to spare us the horrid scree-descent and enable us to romp down the grassy ridge above the Western Cliffs after the route. Expiation, I thought, as any good Catholic comrade might when caught in a trial of conscience. On a much more relaxed basis, therefore, we sat and chattered about climbing before starting on the route.

"How did you come into the sport, Duncan?"

"I did a climbing course on the Sobell Wall in London ten years ago, then left it for a long time until a friend in Edinburgh offered to take me out. I thought I'd better make sure I was competent, so I went on a course at Plas y Brenin, where I teamed up with Gregor MacLennan, whom you'll know—he's Gordon MacLennan's son—and had a fantastic time, though I was frightened very badly at one point in descending from the Idwal Slabs. We were with Rob Collister for most of the week and if he took us on things which were too hard for us, on the way down we would deliberately make it hard for him to follow the intellectual content of our discussions."

"Coming from Scotland, did you start out in the traditional manner as a teenage Munro-bagger?"

"No—there was no tradition of hill-walking in our family. But I do feel a very strong affinity for the Highlands and get up there whenever I can."

I told him something about the route we were to do, what it was like, and about Menlove Edwards's first ascent of it in 1931. He came back with a comment which I've found amusingly recurrent in a particular context over the last couple of years, since the publication of *Menlove*:

"I've always wondered how someone who's obviously straight could write so perceptively about someone who was gay?"

"There are certain basic human problems in communication and integrity which cut across the specifics of sexual orientation, aren't there?"

He pondered that one. I uncoiled the rope, handed him the end, and he got to grips with the Direct Start, which leads from the toe of the buttress to the first pedestal stance. It was wet. There was a difficult move up and across on small and awkward holds. He wobbled, made it, gasped. A cold wind was blowing, I followed chill-fingered and cursing, heaving inelegantly on whatever came to hand. We ceremoniously read the guidebook and he started up the magnificent second pitch.

Outside Edge is literally that—the outside edge of the Great Slab of Craig yr Ogof before it cuts away into the sheaf of overhanging ribs and grooves which make up the Ogof Nose. So very quickly the position becomes sensationally exposed. This second pitch makes a rising traverse out left on good, square-cut holds, slightly awkwardly placed at times, and leads in 90ft to Sunset Ledge, a long strip of grass running across the front of the Nose and marking the end of the harder climbs—Crucible, Eureka, Jabberwocky. You traverse this, past the very much inferior finish to the Great Slab Ordinary Route which is often climbed in mistake for the top section of Outside Edge, and step out on to a rib which hangs in space.

I belayed on a thread just before the rib and watched Duncan move across. The guidebook description I'd written years before was of no obvious assistance. He read it, ignored the scratches and holds going out left and tried to climb a smooth, wet groove. After half an hour's inactivity I timorously suggested he step round left. He gratefully accepted the invitation. It was the turning point in our partnership, lancing a sliver of cosmic jokery into the ill humour of the past few days. He smiled a benign smile and surveyed me from the corner of an eye, then climbed on in fine, sunny mood up the cracks and grooves above. When the rope ran out, I untied the belay and followed. At the top I scrambled past him and we romped on up the ridge and into the sun. As we coiled the ropes he planted a delicate kiss on my cheek and thanked me for his choice of route.

"That was better than Kirkus's," he said.

"Ah yes, it's the best V. Diff. in Wales—that's why we did it last," I responded. "There's nothing quite so bad as an anti-climax!"

We took the flask out of the sack, drank tea, ran down through the blonde grass of the ridge and looked back on the fine features of the cliff and cwm.

"This is the life, hey, Duncan—to get out climbing two days in a row!"

"Yes—you know, I'm making so much money these days out of re-editing the Zircon programme for the Beeb, I think I'll retire to Scotland."

"Good Socialist, eh—Edinburgh tenement block and London pied-a-terre?"

"Oh, I'll sell off the London house. That'll get Special Branch confused!"

I skipped off down, laughing. I'd come quite to like Comrade Campbell. And all that pernicketiness, attention to detail and text, it's only the reverse side of a coin which pays for all our liberties, and pays for them dearly at times.

Perception as Therapy: John Beatty
Climber, 1987

John Beatty.

We were supposed to be going to Laddow, but driving over from Wales that morning the news on the car radio was of the Moors Murders victim whose body had just been found. There was a cloud in my mind hanging over the northern Peak District. I had been looking forward to a day on Laddow, wasn't going to say anything, but half-knew there would be no need—an intuition which John's first words, when I arrived at his house above Whaley Bridge, confirmed:

"Have you been listening to the radio?"

"Yes."

"Let's go to Windgather—that was the first place which sprang to my mind anyway."

One of the pleasant surprises about this series for me so far has been that the subjects haven't made the obvious choices. Certainly Windgather would never have been a chosen venue for anyone conditioned into the status-and-collecting-and-tickability view of climbing. It just isn't a fashionable place and the general perception of it is that it has no worthwhile climbing above V Diff.

In fact it has two very good routes at the top end of VS—the Joe Brown problem, Portfolio, and the Right Hand Route on Overhang Buttress, both of them 5a, and there is also some excellent hard bouldering at the left hand end. It's not that these are beside the point, it's just that the accent lies elsewhere. If you like good-quality steep slab or easy-angled wall and arete climbing at Diff. or V. Diff., if you rejoice in the sort of relaxed, flowing movement into which you are encouraged by that style of route, then Windgather's the place for you. And here and there, when you've gathered confidence and keyed in to the rhythms of its particular dance, there are some more intricate sequences of steps to keep your interest going.

So much for the merely technical aspects. If you can say one thing about Windgather with absolute certainty it's that these are unimportant compared to the forms, the position, the atmosphere, the *spirit* of the place. I was delighted to be going up there. Into the car and up the road from Horwich End we drove, with the Toddbrook Reservoir down to our right and John holding forth about kingfishers and the courtship of the Great Crested Grebe, to arrive at the green roll of moorland with its spraycrest of brown and silvery-green gritstone which was our objective.

"Why do people come here, John?"

(There was an outdoor pursuits group busily toproping Portfolio, and a few other climbers dotted about along the length of the crag.)

"For the healing . . ."

He cocked his head on one side to study my reaction, eyes sparkling with good humour. You can't be long in John's company without identifying a personal vocabulary, in which concepts like healing, therapy, the subliminal power of the image, are central. He gains tremendous enjoyment from volleying around gnomic phrases. I swatted his service idly back over the net:

"Go on, explain . . ."

He shakes his head.

"I like the people who come here. There's none of the dreadful tension and ego-nonsense that modern rock-climbing's all about. The ones who come here come because they like the place, they like being here. That's important. There's nothing here for the ego-boys."

This set me off musing about the people you do meet at Windgather. When I lived in Buxton recently, on fine evenings I would often—despite the "beginners' outcrop" sneerings of the middle-aged ego-boys with whom I might have kept company—come out here to solo around. I'd never arrange to meet anyone, but generally someone I knew would turn up, and the people who did turn up would be just the sort of relaxed and easy company you would have wished for: Nat Allen, John Robson, Ray Greenall, Ally Cowburn, Malc Baxter, Tony Shaw, John Beatty himself—those with whom you'd most willingly go for a pint in the Shepherd's Arms in Whaley when the sun had gone down and the last cars had slipped away down the road into the shadows and the city lights. And conversely, those who were most scathing about the place when it was suggested were those with whom it would be a penance and a purgatorial experience to tie on to a rope. Their screaming egos can shape no bolster and detect no echo from these stern, simple, little light-infused and wind-breasting buttresses, so they do not come here.

"So what's your chosen route, John?"

"It's not that sort of place, really, is it? You come here more for the flow. You don't bring ropes and gear and all the other stuff that climbing nowadays is cluttered up with. But since you ask, I suppose the best route here is North Buttress Arete. There's something about it . . ."

North Buttress is the quiet end of the crag. Beyond it are only the boulders. We went along and sat on a large rock to put on our climbing boots. Four years ago, I reflected, I knew nothing at all about John Beatty other than a vague notion that he was one of those few lucky people to have done the Skye Ridge in perfect winter conditions. Then came the 1984 Buxton Mountaineering Conference, at which he was one of the first people on the Saturday morning programme, and by the time I arrived the buzz was all of an extraordinary audio-visual presentation called "Touch the Earth".

"What is it?" I'd asked, of one of the large band of people who were wandering around the conference provoked into islanded wonderment.

"Well," she'd replied, "It's sub-titled 'a celebration of wild places'. All I can say is that it's the most stunning set of visual images I've ever seen."

John Beatty on his chosen route at Windgather, re-graded as VS and re-named Arête Direct in the latest guidebook.

With this information logged into memory-bank, the next I heard of him was a phone-call out of the blue one morning. He was passing near Dolwyddelan, where I then lived. Could he call in for a brew? We spent a day sitting in my garden, under a *philadelphus* in flowering crescendo, talking, talking. I was amused, touched and stimulated by his outpouring of ideas, enthusiasms and creative energy. There was something of the Quattrocento artist in his nervous vitality, and in a strong-featured face, sharp-hazel-eyed, framed by a neat beard and a thinning scatter of brown curls. Since then a friendship has grown between us and John's reputation has gradually won through to deserved prominence as Britain's finest wilderness photographer. So in my turn, sitting beneath North Buttress Aretc at Windgather, I was a shade nervous at the prospect of having to use the instrument of his own craft to depict a master-craftsman:

"As someone who's completely cack-handed with a camera, I often wonder how people like you get on with the technical aspects of photography?"

"I find them *quite* trying!"

"Necessary, though?"

"Necessary to convey what rock and landscape *do* to me. What's difficult is to get those intuitions into still images. I'm going through processes all the time just like my audiences do, and to create those images—which is what you must do—is an evolution. Recreating is inconclusive. I can't go on seeing and saying the same thing."

"That again's a question of necessity, isn't it, and an escape from complacency? My strongest objection, for example, to a particular style of climbing writing that's emerged over the last two or three years is that it seems so satisfied with itself, so pleased and cocksure about the images it forces into being."

"Without them having the real sense of rightness, you mean?"

"Just that. It's a thing you recognise instinctively. It's all very well to applaud cleverness, but this stuff takes you into a very odd area of the is-and-the-ought."

"Yeah, I guess. And if you think about it, that's an aspect of this insistence on *doing* rather than just being. When I sit up here, and I come up here a lot for the healing power of the place, it's often enough for me just to look across at that hillside and know that on it there are woodcock, badgers, curlews, trees that I know. It's like Gifford's writing. He's desperate for his audience to know he's an active man. Doesn't he know it's as good to lie back against a rock? One of the great lessons to learn is why the Buddha is fat . . ."

"You wouldn't appreciate being fat in five minutes' time, John, when you're on this route."

The last comment won his good-humoured acquiescence. We stood up, only to see Nat Allen racing along the path towards us to enjoy a few quick routes in his lunch hour. More talk, banter, humane concern for the plight of Doug and Anne Moller of Rock Hall Cottage at the Roaches. (One of my abiding images of John is of him struggling up through the snow in February last year with a hundredweight of coal on his back as a gift to the Mollers.) Then, shamed into action by Nat's enthusiasm, we turned to the rock, and North Buttress Arete. Nat set off up Green Crack, alongside and to the left. John addressed himself to his route.

I'd come, on this particular morning, from the western perimeter of Snowdonia. Was it worth it, just for 35ft of gritstone? I asked myself that as John moved up it, no rope attached, using his legs and feet gingerly after a recent tendon operation, but nonetheless elegant, deliberate and patient. There was something of the large raptor about his stance and countenance, poised there on the rock as I asked him to pause, for me to focus, change a lens, alter an aperture.

He arrived at the top, sat on the edge, and I put aside my camera bag and thoughts of text and pictures to savour the thing itself. This route, North Buttress Arete, is a Severe, whatever that means. More importantly, miniature though it is in the larger scales of things, it has a presence, an architectonic being, a pleasing arrangement of edges and angles on which the knowledge of the climber can play. There is something powerful, imposing about it. I have seen it repel good climbers: Peter Boardman one biting-cold spring evening years ago; a young cockerel of a lad who'd strutted and crowed along the crag on a warm summer night last year, until he'd struck and foundered on this seventh wave of swirled-up sediment set into an eternal gesture of opposition and aspiration.

When you stand beneath it, a thigh-height overlap masks your feet from view and above head-height in the orangey rock are two large pockets hollowing underneath a further outjut of strata. You pinch them, you press flat-handed on the arete, you skip up a foot, you smear on friction holds, undercut the pockets, adjust your right hand up the arete, and end up reaching for a great horn of rounded rock. The ground is fast receding and the intricacy of attaining balance out beyond the vertical on this rounded everything is a joy. Your feet jag boldly in, knees out like a motor-bike racer, to gain friction, and you reach a ledge. Step back round the front with difficult balance and awkward, fragile pinch-grips for the hands, and you can move up into a ripple of incuts and an easy ending. And that's it. When I was a kid of fourteen in Manchester, after a weekend up here this would be one of the climbs whose moves my mind relived in dreams. We sat together on top.

"It's that near, green ridge which fulfils this place. It hides all the city away and just launches you out west."

"Did you ever stay down there at Windgather Cottage, John, when it was a youth hostel?"

"Oh, yes. I got all my youth hostel badges. And I saw these rocks and came back and told my parents that I wanted to take up a dangerous sport. I bought a dangerous rope for it, too—one of those polypropylene caving ropes from a shop on Piccadilly Station Approach."

"And you came out here at weekends?"

"Yes, or to Laddow, or The Roaches. I remember the first time I went to Wales. We went on the Gribin Facet in the rain and I wore socks over my boots like I'd seen Nea Morin doing in a picture."

"Did you mostly stay in Derbyshire?"

"Yes, and I still love it here, even after The Alps, The Antarctic, Greenland, The Himalayas, all those places. When I was in my 'teens I was a Voluntary National Park Warden . . ."

"What, one of the wobbly aerial brigade?" I asked, incredulously.

"Yeah, but they wouldn't give me a radio. I was the youngest ever. I had an NSU Quickly and one year I went out on Kinder 43 times. I loved it. It's a sad confession when you put it against the way we feutel about them now, but to me it was looking after my land."

"Which is what you're still doing, except you're no longer enforcing regulations but stimulating awareness?"

"Perception itself is a therapy. When I worked in the outdoor centre at Crowden after I'd left teaching in schools, if you went out with a group of kids and just talked, just explained, just communicated, you could see it shining through in them, the healing. And the people who come along to the shows—there's some sense in which they want to be told that the basic, the instinctive way they respond to and feel about landscape is good, is right, is O.K. When someone says, in that horrible, sneering way, that my work's precious, it doesn't matter really, you know. It's the right word used the wrong way. What's precious is out there and what's out there is precious . . ."

We drifted along the crag, climbing here and there, John telling me of his trips and climbs and adventures—the winter epics, the intense phase of working through the hard classics, Vector, Big Groove and so on, the new insights brought to him by the other perceptions drawn from his relationships with his wife Jan and baby son Robin. We watched a wheatear collecting insects.

"D'you know wheatear's supposed to be a bowdlerised name, John. The countryman's name for it, perfectly descriptive, was the white-arse, but it was felt Queen Victoria wouldn't have approved, so the naturalists changed it."

"That fits, I guess" he chuckled, "as if it mattered. It's like the antagonism, the wariness you sense in people. They've been conditioned against sensitivity, against people with something real to say who are trying to say it. I'm fighting against that to maintain the integrity of my work all the time. White-arse is a much better name than wheatear anyway."

He chuckled sporadically all the way to the car.

In no sense is John a po-faced, self-indulgent and self-regarding aesthete, but a man who is alive and funny and warm, whose acts of attention are profoundly concentrated upon the *natural* universe around him. And who is courageous enough to stand naked in saying what it means to him. On the way down to Whaley Bridge in the car he talked of the U2 concert he'd been to in Leeds the previous night. He talked of the bravery of the band's witness to being Christians, of the whole, proud way they walked on stage, like Red Indians, of their music, with its mixture of heavy rock, melodic guitar riffs and intricate bass rhythms. He told of the tremor he felt at hearing 80,000 people singing aloud and along with a single line:

"But I still haven't found what I'm looking for . . ."

"That's where the healing comes in. That's how I think these images I try to create through my photography can help."

And he talked, with a professional's interest in the subject, of the band's presentation, telling of how at the end Bono had picked up one of the stage lights and shone it out so that it touched each one of his audience, so that each one of them felt touched by it.

No bad image, that, for John's own work.

Cathy Powell: A Character Re-written
Climber and Hillwalker, 1988

We each of us have gaps in our education, and The Grooved Arete was just that for me. You know how it is—inexplicably, there are some routes you've never done. Perhaps you've resisted the urge to collect them. Perhaps some memory of accident or things said warns you away. Or perhaps it's just that, on that part of the mountain, your plans always stick in a different groove—the Terrace Wall, the Belle Vue Bastion, but never the soaring rib away on the right. You'll come round to it eventually—that much you know. It's just a question of when.

This is how it happened (things start in prosaic ways, so don't scoff). I was listening to the five-to-nine weather forecast on Radio Four. It was October the eleventh. The weatherman was promising rain, gales, flood for perhaps days on end and I had one of those thirsts for physical activity on me which have to be satisfied. Besides, the sun was still shining—fitfully, yes, and the massed clouds were rolling in over the sea. But there was a golden light that morning, and if I was to cower behind rain-dimmed windows for the rest of the week, the need was to get out now. So off I went to Tryfan. There was, of course, the minor inconvenience of not having anyone to climb with, but that turned out to be an advantage. If I'd been with a partner I'd have been thinking of the old favourites—Munich Climb, or the Belle Vue Bastion again. As it was, I was unapologetically alone and glad to be so—why should you not take your mountains undiluted once in a while, instead of cooling the heat of the experience on the rocks of company? And even the moderation of ambition which solitude entails can be turned to advantage. What was it Moulam said—"As good as anything of the kind in Wales"? And Tom Leppert has it down as a three-star route, "the most inspiring on Tryfan". That gap in my education was about to be filled. It had to be The Grooved Arete.

Half an hour later I was round in Ogwen, pulling the Honda on to its stand, stowing helmet and leathers away in the box and jumping up and down to get warm. A fierce easterly was gusting even at this level. Tryfan, its fine crown hidden, sat in lumpen judgement on my plans under a black cap of cloud. There was fine weather to the west and I flogged up the squelch and gravel to the Heather Terrace hoping it might push a salient through. One by one the gullies ticked by: Bastow, Nor'Nor',

Tryfan's North Peak: "No figure on the North Buttress traverse".

Green, and then I was there, with not even the route's initials scratched on the rock marring the good mood which exercise builds up.

Not only that, but as I sat down to tighten my boots and put on my climbing helmet—the latter a concession to being sensible as you grow older and the sense deepens of how dangerous this soloing is—there in front of me, right between my feet, was a silver sixpence: "That's strange," I thought, as I picked it up and rubbed it on my sleeve. "What on earth is that doing here." But there it was—the King's head, 1951, and a gleam upon it as though it was new minted, the milled edge sharp as a file. I put it in the pocket of my shirt along with the bike keys, strapped on my camera-case, fastened the waist-strap of my rucksack, and turned to the rock.

Tryfan rock! It was made for climbing. There are the textures, from marble through to pumice. There are the holds, often quite subtle, hidden, but absolutely reliable, and all of them buffed to a pale ochre sheen by the grinding of nailed boots through decades. The thought brought me up short. In that first slightly awkward crack which commands you from the outset to summon your forces and concentrate, there beneath the

flat hold at half-height out on the right were nail-scratches—quite unmistakeable—number 6 Tricounis, a fine grey dust of gouged rock on each side showing how fresh the marks were. I laughed aloud. In this world of Lycra tights, butyl rubber and climbing competitions, here on Tryfan, somewhere up above me at this moment, someone was climbing in Tricouni-nailed boots.

People complain about Grooved Arete. They say that after the first two pitches you have to walk across to the left, and after the next two pitches you need to amble over to the right. So you do, but that's the nature of Tryfan and what you're making for in both cases is the next obvious continuation of the line. And why complain when the climbing is as good as it is. Take the rib of the middle section, for example. There's not a dull move on it, and you have to think it out all the way. The guidebook gives it as 100ft, but it feels more than that. You climb a slender, tall riffle of edges and grooves, often with delicate moves on rounded edges, and you're so totally absorbed that you scarcely notice how much height you're gaining, how steeply the ground is dropping away beneath. Or at least, you don't notice it until—high up on the rib and with a fall-factor now which would bounce you way beyond the Heather Terrace—it gets hard. "What's this climb supposed to be," you mutter to yourself, "V. Diff?" You wonder where the holds are. After all, your rule of thumb for grading is that on a V. Diff. there is always a good, positive hold to hand. Not here, though—there's a greasy finger-jam in the groove, a toe-scrape at thigh-height on the right, and a hold of unknown worth four feet out of reach. And there in the toe-scrape were those tricouni-imprints again! "If someone can do this in nails, I should be ashamed of myself" I thought, and hoisted on up.

At the top of the rib is a last steep little tier before the grass ledge which leads off beneath the Terrace Wall. You step out and bridge up a shallow groove near the gully edge, pull over a bulge at its top, and the true glory of the Grooved Arete confronts you. The most elegant of curved ribs runs up into a blocky maze of roofs and black grooves, and keeps its continuity throughout. I wandered off to the side to sit down and study it at leisure, and it was then that I saw the figure—fleetingly, high up, improbably stepping round the edge of a slab into a groove.

A lull in the blustery wind let the precise click of boot nails drop down to me, and then she was gone—just a suggestion of movement left in the shadows. I was left pondering the route.

It quite scared me. I blew on my fingers to warm them up and found myself chewing the nails. Cloud-dapple and sunshine played across the ribs above. The line enthralled me. The Knight's Slab—the crux—it was right up there under the roofs. The exposure must be tremendous, and the moves—if they're harder than those down below then the issue's in some doubt. The wind was fierce up here, blowing me across to the foot of the rib where I cast about amongst the alternatives to start. Cracked leaves of rock, hollow to tap, curved up, the holds fractured into them comforting and large. At first I was out on the edge above Green Gully, then forced more and more into the corners on the left. At each large foothold, between each burst of activity, I stopped and worked out the moves ahead, climbing slowly and deliberately, learning the moves in case I had to reverse them, enjoying the precision of boot-climbing. The rock steepened. Given a second, runners, rock-boots, you could have climbed straight on at any point but the need was to balance expectation of difficulty against likely line. The figure ahead was nowhere to be seen. I found myself stepping out on to a foothold slippery with damp, with the way ahead concealed out left. Just above was a ledge—The Haven. There are times when you know

how features gain their name.

This time there was no stopping. I didn't want to get caught on the crux in the promised rain. The ledge swelled up into broken rocks, above which a wide, shallow crack with jammed holds ran up the left side of a slab. From a standing position in the crack the slab looked like a friendly interval. There were holds. A single delicate move, with good finger-edges and a sloping foothold, took me into its middle. Up and across, up and across and I was near the edge. The position was terrific, the gully-bed 300ft below. The wind nagged me on. Beneath the capping bulge at full stretch was a hidden fingerhold, sharp and untrodden. I explored it, relinquished it, stepped up and used it, sidled round the arete into the base of a black groove—the second of two, for the first was bald and unfriendly. It was anti-climactic. Or was it? To look down the slab was to glance back on those expectations of difficulty confounded. This traditional crux had been the easiest pitch on the route. But it had also been the best. I scampered up the rest—the groove, the airy black lava-edge above, in thrilled relief, and felt as happy about it as perhaps I had about any route for years. And there was still the summit to come.

Which is where I met Cathy. I popped up directly between Adam and Eve and there she was with her back to a rock, out of the wind in the flat area down from the top. "Good", I thought, "the perfect let-out! If I go through the Adam-and-Eve ritual now she'll think I'm showing off." I went down and sat on a rock beside her. She was dressed in thick corduroy breeches and a fading anorak. On her feet were a dinky little pair of hand-made, tricouni-nailed Robert Lawrie boots of the sort that I hadn't seen for years.

"Where on earth did you get those boots?" I asked, suspecting I'd met with the presence who'd preceded me up the mountain.

She'd been watching as I came down. She could have been in her early fifties, hair the colour of a bracken slope in late October and wrinkles gathering round her sharp features, enlivening the texture of a skin with a curiously translucent gleam of grey about it. And the question, too, had brought a little warmth to her cheeks.

"I got them from a travelling salesman, actually—a long time ago."

"Did he give away a free alpenstock with every pair?"

"Who?"

"The salesman."

"Oh, him—I've not seen him for years."

She sat back and looked at me. She had the strong

Liverpool undercurrent to her accent and the Irishness you often get in people from that city, a mane of red hair, eyes a greeny moonstone grey and the cheekbones high. She was volunteering nothing and I was feeling chatty, so I got an orange out of my sack, peeled it, offered her some—she refused—and asked if it had been her on Grooved Arete:

"Yes—and you came that way too."

"I was following you."

"It's fantastic, isn't it. I love that slab. Of all the routes I've ever done that's the one sticks in my mind."

"Best route on the mountain!" I enthused. "I'd been saving it up for my old age—hadn't done it before today."

The atmosphere between us had changed, as though the warmth of shared enthusiasm had thawed her reserve, and the shared experience had made us joint parties to a conspiracy.

"Why not?" she asked, "How long have you been climbing for?"

"Oh, years—I'd just never got round to it. What about you."

"I started in 1949."

"There weren't many women climbing then, I suppose."

"I don't see many up here now. I used to stay down there, you see, at Cae Capel . . ."

She pointed to the youth hostel amongst the trees. I wondered at the strange name she used. Then she went on:

"There were a few women used to come there at weekends. There was a girl called Doreen . . ." She gave a long scouse snarl to the name. "The warden was a woman, Dorothy Elliott she was called, then there was my author. The reason I like Grooved Arete is that she never sent me up it."

Over by Llyn y Cwn there was a bright patch of sunlight beneath the bales of heavy cloud. I watched it intently, turning away from my companion in confusion. She'd been talking so heatedly, so incomprehensibly—the whole tenor of the conversation had changed. I was sitting up here on top of Tryfan with a woman who talked in riddles, and feeling that strange response, where embarassment mixes with mild fear, which you encounter when you start to suspect that the person you're with is mentally ill. Perhaps there was an explanation for what she said. I faltered out the question which asked for it.

"Who was your author, then?"

"Elizabeth, of course—you know! You must have read her book. I'm Cathy—Cathy Powell she wanted me to

be. I call myself that as a sop to her for not doing what she wanted."

"Oh," I replied, non-committal and uncomprehending, "So how d'you get on with her now?"

"Badly, considering what she wanted me to do."

"What was that?"

"Look, I'll give it to Elizabeth—she made the effort to understand, but she couldn't really. In the end she sent me back there and I couldn't understand it. And she posted Dorothy at a window to make sure that I went. Mind you, I was never that happy about Dorothy being in the book—it always struck me that she was a bit too close to Elizabeth, with all this dutiful streak she had. And all the time Elizabeth was taking out her—what would she call it?—her sociology and her libido on me. She got me to jump into bed with the chaps for her—maybe she did it herself, I don't know, or maybe she was afraid of it—and then she sent me back to Tooley Street to marry Borstal Billy. But you see, it couldn't have worked. Because I'd been out here. It's not just that I'd been climbing, and got the confidence from that. It's that I'd been brought alive to show how alive you can be through all this . . ."

Palm up, she followed the horizon slowly round with her index finger, and turned to me, smiling mischievously. I was fascinated, enthralled.

"Want to know what I did instead?"

"Go on!"

"I re-wrote the ending. You see, she didn't know enough to realise that it could never have worked the way she wanted it. She thought that, full of strength through joy, I could go back to Birkenhead and reform everybody with my new-found sense of duty. What happened after her ending was that Billy got fat, drank too much, smoked fifty a day, beat the hell out of me when I told him about Len and Chris, gave me six kids he couldn't support and died in Clatterbridge of cancer at the age of thirty-eight. I didn't want that."

"So what did you do?"

"I just told you. I re-wrote the ending."

"What happened in your version?"

"Simple—as I was walking along by the lake, with Dorothy's eyes drilling holes in my back from that window, I realised that Elizabeth had never let me do Grooved Arete, and I was buggered if I was going to stand for that. As soon as I was out of sight of the hostel, I stuffed my rucksack under a boulder and came up here to do it."

"Oh!"

I was lost for words.

"So you've been doing it ever since?"

"Well—there's not much else a character can do when she runs away from the plan laid out for her. But I'll say this—when she had me lead Great Slab, she thought anything after that would be an anti-climax. But that's not how it is—I knew that much, for all her First in French and so on. It's not a battle. It's not some examination . . ."

She put a marvellous drawling sneer into her delivery of the word.

". . . where once you get top marks you're through with it. It gets into your blood. If they give us any, that is. So I came up here and did something I wanted to do, and d'you know, it was wonderful. That's why I turned up for you today. Because I know what it's like, the first time."

I was convinced now that she was one of those people you meet who are—no longer in touch, friendly-crazy, but there was such a sincerity about her and a chuckling humour running through her speech, I could have sat and listened for hours. But she rose to go, boot-nails clicking across the rocks.

"I'm going down North Buttress—how about you?"

"Pinnacle Rib for me."

We set off in our opposite directions. As I went down towards the flaky sheaves leading to the Yellow Slab I caught sight of her on the long traverse over the Terrace Wall—a flicker of neat movement across the rock. I took out my camera to photograph the scene the wall plunging below, a lovely misty light over Pen yr Oleu Wen behind, sun gleaming on the slabs of Little Tryfan and the traffic so infinitely distant on the Holyhead Road. Then she was gone, and I hurried on down. The weather had closed in by the time I reached the Heather Terrace, her nail scratches barely visible now on the first crack of Grooved Arete. There was no sound from the mist above. I rode back in the rain over the Crimea Pass to drop off a film for developing in Blaenau, and arrived home in a downpour.

"Did you have a good climb?" my wife asked, helping me out of the waterproofs.

"Wonderful!" I said. "Any messages this morning?"

"No—except Anthony called. He left a book for you. I told him where you'd gone and he said if you'd never done Grooved Arete perhaps you'd never read *One Green Bottle* either."

"Oh good—I've wanted to get hold of a copy of that for ages."

I put it to one side. Next day the film came back. I put the strips on the light table and looked at them under a glass. No figure on the North Buttress traverse! Just an empty mountainside. I fished in my shirt-pocket for the sixpence. There was the king's head, the date of 1951, milling tangible as rock. And then there was the book. I read it. But you can't *meet* a character out of a novel! And one who re-writes her own ending. Can you . . .?

The Living Philosophy of Colin Mortlock
Climber and Hillwalker, 1990

"Drive him out into the wilderness"!

Between days of sunshine, diabolically there comes one of cold, driving rain. I thrash up the motorway in a downpour, plunging through lorry-born hazards of spray only slightly more anxious at the prospect of a route on Cumbrian rock than at the thundering, swerving juggernauts I can barely see inches to the left. Through my mind there's running the description of life in an inner city comprehensive classroom which I'd read that morning:

"Sporadic fights break out. Someone is kicking, pinching, stealing, lighting matches. Textbooks, scarce now, are ripped up, chucked around. While the girls comb their hair and put on mascara, the boys play cards, flick catapults and pass cigarettes to each other . . ."

What vision, I wonder, will the man I'm going to see

have to set against this commonplace of state education under Mrs Thatcher's government?

Colin Mortlock has been running a course—I won't give its title because that appears to change with each new intake of students—in adventure education at Charlotte Mason College, Ambleside, for the last nineteen years. He's 54 now. When I first knew him he was in his late 'twenties, had a mission in life (though at the time it was not clearly defined), and like an American evangelist, to underpin the style he drove a long-bonneted white E-type Jaguar.

His course is remarkable in the extent to which it is values-based rather than skills-based, promoting adventure as a quasi-religious concept rather than insisting on the acquisition of technique. Opinion about his work is sharply polarised; to the staider outdoor pursuitists he is a major irritant, to the striving and undogmatic faction amongst them a way forward to be considered at least, and often embraced with fervid enthusiasm.

I've known him for 25 years; worked closely with him for two periods in that time; he was my regular climbing partner during one of my more intense phases of interest in the sport. I have always been critical and combative with him, and at pains to tease out the contradictions between action and professed belief which occur in any substantially interesting character. As friend, teacher and inspirational example, he is one of perhaps half a dozen people who have had most influence on my life. Weather notwithstanding, to spend a day with him after many years of only intermittent contact was a pleasure to which I was looking forward.

Oppressed by the continuing rain, we sat and talked in his office. It is *possible* to talk on a wide range of subjects with Colin, but the moment an opportunity becomes available, the default mode sets conversation to a single, recurrent topic—adventure. People were becoming more aware of it, he argued; they were starting to see its necessity as a therapeutic and enabling medium which can help people to cope with the conditions of late twentieth-century life. An appreciation of it was becoming widespread. I jibbed a little at this, querying whether some of our traditional adventure sports were still truly adventurous, suggesting that the stress on tabulation of performance was in truth another manifestation of the acquisitiveness fostered by eleven years of devil-take-the-hindmost free-marketeering, wondering whether the ticks-and-conquests ethos on display was in any sense socially desirable or advantageous?

Surely, I suggested, much of this is not the eternal quest, the exploration of inscape, but more nearly the amoral jockeying for position we might see daily in politics or any of the more dubious television soap-operas. Indeed, adventure in media terms is now such debased currency that it even provides the background situations for a great deal of advertising. I mentioned car advertising in particular, with a wicked grin towards the E-types and Lotuses of his past life.

His response was straightforward: yes, that is all valid comment, but to him, for his uses, the activities are merely the vehicles for the journey, valueless in themselves, of value only inasmuch as they provide the means of escape.

But escape from what and to what? From, he explained, is easy enough. From our fears and complexities, from the Arnoldian "sick hurry and divided aims", from whatever inhibits us from winning through to—and here comes in "to what"—a spiritual and holistic awareness.

"Which will," I challenged, "create the desire to improve ourselves in terms of response to each other and the environments amongst which we live? Laudable, but—notable resisters apart—in any other than a tokenist sense it's against the flow of received values in this country over the last ten years . . ."

He grimaced at the difficulty of the problem and began to tell me of a two-month solo canoe expedition he had undertaken on the west coast of Alaska which had profoundly altered his own views of life:

"The inspiration for it came from John Muir. I went with ideas of adventure and fears concerning safety and the probability of loneliness. There was plenty of adventure, but the overwhelming feeling was the opposite of loneliness. There was this deep contentment at being actually a part of the environment—at least on the sea—even when the sea was dangerous and I was being severely challenged. I'm not a dreamer—I see myself more as a practical, no-nonsense person—yet there was the deepest of feelings that I actually belonged in this magnificent place.

"Eventually, of course, I came to miss Annette and the girls, and my friends, but memories of that relationship-in-isolation were indelibly stamped on my mind. I now accept totally that all forms of nature have their own feelings, and that when I look at a tree, a flower, a rock even, there is the possibility of two-way communication and communion. That there's scant scientific evidence as yet to support such ideas doesn't worry me. I know that, for me, these links exist."

"And could you get the same feeling of oneness *within* society—in the Kop, say, when Liverpool are playing

Colin Mortlock on the final gangway of Overhanging Bastion.

at home in a cup match . . . "

"Something like—the same power of shared ideals."

" . . . or half a century ago at a Nuremburg Rally?"

He winced. I pressed. "Isn't the problem that what I take as your former view, put forward in your book *The Adventure Alternative*—of adventure as necessarily ameliorative, is hopelessly simplistic, and that what you're working towards now is a concept—in which traditional mysticism shares boundaries with the moral lessons of Greek Tragedy—focusing on solitary journeys in which the oneness and interdependence of what used to be called Creation but which we now have to refer to in more scientific, sterile and abstruse jargon can be perceived and experienced, and in which flaws of character are confronted and perhaps even remedied? Which is all fine and beautiful until you consider the circumstances of the educational system through which you might hope these ideals could be implanted. You are, after all, in the business of training teachers. How bitterly do you lament the scantness of their opportunities to fulfil your ideals, and the frustration that must engender in them? Your self-realisation and self-actualisation programmes, if you can stomach that terminology, are as laudable as—to the majority—they are inaccessible . . ."

The political litanies into which we then digressed somehow modulated—I'm not sure by what alchemy—into a discussion about Machapuchare, the holy mountain the top 150ft of which Colin's great mentor Wilfrid Noyce, in company with David Cox, had left unclimbed in 1957. That right deference to proper belief suddenly seemed crucial both to his developing vision and to the essential experience of mountaineering. And it left us with no option but to eschew the further hypocrisy of continuing to talk indoors about adventure, and to go out instead laughing into the cold rain in search of it.

These days Colin does not have an E-type—much though he laments the financial investment it would now represent—but something small, fast, black and Japanese which took us to Castle Rock, Thirlmere, with a minimum of fuss in a matter of minutes.

Colin was one of the significant figures in rock-climbing during its vigorous seasons of the early 'sixties. He had been Whillans's second on the first ascent of Extol, had added a clutch of his own new routes on Clogwyn Du'r Arddu and elsewhere, had made early repeat ascents of most of the difficult climbs of the day, had served as a link between traditional Oxford (where he took a degree in Modern History) mountaineering and the Rock & Ice and Alpha clubs which were establishing the new standards on rock. His article for the Climbers' Club Journal, "Training for the Advanced Sport of Rock-climbing", pre-dated Livesey's approach by ten years. After Oxford, he had gone the anything-but-traditional route of taking a P.E. teacher's diploma at Loughborough, and thence into schools, where he was one of the first to introduce climbing and canoeing as curriculum subjects. He had taken schoolchildren in the sixties on expeditions to Arctic Norway, and from 1965 to 1971 ran the most innovative and influential outdoor educational experiment of its time, for Oxford LEA at the Woodlands Centre in Glasbury on Wye.

It was nineteen years since we had last climbed together. Our partnership, which was the first phase in the development of South Pembroke as a climbing area, had ended at the same time as our friendship for a time was temporarily suspended—in a blazing row above a particularly little cliff at Lydstep. I didn't see the point in wasting days of sun and right tides on trifles when I was climbing well and eager for big lines. Colin, his interest in climbing in decline and frustrated by his seconding role, was weary of the stress of uninspected, uncleaned first ascents on loose and lonely Atlantic cliffs, and worn down too perhaps by the weight of resistance against him in his professional sphere. We both behaved dreadfully, laid unforgiveable charges against each other, and though the friendship had been mended, we hadn't tied on the same rope since.

Judging by my performance at the foot of Castle Rock, you might think that I hadn't tied on to a rope at all in that time. Colin at least had genuinely not done a route for nineteen years. I had no such excuse. The incessant drip of rain was putting me off, as was the lushness of vegetation at the foot of Castle Rock. I couldn't remember how to tie a bowline. We'd come here because it overhangs and might have remained dry. It hadn't, but we were hoist by the petard of our previous discussion. There was no escape. Overhanging Bastion it had to be, though a classic Lakeland VS—and a hard one at that—in the early-season rain is quite adventurous enough for me these days.

A chiff-chaff was jarring away amongst the young larch-buds. I felt like throwing a rock at it. This was not the state of mind of one in cosmic harmony. Colin was silent and obviously nervous. I'd foolishly volunteered to lead until he got back into the rhythm of it all again. So off I had to go.

If my recollection is sound, I had only done Overhanging Bastion once before, and that was when I was fifteen. Since I'm now well into my forties, not many of the brain cells in that particular data-bank are still available for recall. I knew where the line went higher up, because that's obvious—a magnificently narrowing gangway running at a steep diagonal up the front of the crag. What I couldn't figure out was where it started. I remembered stepping from a whippy tree to a slabby wall. Where was the tree? There was a vegetated ledge with a stump or two upon it forty feet up the initial mossy slabs. Was that it? I went to explore.

The stumps were neatly positioned as impalers beneath a steep corner running with water and a repellent black ooze. An infant river cascaded blithely down from the lipping rock which had given it birth above. The general configuration riffled a few chords across the wind-harp of memory. I had a vague sense of having been here before, and so began to climb.

The defining characteristic of climbing on slimy wet rock is the need for a combination of the resolute and the delicate in your approach. At any other time than high, hot summer you take it for granted that your fingers will remain tripe-textured and feelingless throughout. As to your feet—like climbing on very loose rock, it becomes a matter of accuracy and angles. At a precise, given point in the straightening of a knee, its attendant foot will shoot off. When the holds towards which you're sight-guiding numbed fingers are out of reach and require extension beyond the critical point, the whole business becomes interesting.

There was a manoeuvre in this wet corner which required standing on a sloping, slimy foothold at mid-thigh height with an undercut jam at waist height, bridging out to an ooze-filled depression on the right wall, and reaching at full stretch for what, in these conditions, was an inadequate finger-jam. On dry rock it would be a 4c move and you would scarcely notice it.

On wet rock, you simply can't climb in the same style, you can't allow yourself the same joyful, heaving physical upsurge, the same insouciant slapping of bootsole on frictional slab. Power doesn't come into it. Instead you have to substitute the most relaxed (because even so much as a tremor would break the surface tension which keeps your foot in place) and delicate process of upward balancing adjustment. It's not conquest, it's sensitivity and feeling on through.

Making this move on this day to me was an adventure and an act of environmental awareness which—because it was so lingering-clarified—was profoundly satisfying. And because I did it in good faith and with a joyful, tentative heart, the sun came out, forgave me

the ungainly scrabblings where, wet-clothed, I had to re-adjust to dry rock, and pronounced upon us its benediction.

The rope running through my fingers restored feeling to them, and the sun outsailed a stretching net of cloud. St. John's in the Vale glistened into vivid green life. I tied on to a spike and was very happy, though a cold wind gusted now and again to re-assert contingency. Colin followed up, with grievous complaints about the coldness of this rock to the touch and I was thinking, if this is speaking rock its message is a tenuous, icy one, though the moral from its black ooze is crystal clear.

When we had climbed together before there were no harnesses, Friends, RPs, sticky boots, Sticht plates. That now we had all these things was no guarantee that we knew how to use them. In fact, Colin didn't—got the rope as wrongly through the latter as a maladroit novice. With some people this would put you off, undermine your confidence—but not with Colin. I remembered the enabling power, the support that his presence on the rope had brought when, in the 'sixties and early 'seventies, we were exploring, probing, climbing on sight routes up those steep, loose limestone cliffs of Pembroke. It is another form of oneness and sympathy which feeds into his beliefs, and its alchemy was immediately re-instated. I would as soon climb with him as anyone, and that his climbing—and perhaps in its intense practise my own too—are now things of the past is sometimes a sadness to me.

But let the moment suffice. We had belayed just beneath the gangway, and I wanted to be on it. At first it was broad and a few moves of no great difficulty led up to a steepening. Unexpectedly, above this I found myself on a pinnacle, a ledge rich with bluebell and wild clematis below me. I didn't remember a thing about this as I belayed there with the hyacinth scent and the post-adrenalin wellbeing glowing across my senses.

Twenty-eight years since I'd last done it? Fifty-two years since Jim Birkett, with his primitive equipment and his strong, quarryman's hands, had first entered determined and delicate into this secret place. Birkett now old, maybe infirm, but still nearby. How clear are his memories? How short is time (and the rock still speaking to those who come here positively alive to its meanings)? I know too many *dead* men in climbing.

When Colin joined me we changed over belays smoothly and without speaking. The last gangway lay ahead. Did I remember a peg here, and difficulties to start? No matter—at times, when you give yourself to the rock, to its form, bending subtly to its curves, easing into the rhythm of its holds, there are no difficulties, there is only the flowing beauty of the thing and the free space below through which birds fly, and your soul tuning to the granite lyric you must sing and act out in this strange, slow-partnered dance. And yes, you pause to place a flimsy runner here or there, to ponder a move, a fear, a way through, but you have given yourself over to a gladness which is adventure of the spirit and which afterwards makes the sky and the sun and the flowers and the blossoming, imperfect beauty of your own friendships, your relationships with humanity, shine more clearly. Because you took those steps out beyond the edge of the gangway, because you swung over the void—and how large those holds were, despite their creaking insecurity—you came, this once and with ease really, to the peace and the place from where the view spreads wide and you connect with the earth and sky.

Moments! Of course Colin is right in what he is doing and of course he cannot say, cannot define. But this strange, awkward, shy-stumbling-worded man towards whom, for most of my adult life, I have held out a form of love, is inspirational—to work with, to talk with, to know. Continue, society and you critics, to probe at his deficiencies; drive him out into the wilderness; confirm him as wanderer, searcher-out of islands, lone discoverer of aquilegia, the Eagle Flower, in some solitary Lakeland ghyll. Then have him back, renewed, to tell you and to let you know, as Blake knew, that "Everything that lives is holy". And to draw your attention, as the poetic rhythm does, to the Active Word at the positive centre of that insight . . .

Yet still, how do we contend with the dead, unfructifying material values upon which the influences we take into our little houses dwell? And how do we defuse the scalding splash of resentment and negation being heated up in our cities and schools? We do not even have Sport for All. How can Adventure for All ever become a prospect? I do not know and nor, I think, does Colin. If there is any consolation, it is perhaps no more than that in its adventitious strengthening of each few participant's individual consciousness—however infrequently it occurs—is the old glory, anarchy and sedition of truthful witness, upon which no herding politician can ever pour his plausible, vile unction, and which, as it spreads, must scour, succour, mend—and make whole.

Talking About Colin Kirkus
Climber and Hillwalker, 1989

Steve Dean on top of Craig yr Ysfa.

"This bit where he nearly kills himself on Craig Lloer—why don't you put it into his own words? You've only paraphrased the account in *Let's Go Climbing* anyway . . ."

The speaker was me, and I'd been sitting in the sunshine in my garden reading the manuscript of Steve Dean's biography of Colin Kirkus.

"Have you done the route, by the way . . .?"

"No!"

"Have you got your gear with you?"

"No, but . . ."

The 'but' reflected the gleam of enthusiasm in his eye. He'd come down for the day from Derby, where he works in local government on urban renewal or some such, to talk about his book. I'd just been rescued by him from a wrestling match with a recalcitrant brushcutter amongst the virgin jungle of my garden. The day was one of those luminous ones you get between spells of rain. Neither of us was going to need much excuse.

There were a few problems to be overcome first. The main one was the condition of Steve's broken rib, result of a fall from some little shaley horror in the south of Cornwall a few weeks before. His prognosis was that it would last out the day. Second problem was equipment, but we grabbed what there was and shot out. There'd be enough. We stopped in Capel Curig to hire a pair of boots for him—walking, not rock variety.

Monica, the Antipodean assistant in Ellis Brigham's shop, eyed us askance.

"What's this city-slicker and his hayseed sidekick want with a pair of boots?"

You could see her brain formulating the thought she was too polite to voice. She took our names and addresses in case we made off with them. Then we drove up Ogwen.

"So have you done all his climbs, Steve?"

"Not yet."

"Which ones do you have left to do?"

"Oh, Pinnacle Wall . . ."

"You haven't done Pinnacle Wall? Nor have I, and that's a sad gap in our education. We'll do that, then walk round the ridge and drop down to Craig Lloer . . ."

This was rather ambitious, since it was already early afternoon, but why not aim high? We parked at the foot of the tarmac road up to Ffynnon Llugwy, and set off grinding up it.

"How does it go, Steve? 'On the occasion in question I had cycled the ten miles from Betws and then slogged for an hour-and-a-half across the grassy slopes of the Carnedds, over the saddle below Pen Helig, and down to the grand precipice of Craig yr Ysfa.' You know—the Arch Gully incident!"

I should say here that *Let's Go Climbing* is probably the only book I could recite verbatim from cover to cover. All those hours in the school library looking out to the Derbyshire hills in my early teens, when I should have been reading "Paradise Lost" or "La Peste", "Der Schimmelreiter" or "The Prelude", and instead as often as not I'd slink over to get Kirkus's book down from the mountaineering shelf and pore over accounts that I already knew off by heart—the fall from the South America Crack, the avalanche in Tower Gap Chimney, the first ascent of the Great Slab on Clogwyn Du'r Arddu. I gave a copy to a friend once.

"It's a bit childish," was his verdict, after he'd read it, and I suppose he was right. It's written with great simplicity and matter-of-factness. But that's its appeal. It has all the tactile certainty of our first visits to the hills, and all the innocence of an age when leading climbers wrote to each other in terms such as 'Congratulations on CB. It was a most marvellous achievement to lead the Flake Crack direct . . . I have sometimes thought of it, but I expect I would have funked the beastly thing when I got under it. To do it straight off without exploration was a most marvellous feat. Three cheers for the Climbers' Club!'" I recited this letter, written by Kirkus to Menlove Edwards in 1931, and com-

mented to Steve how pleasing I found it that an older climber at that time could write thus to a young pretender.

"Isn't it," Steve responded, "but did you know Colin was a day younger than Menlove? He was older in climbing experience, but Menlove was born on June the 10th, 1910, Colin on June the 11th, and Maurice Linnell on June the 12th. I wonder what the astrologers would make of that? He did Pinnacle Wall up here solo just over a week after his 21st birthday, on Midsummer's Day 1931. It was a Sunday, and the day before he'd made the first ascent of Lot's Wife on Glyder Fach. Apparently he'd weighed up the Pinnacle Wall route during an ascent of Amphitheatre Buttress earlier in the year. He probably rode his push-bike back to Liverpool after he'd done it as well!"

"He probably did, and over the Denbigh moors at that," I replied, amused and impressed at the same time by the rush of information that was released from Steve by any Kirkus button you cared to press. "What else can you tell me?"

"Well you know the accident on Nevis when Linnell was killed and Colin was badly injured. A.B. Hargreaves saw them setting off on the motor bike and remembers having the most terrible sense of foreboding . . ."

"I can remember the same sense in people's minds before Nick Estcourt went off to K2 in 1978."

"Anyway, that accident left Colin's eyesight out of alignment, and when he went for his medical to get in the RAF, he was way back in the queue for the eyesight tests, so he just memorised them. That was how he got in. Otherwise he'd have been rejected as unfit. His younger brother had also been in the RAF. He was killed flying a daylight bombing mission on the first day of the war. There's only Guy still alive out of the three brothers . . ."

"It always seems to me such a plain, sad life he led—the great climbing days ended by that accident when he was 23, then dropping out of the Climbers' Club scene more or less, spending his time at Idwal Cottage—and the social distinction inherent in that is fascinating—and then his brief marriage, and he's dead by the age of 32. Yet for me the Welsh hills are haunted by him—by this awkward, Chaplinesque figure who was everywhere amongst them. It's strange how he and Menlove still inhabit so powerfully here, how what they did and who they were still resonate around the place. You can't imagine, somehow, that people will say the same in fifty years' time of today's climbers. They just don't have that same loving, intimate acquaintance and association with

the hills . . ."

All this talk had brought us to the point where the path leaves the new road to contour round above Ffynnon Llugwy and strike up to the bwlch. There was an outdoor pursuits group lolling on the tarmac, maps spread out before them. They eyed us askance. I was still wearing the clothes in which I'd been gardening, scratched and torn and spattered with juices, pulp and sap, leaves and grass in my hair, face and arms stained in greens and purples, and a battered old sack on my back. Millican Dalton would have acknowledged kinship. Steve was smartly dressed in his clean city jeans and shirt. The last people we looked like were climbers. The leader of the group piped up:

"Do you work here? Can you tell us where we are? We're lost . . ."

Steve and I looked at each other, at the cloudless sky, the tarmac road, the clear horizons, and just burst out laughing. We reassured them, and skipped away still sniggering. Maybe we were uncharitable, but what can you do? The tarmac, the gabions on the zig-zags up to the bwlch, their inane enquiry, were alienating mechanisms which somehow were making the past more real and desirable to us than the present.

We arrived on the col, Steve crammed his feet into a three-sizes-too-small pair of rock-boots, I slung my antediluvian rack over my shoulder, we grabbed the single, stiff 11mm rope we'd brought, and looked . . .

Pinnacle Wall was throbbing with sunlight, the quartz ledge all aglint, the upper slabs a sensuous invitation. I haven't seen a piece of rock look so seductive in years. We picked our way along the traversing path under the cliff, made the usual route-finding errors, ended up descending something frightful, and eventually found ourselves scrabbling up the scree into the Amphitheatre. There was no-one else on the crag, in the cwm, on the mountain.

If you've never been to the Amphitheatre, you're missing one of the sights of the Welsh hills. On the one side is the huge bulk of the Amphitheatre Buttress, one of the great easy rock-climbs in Snowdonia. The Amphitheatre itself is a bowl of scree narrowing down into the stone-chute gully up which we were climbing. Its north wall rises for five hundred feet in two south-facing tiers split by the Bilberry Terrace. It has the same feel of majestic size and integrity which you find with crags like Cyrn Las, Cloggy, Llech Ddu—and it is far less frequently visited. Steve was overwhelmed.

"Look at that! I just never knew . . .!"

I knew. I'd been here twice before to climb on this

Steve at the start of the ramp on Pinnacle Wall.

wall. The first was on one of the earliest visits I made to Wales, when the people I was with had some sort of an epic on Pinnacle Wall, with the second refusing to follow the Quartz Ledge pitch and the three of us then retreating to climb the Amphitheatre Rib. ("I found a good new climb on Craig yr Ysfa, the Amphitheatre Rib, that was no more than Very Difficult. Thousands of climbers had passed without really noticing it . . ." Kirkus wrote about it.) The second occasion was in the 'sixties, which I'll come to in a minute. Since Lawrie Holliwell was killed here in 1973, I'd not been back.

The base of the wall was in shadow, the sunlight imperceptibly retreating up the crag. It lay warming and celebratory across the traverse of Mur y Niwl, the Wall of Mist, which, to add to the redolent simplicity of its name, has the reputation of being the best VS outing in Wales.

"Have you done Mur y Niwl, Steve?"

What this question actually meant was something along the lines of, "Oh, that looks good! Why don't we abandon previous plans, stop sweating our way up this hideous gully, and launch out across that sumptuous, golden wall?" Steve was certainly picking up on the alternative discourse. He smiled and shook his head.

"What would Colin have done?" I teased, picking up on his familiar, first-name relationship with his biographical subject.

"He'd have said, 'Oh, that looks good—let's have a change of plan!'"

"Just what I was thinking. Come on then!"

We sloped across to the foot of the route, or rather, to where we hoped to find the start of the route.

"Have you done this before?" asked Steve.

"I've been here before . . ."

I was remembering back to a June Saturday in 1967 or 1968 when Julie Collins and I had come up to do the classic Mur y Niwl/Pinnacle Wall combination.

". . . do you remember Julie Collins? She was a P.E. student in Liverpool, a really good woman climber. She had long golden hair and a lovely body and every male climber in Wales lusted after her—all quite hopelessly. She was good to climb with, competent and great fun. Brown did that outside broadcast on Vector with her. We came up here because it was wet and we were young and arrogant and thought VSs on mountain crags with your rucksack and big boots on were the things to do in the pouring rain. We quite properly failed on it. It was all soapy lichen, swirling mist and little holds, with your sodden sack pulling you off into space. She went off and married a golfer after that, but I don't think

the two experiences were connected."

The rope, in the course of this soliloquy, had been uncoiled, I'd been handed the end of it, Steve had belayed, the moment of truth had arrived. The route, remember, is a mere Welsh VS, yet I was oddly discomfited by it. There was a combination of factors at work in my mind: that early failure, the atmosphere of climbing out across this forbidding gully wall, remembrance of Lawrie's death, of John Kingston desperately administering him the kiss of life as the breath frothed out of his broken body; there was the impromptu nature of the present day, the uncertainty of not having climbed with Steve before, no bond of trust yet built up. There was the necessity for careful management of a single rope on what's predominantly a traversing climb. And there was also, and most significantly, the difficulty of the first pitch. You don't expect a Welsh mountain VS to start off with boulder-problem moves on tiny hand and footholds, off-balance on a bulging wall, with dynamic reaches to creaking holds and unsatisfactory protection behind them, followed by traversing out to a belay. already exposed and out over the plunging gully bed, with nut belays which are neither large nor encouraging nor conveniently placed. I was impressed.

I was also impressed by Steve's performance in following. Because of his rib and lack of equipment, I'd been elected leader for the day, but the neat competence of his climbing suggested that that state of affairs was by no means the natural one. We changed over belays, and I set to on the crucial pitch above.

The entire first section of Mur y Niwl makes a concerted attempt to shoulder you away from the balanced delights above. The crucial pitch starts with a leaning groove. The holds are good enough, it's just that they're in the wrong place. You want to move straight up, the groove slants left, and the holds are out left again. This makes for a certain awkwardness in the relationship between you. After 20ft a large spike improves matters. You embrace it. It warms to your embrace and shows a desire to move closer. Aware that this intimacy could have disastrous consequences, you hastily release it from your clutches and grovel past an awkward little overhung niche to a ledge system running out across that glorious, golden wall. Suddenly the whole character of the climb changes. You're standing in balance. There are good runners. The rock is sound and rough. You have a choice of route. There's a hand traverse line above, there are footholds at a lower level, and the exposure is achingly present beyond the gully confines. Some dim memory of a reverse mantelshelf registered in my mind so I sat down on the ledge, dropped off its end, and swung across to an ample and dignified foothold in the middle of the wall, from which an easy flop over into a groove and a frolic up the side of an unnervingly detached block which will depart its parent body in some coming spring leads to—new territory for me—the pulpit stance, where the belays are rotten pegs or nuts of a size I'd used up lower down on the pitch. I draped a tape round a sound and slender spike, tensioned the belay to keep it in place, and brought up Steve. He was protected for the first groove, but thereafter the runners had inevitably, on a single rope, pulled out. Sitting on a loose block with a poor belay, 200ft above the gully bed, with Steve at the farther end of an unprotected 40-ft crux traverse, the seriousness of the route started to creep home to me. As did the knowledge of the two Bangor students who had fallen to their deaths from this stance in the 'seventies.There are VSs and VSs in the world, and as VS's go, this one might not be technically desperate, but it's good E7!

Steve followed with calmness and aplomb. We supplemented the belay and felt better for it.

"Who was this guy Moulam? Do you know him?"

"Certainly do! He's a good fellow. I climbed with him once at Stoney Middleton years ago. He wore a tie and climbed without a break all day. Very solid. Good conversation too. This was some route for its time! All these stances with nothing more than nylon line and ex-WD pegs for belays! Can you imagine? I wonder what's next on the menu . . .?"

What was next was a brief hand traverse with a tendon-slicing edge and good jams, after which the route faded a little into technical grooves interspersed with ledges which robbed it of the exposure. There was a dripping, filthy wall at about 5a to finish, running with water after the previous day's rain. But there was a compensation in this anti-climax. As we had been following the retreating sun out of the blackness, so too had the amphitheatre filled and rung with a wild, wild screaming from all its corners and ridges, with a rush of wings, a whistle of cleft air, with tail-feathers fanned out against the light. Peregrines! Not one, but four of them, the juveniles red-plumaged, playful, the falcon and tiercel teaching them to hunt, to stoop, to fly. In this majestic arena we were being given the privilege of watching from closest quarters one of the grandest sights in nature. And the birds came close and looked and cocked their heads and wondering and unafraid went on their way.

You might think, after all this, that Pinnacle Wall, the route we had come to do, would have been a let-

down. It is not. It, and Main Wall on Cyrn Las, are the two best Severes in Wales.

And by ourselves on the crag in this mood, chasing the sun, we had the excitement of Kirkus's solo ascent almost exactly 58 years before being re-enacted in our imagination. The Quartz Ledge, unnervingly damp, sloping and protectionless:

"How would he have felt when he got here?"

The groove leading up to the crack behind the Pinnacle:

"There are moves on this which you wouldn't quarrel about if they were graded VS."

And the final slab in the evening sun, having stepped off the ridiculously sharp point of the pinnacle, with Cwm Eigiau a gilded chalice of light below and the Carneddau stretching majestic and shapely all around. At times like these there's no more beautiful place on this planet than the little mountains of Wales. We loped off back towards Helyg, and beyond that to a few beers in the Bryn Tyrch, with skylarks scurrying in crested pride, soaring in an ecstasy of song, and the stonechats tsip-tsipping away amongst the quiet rocks of the hills.

"At least we don't have to ride our bikes back across the Denbigh Moors to Liverpool, Steve."

"You know, on a night like this, I don't think I'd really mind!" came his reply.

Grappling with Ken Wilson
Climber and Hillwalker, 1989

The Adversary.

He began arguing from the outset, of course:

"OK then—I can see that it'll be a valuable opportunity for me to put across my views on this competition issue—but no gush, and it'd be very useful to me if you could get in a plug for VS Rock."

This is an entirely typical example of Ken Wilson laying it on the line—brusque, direct, unchallengeable because if you do it's to release a cascade of irascible abuse: "mealy-mouthed . . . beating about the bush . . . fine words butter no parsnips . . . genteel bullshit." It pours out upon you, withering scorn directed upon any fine and mellow human feelings in which you might momentarily feel inclined to indulge.

Ken is one of the stock-characters in the long-running farce at the centre of British climbing. At times he resembles nothing so much as one of the more choleric humours from Jonsonian comedy—Kastril the Angry Boy in *The Alchemist*, say, or Val Cutting the Roarer from *Bartholomew Fair*, engaged in an unending, years-long game of the vapours:

"Don't come out with any of this crap about us going back a long way. I know that you and I go back a long way but the point is, we *grapple* with each other . . . "

That's a fair enough summing-up of the situation. Since I first became aware of a force of nature frothing and fulminating amongst the murky waters of climbing politics in the early 'sixties, there has been a strongly adversarial element to our acquaintance. I have thought him, throughout his career as photographer, editor and publisher, by turns rude, overbearing, bullying, impervious, loud, aggressive, Machiavellian. But I've also had some very good times out on the crags with him. I've admired the graphic revolution he brought about in climbing publishing. I've respected the doggedness with which he's stuck to his causes (even though on occasion the tactics he's used have appalled me), and I've always relished the combative glee he brings to debate, and the resultant raising of his opponents' game. If you 'grapple', as he chooses to call it, with Ken, then you'd better not be—as he also chooses to call them—one of life's delicate flowers or wimps. You have to know your stuff and be fully prepared to justify it in detail and at full volume for hours if necessary. And then you'll win a temporary truce and good-humoured civility before he sets to revising his position and the bell rings for round two. This, however, hasn't even got us to round one. The day was propitious, the moon on the wane, the sun shone and his chosen venue was Ravensdale.

"No, no, not Raven's Tor—Raven Crag, Ravensdale, it's called. What I like is a route with several pitches that you can get your teeth into, get to feel the rhythm. Now Ravensdale's perfect for that. We'll do Mealystopheles—it's the grade I like climbing at and a lot of other climbers do too—middling VS or amenable Hard VS—that's the grassroots grade of British climbing and that's what *VS Rock's* about."

I had good memories of Ravensdale—of climbing lots of VSs and HVSs in amazing positions on wobbly holds and rough rock back in the 'sixties with Jimmy Curtis and Emmett Goulding. So I was looking forward to it, and arrived in the kitchen of Wilson Towers at an unwontedly early hour for a Derbyshire Sunday to find Ken nursing a hangover from the previous night's party. Aggression aside, he's a gregarious creature. He slid a mug of treacly black coffee—with Ken all sensations come undiluted—across the table at me and began to explain why the Gibraltar Inquest outraged him. Ken argues with his body. It's obviously a good way of loosening up for climbing, as well as of imposing his physical presence on the dialogue. Jerky and staccato gestures—jabbing fingers, sweeping arms—accompany the thunderous rush of phrase, his lips growl and curl around the points, eyes pop at the unexpected turns he finds his arguments taking. It's bravura stuff, but I won't go into the detail of this particular issue, because we're off to the crags.

For many years Ken lived in London, which is a long way from the crags, which means long car journeys, which gave rise to the tradition of "revving". Revving has nothing to do with car engines, everything to do with company. On Thursday nights in the Crown on Highgate Hill you chose your partners for the weekend, not only on the basis of their climbing ability and the speed and comfort of the car they drove, but also you vetted them for how good an argument they could sustain. This was known as "revving up", started at Hendon and continued to Ynys Ettws or wherever else you were bound. It is one of the absolutes in Ken's world still, and as soon as we were in the car he got down to the agenda:

"What do you think of this business with the BMC and competition climbing?"

Ken always gets the opponent to speak first and outline a position which he, Ken, can then attack. So far on this day, however, the martial auguries were inauspicious—we'd already found ourselves in agreement on several topics. I set out my stall:

"I can understand the feeling in the BMC that they have to be very careful not to alienate the younger climbers who are interested in competitions, and also that they fear their power-base might be eroded if a media-conscious organisation were set up to control climbing championships. But this competition they're organising in Leeds in February—the BMC's got no remit to do that! It's just squandering its limited staff resources and there are far better uses for those. I've no objection really to its taking an observer's role, but actually to set one up is carrying appeasement a bit far . . . "

That was the entrance he required and he thundered in on cue:

"Appeasement! That's exactly it! You mark my words, this BMC executive will go down in climbing history as the Men of Munich . . . "

I clapped my hands with glee at this and set Ken to working out the cast:

"Bonington as Chamberlain, Dennis as Halifax—you can just see it, can't you? 'Peace in our time' and whaddya get? I'll tell you what sort of can of worms you get. You get the birthright of a generation sold down the river and for what? For quickdraw climbing, that's what! You mark my words, if competition climbing comes in, we'll have bolts over every crag in the country. Have you been to Buoux?"

I demurred.

"Well if you'd been to Buoux you'd know what a state French climbing's in. Bolts everywhere, six feet apart. Climbers who can only climb where you can clip a quickdraw."

"So what happened at this meeting where you resigned, Ken?"

"I want you to get this straight. I resigned as Climbers' Club representative on the Lancashire and Cheshire Area Committee and Area Committee representative on BMC Management because I felt my views were out of step with the expedient line they wanted to pursue on competition climbing. But I think they now realise that the BMC's gone beyond expedience and keeping open the dialogue here, and it's now actively promoting competition climbing in this country. In my view that's outrageous, and so was the manner in which they achieved it. The Executive held a meeting beforehand in which they decided what their policy was going to be, they set up a motion from the floor which was circulated halfway through the meeting. MacNaught Davies beat me over the head throughout, just straightforward political thuggery. They'd fixed themselves an inbuilt majority and because of that and because they thought I'd be out to cause trouble it was pushed straight through, and any proper debate on the issue was stifled."

"Sounds like just another example of the grand old BMC tradition of political fixing which we've grown to know and love ever since you were a member of its inner circle in the 'seventies."

"If you're suggesting I set that tradition up, then that's a charge I resent. I have always believed in open and full debate on serious issues."

"You've also always believed in the value of widespread lobbying before the debate. I'd find it hard to accept a claim from you that your hands are entirely clean in this respect."

"That's part of the debating process. What I'm saying about the present BMC Executive is that they set up the decision on competitions beforehand, it wasn't adequately debated, it was just pushed through on the nod. On a crucial issue like that, those tactics are completely unjustified. What they don't seem to realise is where it leads. It's not just a matter of protecting the natural crags by hiving off competition on to the indoor walls. It gets us into the whole ball-game of World Climbing Championships, and that *is* a real can of worms, and that's what you get when you have political naives— and these are my friends, mark you, but I still think they're wholly in the wrong over this—trying to usher in a period of strong government in the BMC. What they're doing is not strong government. It's weak, because it fears proper debate. They've landed us with this now, and God knows where it'll lead. And incidentally, get this straight, my resignation has been refused by The Climbers' Club because they've looked closely at the issue and concluded that their position may well be closer to mine than to the one in which the BMC has landed itself. And it also seems likely that the CC, the Fell and Rock, and The Scottish Mountaineering Club will be issuing a joint statement to that effect in the near future! I think they're coming to realise that the Men of Munich's line isn't the proper one to follow and that we've got to stand and fight on this one. I mean, look, over this Malham business which started it all off, we won! We formed a very effective alliance with the National Park Authority and we saw off the threat, and it'll be easier next time around . . . "

Sound or unsound? Consider his views as set down in cold print, without the intrusion of character, approach, and other such irrelevancies which tend to cloud issues where Ken's concerned, and I think you have to conclude that what he says is very much the former and the present Executive can be seen to have behaved extremely badly. An Executive of a representative body which promotes something of which a vast majority amongst those whom it represents strongly disapprove, has manoeuvred itself into an untenable situation and has only two courses of action open to it—to reconsider, or to resign! Enough of politics—let's get to the crag.

It towers up, a seamed and wrinkled bastion of white rock against the dark valley woodland. To the left, a trickle of diminishing buttresses lend power to the major theme. I knew where the routes went, but Ken went over them anyway for my benefit, and then . . .

"The thing is, I've gotta change the formula. Single routes were O.K. for *Hard Rock* and so on, but with VSs, you've got to spread the burden because the individual routes often don't have the stature, and particularly with limestone, the dangers of over-use are obvious—the holds get polished and your nice V.S. of one year's your marbled horror of the next. So what I'm aiming to do is put it across in chapters which dwell on groups of climbs, get the character of the place across."

As Ken was rehearsing his future publisher's blurb, we scrawped up the scree path through woods with the scent of ramson heavy on the air to the foot of the crag. High above us someone was launching out on to the "Edge of Insanity" and Ken was bubbling with enthusiasm.

"Fantastic . . . look at that . . . that *must* be the best thing here."

We changed into boots at the toe of the buttress, Ken offering advice, interrogating, encouraging anyone within earshot. He's the most terrific busybody when out on the crags, always spoiling for banter, but it's immensely amiable on the whole, despite the loudly aggressive front. If there is a vicious side to Ken's character, it's definitely restricted to the depths of political intrigue, and even there it may be as much a function of misdirected zealotry as anything else. So much for the mephistophelian. We were bound for Mephistopheles, the first pitch of Mealy Bugs—which had been the original plan—being occupied.

Ken set off. He is a big, square-framed man with such a surplus of nervous energy coursing through him that his movements have a certain rigidity and stiff awkwardness about them. When he's climbing well he gets up by the barnstorming approach, beating the rock into submission before its subtleties have time to assert themselves. Competition between friends in particular—especially where he scents the chance of scoring points—winds him up to the appropriate pitch. One incident I remember which took place on the Aberdeen sea-cliffs years ago, when Ken, Greg Strange and myself had gone out to get some exercise on a filthy day after a night

Ken Wilson from a suitable distance.

of appalling drunkenness. We arrived at the foot of a classic V. Diff. and Greg told the tale of a solo-climber who'd fallen from it into the sea a week or two before, the waves trapping his drowned body beneath the cliff's undercut base for days thereafter. Greg produced a rope, and he and I tied on with alacrity, but not Ken. "Effing Pansies!" he'd bellowed, and shot off up the route to hurl abuse and sods in equal measure down at us from the top.

There was no such performance today. He was jerky and nervous, ground to a halt by a fixed sling on some pegs where the pitch steepened:

"No—can't do it! I'm going to traverse off into Mealy Bugs. Look at this tat! It's disgraceful. Climbers just don't realise their environmental responsibilities. This stuff is basically litter, it's not necessary. British climbing's not about pegs and bolts and tat all over the place, it's about nuts—the thing about nuts is that they're an ecologically desirable form of protection . . . "

With a final and conclusive "humph!" he set off on a long downward traverse into Mealy Bugs. The ropes threatened to jam. I climbed up to take off his first runner and relieve the situation. He carried on up Mealy Bugs, finding his rhythm now after the false start, looking like nothing so much as a rock-and-roller flinging his invisible partner around on the vertical dance-floor. Once Ken gets into his act, he is very competent. It's the same story as the other areas of his life—no messing about, just get on with it and if you can't do it, then get straight out with the minimum of fuss. He was at the stance in no time.

The party ahead was still engaged on the top pitch so I picked and dawdled my way up, savouring the steep bits, treating the rock with circumspection—Ravensdale has all the unpredictable looseness of a certain type of limestone. The necessity for cautious adjustment adds to the pleasure of the climbing, instils an air of uncertainty into proceedings. There are no memorable moves or passages, as with the great routes on the nearby grit. But the whole thing—position, atmosphere, insecurity—adds up. And as Ken says, with more than one pitch, you get into the rhythm of the thing.

I got to the stance, lashed myself in using all the best nuts from the first pitch, and handed the remnants to Ken:

"It's your climb so you can lead."

Off he went up a slabby, leaning groove. It's an odd thing, but although this crag supports a lot of vegetation, even where it flourishes the climbing is still continuous. It's a case of flower-power working a con-trick.

There was Ken, out of the groove and grazing amongst the plants, but he was obviously still climbing. He went out of sight. Some time later he reappeared above my head gurgling. He was back on the top section of Mephistopheles and it seemed to suit him better than Mealy Bugs. It suited me too when I got there, after some pleasantly undistinguished V.S. stuff with plenty of grass to chew on. You stepped round a corner, very airily, and there in the back of a corner was a steep crack running up for 30ft to the top of the crag. The sound of voices came from above:

"What you've got to understand, Derek, is that your mob effectively scotched a free debate around the most crucial issue affecting contemporary climbing . . . "

I put my head over the top.

"Geddaloadathis, Jim—two ex-CC presidents out climbing together! *What* a historic picture! Get your camera out!"

I looked up. Trevor Jones and Derek Walker were there, looking vaguely abashed, trying to sneak away while Ken's attention was diverted.

"Hang on, Derek", he roared, and launched in again. If Derek hadn't realised the responsibilities of being a BMC vice-president and Executive member before, they were dawning on him pretty fast now. We'd wasted a lot of time and Ken had to be back early, so I dangled the bait of another route to draw him away:

"Oh, right, it's your lead. We'll do Beachcomber. Come on."

"Where's that?"

"Just follow me."

We scuttled down and along the base of the crag to a white pinnacle rearing out of the grassy slopes at the left-hand end. I grabbed the ropes and climbed. It was an ecstatic little pitch. You climbed a steep groove, moved delicately across a slab under a roof to a crack, wedged up this, stepped boldly out on to the front face and then thought your way up the narrow buttress using brief incipient cracks and sharp, tiny edges to a real, pinnacled summit—limestone climbing in what for me is its best style. And at the bottom Ken was all encouragement, enthusiasm, consideration and advice. You can bear with a great deal from someone when they're good companions on the rock. Just as you can find sound and considered judgement in even the most officiously antagonistic of manifestations. And after all, he and I go back a long way. But let's not gush . . .

On a Summer's Night
Climber and Hillwalker, 1989

Judy Yates.

Think of the best times you've had climbing. When have they occurred? It's a fair bet that many of them have been in the evenings—at the end of those long, warm days of summer when the satisfaction grows on you at the end of a full day's session, or when you've hurried out to refresh yourself in a little oasis of climbing amongst the weekday deserts of work. I like the spontaneity that often comes with the latter—the sudden realisation that you've a few hours free, the 'phone-call to a friend, the impromptu combinations of companion and crag. Take yesterday, for example. I'd finished my stint in front of the flickering green screen, the concentration and isolation of which had left me with the usual headache and need for company. But the company had to be right—there are times when you grow weary of pandering to or tussling with the competitive egos of famous or would-be-famous men. So I rang up my old friend Judy Yates, whom I've known since I was a schoolboy and with whom I was always guaranteed an unhurried and relaxed adventure out on the rocks, with the zest of modesty and pleasant conversation to bring out its flavour:

"Judy, you're to take me out climbing tonight!"

"Oh, very well then, if you insist," she teased, "but only something easy, mind—I've been working hard and I'm feeling knackered."

"We'll do the East Wall Girdle then—how about

that?"

"Lovely—I've never done it. Will it be in the sun?"

I drove round to meet her. Judy's a capable, independent woman in her mid-forties, one of a definite breed you come across from time to time in the climbing world—lined face, laughing eyes and strong forearms. She has a mother who's a version of herself thirty years on. You meet them together from time to time, out walking on the Nantlle Ridge maybe, or swimming in one of the remoter lakes of the Carneddau or Rhinogydd in the full heat of a summer's day—and you're always glad of their graceful, merry presence in those places. You feel that they know something of the pleasure which wild country affords, and that's a gift which many people you encounter amongst it do not perhaps so fully share. Judy lives on a smallholding above Bethesda, so prising her away for a climb entails much rounding-up of goats and shooing of chickens and ducks, feeding and petting of cats, all taking place to a running commentary on their condition, character, history and latest naughtiness. It makes a change from climbing gossip and who won what at Leeds or Lavecchia.

Eventually she is ready. We drove up the Nant Ffrancon. The East Wall was seeping, sunless, shadowy:

"Sacrilegious to go there now, Jude! We'd better re-think."

"What do you know that will be in the sun?"

"Carreg Alltrem?"

"Ooh!" It was a note of anticipatory pleasure—"I've never done Lavaredo Wall!"

"Off we go, then!"

It wasn't as easy as all that. You see, to get to Carreg Alltrem you have to drive through the Lledr Valley and every coach operator on the North Wales coast every evening from Easter to October runs a mystery tour, the only mystery about which is why they should all go through the Lledr Valley. It wouldn't be so bad if it weren't for the fact that every coach operator between Barmouth and Pwllheli also runs evening outings to see Alex Harvey and and his Amazing Dancing Barbie Dolls in summer season at Llandudno's Astra Theatre. These two opposing armies inexorably converge at a point on the A470 approximately above Craig Rhiw Goch, where the road is wide enough for two coaches to pass so long as each driver is prepared to think millimetres and not no-claims-bonuses. Do you take my drift? The drive becomes a test of fortitude, character, patience. All are qualities Judy and I possessed in abundance since we'd taken the sensible precaution of laying in a supply of cream cakes in Betws y Coed. So our mouths became sticky and white as the bus drivers' faces became correspondingly hot, sweaty and red. By the time the coach-constipated road had unblocked itself I'd sketched out a treatise on the use of the cream cake as an aid in meditation.

The Great Coach Battle was only the first difficulty to present itself on this evening. Traditionally these come in threes, and there was no obvious reason why this evening should have been an exception. Everything in Wales comes in threes, anyway: rain, wind and mist; cafés, chips and cigarettes; tourists, trains and traffic-jams—the list is endless! They're known as the Welsh triads and scholars at our ancient universities have made special studies of them.

To the student of Zen Buddhism, difficulty is simply a function of attitude. I knew of a way up to Carreg Alltrem which almost completely negated the need to walk. It all hung upon a gate, and whether or not it was open, so we drove to the gate and open it was. We should not, perhaps, have been so easily deceived, because a half-mile up the forestry track beyond it a man in red overalls with an angry face stepped out from the side of the track and stood in its middle with his hand raised like a traffic policeman. I'd just seen the film-footage of that lone student in front of the tanks in Tiananmen Square, so it was a gesture—if not a facial expression—I was inclined to respect:

"Where do you think you're going?"

"To the foot of Carreg Alltrem."

"Oh no you're not!"

"Well in fact we are, though whether or not we drive there may be a point at issue."

This eminently reasonable response seemed to make him more angry, and he came out with the usual amalgam of references to copulation, departure, illegitimacy and Forestry Commission regulations.

"There you go, then," I answered mildly, "regulations is regulations, ain't they?" We drove up the track, turned round, and headed up the road along the other side of Cwm Penamnen.

"Judy," I said, "we could still drive there quite easily by the head of the valley—the Forestry gate's always open up there. But it's a long and weary haul and I'm rather inclined to the Middle Way these days. Let's walk up the normal path."

She agreed. We parked, by the ruins of an old farm now deep in the conifers. When I first went there, in 1964, it was a light and open space. I remember sitting here in the evening sun with my girlfriend of the time, and Don Roscoe coming up from the river, where he'd been with his fly-rod, giving us some trout for our supper. In the present deep, resinous shadows you wouldn't have been able to sit and cook them. As soon as Judy and I stepped out of the car, the third difficulty of the evening presented itself—midges, swarms, clouds of them, swirling spirals of the venomous, shrieking infinitesimals.

"Judy, run for the sun!" I yelled.

The midge, I suspect, is the originator of the vampire legends, the ultimate manifestation of gratuitous evil. Like its draculoid embodiment, it cannot bear the full light of the sun. Move yourself through warm sunlight and the midge cannot prevail. I offer this hypothesis as one which I've found personally useful, in the knowledge that it is really an admission of failure since it evades rather than accepts the test. We trotted off towards the crag whistling a little duet about keeping on the sunny side, always on the sunny side, keeping on the sunny side of life, and the crag smiled down on us and the river chuckled over the stones and we were very happy. The flat pebbles glinting under the water reminded Judy of streams she'd slept beside in the High Sierras, the scent of rowan blossom hung heavily intoxicating on the air, and a breeze blew like the settling of clean, cool sheets around our grateful bodies. We arrived beneath the crag in great good humour, with Judy chatting away about what she'd done recently with the people with whom she climbs, Clwb Dringo Porthmadog:

"Have you been to Craig Cywarch? I went down there last weekend. Emyr and I started up this supposedly two-star VS called Man of Kent. There was about 20ft of rock on the first two pitches and then you came to what's given as a 4c pitch. There was no protection and Emyr couldn't see where to go. He came back down from it eventually and we had to abseil off. From a 4c pitch, and Em's leading 6a at places like Tremadog! Anyway, we went and did Doom then instead and that was superb, have you done it, it's marvellous, 4b pitch after 4b pitch up this huge corner line . . . "

There's something delightful about someone who's been climbing for over thirty years and still has that degree of enthusiasm for the sport, for the new experiences it has to offer. In the 'sixties Judy was climbing routes as difficult as any woman at the time, and here in the late 'eighties she's still enthusing about what she's done, whether it be VS or even some out-of-the-way Diff that she and the people she usually climbs with have unexpectedly unearthed from decades of neglect. When I was involved in writing the Cwm Silyn and Cwellyn guide with her husband Mike, from whom she's

Judy on the top pitch of Lavaredo Wall.

now separated, in 1970, it was Judy who was the motivating force in sending us out day after day and as often as not in the drenching rain on to some awful, vegetatious scramble or other which needed to be checked, included or dismissed on Llechog, Craig Cwm Du, or the East face of Moel Hebog. Sometimes I get flashbacks to the horror of soloing around in those places and fetching up against something like the short, bald groove on Llechog's Mermaid Climb, which was graded Moderately Difficult and came on like a half-century-too-soon version of First Slip. Still, we survived, and here we were in the sun, a sweet, sound classic in front of us.

Carreg Alltrem is not a large crag, but it is exceedingly well-presented. It has a strong, classic line which gives one of the great Welsh off-widths—Penamnen Grooves, climbed by Bob Downes in 1956, the year before he died of oedema in Whillans's arms on Masherbrum. Molly Roberts once told me that after his death, there wasn't a dry handkerchief in the house of any woman climbing at the time:

"He was a lovely boy," she said, "we were all after him!"

There's a sort of solace to be had in the notion of a young life's waste balanced by the continuing association of his character, vibrancy, sexual energies I suppose, with this boldly-offered great Gaia-vulva up which he'd fought his way all those years ago. Strange, too, yet satisfying and expressive of what he must have been, that this should have been the only new climb he did here, and one of the first on the crag.

But Penamnen Groove wasn't what we'd come to do. Lavaredo Wall climbs a sort of pillar or faceted wall which bounds on the right the main section of the crag. In the low sun the crag was gleaming pale green and silver, pulling itself up proud across the slanting light. In its quality of upthrust into the blue heavens, it could have been one of the Tre Cime. It made you want to climb it.

"Why is it," asked Jude, breaking into my thoughts, "that every harness you buy becomes an intelligence test in spatial awareness if you're to get it on right? Which bits do your legs go through? I've had this one for six years, and I still don't know how it should go."

Old climbers always moan. If they're not moaning about the difficulties of using modern equipment, they're bewailing its devaluation of the heroic routes of their youth, and once they've exhausted that theme they get on to the one about how fit people are these days, or how is it that people who couldn't get up a Diff. without

a tight rope in the 'sixties are now cruising E4? The only thing they agree on is what a good thing competition climbing is, because it will lure the crowds away from the crags and free their aged efforts from the prying eyes of younger generations. With this thought in mind and not another person visible on the face of the earth, I set foot on the rock.

The first pitch of Lavaredo Wall is graded 4a. It is probably vertical, but since it lies up a groove where the holds are both good and numerous, that doesn't make things difficult, it just makes them enjoyable. The ropes hang cleanly from your waist and run down with a satisfying directness. You can plot your moves with relaxed precision. I think there are few things in life quite so enjoyable as climbing well on relatively easy rock, weighing up the elegance of each alternative, not giving in to panting haste but thinking smooth movement, thinking balance and flow. I've seen people capable of climbing the hardest routes of their day who never attempted, or were even capable of this minimalist grace, and I've seen people on easy climbs who'd probably never experienced anything harder in their lives who were perfectly attuned to the style. It is the best thing to watch in climbing when it's done well, and the most perfectly satisfying to attempt. In the warm sun, I immersed myself in the particularity of each hold, its feel and form and the body's potential use of it, and it felt quite effortless. Considering and exploring my way thus up to the first stance, which is comfortable and large, I sat and chewed the sweet grass.

Judy in her turn set herself into aesthetic mode, shunned the thrusting version of functionalism, and drifted up to the accompaniment of enthusiastic utterance on the satisfaction given by the jams in the crack at the back of the groove, and the ideal positioning of foot- and hand-holds on the difficult step out left at 40ft. I thought back on the pleasure this climb has given me time and again over the years; the people with whom I've done it, the springtime conversations with the ravens who've nested for years atop a great untidy pile of sticks in the groove round the corner; the capacity for surprise on each fresh journey of discovery—new ways to make familiar moves, handholds previously unexplored, all the texture that accrues in your mind around a favourite classic, and over which Judy and I gleed as she climbed steadily up to join me.

There are two pitches and it is the top one which makes the route. It has every quality—apart, perhaps, from difficulty—that you could require from a rock-climb: surprise, delicacy, discovery, effort, exposure—

they're all here to be experienced. It looks as though it could be any grade from VS to E6—there's no way of knowing until you get to grips with the rock, and when you do, wherever your hands wander they sink two-finger-joints-deep into the sharpest holds imaginable and at the lowest level all you need do is pull. Judy had never been there, out on that top wall, before, and for her, initial nervousness rapidly became revelation. She pulled out at the top with the biggest grin I've seen on her face in years:

"The only thing wrong with that was that it ended too soon!"

We coiled the ropes and even the descent down the fingerstone gully was a thoughtful, pleasurable experience. As we crossed back over the river by the stepping stones, with the crag emanating light and aspiring behind us, an alder bush in front of us, the rounded perfection of its sage-green form picked out, accentuated by the light, had us both rocking with the laughter of well-being. All on a summer night, with the experience of a climb somehow at the back of it all, and valuably so.

We went to the pub to celebrate. It was the Bryn Tyrch in Capel Curig, which has undergone a renaissance of late and is reliving its great days of the 'thirties as one of the truly welcoming climbers' pubs. The people in the bar had the happy faces of good hours out on the hills. The barman is a poet. At the bar there was a lovely woman with red hair smoking a roll-up, who'd been climbing at Tremadog that day, been parched by the sun, done Barbarian and Poor Man's Peuterey, the former "a bit heavy" for her. Equally enthusiastic about a Severe or an Extreme, she was going into the shadows the next day, on to Cloggy she said, rapping her knuckle gently, decisively, on the open page of her guidebook. Such is the texture of climbing life, and such its rare, frequent beauties . . .

No Pain, No Gain: Ron Fawcett
Introduction to Fawcett on Rock, 1987

Fawcett with child — no pain, no gain!

Stoney Middleton Dale: a thicket of straggly elder, ugliest of winter trees, screens the rock buttress from the road. Thirty yards away lorries clank past, laden with aggregate, bottoming on their springs. Vegetation encroaches on to the limestone walls from either side— ash, hawthorn and ivy. A cold fret of mist, characteristic of March days in the Derbyshire Dales, hangs in the breeze and a scurf of dust from the quarries opposite settles on dark leaves. The rock face is an open angle fifty feet high. The left wall overhangs, the right is slabby and smooth. Its colour varies from a chalky grey through beiges to patches of bright ochre. Dark stains weep from discontinuous cracks. The tide-marked hole of a cave entrance punctuates the base. A semi-circle of ground under the cliff is glutinous with mud, islanded with fertilizer bags, squares of carpet, filthy towels. It is the most unprepossessing of gymnasiums.

But that is exactly what it is, and on this cold grey morning there are eight gymnasts working out here at a changed sport. Two of them are wearing shorts, the others candy-striped or floral Lycra tights, or more sober tracksuit bottoms. A ghetto-blaster is thumping and tin-

ning away, propped against a tree stump out of the mire: ' Relax, don't do it . . .''. Three of the climbers are in various states of dependence on ropes hanging down the cliff. Two more stand at the bottom belaying, one watches, a couple more boulder across the foot of the less steep wall. Of the eight, five are tall and slim, long-limbed and lightly-muscled; the other three are muscular and compact. The distinctiveness of the two body-types is pronounced. Concentration is so intense that a general silence prevails, broken by sporadic supportive comment: "It's just a bit of oomph—once you know it's really good, you just spring up." Or again: "Just push right up on that hand and slap for the jug. Go on . . .!"

The climber who voices the latter encouragement, oldest of the group, is himself thirty feet up and midway through a sequence of 6b moves. Even at ground level an untrained body would barely be able to hang on holds of this smallness on rock at this angle—let alone reach them, rest there, then move on through. This gymnast, this athlete, however, completes the climb, abseils down, replaces a sliding self-protection device on the rope, and then repeats the whole process before taking a brief rest. After five such sets—five hundred feet of climbing up a severely overhanging wall on the smallest of finger pockets and edges, he will allow himself a break.

He squats by a tree, rolls a cigarette, watches the other climbers at work on the wall. After five minutes he gets back to work, traversing this time across the base of the steeper wall—across, back, across again, his breathing exaggerated now, sharp exhalations. Eventually he drops off, ruefully rubbing his finger ends, and turns to speak: "It feels as though my biceps are going to explode when I pull on that", he explains, pointing to the hold at which he jumped off. The move to which it is crucial is across a scooped hollow in the rock. There are no real footholds, just the friction of rubber pressed on dimpled patches in the slick surface. The hold in question is a shallow pocket, three-quarters-of-an-inch deep and an inch-and-a-half across, sloping, damp, and rimed with a chalky paste. He demonstrates its use. Two fingers, with the thumb curled behind them, clip into it at the precisest of angles.

"Like this!"

He grimaces, blows air out of his lungs, feeds in the power, and completes the move. "No pain, no gain," he gasps, before stepping lazily off on to a boulder and suggesting a cup of tea in the café down the dale.

Commanding figure in this performance is Ron

Fawcett, the outstanding figure in the revolution which has taken place in the sport of rock-climbing in Britain over the last fifteen years. He was born in the West Riding of Yorkshire, at the little village of Embsay, three miles out of Skipton, in 1955—the year in which Joe Brown reached the summit of Kanchenjunga and Don Whillans made the first ascent of Woubits on Clogwyn Du'r Arddu—the second of five children in a family of Yorkshire Dales farming stock, and has the "mould of man, big-boned and hardy-handsome" of those people. His hands in particular are huge and powerful—almost to the point of being a standing joke in the climbing world, with tales abounding of visiting Japanese enthusiasts as eager and clamorous to see the outsize Fawcett fingers as earlier pilgrims must have been over saints' relics. Other stories tell of his being reduced to desperate straits by thin finger cracks or small limestone pockets, accessible to ordinary-sized fingers. That's one side of the benefit/detriment equation. Massively outweighing it on the other is the obvious strength and durability of his physique. Almost alone amongst his own and later generations of rock-gymnasts and athletes (in no sense is the term of mere rock-climber adequate to the activity in which he's engaged), he is untroubled by the crippling finger-tendon and shoulder injuries which others have suffered.

He first intruded himself on the attention of the climbing public through an article published in *Mountain* magazine at New Year, 1972. Dave Cook, writing on "The Sombre Face of Yorkshire Climbing", introduced him as follows:

"My mind, remembering the days when a long Ogwen apprenticeship preceded VS climbing, also boggles at the speed at which young climbers race up the grades. Ron Fawcett from Skipton was fifteen when I met him in Ilkley Quarry soloing HVS routes. He was already doing first ascents of this standard on limestone. His walk home from school led him beneath a limestone quarry on which he constructed an alternative path of VS standard in order to vary his homeward route."

Down in the café in Stoney Middleton Dale during the break from his training, Ron himself talked about his beginnings:

"As a kid I used to play in Rock Wood, across the road from our house. My mate Martin Brewster (he's dead big now—likes his pop! It's frightening to see the physical state of lads I was at school with) and I used to get up to all the usual things—climbing trees, making swings, lighting fires, making bombs out of weed-killer and sugar. There were some big limestone slabs in the wood which used to be popular—it's called Haw Bank Quarry. We used to see fellows with ropes and bright clothes there at weekends. We were too stroppy to ask them if we could join in, so we used to roll rocks down on them or solo the things they were doing—I was a right little tearaway. One day Brewster decided he was going to run down one of these slabs. It was about 100ft. He set off but he'd forgotten about the barbed wire fence at the bottom. He made a right mess of himself and got a real bollocking off his mum.

"There was a climbing club at our school, but they wouldn't let me go at all, because the Games Master ran it and I never liked team games. I like to do it myself rather than depend on other people. I did go to the Lake District with the school, walking, though. We walked up Coniston Old Man and saw climbers on Dow Crag. That really impressed me—to a youth Dow Crag looks absolutely enormous. I fancied having a go, and in November or December, 1970, I got to know about a group of Venture Scouts that met in a cottage in Skipton Bus Station. The first time I ever went out was with a lad called Arthur Champion. He was about five years older than me and a really good caver. He said he'd take me out one Saturday, told me to turn up and bring a pair of pumps. We went up to Rylstone and did a few Severes, then I led a VS. It had a hard start but was easier above. That was my first proper day's climbing, and the next day we went to Malham, which seemed more of an adventure."

The enterprise, determination and distance from convention displayed here are characteristic of the entry into the sport of most of the really great climbers. That the young Fawcett had the commitment and drive which are perhaps the most important factors in achieving that status was soon readily apparent. Here is Dennis Gray with an early reminiscence:

"I held a housewarming party in Guiseley at which there were people like Nat Allen and Speedy Smith. Bev Barratt, a local youth club leader and Yorkshire climber, brought Ron along because he wanted him to meet these famous climbers. The next day a group of us old men and some younger climbers, including Ron, went bouldering at Caley—it was a terrible day, wintertime and wet and cold. I remember Ron climbing on a boulder called the Sugar Loaf. At that time he was not by any means the best of the young climbers in the group— there were others with more natural ability than him—

but I can remember his great determination. There was one particular problem which Speedy Smith had done in these streaming conditions—we were all climbing in big boots in the pouring rain. Ron, in something like a pair of Tuf Boots, just made it. He forced himself up this thing and all the other young climbers backed right off."

Within six months of starting to climb, Ron was starting to seek out the new routes, or the free ascents of the old aid climbs:

"Being a young whippersnapper and wanting to get in on the action, I attempted to free climb Mulatto Wall at Malham, On the first pitch I attempted to clip the bolt with an overlarge krab. It would not go in and I could not go up so down I flew, ripping out all my gear, making a hole in a tree and knocking out my second as we collided. I had my helmet on at the time. A week later I returned with a stitched hand . . ."

This time he succeeded on the route. Another incident from the same period reveals the same combination of fortitude, application and luck. It took place on Kilnsey, the great overhanging buttress of limestone in Wharfedale. One of the practices of the group of climbers Ron had joined was to spend much of the winter on the big aid routes with which the major Yorkshire crags abound. The efficient rope handling these demanded, along with the breathtaking situations into which they lead, were both important elements in a young climber's apprenticeship.

On this occasion he was alone, playing truant from school (having thrown his climbing gear from his bedroom window in the morning and picked it up on the way out so that his mother wouldn't know):

"I went to solo the Superdirect, which is the hard one across the roof at Kilnsey. I had two short ropes, probably 100ft or so. I got round the roof, abseiled down and pulled myself into the stance, then seconded the pitch on prusik loops. There was a free-climbing pitch to finish, it was pissing with rain, and I didn't want to miss the school bus back down to Skipton. So I abseiled off but the ropes ended forty feet short of the ground. I tied a knot in one of the ropes and abseiled on to it, letting the other go. It took about five feet to burn through the bit of bootlace I'd used as a belay sling on the pegs above, so I fell over thirty feet and hit the grass bank below—I used to be able to land well. Anyway, I then set off rolling down the bank and ended up cocooned in the rope in the beck below the crag. I nearly drowned."

It needs to be understood that the regionalism of British climbing (thanks to the magazines and greater mobility of climbers the situation obtains to nothing like the same extent today) in earlier decades had led to some remarkable aberrations in local gradings of climbs. Yorkshire limestone, on which Ron's early attentions were mainly focused, was more competitively graded perhaps than any other rock-type in the country. There were VSs on Malham which were technically 6a, and which would have been given Extremely Severe in any other region. If a climber was going to survive in this hard school, he was going to improve very rapidly indeed. Just how rapidly is illustrated by an account given by Al Evans of his first meeting, in the Lake District, with Ron. Again, weather is an important factor— before climbing walls and training in gyms had their present currency it was fairly commonplace for climbers to moderate their ambitions and ascend a token route in the rain:

"It was a miserably wet Sunday and we decided to splash up one of the easy routes on Castle Rock of Triermain before going home. When we got there Ron was on The Ghost, which was probably the hardest route on the crag at the time. I felt quite worried for him, because although the traverse is safe enough, on the top arete there's no protection. Anyway, he did it straight off, no trouble.

"Afterwards we got talking to him and asked him what he was doing on that sort of route in this weather. Apparently someone had told him that Lake District Extremes were easy, which some of them are, but instead of going on to one of the easy ones he'd gone straight on to The Ghost, which definitely isn't. We could see he was young, but just how young we didn't realise— he'd be about fifteen at the time."

It is natural in the sport for climbers to get to hear about, and team up with, their peers. The few who do not are invariably, and often with very good reason, treated with suspicion. Probably Ron's only peer in the country at the time was Peter Livesey, a fellow Yorkshireman and one of the most extraordinary characters ever to have graced and inspired the climbing world. Livesey, in his late twenties when he came to prominence in climbing, was the most rigorous of trainers—he virtually introduced the concept of training along athletic lines to the climbing world (though others, notably Colin Mortlock at the beginning of the sixties, had attempted to do the same before him and been laughed aside by the temper of the times). He was also the slyest of tacticians—question marks crowded in his wake like hens cackling over spilt grain. An enigmatic smile and a Gallic shrug were his usual response. His legacy was a roll-call of the great routes which stimulated climbing's mid-seventies revolution: Face Route, Footless Crow, Claws, Right Wall, Cream, Fingerlicker, Downhill Racer, Wellington Crack—all of them still test-pieces for the aspiring extremist.

"I knew from when I first climbed with him that Ron was better than me," he jokes. "The thing was, not to let Ron know that."

It was not a fact which could long be kept hidden. Ethical pressures intruded as well—an argument, for example, over whether or not a sling had been used on a particular first ascent. The partnership, without any great degree of acrimony on either side, fell apart. But not before it had given Ron the confidence to know that he was up there with the best, and that any existing route in the country was now within his powers. If Livesey had been the father-figure, the Old Testament God full of flaws, character, humour and magnificence, Ron was the young prophet of the New Testament, and his creed was purism.

It *was* a creed as well in the mid-seventies, and forcefully expressed. There were the old Yorkshire aid routes to be free-climbed. There were the impure routes of others to be cleaned up and commented upon in the magazines, one of which in particular had begun to idolize him. In article after article his now-proven ability gave him the confidence to castigate the less praiseworthy activities of his predecessors and contemporaries:

"Undoubtedly there are some brilliant routes in Wales, but a lot of them fall short of the ethical purity line. Really fine routes like Resurrection and Grasper were sadly over-aided by their first ascensionists and considered free routes, only to be cleaned in later ascents."

Judgements on individual routes took the same severe line:

Medi: "Climbed originally with a tension move and peg."
Resurrection: "Rather overaided on its first ascent."
Wellington Crack: ". . . regrettably used a sling for aid near the top."
Great Arete: "An overpowering line that was pegged into submission by Drummond, later free-climbed by Livesey and Foster."

The Moon: ". . . another Drummond attempt, was another to succumb to a later pure ascent."

His assessments of the quality of routes were no less terse:

Positron: "rather overrated."
Creeping Lemma: "vastly overrated."
Ordinary Route: "hardly a brilliant line."

Obviously, statements as rigorous as these demanded individual achievement to back them up. The lines were still there to be climbed, albeit at a higher standard than had yet been fully achieved. One of them was at the Cow and Calf Rocks, just outside Ilkley, where in 1978 the 23-year-old Fawcett was taking a teacher-training course. A 60-ft-long overhanging crack, starting insignificantly and widening beyond a half-height four-foot roof to unusability, it had been pronounced by Livesey to be "too hard for now". Fawcett's willingness to suffer for his art comes out strongly in his description of its first ascent:

". . . on a rather damp Saturday morning a tense leader launched out. It just had to go. My meaty, overlarge fingers are stuffed into tiny cracks, skin tearing, until they find a slot that accepts them up to the first joint. The crack then kinks slightly and narrows nastily; the line of holds leading to the roof is out of reach . . . a move in desperation, cramming poor digits in to the end of the nail, sees me panting under the roof. My forearms ache as I hang sloth-like from the lip, a runner sinking like a dream but my jams not.

"I try to get my foot round the lip, but no go. My arms don't obey and they let me fall—only a short drop but pride is hurt and I storm back up in rage. I can feel every heartbeat as my jaded muscles try hard to do their stuff. I sweat and curse, and just as I'm all-in the jams sink. Well done, arms, you deserve a medal!"

Throughout the late 'seventies and early 'eighties Fawcett was the ubiquitous, unrivalled Master of British rock. There were other notable figures around—Pat Littlejohn continued to produce major classic lines throughout the country, Pete Whillance specialized in cool, remote leads, and John Redhead was spectacularly audacious on the thin wall-climbs of Wales. But it was Fawcett who dominated, and who opened up the blank walls of difficulty's new order: the Vector Buttress head-wall taken by Strawberries (1980); the series of routes in the remaining bare spaces on the walls of Cenotaph Corner, particularly that to the left of Livesey's Right Wall which gave Lord of the Flies (1979); the bleak stretch of white rock beneath Anglesey's North Stack lighthouse, up the centre of which went *The Cad* (1978), where two controversial bolts were placed for protection; the smooth verticality between Gargoyle and Octo above Clogwyn Du'r Arddu's East Gully where Psychokiller (1980) found a way; the technically desperate and ferociously overhanging twin starts to Gordale's Cave Route (1982). And perhaps above all, the soaring lean of Derbyshire's Raven Tor in the words of one magazine writer of the mid-seventies "the ultimate outcrop [which] defies all attempts at free-climbing it". Fawcett climbed seven routes here between 1976 and 1982, culminating in The Prow, still regarded as one of the desperates, "the ultimate body-pump".

Chris Gore, who was a front-runner in the pack which began to catch up with Ron in 1982, makes the following assessment of his contribution to climbing up to that time:

"The thing was that after Livesey faded out it was always Ron who was pushing his own standard, and that's the hardest thing in the world to do. In running you have pacemakers, but he had no one but himself. What he did, despite that handicap, was absolutely brilliant and will be looked on as one of the watersheds in years to come."

The year 1982 is significant in that a rival for the crown emerged. The following year this young pretender, Jerry Moffat, firmly seized the initiative with his ascents of Revelations, a technical masterpiece which created a direct start to the Prow on Raven Tor, and Master's Wall on Clogwyn Du'r Arddu, a long and serious lead which had been bravely contested by John Redhead prior to Moffat's ascent. Not only had Moffat taken the initiative, but in 1983 Fawcett was put abruptly and seriously out of the action. He had been working on a television broadcast from Dinas Cromlech on a wet day, and in the evening, restless as ever when under-exercised, he went up to Clogwyn y Grochan alone for a work-out:

"It was a dismal evening, the crag deserted, routes with crucial holds coated in slime, jams sliding down wet cracks. Darkness. I was woken by the dog licking my face. All around were jagged boulders spattered with blood; my left hand had no support, it hung limp and hurt like hell. I wrenched it into some sort of shape, which nearly made me pass out, stuffed it into my pocket, and walked to Llanberis."

"A broken radius and ulna put me out of business for quite a while . . ."

This was by no means the only broken limb in Ron's career—the number of those runs into double figures. But it was one of the worst, and psychologically it came at a crucial time. What follows gives the measure of the man—his ability to rise to the challenge when it presents itself. Ron was seriously injured. Moffat was acclaimed as, and revelling in the position of, the New Star, and was casting his eye around for suitable new conquests. One of the most obvious lines in the country was the arete to the right of Green Death on Derbyshire's Millstone Edge. It was virtually holdless, protectionless apart from the possibility of placing a camming device in one of two old quarryman's shot-holes too low down to give much security on the crux moves. Extensive practice on a rope enabled Moffat to climb it without top-rope tension and pronounce it possible. He then declared his intention of returning to make the first ascent when the good weather came, and proclaimed that whoever led it on sight would have to be The Master. When he climbed it, therefore, he would name it The Master's Arete.

Fawcett meanwhile, the break healed, was training obsessively to regain his fitness. In December 1983, he climbed a series of extremely difficult new problems on gritstone, his account of one of which conveys the intensity he was bringing to the task:

"I could always come back tomorrow. In ten minutes I could be by the fire with a brew. One last try. I committed myself. One move from the break and an impasse; no way could I climb down and by now I was too far up to jump. Go for it, but with which hand? My fingers burnt with the pain of that edge but I kept on cranking way past the level of acceptable pain . . ."

On December 29th, he drove up to Millstone and inspected Moffat's unled line. He set off up the bottom section, arranged some protection in the shot-hole, and moved on past it:

"Smearing with my feet I snatched the arete and put my right toe in the top hole. My left toe went on to the arete and I pressed hard. It had picked up some lichen and it shot off. I followed it. The runners held and I was lowered to the ground. I chalked up and got straight back on it. Up to the holes it was much less gripping but harder because I had blocked the bottom one up with a runner. Once established at my high point the motor drives started firing. I laybacked the arete in classic style. Somehow I got my foot on a very sloping edge on the arete ten feet above the holes. I started gibbering. Only two moves to a jug. Could I step up and reach it or was it too far? Failure would be painful to say the least. The hell with it. I stepped up and grabbed.

"It was all over, bar the shouting . . ."

At the time of writing, more than three years on, The Master's Edge has been repeated only once, in the course of which ascent the leader, Mark Leach, took a long fall from high up on the route. The steely impetus and total commitment of Fawcett's ascent underline the fact that, although he may now have a peer group around him, he is still unquestionably one of the great climbers of this (or any) era of climbing history. There is a sense in which, with The Master's Edge, Ron finally gained a proper recognition of his dedication and contribution to his chosen sport. Here is Chris Gore again, with an extremely intelligent and valid assessment of his developing position:

"Ron initially had a disservice done to him by the profile and hype given him in *Crags* magazine. He was *expected* to be the best, but really it was more political. The magazine deliberately associated itself with its own created star, and obviously the star believes in the image he's given. I remember once on Windy Ledge at Stoney, Ron was on the start of Special K, which for 5c is way out, and he messed up a move and had to come down. So he went, 'Tut—slapped wrists—shouldn't have done that,' which was ludicrous. He was taking on himself these imagined expectations of the people watching, in whose eyes he should have been flowing up the routes. Because he'd just become a media-machine, the character didn't come out.

"He doesn't care about that now so much—he just gets out and goes climbing because that's what he loves doing and what's more important to him than anything else. He's got the personal confidence now not to be scared about failing or having a hard time. Ron can say that he's done it now, and with routes like Zoo Look at Malham, is still doing it."

Let's pick him up again where we left him a few thousand words ago, in Stoney Middleton Café, He's finished a meagre lunch of tea and a sticky bun, smoked a few roll-ups, and the sun's filtering through, promising warm rock on the gritstone edges. So it's up to the west-facing slabs of Froggatt for the afternoon session. Once there, the sun breaks through and he takes off his shirt to bask

in it, lean-bodied, with great ropes of muscle at the rear of the rib-cage on either side. They stand out in perfect definition as he solos, relaxedly, contemplatively, up Livesey's route Downhill Racer (E4, 6a) feet angling on to the quarter-inch sloping holds with careful precision, then down Long John's Slab (E3, 5c) up Hairless Heart (E5, 5c) and down Synopsis (E2, 5c). Bouldering, he strolls, hands off the rock, across the old 6a moves of Joe's Problem. His body instinctively places itself in the correct positions. He comments, on the grades of the Extremely Severe routes around which he's wandering at will, that "I can't make a proper judgement and I don't think the people who write the guidebooks can either," and further berates the guide writers in saying that "when I was doing my 100 Extremes in a day on grit, the main difficulty was finding the routes from the guide." Bare-chested, despite snow still lying in patches on the ground, he smiles at the thought that "they'll all be back in Sheffield whingeing about how cold it is today". You watch him with an underlying awareness that his eleven-and-a-half stone of lightness, elegance and microdot foot-precision could so easily—has too often—become so much dead weight hurtling into the boulders. Yet the compulsion lives on. On Artless (E4, 6b) he looks down after completing the crux, and musingly tells me that "I hate that—it's one of my little purges that I make myself do it. I always feel so gangly on it. If I find it hard to reach the holds, and I'm six-foot-three, how the fuck did Whillans do it?"

The respect for the great pioneers and his own innate modesty continually shine through. As does his pleasure and enthusiasm: "All these numbers, all this talk about what grade they are, as if it matters. Why does nobody talk about quality any more. Why don't they realise just how good it is just to be out here . . .?"

On the technical side of rock-climbing, *Fawcett on Rock* is probably the best treatise ever written. Yet the single last comment above is the most important that its author makes. It amplifies, underscores, and to a large extent explains Ron Fawcett's continuing greatness as a climber. Learn what you can from his enormous technical expertise, but bear that simple philosophy with you as you do so. It's the key to the real enjoyment of the sport. And enjoy it I hope you do.

The Character, Life and Times of H. W. Tilman
Royal Geographical Society Lecture, 1988

H. W. Tilman.

I'm honoured to be asked to speak about H. W. Tilman tonight, and very pleased to do so in aid of the Wishing Well Fund—which is probably the only aspect of tonight's proceedings of which Tilman himself would have approved.

I'm also conscious that my acceptance of the invitation is slightly fraudulent. I knew Tilman only for a very short period right at the end of his very long life. There will be others here tonight who knew him far better and for much longer than I did. It would nonetheless be bogus to pretend that I'm anything other than delighted to be able to speak here, at the RGS, about a man who held the highest award, the Founder's Medal, of The Royal Geographical Society, and who certainly had a more profound effect upon me than any other man I've ever met.

The question is where to begin. There is, as you'll know, a 350-page biography and even that's only a more-or-less cursory narrative of the events of his life. There are his own books—fifteen in number and each of them a distinguished contribution to the literature of travel, or mountaineering, or sailing, or all three because really they're impossible to categorise. And then there's Tilman's character, and it's with this, as it came through in his writings, in his conversations, and in the response of others to him, that I'd like chiefly to deal.

I'll presume that you're familiar with the simple record: with his mountaineering in the 1930s, often in company with Eric Shipton, which took in first ascents such as that of the West Ridge of Mount Kenya—as a novice—in 1930; and of Nanda Devi, the highest summit to be climbed in the pre-war period, in 1936;

with his explorations in the Himalayas—up the Rishi Ganga to the Nanda Devi sanctuary in 1934; or on the 1935 Mount Everest reconnaissance expedition; or with the 1937 "Blank on the Map" trip with Shipton, Auden and Spender which contributed so much to knowledge of the Karakoram. And finally as leader of the 1938 Everest expedition—as a single decade of mountain exploration it's unsurpassed, and only equalled by his friend Shipton, with whom so much of it was shared.

Then there's his war record—on the Western Front in the Great War; in the Western Desert—which he found boring—and behind enemy lines in Albania and the Dolomites in the Second World War, for which he was awarded the DSO, the MC and bar and made a freeman of the City of Belluno. After the last war there's brief service as a British Consul in Burma and then an extraordinary period of five years when he was continually travelling; through China, Nepal, Sinkiang, Kashmir, the Gobi Desert, Afghanistan.

Finally, twenty-three years and 150,000 miles of sailing—in Bristol Channel pilot-cutters built at the turn of the century—to the Antarctic, Patagonia, Greenland, Spitzbergen. It is not an ordinary life and it was not an ordinary man who lived it and you knew that from the moment you first met him.

In my case that was on top of Cader Idris on a snowy day in the 1970s. I'd come up a snow gully with my dog, which was fortuitous—he liked dogs. One of his favourite quotations was the supposed maxim of Frederick the Great—"The more I see of humanity, the more I love my dog". I went into the summit shelter, which was banked high inside with driven snow, took out my flask and sandwiches, and then one of those meetings which are amongst the greatest pleasures of being in the hills took place.

A short and rather shabbily dressed old man with an old-fashioned rucksack came in. My dog barked at him, and his face, which was alive with good humour, registered an amused displeasure at finding another person there. He sat down, made friends with my dog, drank my coffee, and grumbled aloud at the intrusion on his privacy.

There is, you should understand, a sort of freemasonry about mountaineering. It doesn't consist of rolled trouser-legs, bared breasts, rubbed knuckles or any of that nonsense; it exists through mutuality and not propagation of interest; and the induction process is utterly straightforward. You have to be in the right place at the right time and that in itself is a declaration which establishes a degree of trust.

So for the next few months after this winter meeting, I saw Tilman quite regularly and talked with him at considerable length.

I didn't initially know very much about him. I'd heard about him from a friend of mine who'd sailed with him—Ian Duckworth—who'd told me that "he's a bastard, an absolute bastard," and then modulated his criticism by adding "But he's a hard old bastard!"— which to Ian was the highest praise.

I'd read perhaps half-a-dozen of his books and I had the feeling that they were the best thing in mountaineering literature.

I should say that at that time this point of view was heterodox. Mountain writing in the 1970s was dominated by a new style of breathless, tell-it-all solipsism and self-aggrandisement and Tilman's cultured clarity, detached irony, wit, and self-effacement were entirely unfashionable.

He lived in a house called Bodowen near Barmouth, and I began to visit him there. I was rather intimidated by him at first—not through any action of his, but through an aura of moral solidity which someone brought up as I was, in the 'sixties on sex-and-drugs-and-rock'n'roll, would inevitably find rather bracing.

We did, however, have two great loves in common— one for the mountains and one for eighteenth-century literature, and it was the latter which for those few months brought us together.

You'll be aware of the language and the ideas of eighteenth-century literature—its ironies, its moral questioning, the vein of misanthropy which runs through much of it. Tilman to me was an embodiment of these, and to him I was a partner in an extended conversation which could be conducted in those terms.

When I met him he was 78, and within the year he would be dead. Our conversations were retrospective over the matter of his life. He was old and lonely. He felt isolated and anachronistic. His last boat, *Baroque*, had been left in Iceland because of crew trouble. He needed someone in those last few months to whom he could talk and to whom he could vindicate himself.

Don't take from this the impression that these conversations were solemn—they were far from it. If Tilman ever caught himself out in the act of being po-faced, you could be sure that a joke directed against himself would result.

The most celebrated instance of this is the famous line about himself and Odell reaching the top of Nanda Devi:

"I believe we so far forgot ourselves as to shake hands on it."

Where he obviously feels that the solemnity of the preceding climbing account now needs to be punctured. It's a curious comment on the critical acumen of readers of mountain writing that for many years this was taken literally as an example of how pukka sahibs behaved on reaching the top of their mountains.

There was a quality in Tilman's humour which, both when you read it and when you talked to him personally, was somehow disturbing. A lot of it's concerned with making a joke about misanthropy, but the joke is ambivalent, has a sub-text. You laugh, yet you sense the laughter's really a way of accommodating yourself to the fact of a very deep-seated dislike of the human race. As an example of this, I once asked him how many of the stories told about himself were apocryphal and his response was this:

"By far the greater number, but there is one which is substantially true.

"It was on an expedition in the thirties. We embarked at Tilbury, and I am said to have stayed on deck until we rounded the North Foreland, whereupon I was heard to mutter the words, 'H'm, Sea!'

"After this I went below decks and was not seen again until we hove in sight of Bombay. I then came on deck once more and was duly heard to utter the words, 'H'm, land!'

"It is asserted that these were the only words I uttered on the entire voyage, which is more or less the truth of the matter, and the reason, quite simply, is that I could not stand the other chaps on that trip."

He looked at me long and hard to study the effect, then burst into an alcoholic chuckle. (The drinking of beer in Tilman's house began at twelve o'clock sharp—it being decadent to drink in the morning—which meant that by one o'clock I was generally drunk, which explains why my pictures of him are often out of focus. He remained unaffected.)

I've never heard anything like this story from any other source, and I'm fairly sure that it was a piece of extemporisation on Tilman's part. Of course, it's not a joke, not really—it's a parable, in which, if you like, he's setting forth his moral relationship with the world: the voyage; being below decks; seeing sea; seeing land; but above all shunning the company of his fellow-men.

Why?

Consider these images from his life: Berkhamsted School, 1914; the military academy at Woolwich, 1915; his eighteenth birthday, on February 14th, 1916, which he spent in a dugout on the Somme:

"We lost our best sergeant the other day, up at the

Observation Post. A whizz-bang came through the window as he was looking out. It's always the way—the best fellows get done in, the rotters escape.*"*

Nobody as sensitively intelligent as Tilman could have hoped to have survived this experience at this time of his life unscathed. I asked him about it once:

"What about the Great War?"

He looked at me very sharply, shook his head, and in the heaviest silence turned away. This was *sixty* years after it. To my knowledge, the only thing he wrote about it was this.

"After the first war, when one took stock, shame mingled with satisfaction at finding oneself still alive. One felt a bit like The Ancient Mariner: so many better men, a few of them friends, were dead:
'And a thousand thousand slimy things
Lived on; and so did I.'"

A part of the fascination of Tilman's life is that it has about it an almost mythical resonance. Little more than a month after his 18th birthday, this Valentine's-Day-Child misanthropist is wounded for the first time—a flesh wound in the thigh. It's King Pellinor. It's Philoctetes. You see the start of the process by which the man ultimately seeks to understand this incomprehensible world through myth, and indeed the mythopoeic tendency in writers who endured and survived the Great War is startling: Robert Graves in pursuit of the White Goddess; the Celtic Synthesis of David Jones. With Tilman it's the modern Odyssey, which takes him far away from what we presume to call civilisation—his attitude towards which, particularly after the Second World War, had hardened into an almost Swiftian rage and rancour:

"There is a good case for dropping bombs on civilians because so very few of them can be described as inoffensive . . ."

(I can relate to that sentiment—I feel much the same way whenever I see a member of the Conservative Cabinet.)

It's interesting to observe in Tilman's language that he frequently uses the inflated vocabulary of Great War reportage and non-participation—gallant, ardent, warriors, vanquished, radiant and so on—when his ironies are biting most deeply.

I don't know how many of you have been reading the Falklands war memoir of Captain Robert Lawrence which has been serialized in *The Observer* over the last couple of weeks? In that memoir you have the same

Mischief at Ubekvendt, Greenland.

process at work, this splitting off of private from public perception in the mind of the highly intelligent young officer. The image with which Lawrence presents us, of a man rejected and humiliated by those on whose account he has had half his brain shot away, and who can yet see more clearly and sensitively than those who have used him thus, is startling, shaming, and obscene.

"In the Country of the Blind, the one-eyed man is king."

It is something like this, in my view, which caused Tilman in 1919 to shake the dust of Europe off his shoes and set out for a new Eden, wherever it could be found.

Once he'd found it, years later amongst the Sherpas and hill-people of the Himalayas, he was concerned to keep it undespoiled. Here's what he has to say in *Nepal Himalaya*:

"Like Tibet Nepal has always sought isolation and has secured it by excluding foreigners, of whom the most undesirable were white men.

"A man fortunate enough to have been admitted into Nepal is expected to be able to explain on general grounds the motives behind this invidious policy and, on personal grounds, the reason for such an unaccountable exception. But now that the advantages of the Western way of life are becoming every day less obvious no explanation should be needed. Wise men traditionally come from The East, and it is probable that to them The West and its ways were suspect long before we ourselves began to have doubts."

It's very notable in his writing that the only period in which he indulges himself in celebration of his fellow men is that of his Himalayan travels and even then it's only one faction amongst them about whom he writes with attentiveness and affection—the Sherpas and native porters—Pasang Kikuli, Naiad Shah, Nukku, Norbu, Mir Hamza, Da Namgyal, Tenzing, Angtharkay.

And the affection was reciprocated. Here's Norbu, forty years on:

"Tilman was always first away in the morning, carrying a load in excess of the standard Sherpa load. He always arrived first at the day's destination. Sometimes he would run along parts of the route. He would have tea brewing by the time the rest caught up with him and then he would praise those who had made good time and yell and scream at those he thought had been lazy or lacking in some way. On at least one rest day he made all his Sherpas a cake. Tashi, the Sherpa who was translating what Norbu said, was made to repeat this fact several times."

It was an idyll, and it couldn't last. By the early 1950s those Europeans whom he sought to avoid had begun to catch him up:

"The Himalaya are extensive, no less than 1,500 miles in length, but a quiet man might well shrink from going, say, to Katmandu if he thought he was likely to meet there eleven other parties with their 5,000 porters."

So he took to the sea and he did so, appropriately enough because there is a mischievous, subversive or even seditious element in his writing, in a Bristol Channel pilot-cutter built in 1906 and called *Mischief*:

"In the years between 1954 when I bought her, and 1968 when I lost her, the possession of an old pilot-cutter called Mischief enabled me to visit some remote regions north and south. In those fifteen years she sailed some 110,000 miles. She was not that big, 45ft long over all, but she was an able sea-boat, kind on her gear and kind on her crew."

The problem with boats is that if they're of a certain type and above a certain size, you have to sail them with other people, and you'll know Dr Johnson's thoughts on that:

"No man will be a sailor who has contrivance enough to get himself into a jail; for being in a ship is being in a jail, with the chance of being drowned."

And at another time:

"A man in jail has more room, better food, and commonly better company."

Post-war sailing carries with it, of course, a set of social attitudes ranging from the Neanderthal to the palaeolithic. It's a true-blue sport where pride of possession takes pride of place. So again, we have what this time is a very amusing distancing effect between Tilman and the society of his time. On the one hand he was making phenomenal voyages in ancient wooden boats to some of the world's most inhospitable waters, and being recognized and honoured for doing so—he was given the Fellowship of the Royal Institute of Navigation, the CBE, the Blue Water Medal of the Cruising Club of America and the Goldsmith Award of the Royal Cruising Club.

On the other hand, his style of voyaging and the reports of his more disaffected crew members were drawing the wrath of the yacht-polishing fraternity. In the trade journals which masquerade as their magazines members of the latter were earnestly seeking to polish off his reputation. There were scurrilous representations of him as "a desperate old man, repeatedly wrecking his unseaworthy old boats and maltreating his crews."

Andrew Craig-Bennett's reply to one of those attacks in the correspondence columns of *Yachting Monthly* for January 1982, gives in passing a very clear picture of what it was like to sail with Tilman:

"Mr Beavis's article raises a rather important question. What does constitute safety in yachting? We have grown accustomed to long voyages made in sponsored boats with every possible facility and for years past the safety industry and the RYA have been trying to persuade us to buy expensive safety equipment, and to obtain expensive pieces of paper called Yachtmasters' Certificates.

"Accidents have continued to happen—the possessor of an RYA ticket is just as likely to do something daft as the next man. I am appalled by the attitude of those numerous yachtsmen who seem to imagine that because they carry liferafts, radio- telephone, lifejackets and so forth they are thereby safer.

"Safety is an attitude of mind, and Tilman was a very safe man to sail with.

"He never sought publicity or sponsorship. He sailed to the places he wanted to visit without fuss and in doing so enabled a number of young men who would never have been able to do so in their own boat to share the experience.

"No-one was compelled to sail with him. All he asked in return for providing the boat and the provisions was that one should muck in and get on with the job in hand. His irritation with those who, having eaten his food and perhaps deprived others of a place, decided to tell him how to sail his own boat is quite understandable.

"His safety record compares rather well with that of certain competitors in recent offshore races, despite all their safety equipment. Sailing in high latitudes is bound to be more dangerous than crossing The Solent, but he always took care to minimise the risks and act prudently. His achievements speak for themselves."

It was a teasing irony that the annual Fastnet Race of 1978 to which Craig-Bennett is referring and which ended so tragically, took place on the weekend of Tilman's memorial service. Tilman's own view of the matter was succinct:

"In my view every herring should hang by its own tail.

"Anyone venturing into unfrequented and possibly dangerous waters does so with his eyes open, should be willing to depend on his own exertions, and should neither expect nor ask for help. The confidence that is placed, and successfully placed, in being rescued fosters carelessness or even foolishness, and condones ignorance . . ."

Be careful how far you give your assent to that judgement, because it's more astringent than most of us here

can stomach. Interpret it in socio-political terms and you have one of the operative levels of Mrs Thatcher's dream society.

It's a stance which *reads* us, which exposes our fears and inadequacies, but which also reflects our longing for that strength and independence of spirit. You see in it the sustaining power of myth, but to live out that myth is beyond the spiritual resources of most of us.

I last saw Tilman in the summer of 1977. His last boat *Baroque*—third and last of his pilot-cutters—was back from Iceland. He was calm and a little morbid, curiously resigned and prepared for his own death. I spent a morning with him. He talked about Christianity, the deaths of friends and particularly that of Eric Shipton, with whom he'd shared much of his mountain exploration in the great decade of the 'thirties. He told a few jokey stories, but was otherwise quiet and subdued.

A week or two later the house was shut up, the dogs kenneled, and he was on his way from Southampton to the Antarctic as a crew member of the 24-year-old Simon Richardson's boat, *En Avant*—a steel-hulled tug converted to a gaff-rigged cutter. They arrived in Rio de Janeiro on 25th October 1977, and left for Port Stanley on 1st November.

Thereafter, no sign, no signal, no trace. If you believe in extra-sensory perception, there's the dream of Simon Frazer—a young explorer in the Tilman mould. He woke from it on an early November night in the Himalayas—a dream of a hull upturned and keelless, rolling in heavy seas, which he somehow knew to be connected with Tilman. The myth ends in Avalonian uncertainty, but its pattern holds:

"Come, my friends,
'Tis not too late to seek a newer world.
Push off, and sitting well in order smite
The sounding furrows; for my purpose holds
To sail beyond the sunset, and the baths
Of all the western stars, until I die."

Playpower and The Cosmic Rascal
Climber, 1987

Some weeks ago, in the course of one of those greybeard laments in which older generations find solace for their lost youth, Dennis Gray and myself happened on the theme of characters: "Where are the characters these

Johnny Dawes.

days?'' we chimed in unison, "Ah, where have all the characters gone! Climbing used to be so full of them . . ."

The premise stated, we sat there like a pair of old crones, nodding and chuckling over old anecdotes and fond memories.

"Of course," piped up Dennis, "there's always that little rascal . . ."

". . . Johnny Dawes!" I snatched the words from his mouth and our chuckles became guffaws.

"He took me along to a party the other night," continued Dennis, "Said he'd been invited, walked right in, big posh house in Didsbury. Started stuffing himself with food, swilling down the liquor, fondling any breast that came within arm's reach. I was trying to make polite conversation with the hostess, distract her attention, when someone came up and asked her who'd invited *that*! We were out on our ears in no time . . ."

The conversation develops into a cornucopia of car crashes, parties, outrageous behaviour in all sorts of situations, which I won't describe for fear of libel or intrusion, but all of it centrally involving the diminutive figure of Johnny Dawes, whirling away like some impish, all-licensed fool or jester to the court of climbing. Dennis and I were reassured that the Old Adam still reigns, the proper men have not taken over total grey control. So we can get down here and now to the serious business of talking with and about Johnny Dawes the climber.

How would they do it in one of those pop magazines? "Johnny Dawes: Height 5ft 5 inches; shoe size 5; eyes hazel (and disconcerting—they look at you sly and side-long, roll round and wrinkle into laughter); favourite

food Chinese takeaways, eaten on doorsteps in Llanberis; favourite music Tchaikovsky and Paganini; dislikes limestone hype; loves millstone grit (in all its many and weird manifestations, and also talking, which he does as incessantly and eccentrically as anyone I've ever met)."

No, that's not it! Let's try it in DNB or *Burke's Peerage* style instead: "John Dawes, the rock-climbing innovator, was born on 23rd May, 1963, at Eastington Manor, Upton-on-Severn (coincidentally the one-time home of the lesbian novelist Marguerite Radclyffe Hall [q.v.]). His father came of an old-established Worcestershire family and his mother of Italian-American stock, her father having been a Massachusetts police chief in the era of prohibition. John and his elder brother Michael were educated at preparatory school in Malvern and later at Uppingham School, Leicestershire, Michael going on to Oxford whilst John matriculated in the University of Manchester. Both brothers began their climbing careers on the back wall of the fives court at Uppingham, a nursery which was to launch John into extraordinary national prominence . . ."

Trying on hats! I vouch for none of the facts in the above—they're approximations, some truth, some convenient fabrication, like the average record of a modern climb. The point is, that being around Johnny Dawes inclines you to playfulness. There's an element of the clown in the tiny, gymnast's physique, clad in baggy tweeds several sizes too big. Let's stop playing about, and let him speak for himself. But with the advice that if you find any of what follows too coded, airy or inflated–pretentious for your taste, make some effort of understanding and don't just smirk and dismiss it. (Unless, of course, you've *been* there, and regard his attempts to capture and define experiences which have stamped themselves upon his soul and cost him blood and savage fear as just so much hot air.)

We'll start with the grit. This is entirely proper because gritstone is the essential rock for climbing. Nothing else comes close and the band of exponents is select. There have only ever been four great gritstone climbers. There are lots who have made their—often considerable—mark: Frank Elliott, Peter Harding, Peter Biven, Allan Austin, John Syrett, Ron Fawcett, Simon Nadin and so on. But the four immortals are Brown, Whillans, John Allen and Johnny Dawes. The reason for this is that any one of these gentlemen's routes has a quality of character and vision about it which marks it out as being *of* its progenitor, and by no-one else. Whose route is The Dangler? Or Forked Lightning Crack? Or Profit of Doom? Or Gaea?

"Gritstone is not limestone and is consequently lots of fun to climb. The friction and windblown shape make it a uniquely absorbing medium for climbing. One climbs features rather than series of holds and that's at the root of why it feels so simple and, as they used to say at Woodstock, 'spiritually satisfying'. There's something incorrigibly playful about it; but for its excessive danger it would be one of the great adult toys."

I pull him up short at this point, try to sound peremptory and schoolmasterly:

"Johnny, you're reading from your notes!"

(He has a sheaf of scrawled-over foolscap in his hand from which he has haltingly deciphered the above.)

"Oh yeah, O.K."

"Now what is it about limestone that you don't like?"

"I'm too small to reach the holds."

"Why can't you jump—sorry, dyno—for them—you jump for holds on every other sort of rock!"

"It's not obvious where they are on limestone. No, seriously, though . . ."

"I thought you were being serious."

"I am. I'm building up to some historical analysis." (What the little rascal's really doing is dancing all round the ponderous format of an interview.)

"Go on, then."

"Well 1984 was the end of the time Ron was doing routes like The Prow, Vision, Eye of the Tiger. They were definitely a step forward. But I think what happened was the next step—Jerry's and Ben's routes, Revelations, Master Class, Statement of Youth and so on—just required more finger power, and that finger-power was able to be got clinically. If you train on a wall and work at it, you can definitely get up those climbs, whereas the same is not true on the grit."

"Sing us a song of gritstone, Johnny!"

"It's like classical music." His eyes widen into swimming pools and he smiles a long-toothed smile. Laughter seems imminent but gravity intervenes: "When you're young you say 'what is this stuff!' Then suddenly it comes into you and you realise it's totally climbable. It's like the Roman idea that the gods are not creatures out there in space, they actually come into people and the people become gods—gods of love, gods of war. There's definitely a climbing god which comes into you in the Roman sense. You don't know why you're climbing so well—it's nothing physical, you could have been porking away for two or three weeks and suddenly you're climbing brilliantly. It's not mental, it's soul, it runs deep. That's why on-sight climbing is so much more

compelling and important than any other climbing. If you want to produce a piece of climbing art, you've got to compromise everything, you've got to bleed to produce it. That's what the Indian Face was . . ."

Voice tails away. I ask some footling question about pride in achievement. Four fingers of his right hand flick it aside:

"What I'm most proud of is the feeling that sometimes I'm completely in sync with what the rock can do, that it's almost as if it's asking something of you. It's like impersonal music—it's not written as music but some geological quirk has made it into a piece of music which, when you listen to it, makes you dance. And if you really pay attention to the dance, the harder the route gets, the more blank and featureless it is, the better and more complex is the message you get from the rock—the more idiosyncratic, eccentric, and gritstonely weird."

"The rock's the choreographer?"

"The rock, and the wind and water before it. They set up the coincidental music your body aligns itself to. You can converse with something natural."

"Pulsating cosmic awareness on the grit, eh?"

"Bit 'sixties, that, Jim, but yeah—exactly!"

"So for you gritstone's the focus still?"

"In 1984 Gritstone was massively important. I felt I had a mission. I had to go out and climb it. All the time the philistines were crying up the limestone. To try to be accepted as a climber in the political and ego senses was so much more difficult if you were operating on the grit."

"Those were important to you?"

"Oh yes—I resent my ego, but that's the point. You feel sad about your ego, especially if it crowds out the central reality."

"But it's the ego-drives which take you into the final disciplines."

"Yes, if you're into the final, total disciplines. But I think, for example, that a sketch can be better than an oil-painting, that Picasso's and Matisse's sketches are better than their finished works, that grit's better than Wales. It takes too long to climb The Indian Face. It hasn't got the same fine, smooth movement made out of simple lines."

"Do you feel miffed that people will remember you more for a route like The Indian Face than, say, Gaea or The Braille Trail?"

"Yes, in a way. Also I had to cheat more on Indian Face—I rehearsed two sets of moves on a rope—because other people always cheated as well on those routes. But

*Dawes gets his head down on the first ascent of Big Things,
Little Things, E9 7b, Rainbow Slab, Dinorwig Quarry.*

what I was left with was the most beautiful route in
Wales. There was a friend of mine on Great Wall when
I did it. We looked across and tried to smile at each
other but we couldn't smile. It was as though he was
saying 'Oh my God, what a sad case.' That brings it
back to you that perhaps he was right. At the end there
was a sort of solid feeling that you'd done your bit for
Cloggy, that some old Grandpa sitting over on top of
Curving might come across and say 'Well done, son!'
You only live once, and I really wanted to do the route.
With eight bolts it would be E6, 6c.''

"Do you think your route and the style of climbing
that others in Wales—Stevie Haston, Andy Pollitt and
so on—are practising can revitalise the sport?"

"I hope so. If it gives people an eye for what they
can do, it's done some good. Things like competitions
are good in context, but bad if young climbers are
seduced into thinking that's what climbing's about.
When I think of climbing I think of gritstone and
Gogarth and Cloggy, of Pat Littlejohn and Mick Fowler,
of Ron in his early days—of people going out and putting themselves in risky positions and by subtlety and
trickery getting themselves out of them. I respect limestone climbers for their stamina, but they're going to
have to find a new name for their sport. They can't call
it rock-climbing any more. It's no longer anything to
do with crags and danger, it's just hard physical tasks.
That's not what I want from climbing. I like routes
which are dynamic and frictional with big fall potential, preferably done on sight. Climbers have almost
become too good. The things that are most enjoyable
are pummelling up 5bs on a sea-cliff, or soloing HVS
on grit.''

"What do you think are the most important attrib-
utes for a climber?"

"Sensitivity—he's got to realise that it's a bloody sight
better climbing on Cloggy than on Wilton—natural ability and ambition. It's also linked with character—you
don't get good climbers unless they're characters.''

"How did you feel after The Indian Face?''

"It enabled me to put away my climbing as a past
thing. In order to be rid of a massive fatalism and a
massive cosmic depression, I had to go and do a route
like that which would stress me more than any other
route before, so that I could relax and go on to express
myself in a different way—that's how I feel at the
moment.''

The next moment he was listing all the new routes
on grit he had left to do. They'd fill the rest of this
magazine. And performing a pantomime, in his tweedy

clown-suit, of climbing The Quarryman, E7 7a ("Shit—I hate numbers!"), in the big hole at Dinorwig. Nijinsky. A little madman, a little clown, gambolling about on the carpet in unutterable, elastic glee. Don't send him grey hairs too soon, you Roman gods! Don't gripe too hard, you fellow-men. This is Brown in his youth, self-possessed of his huge talent. This is Streetly at the lonely end of a long rope, enacting a dancing step.

As he moves on through . . .

Benny Rothman: The Making of a Rebel
Climber and Hillwalker, 1990

Benny Rothman.

There is a picture dimly in my mind of one of those Dark Age monks—Gildas, perhaps, or Cybi the tawny saint, preaching to a huddle of people from some rocky knoll on the wild rim of these islands, or labouring over a manuscript in which, with long strokes of rhetoric, he castigates the venality, voluptuousness and corruption of some petty king. In the mind-image, the face above the rough habit is calm-eyed but watchful, attentive, its features strong-set without harshness. The abstracts from this flesh are the obdurate, the indefatigable, the unassailable because rooted in passionate and selfless moral conviction. It is not a face I recognise often, but each time I sit down with one man amongst my acquaintance, I re-encounter it with a shock of respectful surprise.

Benny Rothman was prime mover behind the Kinder

Scout Mass Trespass of 1932—the great, solitary and crucial *event* in the history of the access movement in this country. For his part in it he was charged with riotous assembly and received a gaol sentence of four months. The story is part of our folklore. What is less well-known is the life-history of Benny himself—the forces which acted upon him, the times he has lived through, the wider contexts in which the well-known events took place. His character merits that depth of treatment rather than the sloganised celebrity which is the currency of our contemporary personality cults.

Over the last several years I've spent considerable amounts of time with Benny. As often as possible when passing through Manchester I call in at the semi-detached red-brick house in Timperley where he lives with his wife Lily. We've spoken from the same platforms, walked together on his beloved Kinder Scout, we harangue each other at length on the 'phone most weeks, are members of the same political party (not that that guarantees equable political discourse). I value him as friend, model and comrade. What follows is a composite of conversations I've had with him over the years, some recorded, some annotated. In the two dimensions of the printed page some of the texture is lost—the measured, gravelly tones of voice, the grave, teasing ironies of inflection, the resonant depth of feeling in telling some of these tales. But the quality of content remains. The reasons for writing up this interview or profile now will become apparent as you read through. Some of the material may appear superficially to have little right of place in an outdoor magazine. I think that view is as wrong as the man, his example, and the warning he sounds are right. In his own way, Benny embodies much of the history of our century, and history is not a process which ended yesterday, or from which any one of us is entirely dissociated.

It's appropriate to start with the family background. Benny was born in Cheetham, Manchester, in 1911. His parents were both Rumanian Jews, his mother's family smallholders from Piotrnant, his father from Bucharest. They came to England at about the turn of the century, his mother via Austria, where her grandfather was Chief Rabbi and one of a famous family of Jewish intellectuals called Rapaport, and his father by way of America:

"Theirs was probably an arranged marriage, and he settled down as a typical small Jewish trader, with hardware stalls at Glossop and Shaw markets. We lived on Granton Street in Cheetham."

There were five children in the Rothman family: two elder sisters and then Benny, another sister and a

Paddling, even in childhood, his own canoe.

younger brother. The area in which they grew up was one of cobbled streets, "the only grass that which grew between the cobblestones". Sometimes they went to hear the brass bands in Elizabeth Park, sometimes on Saturdays Benny would walk to Heaton Park, though this was frowned on—but not by his father, who was an atheist and who despised what he saw as the hypocrisy of many of the ultra-orthodox Jews:

"We weren't conscious of the fact that we were poor, but we were very poor, particularly after my father's death, which happened on my twelfth birthday, when he was 54. I remember being chosen to play an elf in the school Christmas play—it was a church school—and it was the custom that the parents bought the costume, which cost a shilling, after it was over, but I couldn't persuade my mother to pay for it.

After the death of Benny's father, his two sisters, who were at Manchester Central High School for Girls, had to leave school. Benny had won a scholarship to the Central High School for Boys, and two years later, when the opportunity for a job came up, he had to leave too:

"I wasn't happy about it. I'd been doing well, coming top in most subjects. I remember going to tell the headmaster and receiving the most terrific dressing-down—it was the crime of crimes, I'd undertaken to stay until I was sixteen, didn't I realise what I was throwing away? But of course I had no choice in the matter."

The job was at Tom Garner's garage in Knott Mill, at the end of Deansgate in Manchester's city centre. Benny was "a sort of errand boy, going round the motor factors collecting spare parts." He was paid seven-and-sixpence a week. There was a good deal of family disapproval—it was not the done thing for a respectable Jewish boy to work in the motor trade. He should have been in clothing. And there was more disapproval from his mother when it came to his getting a bike:

"Going to work on the tram six days a week was expensive and took a long time, so I asked my grandmother—Jewish grandmothers always dote on the eldest son of the eldest son—if she would pay for a bike. One of the motor factors I went to—it was on Brasenose Street—dealt in bike spares as well and I asked an old chap there if he would look out for a bike. He said he'd do better than that, he'd get one built up out of spares. Unfortunately he was an old man without a clue about bikes and I ended up with this great, solid, heavy bike with 28 inch wheels, which cost me just under £4. I got it on a Thursday, walked it home— I'd never ridden a bike—and of course I was in disgrace. It wasn't respectable, and respectability haunted our family."

The following Sunday Benny rode out to Knutsford: "You can tell how naive I was—I thought when I got there I'd find some nut trees." He was so saddlesore and weary on the way back that he walked the ten miles from Altrincham to Cheetham. The next weekend, recovered and more practised now, he rode to Southport, the weekend after that to Blackpool, "with a lad—he was a nephew of Louis Golding the author—from a more enlightened family than mine, and we slept out."

In the summer of this year, 1925, he went for a week's cycling and walking in North Wales:

"I remember climbing Snowdon. I had a sixpenny map from Woolworths, and walked up from the top of the Llanberis Pass. I got really frightened on that last steep scree, taking one step forwards and two steps back but eventually I got to the top—I don't think there was a café there those days, and I was the only person up there. It just hit me in the face, that great open view with the sea all around. It was a perfect day and I've never seen it like that since."

He went back down the Watkin Path and remembers climbing down an old cable into a quarry hole—the cable broke and came tumbling down on top of him as he reached the bottom. In Nant Gwynant where he was camping, he packed up his tent and set off for Manchester to be back at work next day. "So that was the beginning of my outdoor career."

I asked Benny how he became interested in politics,

and how the Mass Trespass grew out of that interest? He told me that, in about 1928, he used to attend the YMCA nightschool in Manchester, taking courses in advertising and salesmanship, "which was just rubbish, absolute child's stuff", and economic geography. He became very interested in the latter, and through that interest became acquainted with a Scots mechanic at work called Bill Donne:

"Bill was a very keen debater, always surrounded by a whole crowd of people trying to shout him down but he could wipe the floor with any of them. He knew I was interested in economics, and he invited me along to the Sunday night debates held at the Clarion Café on Market Street—it's gone now, which is a great pity because all around its walls it had the most beautiful murals painted by socialist painters. These were very exciting meetings with a good mix of people— Trotskyists, ILP people, people from the Socialist Party of Great Britain."

Bill Donne was a member of the Communist Party, and under his influence Benny soon became a member of the Young Communist League. In the English society of that time, it was inevitable that this would get him into trouble. The first incident occurred at the time of the launch of the *Daily Worker*:

"I went out chalking—writing things like 'Watch out for the Daily Worker' on the pavement with big slabs of chalk. I was a bit green at that time and chalked outside London Road Police Station. Chalking wasn't an offence, but I was promptly nabbed by a Bobby and charged with causing an obstruction. There was no obstruction, but I was fined seven-and-sixpence—a week's wages—and that was my first taste of justice."

The YCL in the late 'twenties was heavily committed to organising working class sport—Sunday football leagues especially—under the aegis of the British Workers' Sports Federation, itself part of the Red Sports International. Benny's interests were camping, cycling and rambling, "which I'd been doing regularly at weekends with lads from work from about 1925 onwards. So through the BWSF we started to run camps, generally at places like Marple or Rowarth."

The camps were run on a shoestring, the equipment rough and ready and mostly army surplus from the Great War, "big pans for boiling spuds, an old marquee we'd got from somewhere or other." There was no money in this time of the Great Depression for luxury, and very little for even the simplest recreation. Benny and his companions ran savings clubs so that people could go to the camps. Some of those who came were

hard pushed even to borrow a blanket from home, let alone a sleeping bag. They froze occasionally, got wet occasionally, but there was a good atmosphere and comradely spirit at the camps, and in spite of their facilities being inferior to those of other more organised groups they were a magnet:

"We'd have 50 or 60 people a weekend, all ages from 15 to over 50, and we introduced a lot of young people to the outdoors. Our weekend activities were mainly rambling, with sing-songs round the campfire at night. One of my jobs was segregating the sexes—keeping the buggers apart—quite a job of course, and to what extent we were successful I don't know but we had to try hard because your local authorities who'd come round to inspect for cleanliness and behaviour would be on the lookout for any excuse to close down the camp, so we never gave them any."

It was at the discussions round the fire at these camps that the first glimmerings of realisation about the wholesale process of theft by which the Derbyshire moors fell into private hands dawned. The 1932 Mass Trespass grew out of one particular incident:

"We were running a camp at Rowarth, and some of the London section of the BWSF were there. I think there were six or seven of us, including a couple of youngsters from London, out for a ramble on Bleaklow. When we got to Yellowslacks, we were met by a group of keepers who accosted us in a very nasty, threatening way, telling us they were going to knock hell out of us. They were most insulting and intimidating, which was the way of keepers in those days. It was not at all unusual for ramblers to get very, very badly beaten by them, and of course if you were working-class there was no redress. That's why we're so concerned about going back to those good old days. Anyhow, we went back to the camp and that's where we decided that if, instead of six or seven there'd been 40 or 50 there, they wouldn't have been able to do it."

I asked Benny about the class division over access to the Derbyshire moors in the inter-war period, told him the story about the American Consul Rice Kemper Evans bribing the gamekeepers with barrels of beer to let him climb at Stanage, and put it to him that if you were a member of one of the established gentleman's outdoor clubs—The Rucksack Club, for example—you stood a better chance of being given permission to go on to Kinder than if you wrote as an individual from the wrong address. Did he think a specific policy of exclusion was operated by the owners and agents against people perceived as belonging to the working class?

"Unquestionably. I had no contact with anyone who did get permission to go up there—none whatsoever. You'd only get it if you wrote from the right address."

Did he feel that division to be further underlined by the report—written by a southern, Oxford-educated journalist—in the *Manchester Guardian* on the Mass Trespass, which carried the strong implication that the "trespassers" were a set of hooligans?

"It was a very big movement in those days, and the older clubs did have a tendency to look down on the ordinary, working-class lads and girls who went out to Hayfield and Edale of a Sunday. We weren't the best people. And if we wrote in to Old Man Watts, who owned the shooting rights around Kinder Downfall, all we got was a standard, stereotyped reply saying that he regrets that grouse numbers have been deteriorating recently and he didn't want them further disturbed. They were deteriorating, of course, because all these bloody upper-class psychopaths shot the buggers to bits every year . . ."

How did he feel, then, when the people who were making the pace regarding access after the Mass Trespass in the '30s and '40s were the same people who had castigated Benny's actions and distanced themselves from him, whilst in many cases themselves gaining limited personal concessions, arguing thus a process of natural selection which ensured that anyone with sufficient initiative could go on the moors anyway?

"We were very bitter about our complete exclusion from any of the process of negotiation leading right up to the 1949 Act."

But were they sufficiently organised to be involved?

"We were certainly failing to bond together to get our points across."

Why, I mused, didn't any organisation come out of the Mass Trespass, which must itself have taken a vast amount of organising? Benny's response was sharp and immediate:

"It took no organisation, Jim—it was a genuine piece of spontaneous activity—took us a week. When Wolfie Winnick, who was my sparring partner, and I went out on the Sunday morning on our bikes, we didn't even know what route we would take. Two things had been fixed—time and place of the meeting, and the main speaker, Jack Clayton—very able, professsional chap and quite a left-winger. But when we got to the quarry, he decided he didn't like the way the thing had been bounced on him and decided not to speak."

"Why did he back out?"

"Well, when you suddenly see that there are a couple of hundred policemen all around, not to mention the four or five hundred ramblers who'd turned up, I suppose it might make you a bit timid."

"So they were expecting you?"

"The buggers were certainly there expecting us. There was a third of the Derbyshire Police Force there, and the keepers had been very heavily increased in numbers. When Wolfie and I looked round on our recce that morning, they were all around South Head and in a line right the way along the skyline at William Clough."

I asked Benny about his speech:

"I've still got the notes for that. I told the history of the struggle for access since 1884, made quite an attack on the organised rambling movement of the day—which was probably naive of me, because even though they were getting nowhere they were trying to do something. I said all they were concerned with—as they still are regionally to an extent today—is running nice Sunday rambles and having their annual outing to Cave Dale or Winnats Pass to listen to a few polite fellows saying how we must negotiate. The gist of my speech was that if we wanted something we had to be prepared to fight for it, rouse the outdoor movement and alert them to where we were going. Then I went on to technicalities— how we weren't there to fight the keepers, that we were going up on to Kinder, what our signals were, and off we went—four or five hundred of us—rough and ready as that!"

"And the police were listening?"

"They were making elaborate notes."

"But they made no attempt to stop you or break up the meeting?"

"They couldn't—not until we'd actually committed an offence. The only time they could act was when one keeper—this fellow Beevers, who was probably three-quarters sozzled—got into a tussle with some ramblers, in the course of which he sprained his ankle. So they nailed this unfortunate fellow Anderson for it, who wasn't even sympathetic to us and had just come along as a spectator. From that moment everyone else was involved directly in what had become a riotous assembly. Until then they'd got no legal grounds against us. In fact, they'd got no legal grounds anyway, but that's by the way. They needed a selected jury to get the thing through . . ."

The jury in question comprised two brigadier-generals, three colonels, two majors, three captains, two aldermen—eleven of them country gentlemen. I remarked sardonically to Benny that perhaps the judge was selected, too?

"That chap was a professional, and he was backed up by all the state apparatus to reinforce what he wanted to say or do. When it came to his summing-up, it was masterful. He spoke about freedom in Britain. We'd got the freedom of expression. If we didn't like something we had the right to demonstrate our feelings, but—the magic word 'but'—we were not allowed to do what we did, which amounted to conducting a riot on the moors, in the course of which a loyal servant carrying out his rightful duties of beating hell out of ramblers was caused such severe injuries that he had to hobble down off Kinder into Hayfield. Oh yes—he was that badly injured, the poor chap! Probably had blisters on his palm, too, from putting his stick across a few ramblers' shoulders before they stopped him."

Benny went on to describe how everyone who testified against the defendants was either a member of the police or an official of the estate or water board—"like the Gibraltar Inquest but more blatantly slanted". One of the charges against him personally was that he had incited the crowd to cause grievous bodily harm. He described how he had asked the police inspector who was testifying if he'd been taking notes of what had been said? Yes, he had. He then asked, if he were to say that the testimony of a previous witness completely contradicted this, who would then be right?

"Of course, the judge and prosecuting barristers jumped on me, but it had the effect of making him doubt what had been said, and when I then asked him if it was true that far from inciting violence I had specifically asked the ramblers at the meeting not to use any, he grudgingly admitted that he remembered something of the kind. Well that was enough, and I got off on that one. That man—a police inspector, mind—was just a bare-faced liar, and if I'd been found guilty on his testimony on that trumped-up charge I'd probably have got a couple of years. I was very lucky—he was probably in the same masonic lodge as half the jury as well."

I asked if any overt play had been made of Benny's political affiliations?

"Definitely—Nesbit, for example, on exactly the same charge as two of the others got three months in gaol where they only got two, and I'm sure that was solely because at the meeting he'd been selling the *Daily Worker*. So the police snatched him and it was brought up against him. And in a very subtle way the judge did a lot of racial as well as political stuff: 'Don't be influenced,' he told the jury, 'by the names and the origins of some of these people.' Three of us, you see, were obviously Jewish, so he drew attention to that under the

pretext of telling them not to be influenced by it. He also told the jury not to be influenced by the fact that we were of the communist political persuasion. You can imagine how all these landowners and retired colonels reacted to that. By drawing attention to it, he was deliberately influencing that jury."

Given the present reputation of the English police and judiciary, I remarked that that sort of behaviour would now cause a furore. What publicity did the trial receive at the time? The answer was virtually none.

"It was played down—just a tiny item in a local paper. Even amongst ramblers it was an embarrassment, and swept under the carpet. The Manchester Federation of Ramblers barely gave it a mention in their annual report, and the Clarion Handbook likewise. It was this idea that going in a body on a trespass wasn't sporting, it wasn't British. Our case was that if you wanted to get anything done, you had to have a mass movement behind you. Unfortunately, the former's still a commonly-held position today. People in the outdoor movement are still hostile to the idea of taking action to secure access. Well bugger what's sporting when you're trying to right a wrong!"

At the trial Anderson, the man supposed to have assaulted the keeper Beevers, was given six months. Benny, for having caused a riotous assembly, served four months in Leicester Gaol. Unemployed at the time of the Mass Trespass (the responsible job at Tom Garner's to which he'd risen had gone in reorganisation, and as a potential troublemaker and political activist, no place was found for him in the new structure), Benny came out to a situation where there was no prospect of work for him in the close-knit Manchester motor trade. At the age of 21, he was on the dole in the leanest years of the Great Depression.

Rather than sitting down and lamenting his plight, Benny's response was to return to the struggle—not this time for access, but for the right of workers to organise. It was the time of the Moor Loom Strike in the North East Lancashire textile industry. The YCL asked him to go there and work to raise striking weavers' morale. He stayed in Burnley, organising dances and Sunday rambles. Years later he met a woman who told him, "I remember you and your Sunday rambles, Benny—you said we should come on them wearing clogs, but there was a tradition that you didn't wear clogs on a Sunday so we never came." He also set up a Sunday football league:

"People were very keen on that, but the local religious leaders brought pressure on the local Football Associa-

Benny in his natural environment—with a platform to speak from and an audience attentive to his message.

tion to disaffiliate anyone who played in it, and the local press took it up as an affront to God, so it came to a sudden end. The strike was defeated, the workers were forced to accept the Moor Loom system, lots of people were sacked and the poverty was terrible. The YCL recognised that it was too much to expect one person on the dole to organise effectively, so I drifted back to Manchester, where eventually I got a job at a garage in Cheetham—Syd Abrams'. Lots of small market traders and shopkeepers whom I knew were getting old cars by this time, so I kept them going and the boss was pleased with me."

He was still actively rambling and involved in countryside access, and through the BWSF played a part in defeating the Government's 1933 bill aiming to restrict all camping to official sites.

"The government wanted to control it all, and at that time a lot of wind had gone out of the sails of the access movement. It was now a cosy negotiating affair smoothly going on between the big organisations and the landowners, and getting nowhere. We were maybe a bit more militant than before by now, chancing our arm whenever we went out on to the moors, breaking off

the footpaths to a much larger extent. But I have to link all this with the main direction in which my life was going in the '30s. I'll tell you about one incident to illustrate how it started.

"I'd been out for a Sunday ramble and when we got back to Manchester I'd gone straight to a meeting held by the New Party at the Free Trade Hall. I was still in shorts with a rucksack on my back. John Strachey was the speaker and Cynthia Mosley, Oswald's first wife, was there. It was very obvious from their attitudes towards organised labour that here was the beginning of a fascist movement in Britain. We heckled and barracked and when the meeting ended a strange thing happened. For the first time ever at a public meeting in Manchester the police came into the meeting to snatch up the hecklers. I stood out a mile, dressed as I was, and the Superintendent with them made a beeline for me. He was tripped and fell to the ground and to my horror and shame the people who were rushing out proceeded to kick him. It was a nasty incident and showed how the political atmosphere was hotting up. There was a lot of anger and frustration around, with unemployment and the means test. I was speaking from a platform with John Strachey years later when he was a member of the Attlee government, and he said 'I'm sure I've met you before, Benny.' When I reminded him where it was—at the meeting with Lady Mosley—he walked off without another word."

From this time on, the fight against fascism was the focus of his energy. Mosley's Blackshirts were establishing a reputation for viciousness unparalleled in British political life of this country, and Manchester was a headquarters for them. In parts where there was serious unemployment they had set up clubs with cheap beer and worked on anti-Semitism, blaming the Jews for the economic ills of the country.

"On one occasion I went to a rally at Belle Vue where Oswald was speaking. I was in my overalls straight from work and as I was walking along Grey Mare Lane a chap came up and handed me a bundle of leaflets: 'Here, Benny, can you take these? I can't get in.' I tucked them into my overalls and went on in to the King's Hall. I was up in the gods and there was a very large number of blackshirt stewards, two or three to each row. I got talking to one of them, an engineer from Birmingham. 'How's it possible for a trade unionist like yourself to belong to such a rag-bag organisation?' I asked him. He hushed me and warned me not to start anything here. 'We've orders to knock the hell out of anyone who interrupts, stop 'em quick,' he told me. There were some lads from Stockport in the row below me at the front of the balcony. The stewards were absolutely vicious, knocking people senseless who heckled and hurling them out. Eveline Taylor, who later married Jack Jones—I knew her from the YCL—stood up and started to barrack Mosley. They set some blackshirt stewardesses on to her but she was a big lass and just lashed out and knocked them down. The men went for her at that, and it was mayhem. 'Leave her alone', the crowd was shouting as these thugs were hammering her. I leant over to the lads in front and said 'Will you keep the buggers off me while I get rid of these?' and threw the leaflets in a great sweep from the balcony. Well half a dozen of them came to get me, and they swung me out and threw me over the balcony down into the crowd where I landed on a couple of the buggers who were waiting for me and half-killed them. I was winded, but unhurt, and another great lout with cauliflower ears frog-marched me out of the hall, snarling 'Come on, yer Yiddisher bastard, I'll knock hell out of you.' Well the Birmingham lad came along and I got free, landed a few good clouts on this other one before I had to cover up, and this Birmingham lad called me a silly bugger and shielded me through the two rows of stewards with coshes which was the gauntlet you had to run. Outside it was like a battlefield—people everywhere with their heads cracked open and not a policeman in sight. That night Mosley travelled down to London in a first-class carriage with the Chief Constable of Manchester!"

On another occasion the blackshirts tried to hold a meeting in Halliwell Lane, Cheetham, right in the heart of the Jewish area, and in the course of it Benny was arrested and taken to court:

"After the Mass Trespass trial I was warier, and got loads of witnesses this time who could prove that the police were telling lies. The whole thing was set up, they knew of my YCL connection and that's why they arrested me. They found me not guilty, but I was bound over. My boss said to me—he was Jewish as well—'I didn't know you went in for that sort of thing, Benny. Of course, what you do in your own time's your own business, but I hope you won't let it affect our trade.' I told him that his customers were very supportive indeed of what I was doing—and they were."

For Benny—working-class, a Jew, a communist, the '30s was not a decade which gave much further opportunity for leisure. He left the motor trade and went to work at A.V. Roe's aircraft factory—where he was further victimised for his political beliefs, eventually leaving to work at what was then reputed to be the most highly organised—and the most enlightened towards its workers—factory in Britain, Metropolitan Vickers in Trafford Park. He met his wife Lily at a peace camp, volunteered as an ambulance driver for the International Brigade in the Spanish Civil War, volunteered for the army in the war but was rejected as being in a reserved occupation. The more you get to know Benny, the more you appreciate the range and altruistic effort of his activity on behalf of the underprivileged and dispossessed in society. I remember him at a rally against the Water Bill, where his was the sole voice to point out that yes, this would affect us as users of wild land, but it would also, through increased charges and reduced services, affect everyone in society, and especially those least able to pay. The connections with mountains and the environment have been so slender a part of his life's work, however pivotal his actions on behalf of our community. But perhaps, therefore, his perspectives on what will affect us, and how, will be the more sound.

I asked him recently for his views on the present situation, and how it compared with that which obtained in the '30s:

"In the '30s we were excluded from a great deal of land, but that land on the whole was well looked after. People were concerned to protect it for their private benefit, but the land wasn't ruined. Now we have a new and very serious situation where people are prepared to exploit it to the uttermost degree, and to buy it for exploitation. With the Water Bill, for example, the outdoor movement didn't want to know at the outset, and only gradually came to see the threat, both to the fabric of the land though they've still not clearly grasped even that—and to the access they've enjoyed over those half-million acres increasingly since the '60s and '70s. One of the main attractions for shareholders in the new water companies is the value of land owned by them, and that value is lowered by public rights of access over it. Of course the Ramblers' Association and the British Mountaineering Council fought hard to secure amendments to the bill guaranteeing access, but what they secured were just codes of practice without legal enforcement, and those aren't worth a row of beans. David Trippier, the Junior Environment Minister, went on record a fortnight ago as saying that there are no guarantees on free access to Water Companies' land, and further, that there are no guarantees of continuing access with or without charge. Then there's the splitting up of the Nature Conservancy Council, which for all its shortcomings has been the most effective voice of opposition to the despoliation of the landscape—too good, in fact, for its own

"What sort of a red flag do we want to keep flying over our moors and mountains?"

good, which is why the government wants to get rid of it and divide it up between its tame, fixed organisation, the Countryside Commission. And that last organisation's stance on footpaths has been very suspect in recent years. Wherever I look I see evidence of deliberate government interference with the rights of access we've either enjoyed for centuries or begun to enjoy these past few years, along with the handing over of the best land in the country into hands which can't be trusted with its care. At least in the 1930s the land wasn't in such danger of being ruined. But the situation is worse today in almost every way, and when our people object, they just stroke them, make them feel important, buy them off with a few meaningless concessions, and carry on their filthy, damaging, restrictive way. If we let the buggers get away with it, perhaps we don't deserve the enjoyment of the land anyway . . ."

Exploring Eric Shipton
Introduction to Eric Shipton: The Six Mountain-Travel Books, 1985

Eric Shipton.

Early in 1930 a young planter in Kenya unexpectedly received a letter from an ex-soldier ten years his senior, who had settled in the colony after the Great War. The letter mentioned that its writer had done some climbing in the English Lake District on his last home leave, and asked advice about visiting the East African mountains. Its immediate results were a meeting between the two men, an initial jaunt up Kilimanjaro together, and the first ascent, later that year, of the West Ridge of Mount Kenya—one of the major achievements of pre-war British alpinism.

The two men were, of course, Eric Shipton and H.W. Tilman, and their chance meeting, out in the colonies at the very beginning of the decade, led to one of the most fruitful partnerships and entrancing sagas in the history of mountain exploration. Indeed, the centrality of their role in that history throughout one of its vital phases is unarguable. The chance of their acquaintance and magnitude of their travels aside, another aspect of these two men is perhaps even more remarkable. They were both inveterate chroniclers of their climbs and journeys, and the quality of the writings they produced places them both absolutely in the forefront of mountaineering and travel literature. A previous volume in this series collected together Tilman's seven mountain-travel titles. Here, for the first time under one cover, are the six mountain-travel books of Eric Shipton.

Shipton was born in Ceylon in 1907, his father a tea-planter who died before his son was three. Thereafter, with his mother and sister, he travelled extensively between Ceylon, India, France and England before the family finally settled in the latter country for purposes of the children's schooling. Shipton's mountaineering career began in 1924 with holidays in Norway and Switzerland and was consolidated through four successive alpine seasons in 1925–1928. His first ascent of Nelion, one of the twin summits of Mount Kenya, with Wyn Harris in 1929, and of the same mountain's West Ridge with Tilman the following year, brought him to the notice of the mountaineering establishment of the day and elicited an invitation to join Frank Smythe's expedition to Kamet in 1931. Shipton distinguished himself on this trip, being in the summit party on eleven of the twelve peaks climbed by the expedition, including that of Kamet itself, which at 25,447ft was the highest then attained. His performance in 1931 led to an invitation to join Ruttledge's 1933 Everest expedition. Thereafter the milestones slip by: the Rishi Ganga 1934; Everest Reconnaissance 1934, which he led; Everest and another sortie to Nanda Devi, 1936; the "Blank on the Map" expedition to Shaksgam with Tilman, Auden and Spender in 1937; Everest 1938; Karakoram 1939—virtually the whole decade was spent in Himalayan travel, and the extent of his exploratory achievement perhaps even now lacks full recognition.

He spent the Second World War in Government service in Sinkiang, Persia and Hungary, went back for a further spell in the former—accompanied this time by his wife Diana—from 1946 to 1948, and was Consul-General at Kunming in southern China from 1949 to 1951. On his return to England he was asked to lead an expedition to reconnoitre the southern approaches to Everest, in the course of which he and Ed Hillary plotted out the eventual line of ascent up the Western Cwm to the South Col from a vantage point on the slopes of Pumori. The following year he led a tense and unsatisfactory training expedition to Cho Oyu. In the late summer of 1952, Shipton having been urged to lead a further expedition to Everest in 1953 and having accepted, the joint Himalayan Committee of the Alpine Club and Royal Geographical Society performed an astonishing *volte-face*, appointing the competent and experienced but at that time virtually unknown Colonel John Hunt as leader, and accepting the inevitable consequence of Shipton's resignation.

This sorry episode effectively marked a watershed in Shipton's life. After the break-up of his marriage and loss of his post as Warden of the Outward Bound School at Eskdale, which occurred shortly after the events of 1952–1953, he lived for a time in the rural seclusion of Shropshire, working as a forestry labourer. He was enticed back for a last trip to the Karakoram in 1957, and thereafter developed a new grand obsession with travel in the southernmost regions of South America, which absorbed most of the next decade of his life. Finally, in his sixties, he was a popular lecturer on cruises to such places as the Galapagos Islands, and leader of mild Himalayan treks. He died of liver cancer at the home of a friend in Wiltshire during the spring of 1977.

This, then, is the bare outline of an outstanding life. The man who lived it, through his involvement in the 1931 Kamet and 1933 Everest expeditions, had attained a degree of national celebrity by the early 1930s, yet at the time was a professionless pauper and a kind of international tramp, whose possessions amounted to little more than the clothes in which he stood. There is a passage in *Upon That Mountain* where Shipton recalls the dawning realisation that the way of life which most appealed to him perhaps presented a practical possibility. It occurs on the way back to India from the North Side of Everest in 1933. In company with the geologist Lawrence Wager, he had made his way across a strip of unexplored country and over a new pass into Sikkim. Wager was instrumental in shifting the emphasis of Shipton's interest away from the climbing of peaks to enthusiasm for a more general mode of exploration, to a fascination with geography for its own sake. Twenty years later, this shift was to provide his detractors with an easy target. For the moment his mind works over the ground thus:

"Why not spend the rest of my life doing this sort of thing?' There was no way of life that I liked more, the scope appeared to be unlimited, others had done it, vague plans had already begun to take shape, why not put some of them into practice? . . . The most obvious snag, of course, was lack of private means; but surely such a mundane consideration could not be decisive. In the first place I was convinced that expeditions could be run for a tithe of the cost generally considered necessary. Secondly, if one could produce useful or interesting results one would surely find support . . ."

When he took into account his reactions to the large expedition ("The small town of tents that sprung up each evening, the noise and racket of each fresh start, the sight of a huge army invading the peaceful valleys, it was all so far removed from the light, free spirit with which we were wont to approach our peaks."), then the virtue to be made of necessity was obvious, and of it was born what came to be known as the Shipton/Tilman style of lightweight expedition. When he describes the result of putting his belief into practice in his first book, *Nanda Devi*, the result is a revolutionary text. I doubt if there has ever been a less formulaic account of an expedition. It has a fresh, get-through-by-the-skin-of-your-teeth spontaneity and candour, an excited commitment, a clear rationale and elation about the enterprise undertaken which previous mountaineering literature had seldom approached. From the outset the terms are made clear: five months in the Garhwal Himalaya to tackle some of its outstanding topographical problems, 'climbing peaks when opportunity occurred', on a budget of £150 each for himself and Tilman (some of Shipton's share of which is advanced by Tilman 'against uncertain security'). The scenes throughout, from the broken-toed, frock-coated setting-out from Ranikhet to the final descent from the Sunderdhunga Col to Maiktoli, are evoked in clear and economical style. But it is the message—the simple moral that it is possible, and in terms of response to landscape and its peoples even desirable, to travel cheap and light, to move fast and live off the land—which is the book's revolutionary charge, and which was to make Shipton and Tilman, in the words of the American writer David Roberts, 'retroactive heroes of the avant-garde'.

Two major characteristics, already present in *Nanda Devi*, distinguish Shipton's writing. The first of these is an intense curiosity—which remains with him, his conclusions growing more authoritative with increase of experience—about natural landforms, whether they be mountains, valleys, rivers, volcanoes or glaciers. This curiosity acts as a stimulus, a fund of energy continually to be drawn upon and used as a basis and point of reference in his explorations: "It was enthralling to disentangle the geography of the region . . . for me, the basic reason for mountaineering"; ". . . a desire to leave the route and wander off into the labyrinth of unmapped ranges that stretch away on every side"; ". . . to follow any river throughout its course is fascinating to me". Or perhaps clearest of all, "Tilman and I climbed a peak of about 21,500ft. It was an interesting ridge-climb, but the pleasure we expected, and in fact received, from it was secondary to getting the hang of the Arwa glaciers onto which we were about to descend."

Alongside this drive to understand the physical make-up of a landscape there operates a more reflective principle, sometimes very close to traditional nature-mysticism, which Shipton can carry off with great poise and delicacy, avoiding the pitfalls of bathos or inflation. As in this passage from *Blank on the Map*:

". . . we settled down on a comfortable bed of sand, and watched the approach of night transform the wild desert mountains into phantoms of soft unreality. How satisfying it was to be travelling with such simplicity. I lay awaiting the approach of sleep, watching the constellations swing across the sky. Did I sleep that night— or was I caught up for a moment into the ceaseless rhythm of space?"

There is a satisfying irony in suggesting an affinity with mysticism here, for Shipton professed an agnosticism throughout his adult life, and even if only for the joy of argument—which was one of the pleasures of his social life—would probably have rejected the contention. Yet perhaps his disclaimer of religious belief was akin to that of Simone Weil, concealing and containing a sense of divine mystery within the universe. Certainly a recurrent point of interest in Shipton's writings is the tension between practical preoccupation with physical phenomena, and frequent lapsing into quietistic modes of thought. *Nanda Devi* puts me in mind of no other text so much as one of the late poems of that most ascetic of saints, John of the Cross (quoted here in the translation by Roy Campbell):

The generous heart upon its quest
Will never falter, nor go slow,
But pushes on, and scorns to rest,
Wherever it's most hard to go.
It runs ahead and wearies not
But upward hurls its fierce advance
For it enjoys I know not what
That is achieved by lucky chance.

Those who knew Shipton well sound a recurrent note in their reminiscences concerning a quality of detachment he possessed. Invariably it fastens on a physical detail, and the following is typical:

"He had the most marvellous blue eyes, very kindly, very amused and very wise. But there was always a sense, when you talked with him, that somehow he was not with you, was looking right through you, searching out farther and farther horizons."

In the course of researching his biography, it has been remarkable and eventually almost comical how often that impression, almost word-for-word, is repeated. Without the evidence of the texts, it could be taken as mannerism, inattentiveness; but in his books, time and again passages recur which describe his response to landscape as one striving towards an understanding beyond topographical grasp.

In this he is very different to Tilman, his most frequent companion of the 1930s, and it is interesting to compare the two men. The ten-year difference in their ages is significant. Tilman's seniority meant that he had endured the profoundly determining influence of the Great War. It was this which made him a master of that most serious of all forms of writing, comic irony, and which caused him to veer dangerously close at times to misanthropy. It explains the prelapsarian vitality with which he imbues his native characters, the neglectful portrayal of his compatriots, and the isolation which identifies his authorial persona. In his personal conduct, it provides the reason for his taciturnity, phlegmatism and unemotional responses to situations. The vulnerability of youth, its lack of circumspection and eager commitment to affection or cause were in Tilman's case the victims of war, and the survivor, psychic and physical, of

that particularly obscene war had need to be encased in adamantine.

Shipton's enthusiasms, on the other hand, operate under no such constraint. He can indulge his feelings as freely as he will, and the zest and gaiety of the twenties glitters around his early activities. He commits himself freely, and as equally to a climb as to a journey of exploration or to one of the many women who shared his life. The following comments written by Frank Smythe in 1931 capture the temperament of the man:

"No one who climbs with Shipton can remain pessimistic, for he imparts an imperturbability and confidence into a day's work which are themselves a guarantee of success."

Or again:

"I saw Shipton's eyes light up, and next instant he went at the slope with the energy of a boxer who, after months of training, sees his opponent before him."

The differences in their characters, by complementing each other, perhaps acted as bond between Shipton and Tilman and account in part for their sharing some of the most ambitious undertakings of their lives. For Tilman, robbed of his own youth, Shipton's enthusiasm and boundless energy must have been inspiriting, whilst the fatherless Shipton would surely have found in Tilman's wry, benevolent maturity a need fulfilled. In mountaineering terms, however, the roles were reversed, Shipton the obvious leader. One very telling indication of this occurs in Tilman's diary for 30 May, 1934. After reconnoitring one of the crucial—and very complex—passages on the route up the Rishi Gorge, they have to hurry back to camp. The subsequent diary entry briefly states, "Shipton's route-memory invaluable as usual, self hopeless."

A change does occur, though, in Shipton's outlook—especially with regard to mountaineering—during the mid-thirties. It is perhaps cumulative rather than associated with specific circumstance. The influence of older companions such as Tilman and Wager must have played a part, as would the long relationship upon which he had embarked with Pamela Freston. But two related events are certainly decisive in the transition from joyful mountaineering innocence to prudent experience. These were the two avalanches which Shipton witnessed on the slopes leading to the North Col of Everest during successive expeditions in 1935 and 1936. Of the first one, he had to say "I am sure that no one could have escaped from an avalanche such as that which broke away below us while we were lying peacefully on the North Col". The following year, as he and Wyn Harris were climbing up the same slope, this happened:

"We climbed quickly over a lovely hard surface in which one sharp kick produced a perfect foothold. About half-way up to the Col we started traversing to the left. Wyn anchored himself firmly on the lower lip of a crevasse while I led across the slope. I had almost reached the end of the rope and Wyn was starting to follow when there was a rending sound . . . a short way above me, and the whole surface of the slope I was standing on started to move slowly down towards the brink of an ice-cliff a couple of hundred feet below . . ."

Wyn Harris managed to jump back into the crevasse and re-establish the belay, the snow failed to gather momentum, and Shipton survived. It was the last attempt on the mountain that year. The point is, that Shipton's faith in the material he was climbing had been undermined. Just as in personal relationships, when the trust has gone the commitment is withdrawn. Shipton's heyday as a *climber* is delimited by these events, and though exciting and perilous escapades happen after 1936—the climb on the Dent Blanche-like peak above the Bostan Terek valley is a striking example—henceforwards, reading these books, we keep company with a much more circumspect mountaineer.

This links naturally into a consideration of what is generally regarded as one of the cruces of Shipton's life—the circumstances surrounding the choice of leader for the 1953 expedition to Everest. It is still, in the dusty rooms of the mountaineering establishment, a controversial issue, and one which is difficult to summarise in brief. Even Walt Unsworth's *Everest* book—the most authoritative history of the mountain—overlooked important material which throws a clearer light on some of its aspects. What emerges, from close examination of relevant Himalayan Committee minutes and written submissions from some of its surviving members, is a bizarre tale of fudge and mudge, allegations about the falsification of official minutes, unauthorized (and not easily retractable) invitations, and opportunistic and desperate last-minute seizures of initiative by a particular faction. It is a perfect illustration of the cock-up (as opposed to the conspiracy) theory of history, and little credit redounds from it upon the British mountaineering establishment of the time.

There are two main themes to be considered here. The first is the general climate of feeling surrounding Shipton's perceived aptitude for, and interest in, the leadership of an expedition which even in its planning stage was subject to a jingoistic insistence that Everest must be climbed by a British party (that this was not to be achieved for a further 22 years after the 1953 expedition scarcely mattered or was noticed in the event). This climate of feeling willingly accepted some of Shipton's own statements at face value. In *Upon That Mountain*, for example, he had written that "there are some, even among those who have themselves attempted to reach the summit, who nurse a secret hope that Mount Everest will never be climbed. I must confess to such feelings myself". It also drew on more questionable evidence, particularly relating to the 1952 Cho Oyu expedition, where a combination of political circumstance and personal history undoubtedly affected Shipton's leadership.

A synthesis of these points suggested to one faction engaged in the expedition planning that Shipton lacked the urgency, thrust and killer instinct which would be necessary to "conquer" Everest. The case was immeasurably strengthened by Shipton's own submission to the Himalayan Committee meeting of 28 July, 1952, in which he expressed doubts about his suitability for the "job" on the grounds that, being out of work with a wife and two children to support, he needed to consider his own position; that he felt new blood was needed to undertake the task; and that his preference was for smaller parties, lightly equipped.

The second theme—aside from the question of Shipton's likely attitudes and commitment—is that of the manner in which members of the Himalayan Committee conducted themselves over the matter of the leadership. The first point to be made is that the Committee was very weakly chaired. Because of this, the pro-Shipton faction carried the day at the meeting of 28 July, when Shipton—chiefly through the efforts of Laurence Kirwan—was strongly prevailed upon to accept the leadership. The contention then rested with the question of the deputy leadership.

There existed a faction within the Committee and headed by Basil Goodfellow and Colonel Tobin—both of whom had been absent from the 28 July meeting—which had its own preferred candidate for this post in the person of John Hunt, who was, in Goodfellow's quaint phrase, a "terrific thruster", and one who would bring a necessary application to the task. Tobin and Goodfellow lobbied forcefully that the deputy—or assault—leadership should fall to Hunt. Inevitably this would compromise Shipton, whose choice as deputy was Charles Evans and to whom in that role Hunt was therefore unacceptable. The crucial committee meeting took place on 11 September. The pro-Hunt faction was present in force, well-prepared, and determined to reverse the decision of the previous meeting. The more ardent Shiptonians—most notably Kirwan and Shipton's old friend Lawrence Wager—were absent. The choice of Hunt was imposed—and as joint rather than deputy leader. Shipton was effectively compromised and morally compelled to offer his resignation, which was promptly accepted. The rest of this squalid and bloody little episode is history, apart from a few later ripples spreading out from the main controversy, such as the charge of subsequent falsification of minutes levelled by Blakeney against Claude Elliott—in the words of one contemporary observer, "as bad a chairman of committees as one could find; he was hopelessly indecisive and hesitant and was too easily swayed by anyone (like Kirwan) who held firm opinions, however wrong these might be".

What the effect on Shipton would have been had he led the successful Everest expedition is matter for conjecture. John Hunt was patently well-equipped to cope with the ensuing celebrity, and used it tirelessly in the public domain. It could perhaps be considered doubtful that Shipton would have enjoyed, and responded so positively, to the inevitably massive acclaim.

After 1953 his life went through a difficult period, but it emerged into a golden late summer of exploration in an area completely fresh to him. His Patagonian journeys of the 'fifties and 'sixties were a harking-back to his great Karakoram travels of the 'thirties, and would have been rendered immensely more public—and hence perhaps less satisfactory—by the burden of international fame. Instead he was able to slip quietly away to the unknown mountains and glaciers of a new wilderness. It was a proper consummation in the life of this explorer-mystic, whose outlook and progress resonate so closely with Tennyson's "Ulysses", from which poem he took the motto for *Blank on the Map* and the title for his magnificent second autobiography, *That Untravelled World*.

There is a phrase from this latter book which gives perfect expression to one of the great lives of our century: "a random harvest of delight". That is exactly what the books collected together between these covers are. They also give the opportunity to a new generation of readers to engage with one of the most attractive personalities ever drawn to mountaineering—and to keep company with his spare, lithe figure loping off into the ranges, seeking out the undiscovered country, his dis-

tant blue eyes lingering on the form of a particular peak or the passage over to an unexplored glacier. If curiosity, appreciation, aspiration and delight are a form of praise—as assuredly they are—then here is one man's vivid testament of a lifetime spent in worship of the great world around him.

The Essential Jack Longland
Mountain, 1988

Jack Longland "The more he sees of humanity, the more he loves your dog." (His wife Peggy said that.)

A photograph, taken at the old Promontoire Hut on La Meije in 1928, of three young Cambridge Fellows: one of them, Bobby Chew, is wrapped in blankets and slumbering on the *matratzenlager;* another—Lawrence Wager—back to the wall and a plate of food in his lap, looks seriously into the camera. It is the third figure which dominates. He lounges back, but even in repose the athlete's physique is obvious—the neat build, the power in chest and thigh. A book is open on the mattress and the camera catches him as he looks up from it. That passing glance of sixty years ago gives you the measure of the man—the expression of a young falcon on a face intensely alert, strong-featured, wide-browed and quizzical. The eyes are hypnotic in their power. The whole presence of the character speaks not of arrogance—though it could be interpreted as such by a casual observer—but of rigour, honesty, effort. The men to each side—Wager and Chew—were both distinguished in their chosen professions as geology don and headmaster. The one at the centre—Jack Longland— even here at the age of 23 gives promise of being more than that.

It needs to be explained just how central to the British climbing culture Jack is. The familiar form of address is a clue. Formally, he is Sir Jack Longland—he was knighted for his services to education by Harold Wilson in 1970. But he is one of those rare people for whom the near-universal affection in which they are held is expressed by the simple forename address—to everyone he is "Jack". His roots in British climbing go back to the days of Geoffrey Winthrop Young, and through him perhaps even to the Golden Age of British Alpinism in Victorian times. A repository of tradition and value, those raptor's eyes—though older and less intensely focussed now—still scan piercingly over the current landscape of climbing. Personally—both in his mountaineering and professional connections—Jack has not always been popular with every sector of the communities in which he's moved. He is a man of strong principles, great intelligence and devastating wit, who can stomach neither fools nor pomposity and is quite capable of savaging either when they cross his path. The idealist in him is so urgent a creature as still occasionally to become choleric. For all that, there's another side to his character which is more frequently to the fore—an impishness, a sense of fun, a relish for the robust ambiguity and the subtle pun, which made him an ideal choice as Chairman and question master to the long-running radio programme "My Word". There are no emotional or intellectual monotones in conversation with Jack. He can describe human situations which will bring you close to tears, argue a precise and coherent case for their amelioration, then explode the whole tenor of the debate with a perfectly timed joke or even just a fit of giggles at the cosmic absurdity of it all. Even now, well into his eighties, his enjoyment of good-humoured and combative talk has not deserted him, nor has his ability to run ragged even the most sharp-witted of his opponents. In my life he has been one of two great mentors. What follows is neither profile nor interview, but a composite synthesized from correspondence, interviews, snatches of conversation, which have passed between us over a long period of years. They give, in his own words, the rich flavour of one of our great men, the chief and *nonpareil* amongst the elder statesmen of British climbing.

His beginnings as a climber:

"It was all so accidental. We had this Classics Master at King's School, Worcester, who became fond of me and my brother. He had a *gîte* in the Alps and took us out there two years running to read Greek. He was a crypto-homosexual obviously, but not active at all— just the affectionate variety. I sometimes wonder if I'm just fantasizing, but I think I remember that walking along level paths and being told to keep to the inside of them, and reading Homer, was not enough—that these mountains all around were made to be climbed. But I'm a bit suspicious of this—it may be a rationalisation of some kind. These times were interesting, and I did a bit of cliff-scrambling—little pinnacles and things—on family holidays down in Cornwall, but I don't know that I connected the two things up at all."

Anything in the family background to give encouragement?

"I doubt it, though I think my Pa and Ma had been taken out by their relatively rich fathers and mothers to sit about in alpine resorts—there was that amount of recognition that the Alps did exist. And there's some tale of my Ma glissading down some bloody slope with a guide and shouting at him, 'Arretez, Monsieur, arretez!'. But that's a pretty far cry from climbing aiguilles. Anyway, they knew about this sort of thing. Maybe the catalyst for me was this very quiet Alpine valley above the Rhône Valley, with the Diablerets around its head. We certainly didn't have any tradition of walking on the Derbyshire or Northumberland moors—I can't claim that's part of my background."

Jack's father was Anglican minister in Droitwich, just the other side of Worcester from the Malvern Hills.

"I remember making my Papa sit on the rope while I was trying to climb the villainous bit of crag called the Ivy Scar Rock on the Malvern Hills, which I think was the most dunderheaded thing that I've done in my life, at about the time I went up to Cambridge."

He went up to Cambridge as Rustat Exhibitioner and Scholar at Jesus College in 1924.

"They were very busy, my first couple of years at Cambridge. I was an athlete, played rugby for my college, and it all took a bit of time to sink in. I wish I could remember what seduced me when I went to discover where you might find the President and Honorary Secretary of the Cambridge University Mountaineering Club, but even to this day I cannot remember the particular reason that made me think it might be a nice thing to join.

"It was quite funny when I did make contact. Wyn Harris had rooms in Caius and I went along and knocked at the door and a sepulchral voice bade me come in. Most Cambridge rooms have a long corridor with a very high ceiling and there were Wyn Harris and Van Noorden five feet above my head."

"What were they up to?"

"Oh, nothing sexual, or if there was it was in an exceptionally difficult position. No, they were simply practising their back-and-foot work. Van Noorden was a splendid chap and a very good climber, who was killed by Herbert Carr in North Wales on, I think, Dinas Bach below Dinas Mot—damned silly little crag. He led this thing—a diff. or V. diff. pitch—and Herbert Carr, who'd been following, fell off. Van Noorden, who'd been shifting about changing his belay or something, was pulled head downwards and killed.

"That must have been only a few months after the first Swiss meet I'd been to involving the club, which was at Arolla We went up the Aiguille de la Tsa and were descending the easier bit of the mountain facing Arolla. Van Noorden was going down working out the way and while he was doing that the chap above me, who was a novice also, slipped and fell and Van Noorden fielded three of us on quite a steep bit. Good job he did, because otherwise it would have been a very nasty accident. I had my revenge afterwards, though. Traversing Mont Collon Van Noorden himself fell off on a short pitch and was extremely surprised to find that I held him.

"The Alps after that definitely had preference, though I remember the same year camping up in Wasdale with my future brother-in-law Paul Sinker, and we climbed around quite a bit. I lost my nerve completely by falling out of Kern Knotts Crack and had gradually to recover it on Scafell. I was very frightened on the Keswick Brothers Climb, which didn't seem to have any proper finishing holds. But after that it began to come right. This was in 1928, which was the first time I climbed properly with others on a rope."

"The traditional sequence went British hills, Alps and Himalayas. Did that imply a contempt for the rock-climbing this country had to offer?"

"I don't think the Himalayas then entered into the scheme of things, despite the three early Everest expeditions—they seemed so infinitely remote that it never struck me that I should go there at all. When I went to Cambridge I was buttoned-up and callow and shy and as soon as I met him I came very much under the influence of Geoffrey Young. For Geoffrey, the Alps were the place and he himself never bothered with the Himalayas. The doctrine of the long traversing day which you get in Geoffrey's *On High Hills* seemed to me a very good way of treating Alpine mountains, so they were obviously much more important than what I did in this country—though I enjoyed what happened here. But it was a small-scale thing, quite different for me from the Alps."

"Your impetus towards the Alps stemmed in part, then, from a tradition, with a strong literary manifestation?"

"Oh yes, it did, and that featured quite strongly in making them attractive to us. Although we were breaking with aspects of that tradition. You see, we were just at the gap before which it was disreputable to climb without guides. It was no longer damned silly, but becoming reasonable, to do without them, and that's the point at which the Cambridge Club came in to say, 'Look, with reasonable party discipline you can do these things!'. Wager put down the argument in one of the early CUMC Journals. The first time you went out you were just a piece of baggage on the end of the rope. If you were any good at all you could become a responsible second man. And if you were *any* good you were expected, in your third year, to be leading quite reasonable climbs. It was a progress we felt to be OK, but some of the golden oldies in The Alpine Club felt it to be ridiculous—how could you possibly learn to lead alpine climbs starting as a novice three seasons before? But to us it was both reasonable and possible, and that's how we did it. I only climbed once with a guide in my life . . ."

"When was that?"

"It was with one of the Lochmatters—funny little man—good on cutting ice-steps, but I had to lead him down from the Lyskamm in cloud. He was lost. He really was rather cowardly, I think. So I never felt I needed to climb with a guide again. Those of us in the university clubs couldn't afford guides anyway—that had quite a lot to do with the build-up of guideless climbing. The earlier guideless climbers—Todhunter and so on—were regarded as pretty eccentric by the Alpine Fathers. By our time it was becoming more the norm, and was more or less OK, though you had to try not to make a fool of yourself. It was an odd time to come into alpine climbing."

"This integrated tradition whereby you had to pass on your accumulated expertise to an incoming genera-tion must have acted as an inhibiting factor on your own development?"

"Oh probably—but in a university club of young stu-dents that *was* the corporate ethos. You picked up your novice generation and you tried to transmit what you'd learned, however incompetently, to them. I think that still goes on in any normal local club today . . ."

"I think perhaps not—what you describe typified an approach founded on particular social and educational values which have given way to a more individualised drive to achievement."

"I think that's quite true—in a sense, prefects and fags were part of that sort of game. There were those who wanted to learn how to climb, and those who knew only a faint degree more than the novices did thought it was their job to teach and lead them. Without being prig-gish, that was really quite a strong tradition with us— that's what we did. If I look at the CUMC now, that doesn't seem to exist. Anyway, the CUMC Journal now is virtually illiterate, whereas there were some quite good articles in the CUMCJs in our day, and we managed to keep a close watch on literacy."

"And you managed to produce one most years."

"Oh yes—and they had some classic articles in them. Now I find them virtually illiterate, not much fun at all."

"Is the literary tradition on which *you* had to draw for the activity *you* pursued now defunct?"

"Probably, yes—when I started the person you read was Leslie Stephen, who was a considerable literary figure as well as a great mountaineer. We all felt part of a tradition and the more I got to know Geoffrey Young the more anchored that was. Climbing was very much a literary business whilst being a physical one as well . . ."

"And in fact, neither GWY nor Leslie Stephen were writing about events hugely removed from your time, and the social milieu they described was a familiar one to you."

"Yes, if you think that GWY climbed with Slingsby and married his daughter, you're going quite a long way back into the 19th century. And all the people I'd read about he'd climbed with. That was a tremendous influence, and of course there was a link-up between climbing and literacy—Geoffrey in my case gave a tremendous boost to that with his personal knowledge of writers and poets.

"Was that important to you, or just a pleasant adjunct to the activity?"

"Oh I think it was important—when you thought that GWY's grandfather had walked over the hills with Charles Kingsley, it made a real connection between literature and the mountains. The interesting thing for me is the sort of balance you tried to keep between what you did in this country and the Alps, which were then your ultimate goal. And you can see the way in Geoffrey's own writing in which he came to see that what you did in British hills and on British rock was a worthwhile thing in itself, and not just practice for doing, say, the South Face of the Weisshorn."

"There always had been climbers whose primary or sole interest was in British rock . . ."

"Very few. The Abrahams went to the Alps, though they didn't make much of it. Owen Glynne Jones was killed on the Dent Blanche . . ."

"Archer Thomson?"

"Yes! Well he's rather a key figure, since he virtually explored Lliwedd himself, and as far as I know he never went near the Alps—he was the beginning of the new lot—the people who didn't simply look on British rock as a training ground. But most of the rest were bisexual—partly devoted to the Alps, partly to invent-ing British rock-climbing, which is what they did. It took them some time to work out that there might be some-thing worthwhile or worth doing for its own sake in British rock-climbing. If I'd been asked to choose— damned silly idea that it is—I'd have said the Alps every time, of course, and the main reason for that was that it was where GWY had made all these great climbs before the War."

"That suggests that your primary search wasn't for difficulty?"

"No—it was for mountain tops by interesting routes."

"So it was an aesthetically orientated urge—the Cambridge aesthete is an apt tag after all?"

"I think so—though I'm not sure I was aesthetically literate enough in those days. Still, there was the Matterhorn—I remember consciously thinking what a lovely thing it was. When young Perren asked me if I'd like to repeat the Schmidt Route on the North Face of the Matterhorn in 1931 I said 'Yes, I'd love to but I can't afford it'. It's conceivable we would have done the second ascent, but it was too much money at that time. I was also a bit frightened, I expect. It would have been rather fun. I think he was good enough and I was prob-ably good enough too."

"Climbing was only a very small part of your life in Cambridge?"

"Oh yes—I played around with all the usual games as well as academic work. I was a pole-vaulter, which was rather an aesthetically pleasing thing to do. Life was very compartmentalised. Cambridge term time was very far removed from what was done in the holidays. Though they did overlap occasionally, particularly where Ivan Waller was involved as he had an indulgent Mum whose car he could borrow. But there was very little interaction between aesthetic, academic and sporting life at the University."

"Although GWY tried, however successfully I don't know, to embrace several of those spheres?"

"Yes, but again, his Sunday evenings were rather like a French Salon. And when he came to lecture to the CUMC it was rather as though he were trying out whole chapters of *On High Hills* on the dog. The *salon* element came in when you got to know Geoffrey through the club and went to his and Len's Sunday evenings, which were an introduction for me to intelligent conversation as well as to climbing. The Pen y Pass parties came of that. If you'd been to 5 Bene't Place half a dozen times possibly Geoffrey or Len would say 'how about PyP at Easter' and that's how I got there. Otherwise I should never have got near PyP at all. It was a social and intellectual background which is quite foreign to what I know of climbing today."

"And there operated a process of selection by which people from less privileged sectors of society were excluded?"

"Yes, but they'd never have been there anyway. I admit this is elitist, but they had to be at Cambridge first."

"So people like the Abrahams would not have been invited to the PyP Easter parties?"

"Well, be fair—Geoffrey got to know and like the Abrahams, and Frank Smythe, who came from quite a different background, was welcome at Pen y Pass—but yes, I admit I do stop at this point."

(A digression in defence of a man who needs no defender: this background in climbing can now seem almost unbearably privileged. Jack's academic career, too, was one of glittering accomplishment. He took a First Class in the Historical Tripos in 1926 and a First Class with special distinction in the English Tripos the following year. What matters, though, is the use to which he put these advantages. In the 'thirties he was, as he puts it, "tempted out of the ivory tower" by John Newsom to work for Durham Community Service Coun-

cil. To this day, amongst older people in the north-east of England his name is a byword for committed social concern. In his own words:

"I came into educational administration at the end of the squalid and hungry 'thirties, after some years working with unemployed Durham miners and their families. I think that those underfed children, their fathers on the scrap-heap, and the mean rows of houses under the tip, all the casual product of a selfishly irresponsible society, have coloured my thinking ever since . . . I wanted the mainline express to a new world, and fair shares all round."

To anyone who knows Jack, the silent pain he has suffered at the undoing of his life's work in educational administration and development by the squalid iniquities which Mrs Thatcher's successive administrations have visited upon the *community* of Britain has been devastating to witness:

"I watch with appalled disgust what is happening to the education service—the substitution of a reasonably non-pompous altruism by unashamedly vulgar self-interest. I can't remember anything nastier than the Conservative Right in the Commons—and I meet their like daily in pubs—since Churchill lambasted 'the hard-faced men who'd done well out of the War' (1914 18 edition) back in the 'twenties."

Digression over—back to the outdoors.)

"Your own technical development as a rock-climber seems to have occurred with remarkable rapidity."

"The sport was going through changes, from grouting about in these bloody gullies—what Geoffrey Young called The Gully Epoch—to balance climbing. I'm not old enough to have taken part in that, though I did climb a few of them and pretty repulsive they were. But gradually we were shedding our heavy clothes and having lighter nailed boots, then climbing in two-and-elevenpence-halfpenny plimsolls and little tricouni-nailed Hargreaves shoes. We were breaking through on to different angles and types of rock and beginning to adapt ourselves and our equipment to that."

"The new routes which established your reputation as the leading rock-climber of your day were your climb on the West Buttress of Cloggy, and Purgatory on Lliwedd. To a later generation, though, your Javelin Blade, along perhaps with Kirkus's Bridge Groove, now seem to be the only pre-war climbs to deserve a grade of Extremely Severe in Wales."

"The Javelin Blade finish was a kind of comic accident. I'd thought I was doing the original route, but had clearly got lost and failed to see the not very difficult mantelshelves over to the right. So I was committed to something rather harder, but don't remember much except the slightly worrying athleticism of the pull-out on to the top of the Javelin itself. I hadn't done any rock-climbing in the previous six months—so much for training for climbing—being out at a German university and concentrating then on ski-ing and pole-vaulting. It never struck me that the climb was anywhere near as important as the West Buttress of Cloggy—which obviously has much fewer technical difficulties: though nowadays nobody can possibly realise the problems presented by hopelessly insecure grass. All my ambitions in 1930 were focused on the Alps and, just coming into view, the Himalayas. The Javelin Blade was so irrelevant to them that I cannot even remember ever having recorded it."

"You say your ambitions were directed towards the Himalayas, yet the only expedition you went on to them was the 1933 Everest trip."

"I would have gone on '36 Everest if it hadn't been for the underground rebellion amongst some of us who didn't think it was right that Hugh Ruttledge should be leader. So quite rightly he didn't ask me. I was very disappointed not to go on Tilman's '38 trip, though weatherwise it turned out to be a bloody awful year. But I was then in the Social Services job and the Director of the National Council for Social Services said, 'No, I see no reason at all why we should give you leave to go.'."

The Ruttledge Rebellion was one of the earliest of Jack's brushes with various Establishments of climbing and other spheres of life.

"I wasn't heavily involved at first. It had been clear in '33 that Hugh Ruttledge didn't find it easy to make up his mind, but he was a good linguist, knew about Sherpas, and on the ride across Tibet he was a nice father figure. But when it came to mountaineering he didn't know much about it. Obviously, the crucial point was when the two soldiers, Bousted and Birnie, took it on themselves to say that conditions were too cold to establish Camp Five on May 20th. Wyn Harris, who was an infinitely more experienced mountaineer, thought this absolute nonsense. I remember I was at Camp Four at the time and Wyn Harris came down in a complete fury, saying, 'The fucking soldiery!'. And he was right, because on the 20th for the next three days not only was the weather good but it was before the upper slabs were covered with new snow. There *was* a chance then, with that open window from 20th to 23rd May. And those funny bits beyond the couloir they were very much my

cup of tea—I was better at that than Shipton or Smythe. Hugh Ruttledge was a nice chap, and we finished up as friends. It wasn't a personal feud, just that some of us didn't think him the right chap to be in charge of a major mountaineering expedition. His indecisiveness jeopardised our one thin chance of success."

"Did your dissidence put you on the wrong side of Strutt?"

"Oh no—Strutt was a bastard and everyone got on the wrong side of him. He basically felt that the other ranks should keep themselves in order. But I think he was more or less on our side over Ruttledge. Longstaff certainly was—he was on the side of all our youngsters as they came up through the ranks, unlike those stuffy bastards at The Alpine Club!"

"There was no formal structure to climbing in your day. You were partly responsible for bringing about the present situation of representation by the British Mountaineering Council. How d'you feel your creature's developed?"

"I doubt the usefulness now of that particular kind of mountain bureaucracy. I'd be happier if there were just a loose assembly of all sorts of clubs at all sorts of levels in all sorts of places. The public *persona* of the BMC—I wouldn't say I find it repellent, but I can't say I like it very much."

"You and I would agree on the usefulness and admirable nature of the club structure, but sadly it seems to have less and less bearing on the functioning of the BMC."

"I'm with you on that—the strength's in the people who meet, climb, drink, marry together, with luck have a base somewhere in the mountain districts—that's what British mountaineering's about—it's not about a lot of bureaucracy and competition climbing and Christ knows what. Clubbability's better than any bureaucratic national structure. I'd be much happier with a loosely-knit federal structure of jolly, solidly-based and solidly-drinking local clubs who would not be inclined to apostasy on issues like competition climbing.

"And the anarchic tendencies and fratricidal jealousies of top rock-climbers seem divorced not only from the BMC but also from local clubs, which are regarded as being for old fuddy-duddies. The sort of neck-biting between top climbers I find totally distasteful—it doesn't agree with anything I ever regarded climbing as being, at all."

"The fact that you can explain this behaviour as the inevitable result of commercial pressures on these climbers is no excuse?"

"None at all, though I'm sure the pressures exist. But then, who in my day could ever make any money out of climbing?"

"Frank Smythe . . .?"

"Apart from Frank Smythe. Also, I find it intensely *boring,* all these chaps doing something with or without bolts to the left or right of where someone else has been."

"And describing their experience in terms of a limited and repetitive set of numbers? Which is intrinsically much less interesting than the tradition of a diverse use of language in which you were brought up?"

"You mustn't be a snob about this and I find *Mountain* and the magazine you write for better than the others in this respect, but I find the other magazines a frightful bore. I read a page or two and think, 'Christ, I don't want any more of this sort of stuff!'. But that's what comes of being old and awkward."

"You've always had *that* reputation!"

"Bloody minded, in fact—I'm all for being bloody-minded!"

After a conversation I had with him last year Jack wrote to me thus:

"Surely a very large body of climbers would ask, 'What in the world are these silly old superannuated buggers talking about?' I can't escape a despairing feeling of alienation. And yet we *were* talking—not directly, because that would have been vulgar—but glancingly about a system (only that is too formulated a word) of beliefs and fantasies and escapes from *La Condition Humaine* which meant a very great deal to us, so many years ago. But we belong to the irrecoverable past, don't we."

No—where there's something to be learnt, some wisdom to be expressed, some complex continuity of human response to the wild country, the tradition lives, and within it nothing is irrecoverably lost. Let's end with a vision, bleak perhaps, but salutary, of the future, from a letter of Jack's:

"It is heartening . . . that not all today's climbers are oafs—and unutterably selfish to boot. I have an uncomfortable vision of climbing moving inexorably towards total irrelevance—shades of Colonel Strutt dog me here! Incomparable athleticism, plus or minus *finite* areas of rock, plus increasingly competitive bloody-mindedness (plus disregard for the environment and peregrines' nests) and litter and louts and the sheer disfigurement of pristine rockfaces—I remember Samivel and his three-phase picturing of unsullied rocks, followed by an agglomeration of pitons, bolts, pre-fashioned holds and ubiquitous artificiality, and (a century or two later) utterly deserted faces and overhangs, chequered by a few pieces of rusting ironmongery—and the choughs (or 'choucas' who followed the 1924 Everest climbers above 28,000ft) content with their uncluttered domain again. And I saw a splendid Lammergeier sailing untouched at 27,000ft above the squalid mess and shit of our camp on the North Col in '33! I wonder if we climbers have only a short life ahead—even if spared the nuclear holocaust . . .

"Perhaps there's a future still in which we shan't *need* Ken Wilsons and climbing competitions? Of *course* I don't know—but with Ted Hughes and the Bishop of Durham and Voltaire, there might just be a bit of a garden which our great-grandchildren might still think worth cultivating.

But pretty deeply in despair . . .

Yours,

Jack"

THREE OBITUARIES

Len Chadwick
The Daily Telegraph, 1988

Len Chadwick, who died recently aged 72, was perhaps the most gifted representative of that peculiarly northern institution, the outdoor columnist. At one time every regional newspaper in the North of England had one, and several of them—Harry Griffin, Tom Waghorn, Frank Wilkinson, Tony Greenbank for example—built up devoted readerships. Len Chadwick wrote a weekly column for the *Oldham Evening Chronicle* under the *nom-de-plume* of "Fellwalker" throughout the 'fifties and 'sixties which was a model of the columnist's craft and an inspiration to all ramblers and mountain walkers resident west of the Pennines.

Len was an outlandish character. Slight of frame, with streaming white hair, a lantern jaw and hooded eyes, his possessions never seemed to amount to more than the clothes—cast-offs which came his way and were worn until they fell apart—in which he stood. The soles of his boots often as not were secured with string, his trousers held up by an old tie. This dress served him as well for the everyday grind at the menial jobs he took—typist in a pool amongst 16-year-old girls, ice-cream salesman or clerk in a clothing factory—as for a blizzard in the Cairngorms or a wet day on the Welsh hills.

His hardihood, his appetite for miles, were beyond belief—30 or 40 each day of every weekend or holiday, taken at a spring-heeled step which most would term a run was the average, and this over any terrain, not even abating amongst the peat-hags and mires of the Pennine moors which were his favourite haunt. The young boys of 13 or 14 who were his most frequent companions were driven often to the limits of their endurance, but if they lasted the course, the end result was profoundly educative. The classic autodidact, Len could keep up daylong an inspired and informed monologue—often in Esperanto, which was one of his loves—about matters ranging from the history of socialism through his prisoner-of-war experiences to the poetry of Ebenezer Elliott or the natural history of the regions through which he passed. All this, because of schedules precisely worked out which gave no latitude to delay, was tempered at the end of the day by the inevitable race for bus or train from some far-flung stop or station, where a not-infrequent mistake in season or timetable could mean double the miles.

He was unkempt, dirty, poor, accumulated no material possessions, never had a permanent home. He smoked incessantly, talked in a quick jabber through toothless gums and wrote—in prose or verse—with a boundless energy for the physical horizon. His tenuous balance and careering pace of life were cruelly stopped by a stroke ten years ago. Recovering, the bad break of an ankle lamed him. Without material resources, his declining years were spent in an old people's home in Oldham. The frail body crippled, what memories of mist-roll and sunburst among the hills must have drifted across the slow fading of that fine, original mind. He leaves no successor.

John Syrett
High, 1985

John Syrett, one of the leading outcrop climbers of the early seventies, killed himself by jumping from the top of Malham Cove on the ninth of June this year. He had been severely depressed for some time.

John was the outstanding member of a gifted group of climbers—Bernard Newman, Brian Hall, Alex MacIn-

tyre, John Porter and Roger Baxter-Jones amongst them—who came together in the Leeds University Mountaineering Club at the end of the 'sixties. He arrived in Leeds from Dartford in Kent to read Applied Mineral Sciences in the autumn of 1968. During his second year at the university he started training on the Leeds Wall, and on a cold, blustery autumn day in 1970 announced his presence to the climbing world by a faultless sight-lead—thought at the time to be the first, though it later became known that Tony Nicholls had made a similar ascent four years earlier—of Almscliff's Wall of Horrors.

This lead and the publicity it was given had a myth-shattering impact; a twenty-year-old student with less than two years' climbing experience had cruised—and found protectable—the route generally considered at that time to be the most difficult and serious lead on British rock. Whether or not it was so is immaterial; the icon had been broken, but a string of others were soon to be supplied in its place, and the development of grit-stone climbing, which with a few exceptions had lagged behind that on limestone in the late 'sixties, now proceeded apace.

The list of John's new routes reads like the recitation of a Yorkshire gritstone connoisseur's test-pieces: Joker's Wall, The Brutaliser, Propeller Wall, Earl Buttress, Encore, Brown Sugar, Thunderclap, Midnight Cowboy, Syrett's Roof and The Big Greenie—the last of these, the impending, pocketed wall above Frankland's Green Crack at Almscliff, which he climbed in 1972, being one of the two or three most significant outcrop climbs of the post-Brown era. But there was something else about these routes apart from their undoubted quality, and that was the style in which they were done. Uniquely amongst pioneers of his time, no hint of dubious tactics ever attached to John's climbing, which had a majestic quality I have not seen surpassed. He was the best climber to watch on rock that I have ever seen—only Boysen at his peak coming close. And he was rigorously honest. Without once preaching the gospel of purism, John embodied it.

He was no less impressive away from the rock. The most striking thing about him was his physical beauty—the body slim and strong and a miracle of proportion; dark, curly hair; a fine, high bone-structure and quick, dark eyes that could never quite bear to look straight at you—perhaps held your gaze for a second, quizzical and sardonic, and then with a half-smile would flicker away. He was tremendous company, testing, excitable, mettlesome—and wild. Sometimes he would dance out his frenzy—a man to spur you on, drag you in, encourage you along. Days climbing with him were like that. More often than not they were orgies of soloing and bouldering, for he often seemed to look on a rope as a form of restraint. "Come on", he would say, "You're doing well. What's next . . .?"

The time at Leeds was so very short. There was a ridiculous accident—the tendons of his fingers cut through at a party in opening a can of beer. Operations. A trip to America ruined. He went up to Newcastle, took a three-year course in physiotherapy, afterwards worked offshore on the rigs. The inner violence you had always sensed turned back upon him. There were frequent, savage bouts of drinking.

Pete Livesey, in one of his articles, wrote of John's "blue-eyed god-like expression", and then referred to him as "the reincarnation of JME". The latter has proved tragically prophetic. I can scarcely bear to think of him as dead—all his bright promise come to this, the sheer, tragic waste of it all.

Surely, for those of us who knew him, he will still be there at Almscliff or Brimham as he was when we were in our young twenties—the flared jeans trailing in the peat, his black curls blowing about his face, and just as you catch his gaze, his eyes flickering away to direct you at some new and more desperate creation?

"Mo" Anthoine
The Guardian, 1989

Julian "Mo" Anthoine might have remained unknown outside the closed, atavistic world of mountaineering had it not been for a remarkable profile of him by Al Alvarez entitled *Feeding the Rat* and published last year. The implicit dismissal would have been grotesque, for Mo was not only amongst the most experienced and accomplished British Alpinists and Himalayan climbers of the post-war epoch. He was also one of the last stalwart exponents of the best traditions of the sport and one of its enduring characters.

Born in Kidderminster and the son of a carpet designer, Mo started climbing in the 1950s in North Wales, and quickly developed into one of the best rock-climbers of his time. His new climbs in Snowdonia—ascents like the Devil's Nordwand in Cwm Idwal, or The Groove on the huge, forbidding and neglected cliff of Llech Ddu—were not only at the top standard of their day, but they were also notable for the honesty and

frankness with which Mo described the means employed in their ascent, at a time when the other active pioneers of new routes were increasingly concerned to play down the number of artificial aids used and rationalise descriptions in order to inflate the sense of their achievements.

This lack of integrity and the new "professionalism" in 'sixties mountaineering which in part bred it, was something which Mo was concerned to avoid and debunk throughout his involvement with climbing. The stance gives a clue to the strongly held underlying values and beliefs of a man who was a natural rebel against all mere conformity, and who very quickly acquired, even amongst the unshockable ranks of climbers, the reputation of a wild man. His partying, drunkenness, ribaldry, fighting and repartee were legendary.

The small climbing community of North Wales in the early 'sixties was far too tame to hold his interest for long. Late in 1961, Mo and a kindred spirit—a former professional boxer from Derbyshire known as Fox—set off on a Rabelaisian version of the Grand Tour which left a trail of mayhem and epic stories across five continents. Tragically, it also involved a spell working in a blue asbestos mine in Australia which was to result—utterly predictably according to the incubation period—in Mo's death 26 years later.

On Mo's return to Britain in 1964, he went to train as a teacher at Coventry College of Education. There he met Jacky Philippe, and from this balanced and fulfilling marriage he had a daughter and a son. In 1964 he also resumed his Alpine career, and in a poor season made several important British ascents in the Dolomites, including one of the Comici route on the Cima Grande di Lavaredo with Alvarez. Poorly equipped, the two survived a storm high on the face and climbed on to the summit in extremely hazardous conditions. Alvarez later paid tribute to Mo's strength, endurance and skill, and his fictionalised account of the experience, "Night Out", gave the New Yorker a minor classic of mountaineering literature. This climb, and an ascent of the Old Brenva route on Mont Blanc in the great storm of August 1966, established for Mo a reputation of extreme toughness and capacity for endurance. On the latter climb two of Mo's companions died in enforced bivouacs in snowholes. One of his other companions, Richard McHardy, later recounted the superstitious dread which Mo aroused in him by strolling around outside the snowhole in the teeth of the storm and jocularly inviting God to do his worst or fuck off.

Mo's anarchic streak, strength of character and reputation for wildness did not recommend him to the attention of the new breed of professional Himalayan mountaineers which was emerging at the end of the 1960s. Nor did their self-promotion and dependence on sponsorship attract him. From 1968 he worked hard at setting up a small business based in Llanberis to provide high-quality essential equipment for mountaineers.

By the early 1970s this was sufficiently successful to allow Mo to fund his own trips to Himalayan and South American peaks. He took part in the 1973 expedition to the bizarre 1700–ft rock prow of Roraima in the Guyanan jungle, emerging as the most committed and capable climber in a very strong team. In 1977 he went with Chris Bonington, Doug Scott and Clive Rowlands to the Ogre, a difficult, unclimbed 24,000–ft peak in the Karakoram. On the descent from the summit Scott fell and broke both ankles. A storm came in. Bonington also took a fall, breaking two ribs. The responsibility for a safe retreat devolved on Mo and Clive Rowlands. Their skill in getting the two injured men down in a prolonged storm belongs with the great tales of mountain endurance.

On the expedition's return to Britain, the media predictably acclaimed the men whose names they recognized. Those who had brought about its safe conclusion were written out of the story. It is a measure of Mo's character that he felt no bitterness about this, gave all due praise to Scott's and Bonington's fortitude, and restricted his sniping to some wickedly funny tales about the latter's obsession, even *in extremis,* with the commercial potential of the situation: "We're going to make a fortune out of this, Mo!"

"How come?"

"The book!"

In more recent years, Mo continued to visit the Himalayas regularly, taking part in two expeditions to the North-east Ridge of Everest, one of them only weeks after he had undergone an operation for the removal of a brain tumour. The condition recurred after a year. There was another operation. Mo struggled desperately to hang on to lucidity and life. Only his exceptional physical strength and will enabled him to survive to his fiftieth birthday, eleven days after which he died.

With his death, the climbing world loses one of its best-loved characters—a stocky, barrel-chested, vital, robust, warm, sane and humorous man who held true for 30 years to the integrity, humility and fun which he clearly perceived at the root of the mountain experience, and which, by conversation and example, he communicated to everyone who knew him.

Zen and the Natural Subversive: Peter Matthiessen
The Guardian, 1989

Peter Matthiessen.

A few nights ago I witnessed an extraordinary event. It took place at The Royal Geographical Society on Kensington Gore—a milieu which suggests a phraseology of august portals, hushed voices and dark-panelled gentlemanliness. In the lecture hall there, where the varnished gleam of paintings with titles like "The Pandora nipped in the pack in Melville Bay, 1876" breaks up an oppressive acreage of stained oak, a lean, gaunt man with eyes deep-set in a strong, lined face taunted his audience in a voice of laughing velvet about his own lack of authority, and about Authorities' and Establishments' lack of integrity:

"I'm sure almost every detail I've told you is mistaken or wrong or lurid . . . I'm not an authority!"

Or again, on the death of Custer at Little Big Horn:

"A more deserved death has never been seen in history . . ."

Or on the Mormons who run the biggest strip mine in America, on Navajo Indian territory in Arizona:

"Their religion is based on the teachings of the Angel Moroni—as in 'moron'. It's a religion based on making money."

His irreverent asides were delivered in an anthropological shrine where people are "human geography", suitable objects for study. His drift was not that we should be learning *about* "primitive" peoples, but that we should be learning *from* them—and "primitive" is not, anyway, the word he would apply. He talked about "traditional" peoples, who recognise, respect, revere the sustaining earth, and contrasted their attitudes with modern man's crassly unheeding and destructive exploitativeness. The whole performance was utterly persuasive and low-key. Which is exactly what anyone acquainted with his books might expect—and that raises another problem.

The Establishment mind is an orderly, categorising affair of pigeonholes and programmed responses. Take the literary establishment, for example. If you were to canvass literary editors of the major newspapers or the English departments of our universities as to what were the major bodies of work to be written in English in the post-war period, you would inevitably be faced with evidence of the constraints of genre. The same names—novelists, poets, perhaps a dramatist or two—would recur, as though all literary achievement lay within those forms. How would a Cobbett, a Carlyle, a Hazlitt, a Hobbes, a Gilbert White, fit into this limiting scheme of things? How does a Peter Matthiessen—the RGS lecturer that night, whose books range across the boundaries of travel-writing, the essay, natural history, fiction, religious philosophy, social anthropology, and whose intelligence and clarity of prose style, whose impassioned preoccupations with the beauty, wholeness and variousness of life, whose range and imaginative grasp give him fair claim to be considered as one of the very few writers of the last forty years who may ultimately be considered "great"?

Rhetorical questions apart, few of Matthiessen's books are well known in Britain. His most famous is proba-

bly *The Snow Leopard*—certainly the finest book on Himalayan travel ever written, coincidentally a treatise on Buddhism, a spiritual autobiography, a wryly affectionate portrait of the zoologist George Schaller and of Matthiessen's Sherpa companions, and a piece of writing characterised by the exquisitely attentive descriptive powers and humane balance between elegy and ameliorism which are identifying features of his work. Several of his other books are as good as, or even in their differing ways better than, *The Snow Leopard*. *Indian Country*, the area of concern of which provided the subject matter for his RGS lecture, is a sort of Rural Rides through Red Indian America. Cobbett or Proudhon would have recognised and approved of their anarcho-syndicalist successor, whose work resonates as profoundly for its age as theirs did for an earlier one. *Indian Country* reads like a cross between *Silent Spring* and *Bury My Heart at Wounded Knee*, is far better written than either, and in its implicit message on the uses of and attitudes towards the land, should come to be seen as one of the crucial environmentalist texts. Equally impressive is *Men's Lives*—Matthiessen's account of the decline, in the face of pollution, restrictive legislation, selfish recreational lobbies, property development and big business, of the traditional fishing industry of Long Island, New York State.

His fiction, too, is of remarkable quality. *At Play in the Fields of the Lord* (1966) is not only a powerfully expressed and meticulously constructed novel comparable to Conrad at his best, it is also frighteningly prescient about the continuing fate in the late 1980s of the Amazonian Indians at the hands of profoundly evil Christian missionary sects such as the New Tribes Mission. (As an irrelevant aside, it was the actor Jack Lemmon's chosen book when he appeared on *Desert Island Discs*.) *Far Tortuga* (1975), which has just been published in Britain, is a technical masterpiece of experimental fiction, a shimmering, imagistic voyage where only the perfectly perceived suchness of tangible objects guides the narrative on its tenuous course between cosmic hope and despair.

I talked with Peter Matthiessen in London's Green Park the morning after his RGS lecture. A tall, lean man with a strong, resilient physique and—behind the frequent laughter—something of the tragic dignity of a character from a Theodor Storm novelle about him, he sat on the grass in Zen meditative posture (Matthiessen was ordained a Zen monk in 1981) under a becandled chestnut tree and talked about his life and work:

"I was born in New York City in 1927. My father

was an architect. Most of my childhood we lived away from New York on the Hudson River or in Connecticut, where I went to boarding school. My brother and I were brought up close to nature, spent our summers on the seashore, were always interested in wildlife. My father made a clearing in the woods by our house, and its shelving rocks invited every copperhead [a poisonous snake] in Connecticut to get in there. We were fascinated by them, learnt how to catch them and put them in cages. Father fished and hunted, and we were taught to shoot pretty young. I gave up hunting twenty years ago—just lost the taste for it. The ducks were getting scarce and I just didn't like shooting them any more. It was the beginning of a tendency towards Zen attitudes and practice. I still fish—haven't extended my compassion that far—though a lot less these days, and I eat most of what I get. Still, no excuse . . .

"When I was thirteen and still at boarding school I volunteered to be a counsellor at a charity boys' camp for slum kids from New Haven. I'd been very sheltered until that time and that was a real eye-opener. These kids were so deprived that the first night in camp they literally ate themselves sick. They'd never had enough to eat and just didn't know when someone was going to come along and take that food away from them. My social conscience really began with that.

"I went to Yale, started writing in my senior year, afterwards went to France and with my first wife, Patricia, founded the *Paris Review*. I wrote my first novel there, which focused around a young Indian who was the victim of white people's social pressures. My early books were well received but not a financial success, and we had a couple of babies by then. We came back to America and I eked things out by being a commercial fisherman—I took people out deep-sea fishing, had a boat, and also worked as a clammer and on commercial haul-seine nets taking dories out into the ocean."

"Was that a family tradition?"

"In a sense, yes, because my father's family came from the Friesian islands off the coast of Schleswig Holstein. They were whalers and sea-captains way back. I always lived near the ocean, was handy with boats, enjoyed it, and I liked these fisherman a lot. Which is why I came to write *Men's Lives*."

". . . where the affection for them floods through. How did your writing develop out of the fishing days?"

"I went along to the *New Yorker* and asked them to send me round the world to investigate wild places—told them everyone was writing about Europe, how about the Amazon, how about the Congo? To my amazement they sent me off, and it changed my life. They paid well, didn't quarrel about the length, and didn't need photographs. And my divorce freed me for travel."

"It wasn't a product of the travel?"

"It was a product of the fishing."

"How do you reconcile the demands of marriage and child-rearing to your style of life?"

"I didn't—I never have."

"So given Yeats's conundrum that 'The mind of man is forced to choose/Perfection of the life or of the work', for you it's the work?"

"I don't know—I've always had a rather ragged and tumultuous life, but I can't blame that on my first wife. I had trouble with my parents too. Father booted me out of the house at seventeen for cumulative mischief, bad attitudes . . ."

"Of the sort that were on display at the RGS—natural subversion?"

Grey-haired, he nodded rueful, boyish agreement:

"I was always in trouble as a kid, threatened with reform school and so on. I had a lot of fun, though. I was an angry child, I guess you could say . . ."

"Or an unaccepting and questioning one?"

"That was my view. They took me as an angry, difficult, selfish person. I've always needed to scourge the Establishment, I've been a voice in the dark and the wilderness for a long, long time. In *Wildlife in America*, which was a very early book, I was very blunt, forthright and angry about the impact of so-called civilisation on the land. That was thirty years ago—I've been yelling for an awful long time."

"You don't fit entirely comfortably into the 'Green' category—your preoccupations seem much more insistently anthropological?"

"Not entirely—I've written lots of animal, bird and wildlife books, though yes, they have generally brought in the contexts, tribal people on the land and so on. In East Africa, for example, you can't just isolate the wildlife from the people. Most ecologists are now coming round to that view. If you take the work of David Western in studying the impact of people on the forest elephants around Kilimanjaro—he's turned the situation there around because he's befriended the local Masai instead of saying 'Clear out'. He's eliminated their previous killing of animals by working with them, whereas Dyan Fossey, the gorilla lady, by antagonising, hating and despising the local people got them to hate her—that was one of the reasons why the gorillas were threatened, because of the hate she instilled in the people."

"In following that line, do you run a danger of acceding to the myth of the Noble Savage?"

"Not at all—I don't believe in Rousseau's ideas about the Noble Savage. Some of them are shits and some of them are nice people. I was taught this very early, working with Cesar Chavez in the 1968 California grape strike. He was a saintly man and did an extraordinary job for his migrant workers, taking on the massed squads of the church, the railroad and the Establishment. He put his life on the line for his people but he was nobody's fool. I remember him telling me one time, 'Don't get romantic ideas about my heroic Mexican farmworkers. You give that guy that ranch over there and in two weeks' time he'll be just as big a bastard as the guy who's got it now!' Human beings are superb creatures, but as you know, they're animals. The ideologues, who say everything has to be this way or that, are the ones who get everybody killed. Like the Ayatollah . . ."

"A theme you developed in *At Play in the Fields of the Lord*. Fiction aside, how do you react to that colonising effect of religion?"

"I've seen it at first hand in South America and New Guinea. This is not to criticise the individual missionaries, who are sometimes dedicated and extraordinary people, but it's such a mistaken quest, and one which opens traditional peoples up to exploitation, abuse, alcohol, thieving habits. They estimate that in South America, once a tribe has been exposed to missionary contact it has fifty years before extinction. That's kind of scary. I'm hostile to that."

"Yet no-one would doubt your commitment to your own form of religion."

"Zen attracts me because the priesthood, the structure, is really not very important in it. Zen calls itself the religion before religion. It's really the common element in all true religions, and shares many elements with Islam, Judaism, Christianity—the mystical experience which lies at the heart of all those religions really is the same, to do with awe and reverence and respect for the mystery of life which we seem to have been trampling on till it's almost gone. We haven't got any night any more, for example, just glare and shrouding smog. Most places you have to raise your hand forty-five degrees before you can see the stars. Go to a truly wild place and the stars go right down to the horizon. And the silence—you can't hear the birds—the few birds that are left. This seems to me a great pity, that we haven't learned to live with the earth and respect it and treat it properly. We belong to it—not the reverse! This has

to be the fundamental shift in our attitude before we start to solve our problems."

"What comes over most strongly in your writing for me is the intensity of your acts of attention towards all living things . . ."

"That's the basis of Zen practice—when you eat, eat; when you sleep, sleep. If you truly see each thing, everything has its particular beauty. It's through being aware of that detail, that sound, that colour, that emotion you're feeling, even in the dark moments—just through being aware, that you come through to the clear, clear seeing. That's the basis of shamanistic training. And when you see like that, you see through to something much larger behind. The Great Mystery . . ."

"What help are drugs in that quest?"

"LSD can be. When it was being manufactured by a Swiss chemical company in measured doses in the 1960s, a group of us learned to use it in a way that was not dangerous. It's a very foolish thing to take irresponsibly, but taken responsibly with people who know what they're doing, it's enormously instructive and I think almost everyone could benefit from it. But now you can't buy it. It's been made an outlaw thing because of the example of people like Timothy Leary, who made it so through their own ego. It's a great shame, because it could have been a very, very useful therapeutic and also a spiritual tool."

"Because it opens you up and knocks down all the habitual defences?"

"Right—it rids you of all that litter in your brain. We're like bells that have been stuffed with sticks—there's so much preconception and prejudice in there that we lose the note entirely. LSD clears that out, lets you see clearly and believe that you're having a mystical experience. I've had many near-mystical experiences with LSD, but you're always aware of that chemical screening, that revelation behind the gossamer. I find now through meditation that you can arrive at the same place but without the mist. There's nothing separating you any more—you become part of the experience, as you never can quite with drugs. That's why so many people who once used drugs go into meditation experience of some kind, because by using drugs they were assured that something was possible, even though they weren't quite reaching it."

"The seeking out of that holistic experience is a very valid reason for coming to Zen, but do you find that there are others who seek it out simply as an assertion of spiritual superiority?"

"There are spiritual materialists who come and crack

their knees for social reasons, but mostly they drop off, because it really is quite arduous and social reasons aren't enough to keep you going in it. But then others come in by accident and something happens which is very important to them and they say, 'Hey, I've got to know more about this! It's the only game in town!' There's a whole other way of approaching life without being in the future and without being in the past, where life's eternal."

". . . the immediacy of the journey in its every moment—which either literally or metaphorically is the subject of many of your books?"

"Or as St. Catherine of Siena said, 'All the way to heaven is heaven.' "

"Buddhists traditionally have a less than reverential attitude towards the written text. How do you regard your craft of writing?"

For the first time in our interview he was mildly evasive, smiled wryly, and cantered off at the pace of his own response:

"I'm a workaholic, obsessive, an absolute menace. Publishers really hate me. My corrections on galley proofs are as long as the text. I'd be in the printers shouting, 'Wait, Wait!' if they'd let me. The last chapter of *At Play* I re-wrote thirty times. I put twelve years' work into *Far Tortuga*, which is my favourite amongst my books."

"Even down to the ink blots?"

"That was the designer. Of all my books, that's the one most influenced by Zen practice. I just wanted the images one after the other—not metaphors, not similes, just the mystery of the thing as it was, by itself—the antennae of a cricket coming out from underneath a galley shack on a boat deck—those two extraordinarily light, fine things—what they were for, the manipulation, the hearing of them. If you really saw those two antennae, you would see the whole universe quivering behind!"

"Your prose has a very precise, musical phrasing to it. Is that deliberately sought?"

"I'm interested in rhythms and harmonies. I want my sentences to fall into place in an inevitable way."

"Do you think through your writing you've achieved, or will achieve, any geopolitical influence?"

"Not so long as my books are suppressed by lawsuits," he laughed (his recent title, *In the Spirit of Crazy Horse*, is still the subject of an FBI lawsuit). "You don't enjoy being pursued by your own government agencies—they're not a good enemy to have!"

"But you take a certain glee in tilting at them all the same?"

"Yeah," he grinned broadly. "I'm shaking it up! The FBI about every two weeks is caught with its hand in the till yet again in some ugly connection or other, whether it be race or anti-democratic activity or invasion of privacy. They really are a light-wing political arm now, not an investigation bureau. They were totally corrupted by J. Edgar Hoover and even now he's gone it's going to take a long time to eradicate that attitude. Nobody's really touched Hoover yet—how evil he was and how corrupt the outfit he ran. He used police state techniques from his first day in office, as far as we can make out: smears, lies, blackmail, secret files. And of course with the Reagan and Bush succession, that ethos tends to be endorsed."

"As it does in this country at the moment through the codes operated by Margaret Thatcher and her Conservative Party."

"I'm afraid you're right—she learned her trade from Ronald Reagan!"

"Yet you've managed to maintain a free and fierce anti-Establishment polemic throughout the Reagan years?"

"When Nixon messed up, that really freed us from the totalitarian drift for a time. But there's always been the potential for authoritarianism and repression in America, as you got in the McCarthy era. Because of our materialist basis, in times of recession we generally retreat into the politics of fear."

"A fear with which your Zen practice enables you to cope?"

"I've never been that severely tested."

"Not even with a $54 million lawsuit?"

"That's like learning to live with a hunchback or bad eyesight. You have it, so what do you do? People say how can you speak against your country like that . . ."

"It doesn't come across like that. Dissent is surely an honourable tradition. How can we reserve it as a term of praise for, say, Andrei Sakharov, but use it as one of abuse for our own countrymen?"

"All colonial regimes have done the same thing. But dissent's a sign of being a good citizen of your country. It's not that you repudiate your country, it's that you know your country's capable of better. You have an America on the one hand capable of the Marshall Plan, which was one of the most generous and wise programmes of all time—a country capable of that shouldn't be beating up on little countries like Vietnam or Grenada or wherever the hell it is. It shouldn't stoop to mistreatment or neglect of its poor, as we've done under Reagan and your country's done under Thatcher. People said Reagan was old and stupid and lazy and delegated everything and had no programme at all. Well he had a very consistent theme to everything he did, which was to make rich people richer and undercut the poor. The more disadvantaged you were, whether you were black or an Indian, a student or unemployed, the more you suffered. Mrs Thatcher and now Mr Bush have neatly followed along in the same tradition . . .''

His anger, irony and compassion rang out fierce and clear across the park. Even here, on the borders of Mayfair, I felt I'd been breathing the sweet air of sanity. When we stood to go, I parted from him with regret.

Brenda Chamberlain: The Artist Islanded
The Guardian, 1988

Brenda Chamberlain Self-portrait on Carnedd Dafydd.

When she died, in Bangor of an overdose of barbiturates in 1971, Brenda Chamberlain was caught in a temporary void where reputation and admiring reviews had not yet led on to the craved wider recognition. Loverless and

on the dole in the rainy, parochial sea-town of her birth, her ''world'' had narrowed down in image and audience alike.

In the years since her death, this painter, poet and prose-writer has been received, amongst the art-fraught coterie of Anglo-Wales, as a tragic type. More recently there are signs that attention is turning at last to assess the quality of her artistic achievement. Last year saw the re-publication of *Tide-race*—an extraordinary memoir, illustrated with her own line-drawings, of the fourteen years she spent living on Ynys Enlli—Bardsey Island—off the westernmost tip of North Wales. This year an exhibition organised by Llandudno's Mostyn Art Gallery is touring Wales, and publication of a biography from Poetry Wales Press is imminent.

Brenda Chamberlain was born in 1912 of parents from amongst Bangor's comfortable middle-class. Her vocation as painter and writer was clear even in her early years, and from 1931 to 1936 she studied at the Royal Academy schools, where she met and married fellow-student John Petts. In 1936 they moved to Ty'r Mynydd, Llanllechid—a primitive cottage on a shoulder of hill looking out over the drowned land of Traeth Lafan— where they set up the Caseg Press. Petts shared with her his expertise in typography and wood-engraving, and the collaboration between them and the poet Alun Lewis resulted in The Caseg Broadsheets—hand-printed poems and engravings now prized by collectors.

Then came the war. John Petts joined 224 Parachute Field Ambulance in 1943, breaking thus the bonds of a difficult marriage. Alun Lewis, his reputation established by the *Raider's Dawn* volume of poetry from 1942, which Robert Graves had reviewed as ''both illuminating and healing'', was killed at Arakan in 1944. Brenda Chamberlain's closest friend, Karl Von Laer, was a German, living in Germany throughout the war years. By 1945, she was islanded in a post-war world. She visited Von Laer, only to find, as she expresses in a poem dedicated to him, that ''The past with all its host/Of friends and habits/Is a lost threshold.''

She returned to Wales, and in the spring of 1947 went to live on Enlli. Even now, forty years on, getting across the ferocious tide-race in the sound from Aberdaron to the island is an adventure. In 1947 it was unimaginably remote, and her decision to live amongst its tiny population (with a Breton companion, Jean-Paul van de Bijl) was a crucial one which inspired much of her best work, both written and graphic. ''I am a lonely woman/ Living on a lonely strand'', she wrote, yet the isolation enabled her to produce not only her prose-masterpiece,

Tide-race, but also paintings which twice won her the Fine Art Gold Medal at theNational Eisteddfodau of 1951 and 1953, and provided the content for one-woman exhibitions at Gimpel Fils, London, in 1950, 1952–3, and 1954. In addition to these successes, her collection of poems entitled *The Green Heart* received the Arts Council (Welsh Committee) Poetry Award for 1956.

Enlli is a strange place, however, and the effect of her fourteen-year sojourn there was profound. It is, quite literally, a burial place—the bones of 20,000 saints are reputed to lie under its few acres of fertile ground:

"Paul and I; we are all in the danse macabre, the fatal play of life and death. The stained bones underground feel our dancing measure. The brisk feet leap over our own future grave-plots . . . on this small stage, this microcosm, in the middle of a scene, the shadow of death falls on the players."

It's intriguing to compare Chamberlain's Enlli with Synge's Inishmore and Inishmaan. Even the topographical detail acts as metaphor: Enlli is secretive, hiding its green, seaward garden from the mainland behind the bulk of a hill, whilst the Aran Islands turn a fearsome spine of cliff against the ocean and shelter their populations below the bare rock on a level strip to leeward. To Synge the Aran Islanders were cultured, homogeneous, generous; those on Enlli—in Chamberlain's account—are deceitful, disparate, furtive, quarrelsome. The latter society (or the writer's perception of it) is not a microcosm likely to impel that curious love of humankind which nurtures artistic expression. And indeed, after Van de Bijl left in 1953, a morbid or even psychotic element in Chamberlain's art is increasingly to the fore:

"I have lived for many years in a world of salt caves, of clean-picked bones and smooth pebbles. Towards the end of this period of my life, I began to paint salt-water drowned man, never completely lost to view. They are ledges of encrusted rock, an armoured leg braced in silt, the loins of a body changed gradually into a stone bridge, a wounded torso, flood-tide rising on the walls of a cave into the far corners of which a storm has embedded stones. In particular, there is the breast of the drowned . . ."

She left Enlli in 1961, travelled round Europe, lived for four years on the Greek island of Idhra (remaining there at the time of the Colonels' Coup but leaving Greece

Charcoal sketch of a horse by **Brenda Chamberlain**, *in a cottage on Ynys Enlli.*

after a visit to political detainees on the island of Levos), and eventually came back to Bangor and a life of increasing, unremarked bleakness, ending with her suicide.

With Brenda Chamberlain, to dissociate the detail of her life from that of her art is an intense impossibility. In her Greek Journal, *A Rope of Vines*, she wrote that:

"We invent our own lives, but there remains reality outside oneself, and these enduring boats, laden with melons and water-pots, green peppers and cattle, point the way to life through abundant dying."

Thus, perhaps, the ease with which, in *Tide-race*, her prose slips in and out of modes as distanced as high farce and subliminal imagery. And thus too in some of the paintings in the Mostyn Touring Exhibition, where the solid apartness of her subjects, static and statuesque, carry echoes of Gauguin in their bold, flat planes, strength of posture and bright distinction of colour. The best of her mid-period paintings—"The Christin Children", "Fishermen's Return", "Girl with a Siamese Cat" or "Children on a Hopscotch Pavement" (there is an excruciating poignancy in the regularity with which she, as a woman who had never gone through the menarche, chose children as her subject)—are remarkable for the consistent and unique style they create. It is not second-hand Gauguin, but unmistakable Brenda Chamberlain.

Her later work is often in cut-out and gouache, but devoid of colour, like bleached late Matisse. In the powerful "Black Bride" series of ten paintings from the mid-sixties the morbid element is strongly present. The bride is full-bellied yet cadaverous, with pursed lips; the titles—"The Bride Enmeshed", "The Bride enters the Sepulchre", "The Bride Entombed"—point to what texts within the paintings make more explicit: "Children have been menaced (before now) by nightingales, so why should not the Bride be made uneasy by a web of lace and artificial roses?" Towards the end, her work peters out into increasingly disturbed abstraction: "Bandaged Heads", "Jugs"—the latter with heads jammed inside them. They force you back to look again at one of the major pieces in this absorbing and worthwhile exhibition—the astonishing "Self-Portrait on Carnedd Dafydd" of 1938.

In some respects this is a typical Royal Academy student's painting—sophisticated, allusive, technically proficient. It could so easily have been Leonardo pastiche, but is far more fully achieved than that. A golden-haired figure, face half-shadowed, looks sternly out of the canvas from a staggered dream landscape which pays obvious homage to that of the "Mona Lisa". Soft outline and mellow colouring tease at our interpretation and create a lyrical mood, but the overall impression is of questing anguish, a face in a mirror registering sardonic dislike. It is a painting hauntingly impossible to live with—as indeed, ultimately, proved its artist's life.

Rats, Rocks and A. Alvarez
The Guardian, 1988

Al Alvarez is now fifty-nine years old, the brown eyes deep-set and alert; jaw clean-shaven, strong; skin crow's-footed, tanned; lines graven around a grey moustache—the face of a Union Colonel musing on liberty or defeat. Strength and mildness of character start out at you from the aquiline, domed profile of the Sephardic Jew.

Amongst 'sixties men-of-letters, his contribution was idiosyncratic, promiscuous and vast. His first two books, *The Shaping Spirit* (1958—on modern English and American poetry) and *The School of Donne* (1961) were important developments out of that energising literary debate which in America went under the name of The New Criticism. Even by the time of his seminal anthology, *The New Poetry* (1962), with its fiercely polemical introduction, "Beyond the Gentility Principle", Alvarez

Al Alvarez.

was already moving away from the constraints of pure textual study into a peril-fraught area of writing where the appreciation of literature implies an understanding of the peculiar psychological processes whereby the artist relates to, and seeks to understand, the social conditions of his time. This direction found expression in *Under Pressure: The Writer in Society* (1965), and in his marvellous collection of essays, *Beyond All This Fiddle* (1968 and sorely overdue for republication).

His work from *The Savage God* (1971—a classic study of suicide) onwards has been increasingly involved with social manifestations of the extremist aesthetic propounded in his 'sixties criticism and reviewing. *Hunt* (1978) is one of the neatest trips along the edge of paranoia to be found in the thriller genre; *Life After Marriage* (1982) a subtle and ironic study of divorce which abounds in masterfully novelistic impressions around its theme; *The Biggest Game in Town* (1983) is a sharply funny investigation of the laconic insouciance and brinkmanship of gambling in Las Vegas; *Offshore* (1986) an exemplary piece of reportage on life and work as a North Sea oilman.

His latest book, *Feeding the Rat*, extends this hagiology of gamblers, suicides, roustabouts, paranoiacs and divorcees to bring in a character from the wild side of mountaineering. "Profile of a Climber" is its sub-title, and its sub-text is a tirade against the fame and phoney values of those whom the media identify and canonise as mountain men. The subject is a quick-witted, anarchic and extremely funny mountaineer of immense experience—"Mo" Anthoine. In 1977 Anthoine and fellow-climber Clive Rowlands rescued the injured but infinitely better-known climbers Chris Bonington and Doug Scott after an accident on a 24,000ft Himalayan peak, The Ogre. "Yet", writes Alvarez, "between the rescue and the ensuing publicity, a curious conjuring trick took place: Mo and Rowlands effectively vanished from the story."

"Mo" Anthoine may have disappeared from the idolatrous pages of Fleet Street. In *Feeding the Rat* he comes to vivid, rude life as a radical inhabitant of Alvarezland, where the individual is forever pitted against the shallow judgements of system and wins through only by robust refusal to be other than he is. Authenticity—that central piety of the liberal imagination—is, in all its sensual, emotional and intellectual manifestations, at the root of Alvarez's work.

When faced with a body of writing of this degree of power, consistency and originality, it is inevitable that its author's quality of life comes into question. The instinct is to explore his adequacy to his own themes. So how does Alvarez shape up? I went out climbing with him for the day to find out.

The personal reputation is for rapid driving, high stakes, rash climbing. It fits ill with first impressions of the man. He is stocky, laid-back, dignified. In prose and poetry alike, process is the obsession. In conversation too the skull is on display beneath the skin. Tease his apparent unfitness and the counter runs thus: "At my age, the only thing that makes you lose weight is cancer."

He drives, very fast and controlled in a Saab Turbo, from his Hampstead home down to Harrison's Rocks at Groombridge, telling an anecdote about I.A. Richards and his wife Dorothea Pilley on the way:

"I went out for a day in winter with them on Mount Washington the first time I was at Princeton in the 'fifties. At the end of it I was absolutely cuffed and these two sixty-year-olds were still bouncing. In those days I was a *very* bad driver. I had a 1939 Buick I'd bought for 15 dollars. The roads were covered in black ice. Ivor was in the front and I was driving faster and faster, enjoying myself, drifting round the bends. There was an air of tension in the car. We came to a T-junction, no chance of stopping—I went straight across and the car completely buried itself in a snowdrift. Dorothea leaned over from the back and told me, quite coolly, 'Ivor doesn't really like fast driving, you know.' "

At the outcrop he changes into rock-boots, climbing clothes and harness, the state of which beggars belief. The modern rock-gymnast is characterised by garish displays of clothing and gadgetry. Alvarez, by contrast, climbs "With shabby equipment always deteriorating . . .". The rope into which he ties for his first climb—the overhanging edge of an isolated block—is in harmony with the rest of his gear, faded and frayed. When someone remarks that it appears to consist of a sheath without a core, he takes out a knife for exploratory surgery in search of the latter. Once he sets out on the vertical plane, though, this unkempt and haphazard aura is dispelled by a forceful and vigorous physical approach. On climbs of considerable difficulty, he performs with aggression, commitment, skill. It is, he explains, the physical workout in his weekly recreational routine—climbing on Sundays, poker on Tuesdays.

And apart from the recreation?

"The writer's life is that of a hermit—he sits on his ass all day in solitude working and re-working the same thoughts, trying to get some balance, order and intelligence into them. I work very slowly, re-write obsessively . . ."

"Without contact with, or feedback from, other writers?"

"I don't know many writers, in fact—the only friends in that category are Frank Kermode and Philip Roth. And if you live in the London literary world, you find that it's fuelled by envy in the Kleinian sense—it seeks to destroy that which it can't possess. So you try to avoid it."

"Are you dangling the old chestnut of reviewers being failed writers there, or are you just saying that if you're out of line with current preoccupations you're unlikely to get much of a press?"

"There's an element of both and if you throw in a dash of spite it can make for a poisonous situation. I remember when my divorce book [*Life After Marriage*] came out, one editor got my ex-wife to write a feature on it three weeks before it was published. It was a totally unethical thing to do and it killed the book stone dead.

"You also, because it's such a small world, have to be on your guard continually against the consequences of what you say, and that can be unhealthy. For example, on *The Critics* once I said about Maggie Drabble, in reviewing one of her novels, that she can't even construct a proper English sentence.

"When her Oxford Companion to English Literature

came out a year or two later, I looked out of interest to see if I was mentioned anywhere. Absolutely nothing! No *Shaping Spirit*, no *School of Donne*. There was even a list of anthologies which ignored *The New Poetry* and that's been constantly in print since 1962. The two things might not have been connected, but you suspect that they are."

"The trouble with paranoia is that there's usually a reason for it . . .?"

"Or as Delmore Schwartz said, in a rare moment of sanity as he was dying—surrounded by girlie mags in a flop-house off Times Square, 'Even paranoiacs have enemies, you know!' "

"How do you explain the reaction to a novel like Bruce Chatwin's *On the Black Hill*, which is written in exquisitely phrased and modulated prose, but in which almost every incident, every character, every scene gives the impression of being more or less loosely based on something out of Lawrence, Hardy or Mary Webb—to the extent that when you read it you almost lose count of the number of correspondences. Is that a case of an exceptionally accomplished travel writer getting by in a different genre purely on reputation, because the reviewers are still the same as those Edward Young

wrote about 200 years ago:

> 'Unlearned men of books assume the care,
> As Eunuchs are the guardians of the fair.'?

"Almost certainly, and I agree with you—it's a fucking turgid novel by a terrific writer. Literary tradition, and knowledge of it, impinges on the literary *business* hardly at all these days."

"Does this mean," I mock, "that the great work on human evil and the human psyche at which you've been hinting for the last quarter-century will never get written?"

"I'm past that, now –I'm into frivolity."

He expands on the charms of not being serious. You read his books. The intense, resonant energy of the American-influenced Jewish intellectual so evident in the 'sixties certainly gives place to a more relaxed anecdotalism in his recent work. But behind the pared-down, elliptical stories, the marginalised subjects and minimalist, gnomic directness of judgement, the squads of emotion and value are tightly disciplined, flexing their muscle through the gaps and spaces in the prose. A frolicker, yes—but the seriousness *will* keep breaking through . . .

3: GREEN PIECES

The Vivisected Frog
Unpublished, 1988

The roads, tracks, go this way and that between quiet hamlets whose present size is no index of their former importance, and in doing so they square off, separate out, the high land into blocks, wedges, rough-hewn shapes on the two dimensions of a map. The names are almost dismissive—Glyderau, Carneddau, Migneint, Rhinogydd. "What," says their quality of sound, "have these places to do with humanity?" The early travellers were more specific in their complaint. Here is the Reverend John Evans, writing in 1798: ". . . The dreary aspect and awful desolation of this extensive tract of hopeless sterility betrays no vestige of a dwelling, no mark of human footstep."

Climb up to the top of Moelwyn Mawr today and you can trace his route, but the softness of these hills' name as you run it across your tongue belies his words—Moelwynion. I met an old man up here once, by Ceseiliau Duon on the old tramway that runs round the head of Maesgwm. It was a hot June day and his jacket was beside him on the glaciated bluff. He had a scar of dark blue-grey three inches long from by his right ear-lobe to beneath his cheekbone and the skin was tight and puckered around it like old parchment badly sewn. But his eyes were the blue of periwinkle flowers and his hands, set rigid into the grip a heavy hammer dictates, rolled a delicate cigarette and offered it to me.

"Moelwynion," I said to him, "it means bare, white hills, doesn't it?"

"It could mean that," he nodded, "but my father always said it was corrupted from Moel yr Oen—the hill of the lamb—because to him, from down in Tanygrisiau these hills looked like lambs skipping round each other in play."

I've heard the same story from others since, and I'd no reason to disbelieve him then. He was at peace in the place and I was no disturbance to him that he should lie me away. He told me where he lived, invited me for a cup of tea if ever I passed by that road. I left him sitting there, capped and flannelled with three inches of trouser waist above his belt, and I never saw him again. For that November, when I did call as he'd insisted, he was a month dead. "The dust," his widow explained in her tiny parlour, as she gave me delicate white sandwiches of cucumber on her best china plates. "The dust. I don't know how he got about in the hills with his lungs gone—days when he couldn't get his breath. Pneumo-nia at the end, but it was the dust, see. . .?"

Why does he so stick in my mind? Simple—for me, he's the spirit of the place. I see him there still whenever I pass that rock. His shape resolves again—a flannel shirt from quartz seams in the rock, that scar from the blue-grey spikes of slate which pierce the turf. He's still there—him and all the other ghosts of these hills which have felt, in those short nineteen decades since John Evans' time, the tread of thousands upon thousands of human feet.

Have you walked in the Moelwynion? It is one of the special places, and not just on my recommendation. Here's Showell Styles on Moelwyn Mawr: ". . . The view from this top might well claim to be the finest in all Wales for beauty, variety and extent."

"But flawed," I hear you say, "slate tips, spoil heaps, Blaenau Ffestiniog."

Well, it is all going back—over the waste rock the stonecrop grows, and parsley fern, and I could show you here and there bright pink patches of moss campion high on the flank of Moelwyn Mawr. Take a walk with me from the car-park in the chapel-stern, two-terrace quarry hamlet of Croesor, walk south-east with me along the old road to Tanybwlch. As we cross the Afon Maesgwm, there are our objectives at the head of the valley, the two ridges on its each side running up to their summits. We walk a little way on, through a harsh angular slab of forest, and break across sedgy pasture to start our climb up the west ridge of Moelwyn Bach. There is a path forming these days—not that you have much need of it on this smooth and easy ascent. It steepens at the last and there is a broad shoulder for you to pause and take in the view. Traswfynydd Nuclear Power Station pokes its stained and malignant concrete into sight.

"Look at me, look at me—I'm important," it says, "I have a special dispensation to be here—I'm needed! You casual people take note of that."

Beyond it, the enigmatic roll of Rhobell, Aran and Berwyn comments silently on its presumption. When I last came this way, a month ago, I met two people here, walking down from the summit with their dogs— on holiday in November with the sun on their backs, scarcely able to believe their luck. We talked round the hills—Rhobell, Dduallt with that holy place of Waunygriafolen at its foot; the way up to Lliwedd by Cwm Merch; we faced out west and sent our thoughts scudding across to Ireland—was that its coast so faintly suggested out there? I told them of Brocken Spectres on Brandon Mountain and they told me of a quiet day on Snowdon; no haste—just the leisurely intercourse of the

Old bridge beneath Cnicht.

its bald pate, with the summit crags curving round on your left and down to Bwlch Rhosydd.•

Views! You can say a great deal about views and convey nothing like so much as a single picture will. But there are things which pictures can't tell. This ruched land beneath, this lake-studded plateau of ice-scoured bluffs at the 1800–ft contour, this industrial wasteland with its brown grass, grey slate and heaped spoil, with its broken walls and hanging, rusting wires—it reeks of melancholia. When I look at it, it reminds me of a passage from *Wolf Solent*, the great, strange novel by John Cowper Powys, who came to live and who died in Ffestiniog. Here's what he wrote before he had ever seen the place:

"He seemed to see, floating and helpless, an image of the whole round earth! And he saw it bleeding and victimised, like a smooth-bellied, vivisected frog. He saw it scooped and gouged and scraped and harrowed . . . heaving and shuddering under the weight of iron and stone."

Or of waste slate.

Of Man's efforts gone to waste as nature reclaims its own?

Or the grieving spirit which tells how men behave to fellow-men, how laws unhampered by justice (do you know how the great estates of Gwynedd—Glynllifon, Vaynol, Penrhyn, Oakeley—were built up? By entrepreneurs' blackmail! Our jobs for your land! Copyhold in return for your freehold!) can force populations into dependence on means of livelihood such as these? In 1875 the average age at decease of men in Blaenau Ffestiniog who had not worked in the slatemines was 67 years; for the quarrymen, it was 37. Those romantic ruins of the quarry barracks at Rhosydd, which you look down on from Moelwyn Mawr—200 men lived there from Monday morning to Saturday afternoon each week, and this is what the Inspector of Mines had to say about their accommodation in 1886:

"Scarcely 200 cubic feet [less than six feet by six feet by six feet] of space per man in rooms used for sleeping, taking meals and keeping provisions and coal . . . the men were nearly all sleeping two in a bed . . . rooms dark, with a bad floor and an indifferent roof."

Two hundred inches of rain a year fall up here, and the wind! In November 1890 the roof blew off the barracks one night, and the men, half-naked, had to flee down

hills. We parted. The pool above the fierce crag-profile of Moelwyn Bach was frozen solid, but I stretched myself out by it on a sun-warmed rock in the still air and drank tea (the hills are for being amongst, not pounding over). And then I picked my way down the steep gully east of the crag, which can be dangerous in snow and today was glistening here and there with ice, the *chevaux de frise* of a slate hillside below awaiting the onslaught of a slip. At Bwlch Stwlan you could walk back by the track along Maesgwm, but Craig Ysgafn ahead is an inviting scramble, and that great hump of a hill which is Moelwyn Mawr from this angle denies too much to the sight. So you climb it, and somehow it never seems far and you're soon at the OS pillar on

Cwm Orthin in a mountain gale.

There are times, thinking of those things, when I cannot bear to pick my way through the dereliction of Rhosydd or places like it. So I head down the western ridge from Moelwyn Mawr with the two estuaries in front of me gleaming maybe with a low tide and the setting sun. Sometimes, at the big drum cradle by the incline head on Braich y Parc, before dropping down into Croesor again I turn aside and walk along the tramway to Ceseiliau Duon to greet the old quarryman there, and I understand then why his back is to the mountain, his boots on ice-scoured stone and his eyes distant, scanning the western sea.

First Known When Lost
North Wales Lifestyle, 1988

Perhaps you know the poem of that title by Edward Thomas? Perhaps you've felt, when out in the North Wales countryside, a similar sensation to the one he describes:

"I never had noticed it until
'Twas gone—the narrow copse
Where now the woodman lops
The last of the willows with his bill."

It came to me the other day passing by Penllyn, where the Afon Seiont slips out of Llyn Padarn on its short course to the sea. There was something different about the foreground to that famous view of the north-west flank of Snowdon. What was it?

It was that the reedbeds around the borders of the lake had gone, had been grubbed out, uprooted, cast up on the bank—nothing more than that, no great work of concrete in their place, no new curve of insidious tarmac across this favourite outlook—just a little tidying and cleansing and *management*, an afternoon's labour for a few council workmen and their JCB. So why grieve about it?

Oh, I could talk habitats. I could tell you what creatures and birds sheltered and nested there, but that's not it, that's not the instinctive root of my objection—and I do most strongly object—to what's been done. There is something else—another dimension—which in all these debates on the environment and conservation is never allowed a name, and yet which is perhaps more impor-

tant than any of the reasoned and scientific and principled and statutory objections which can always be raised to these acts of improvement or management or vandalism—call them what you will. It's this. Those reedbeds, vibrant with life as they were, changing in colour and texture season to season, were beautiful, were an integral part of an exquisite whole, were preferable to the scarred and muddy bank that's left behind.

That, I imagine, as a simple statement of aesthetic value, is something with which most of you would agree. It is, after all, apparently uncomplicated by issues of priority, safety, employment or industrial need. It seems—and it will take a lot to convince me to the contrary—to have been nothing more than a gratuitous act of harm towards a beautiful, intimate environment. I don't know why it happened. I just know how much I regret that it did.

If you agree that in this case something reprehensible took place, how then do you respond when the issues become more complicated? What have you to say to the dark, square, sterile blocks of conifers which are spreading over the whole of the Migneint (an area every bit as unique and valuable as the Flow Country of Sutherland, the afforestation of which has aroused such anxiety recently)? After all, we *need* the wood to make paper—how else would this magazine be printed? And the planting, the felling, provide employment.

What have you to say about the improvement of roads the North Wales Expressway, the trunk route to Cardiff through the Lledr Valley? After all, we *need* better communications. They will boost the economy of the area. They will facilitate access for visitors. They will ease holiday traffic jams. Their construction will provide employment.

What have you to say to a nuclear power station in that wild, high stretch of country from which Hedd Wyn drew the poetic inspiration which won him his posthumous bardic chair; or that other nuclear power station which juts and steams on a headland of the remote, rugged north coast of Anglesey; or the lines of pylons which strut overground away from them both across the foothills and through the ancient passes of the Carneddau to distant conurbations. After all, we *need* electricity, and in short term they provide jobs—not many, perhaps, and they may have more of a negative than positive effect in the long term, but for now there's work to be had from them for communities where work is scarce.

You know I could go on, and each incursion upon the texture of the land can be justified by *need*—as Hitler

Power lines crossing the Dwyryd estuary to Trawsfynydd nuclear power station.

needed Auschwitz to exterminate the Jews, as the Americans *needed* to drop an atomic bomb on Hiroshima to end the war with Japan. I am suspicious of the concept of need. Generally, we seem to use it much as does my four-year-old son when he tells me, "Daddy, I need a new car from Woolworth's today," whilst in his bedroom there's a box which seems to contain every shape and size thereof under the sun. He, I suppose, could not articulate his real needs—for security, for encouragement, for love—and no more, I think, can we. But they are still there, craving and yearning away in subliminal dumbness.

Which is why it worries me intensely, what we are doing to our infinitely precious and limited resources of country beauty, country quietude. Those of you of middle age or more will know how much of that, these last thirty of forty years, has gone. Perhaps with you it was a case, as in the title of Edward Thomas's poem, of "First known when lost". Perhaps in retrospect you realise how much you owed to what's been swept aside. What happens, then, to those who never knew it? What

happens now to them? What quality will be missing from their lives?

You may think that all this is rhetorical overstatement, but I have known this North Walian landscape for a long time. I knew it before that factory of perilous energy marred the wide moorland at Trawsfynydd; I knew it when the first conifers, the litter from whose felling now strews the acid, raw ground, were planted at Crafnant; I knew it when the road up Cwm Prysor, where the roof-racked cars stream at eighty miles an hour, was nothing more than a track. It has all changed, changed utterly—terrible the way beauty has been killed to service need!

Last year the World Heritage Committee—the international agency responsible for assessing World Heritage sites—considered the Lake District for such a designation. For all that it lacks the dramatic grandeur and variety of North Wales, the Lake District is extremely lovely and—something which cannot be said for Wales—very well cared for and vigorously protected, especially by its enlightened National Park Board.

Its designation as a World Heritage Site was rejected out-of-hand, an "Inventory of Destruction" released to explain the decision. Here it is, with the Government departments responsible in brackets following each point:

"Roads forged through the centre of the National Park against the wishes of the Park Authority." (Department of Transport)

"Quarries scarring the landscape." (Department of the Environment)

"Tourism's paraphernalia of suburbia which creates a growing resort atmosphere." (DoE)

"Excessive motor boat traffic on Windermere." (DoT)

"Low flying aircraft shattering the silence." (Ministry of Defence)

"Damming of lakes for reservoirs." (DoE)

"Overgrazing encouraged by Government grants." (MAFF)

"Forestry plantation which sours the ground and darkens the landscape." (Forestry Commission and MAFF)

Every one of the above points, and several more besides, could equally well be applied to Snowdonia.

Commenting on the World Heritage Committee decision, Brian Redhead, President on the Council for National Parks, said:

"Any National Park which allows such things to happen or has them wished on it by Departments of Government can only expect to be snubbed. There is a reluctance, not least in high places, to endorse and to insist upon the principles of the National Parks. They should not be abused."

They should not! But beautiful places like the Lake District, like Snowdonia, will continue to be abused, annexed, desecrated, until their character and texture has been wholly lost. It is happening. It will continue to happen until we can arrive at a mature and intelligent definition of need which recognises those unspoken but urgent human dependencies on natural forms, natural rhythms, natural beauty itself, and reconciles them—if that's possible—to the endless expansion of appetite, at any cost and ultimately at far too high a price.

Trust is Just a Five-Letter Word
Rural Wales, 1988 (Revised)

A lesson in semantics first—it concerns the word "inalienable", a word of which the dear old granny of all our conservation agencies, The National Trust, is inordinately fond. In terms of strict definition and use, it's applied to "that which cannot be transferred from its present ownership or relation". So where land or property held by The National Trust is concerned, it ought to mean that land is held in trust for all time for the nation. Which means us. Which means that it is our amenity. Which means that we, as the people of the nation, must exercise the most responsible stewardship over it.

Within the complexities of our society such a reading of the word is, of course, dangerously naive. We must take care not to place trust in *meaning* to that extent. In terms of the debased monologue which passes for political debate these days it is, after all, almost seditious to expect words to *mean* what they mean. But still, at times we can hope to come close. Inalienable land held by The National Trust and The National Trust for Scotland cannot be sold, mortgaged or compulsorily purchased without the express consent of Parliament. It's a definition substantially qualified from the firm meaning given above, but it seems to retain a certain gravity, a certain integrity. It seems to imply that land held for us by The Trusts is safeguarded for its public amenity.

Is it, though?

After all, there is a loophole through which you could fly a jump-jet, sail a Polaris submarine or drive a Chieftain tank in that form of words. It's simply this. The Executive Committees of The Trusts can *lease* land to whom they please. As the NT Executive did in 1982 to the Royal Air Force in the *cause celebre* of the Bradenham Bunker. That's by no means the only example of such a procedure. St. Kilda, the majestic, rocky outpost of the uttermost Hebrides bequeathed by the Marquis of Bute to the NTS and leased by that body to the MoD, is another case in point. Nowadays on St Kilda, despoliation, discouragement of casual visitors and political vetting are the rule. The cases of Bradenham and St. Kilda illustrate the way in which what Patrick Wright memorably called the "anti-democratic bacillus" of much of the Trusts' activities (*The Guardian*, 1 August, 1987) can infect even the most liberal and valuable gifts made to it.

All this is by way of prolegomena to what for a time seemed likely to become the saddest abuse of trust yet. The story concerns a stretch of the recently designated Ceredigion Heritage Coast between Newquay and Aberporth in Dyfed. This is a magnificent and very beautiful coastline– cliffs of purple and red rock, stark promontories, bracken and heather-clad slopes, slender

Enterprise Neptune coast; MoD installation for monitoring commercial weaponry trials.

waterfalls feathering down into exquisite, sandy coves—one of the holy places on God's Earth, and one to which any civilised society aware of the spiritual value of such landscape would accord due reverence and protection. The National Trust and associated Enterprise Neptune have, both recently and more traditionally, bought land here whenever the opportunity has arisen. And now, it is all under grave threat.

At Aberporth, sprawling across several hundred acres atop a headland looking out over Cardigan Bay, with the appearance James Cameron, writing about Bikini Atoll, described as "that improvised, squalid, tawdry look of anywhere taken over by the Services", is a Royal Aircraft Establishment range—RAE Aberporth.

This is one of three ranges within the Instrumentation and Trials Department of RAE Farnborough, itself a part of the Ministry of Defence. Aberporth has long trailed a secretive aura. In the 1960s there were reports—quickly hushed up—that a pilotless target aeroplane from this range (of the same type as that from the Llanbedr range which crashed on the popular tourist beach of Shell Island two years ago) was responsible for the loss with many lives of an Aer Lingus passenger 'plane over the Irish Sea. This is not strictly relevant to the present theme except inasmuch that if true—as the Shell Island incident certainly was—it illustrates the risk of having military installations of this type along popular holiday coasts or near commercial air routes.

What is known is that Aberporth has extensive facilities for a wide variety of missile and other trials of both military and civilian application, but its main and underlying purpose is purportedly in the development of missile technology "in the interests of national defence". So the old shibboleth, "Defence of the Realm", immediately foists itself upon our consciousness—what chance mere landscape against the imagined foreign foe?

The actual range at Aberporth covers approximately 2,600 square miles, stretching out from Cardigan Bay into the Atlantic. Flight trials are undertaken here of what are vaguely referred to in MoD jargon as "objects launched from land, sea and air". The number of trials conducted each year is about 800, the three armed services being the major users, although civil contractors for the MoD and foreign customers of British companies increasingly number amongst the satisfied recipients of its technological expertise.

It would be a safe assumption that equipment tested here eventually found its way into the conflicts in the Falklands and The Gulf, and that under existing government policies it has an increasing role to play in the highly profitable international arms trade—an export industry in which, in terms of output, Britain ranks third in the world.

For this essentially economic reason, the RAE is forcefully arguing that it is crucial for Aberporth to remain in the forefront of missile and electronics trials capability. Which is where we return to the loveliest stretch of the Ceredigion Heritage Coast, north of Aberporth.

A range covering a sea-area of 2,600 square miles obviously requires rather more than just one monitoring station. In fact it has six, spread along the ten or more miles of coast to Newquay. They are known as observation posts (OPs) or missile tracking stations. Of these six, two are immediately adjacent to Enterprise Neptune land at Ty Hen and Craig yr Adar, and one is within a tiny area of land apparently owned—how it came to be so is unclear, though those acquainted with the Nugent Report might well be tempted into educated guesswork on the subject—by the MoD at Ynys Lochtyn, above Llangranog.

Ynys Lochtyn is the most remarkable feature of a remarkable coastline. It is a bold, craggy promontory with widespread views, a NT possession, a Site of Special Scientific Interest, the location of a scheduled and important Iron Age promontory fort—Pendinaslochdyn—and a place of pilgrimage to large numbers of the public who value their scenic heritage.

In the more casual terminology of the RAE and the MoD, "the Lochtyn site is of the first importance, as it has the best capability of any location on the coast".

We'll come back to these observation posts in due course. For the moment, what the RAE is planning is "to technically upgrade their missile tracking stations along the Ceredigion Heritage Coast . . . [which] . . . will have an effect on the appearance of existing National Trust property and Enterprise Neptune purchases and may have some bearing on public access to Trust property and the coastline in general."

The reason for this is as follows: "The replacement of the existing [radar] equipment is, in the view of RAE, essential if Aberporth is to remain *commercially* viable and capable of meeting defence needs."

First the real reason, then the one to elicit loyalist knee-jerk response!

The RAE justification continues: "The current tracking equipment is no longer capable of effectively monitoring missile trials (it is based on German reparations of World War Two). It is the belief of RAE that Aberporth is crucial to the wellbeing of the British aerospace industry . . . to this end, it is the RAE's proposal to instal electro-optical trackers (EOTs) at observation posts (OPs) along the coast, centred on existing locations already owned by the Government."

Thus the outline, here's the conclusion—"The RAE aim to have their plans completed during 1988." And what work do these plans entail?

"The installation of additional plant and equipment.
"The improvement of access roads to take heavier vehicles, which will necessitate substantial accommodation works.
"The requirement, agreed by the County Surveyor, to improve the width of some public approach roads.
"The requirement of the Health and Safety Executive that when transmitting by high frequency radar, an area of 50 metres radius should be kept clear of people because of possible damage to the eyes from looking directly at the radar."

It could reasonably be asked, with regard to the latter point, that if such serious physical damage can result within that radius, what cumulative damage can ensue within a wider radius, and how well documented and researched are possible effects? The question takes on a particular relevance when the proximity to the most important and presumably most powerful of these electro-optical trackers (that within the ramparts of the promontory fort of Pendinaslochdyn, which is the most popular area in terms of public visits) of the holiday centre of Urdd Gobaith Cymru—The Welsh League of Youth—is considered.

In relation to Pendinaslochdyn, the saga continues. The RAE proposes, in order supposedly to minimise the radar effect, to excavate and level an area of the hilltop—if Cadw, the Government department responsible for ancient monuments in Wales, and the NT agree.

And do they agree?

With regard to *Cadw* (the name, ironically, is both the Welsh verb meaning to guard or preserve, and the Welsh noun for a flock or herd), the question is probably superfluous. It is, after all, a Government department. "He who pays the piper calls the tune" is probably the applicable principle. This may be unfair to *Cadw*, but we shall see.

Here's The Trust's preliminary recommendation, from a confidential paper to its Executive Committee: "If we receive written confirmation from the RAE [that public access at Lochtyn is not affected] and confirmation from Southampton University that there are realistically no alternative sites and the 50m. radius zone is necessary . . ."—a form of words, it should be noted, which invites a specific response—". . . then it is recommended that in co-ordination with the Countryside Commission and others, the proposals as set out are specifically agreed."

Not much talk about principles there! Not much consideration of scenic amenity, long-term public safety, the rationale of MoD and RAE expansionism, or the morality of commerce in weaponry. I wonder what Octavia Hill, the Christian Socialist and Ruskinite founder of the NT, or her colleagues Robert Hunter and the good Canon Rawnsley would have had to say?

The worst, however, or perhaps only the most cynically pragmatic and expedient, is yet to come. I quote from the same confidential paper, unfortunately titled Annexe Thirteen, submitted to the NT Executive:

"The Countryside Commission and The Trust have both been involved with the negotiations, as well as Cadw, Welsh Office Ancient Monuments, The Nature Conservancy Council . . ." (Government 4, Trust 1 . . .) ". . . and representatives of Ceredigion District Council, including the Heritage Coast staff."

So what is the considered opinion of this band of worthies, power-wielders, and honoured-to-be-responsibles?

"It is the opinion of all those involved that the outcome of these negotiations are the best that can be achieved."

So four government departments turn to the National Trust representatives and mouth smooth, predictable platitudes: "Now look here, old chap, this really is the best you can hope to achieve, and their chaps are being most reasonable, bending over backwards, you know . . ."

Annexe Thirteen continues, taking us into the threatening realms of Orwell's Room 101 (even the language is heavy with Newspeak):

"Should the Trust not be able to accept these revised proposals, then the RAE may resort to additional powers to acquire the land they need, either through Special Parliamentary Procedures or on the authority of the Lord Lieutenant (ref. Bradenham)."

The overt threat—it is followed, of course, by the threat consequential:

"As the RAE sees it, the alternatives for them not taking this course of action, could lead to the run-down and eventual closure of Aberporth, as it will no longer be able to function so effectively. This could lead to the direct loss of 400 permanent jobs locally and much wider damage to an area of relatively high unemployment."

The employment case, of course, is not proven, and anyway a good many of those involved are non-local service personnel. But how refreshing it is to see a government body wearing its heart on its sleeve about employment! And how neatly, by doing so, does it catch both Trust and District Council on the horns of a dilemma! And how nervous The Trust is about explaining itself and the position it seems to consider that it must needs adopt:

"A positive step by the Trust to take the initiative would be for the Trust to meet *specific journalists and reporters and explain to them that the proposed plans are the best that can be achieved and why this is the case.*"

Shades of Bernard Ingham and the Press lobby! Not only is this last a blatant admission of apostasy, but also in its manipulative intent it is an absolute denial of democratic principle. The National Trust patently does not like criticism or scrutiny. Its habit, to quote Patrick Wright again, is one of "aligning with a reactionary assertion of private meaning, and identifying the public interest with the rampaging egalitarianism of the revolutionary mob".

What is happening at Aberporth is the proposed blighting of one of the most beautiful *remnants* of our coastal scenic heritage, the rendering dangerous and inaccessible of parts of it to the public, the marring of its every headland and promontory with gross visual intrusions, the ignorant jeopardising of the health of the youth of Wales, the gouging out and implanting with iron technology of an Iron Age fort. And to this filthy and squalid commercial-born process the opposition of the National Trust at first was negligible. Whimpers, self-justification, forelock-tugging, unholy misalliance and abject worship of the great god Expedience! A strange stance from which to "negotiate", that of apparent surrender!

We began with a semantic point. Let's pick up on another. These are some of the meanings of the word "trust": confidence in or reliance on some quality or

Magic mushroom, nightmare-inducing, Ceredigion Heritage Coast.

attribute of a person or thing, or the truth of a statement; that in which one's confidence is put; the quality of being trustworthy; fidelity, loyalty, trustiness; the condition of having confidence reposed in one; the obligation or responsibility imposed on one in whom confidence is placed or authority is vested, or who has given an undertaking of fidelity."

So put "national" in front, and allow both words the significance of capital letters. How many of those meanings still obtain? If the answer is to be any, then the National Trust must raise the standard on behalf of our landscape that its one-and-a-half million members expect of it, and it must raise it now. By doing so, it asserts its role as our senior conservational agency. By failing to do so, it scatters its credibility to the four winds. What, then, does it plan to do?

Before answering that, let me tell you what else I found out on taking a second look at the Ynys Lochtyn and Pendinaslochdyn sites, the latter of which will be affected by the RAF. proposals, at the end of October. It was brought home to me again how breathtakingly lovely and worthy of protection this coast is. In the course of the visit I talked to local residents, who had very little concept of what the proposed developments

entailed. I also visited the *Urdd* centre at Llangranog, and saw what the effect would be of the proposed development at Pendinaslochdyn. What particularly appalled was the proximity to the path used by children from the *Urdd* camp going to the beach of the radar station—used, I was told locally, for tracking missile-launching submarines out in the Atlantic.

The most heartening news encountered came on the day after the visit. Jim O'Rourke, Warden of *Urdd Gobaith Cymru's* camp, had told of a request made by RAE/MoD to build an access road across land belonging to the *Urdd* to Pendinaslochdyn. It had, he said, been submitted to the *Urdd* policy committee. I telephoned the *Urdd* office in Aberystwyth accordingly, to find out what progress it had made there. Speaking for the *Urdd*, Mr. John Eric Williams told me that the policy committee had rejected the request and refused permission for construction of the road—a decision which had been endorsed by the *Urdd* National Council.

"On what grounds was it rejected?"

Mr Williams replied that the *Urdd* was an organisation dedicated to the cause of world peace, and as such could not condone any expansion of military capacity.

The light of scrutiny which this steadfastness on the

part of the *Urdd* must turn upon the hesitancy of the National Trust is searching. The Trust has a membership of one-and-a-half millions and more political clout and influence than any other environmental agency in the land. Its own researches have shown it that commercial considerations and not defence of the realm are the chief factors in this desired expansion on the part of RAE Aberporth. The *Urdd*, by contrast, has a youthful membership drawn exclusively from a small nation, yet is prepared to stand out, independently and on grounds of principle, for that in which it believes.

Judging by its early reactions to these proposals, the Trust was being pressured internally into adopting once again its supine course of recent tradition. Had it continued on that tack, and succumbed to the Belials within, it would have looked very shoddy indeed by contrast with *Yr Urdd*. Fortunately for it, for the strained loyalties of its members and for its continuing reputation, at its most recent Executive (members of which had been circulated with draft copies of this article, as had the national press) it decided to oppose RAE proposals as they affect its holdings in Ceredigion. So perhaps at last we have a credible organisation prepared to live up to the responsibilities of its role and name.

Mending Your Ways
Address at Conference on Footpath Maintenance and Erosion Control, Ambleside, 1990

I want to start this afternoon by reading you an extract from what is beyond any doubt the best account of a long-distance walk ever written:

"Now I saw in my dream, that just as they had ended this talk, they drew near to a very miry Slough that was in the midst of a plain, and they, being heedless, did both fall suddenly into the bog. The name of the Slough was Despond. Here therefore they wallowed for a time, being grievously bedaubed with the dirt, and Christian, because of the burden that was on his back, began to sink in the mire."

As you'll no doubt have realised, this isn't a description of a walk along the Pennine Way, but a passage from *The Pilgrim's Progress*. I want to read you a little more. Christian's companion Pliable has escaped from

the mire and returned back to his own house, leaving Christian stuck fast until the character of Help arrives to pull him out, whereupon the narrator questions Help:

"Then I stepped to him that plucked him out, and said, 'Sir, wherefore, since over this place is the way from the City of Destruction, to yonder Gate, is it that this plat is not mended, that poor travellers might go thither with more security?' And he said unto me, 'This miry Slough cannot be mended; it is the descent whither the scum and filth that attends conviction for sin doth continually run, and therefore it is called the Slough of Despond; for still as the sinner is awakened about his lost condition, there ariseth in his soul many fears, and doubts, and discouraging apprehensions, which all of them get together, and settle in this place; and this is the reason of the badness of this ground.

"It is not the pleasure of the King that this place should remain so bad; his labourers also have, by the direction of His Majesty's surveyors, been for above this sixteen hundred years, employed about this patch of ground, if perhaps it might have been mended; yea, and to my knowledge,' saith he, 'here hath been swallowed up at least twenty thousand cart loads; yea, millions of wholesome instructions, that have at all seasons been brought from all places of the King's dominions (and they that can tell, say they are the best materials to make good ground of the place); if so be it might have been mended, but it is the Slough of Despond still, and so will be when they have done what they can.' "

I don't think anyone who reads Bunyan can be in any doubt that this simple moral allegory is rooted in the direct physical experience of an itinerant preacher—which is what he was—tramping the roads of seventeenth-century England.

There are two strands of argument which I want to interweave here. The first is that where paths, green roads, bridleways are concerned, we subscribe to an idyll which subtly affects our current thinking about them. My favourite statement of this theme is the poem simply entitled "Roads", by Edward Thomas, with its insistence on the goddesses that dwell along them, what the next turn may reveal, the near-autonomy of their existence throughout history. For Edward Thomas, they exist not just in a literal but in a symbolic dimension—as allegory, journey, path through life. His approach is not isolated. When we talk about paths, we're entering a sphere resonant with symbolism.

Coming nearer to concrete reality, I'd like to contrast

The Pig Track re-visited!

two further passages of descriptive writing with Edward Thomas's vaguer, prelapsarian approach to his subject. The first is from W.G. Hoskin's classic work on *The Making of the English Landscape*:

"Roads that carried any considerable amount of through-traffic had to be wide enough, and could be wide enough in unenclosed country, to allow of detours around the impassable stretches that developed in unsurfaced roads by mid-winter. The main London-to-Exeter 'road' was said to have been a quarter of a mile wide by the end of the winter where it crossed—or rather plunged through—the sticky morass of the chalk over Salisbury Plain. It seems to have been a fairly general rule in the later enclosure awards that the minimum width for inter-village roads should be forty feet between the ditches, though local roads carrying more than the average traffic for the district were often laid down forty-five or fifty feet wide."

This ought to give us a perspective on the width of tracks up Snowdon, Helvellyn, Ben Nevis. It is not a new problem. Summits like these probably carry far more traffic than did the main lines of communication—the motorways if you like—of prehistoric, Roman or medieval times. The width of even the post-enclosure roads which Hoskins describes is more than that deemed necessary for the carriageway of a modern trunk road.

Here's the second descriptive passage, from the early nineteenth-century nature poet John Clare's "Lament of Swordy Well".

"The silver springs grown naked dykes
Scarce own a bunch of rushes.
When grain got high the tasteless tykes
Grubbed up trees, banks and bushes.
And me—they turned me inside out
For sand and grit and stones
And turned my old green hills about
And picked my very bones."

Swordy Well, the fate of which Clare is describing, is a small Northamptonshire stream. What's it got to do with the nature, the management, the repair of our mountain footpaths?

If you don't know, then ask yourselves if you should be involved in that work. It is all to do with our attitude towards, our perception of, the landscapes in which we pass our lives.

Let me draw in the other thread I mentioned to this argument here. This is a little more abstruse. It comes from a work by Honorius of Autun entitled *Expositio in Cantica Canticorum*. "The mountains," he writes, "are prophets."

To help towards an understanding of that phrase, you could go to Jung's *Archetypes and the Collective Unconscious*, where he explains that the mountain "stands for the goal of the pilgrimage and ascent, hence it often has the psychological meaning of the self . . . the bigness and tallness of the mountain are allusions to the adult personality." On another tack, this conjunction of mountain and path is one of the recurrent symbols in Buddhist literature. The Buddhist scholar Marco Pallis, whom some of you in the Lakes will remember as Menlove Edwards' second man on the first free ascent of Scafell Central Buttress, called his most important book about Buddhism *The Way and the Mountain*. When a pair of symbols have this frequency of recurrence, they are necessarily powerful ones in our lives. It behoves us therefore to study them with care in all aspects.

But again, what has this to do with the repair of our footpaths? In fact, what has any of what I've been talking about got to do with that?

You men—and I notice that almost inevitably you mostly are men—who are here this afternoon are involved for the most part I would imagine in some aspect of what is nowadays termed "countryside management"—not a term for which I have any affection, and I'm not sure that I wouldn't rather see a good deal more "womanagement". I'm not sure how far traditional male attitudes—assertion, achievement, conquest, penetration, confrontation—are compatible with the responsible stewardship of the environment which is the underlying, crucial discourse in this weekend's conference.

Those of you who've read Fritjof Capra's book *The Turning Point*, will remember his comment about the natural kinship which exists between feminism and ecology. The ecofeminist writer Andree Collard, in a vigorously argued treatise entitled *Rape of the Wild*, which should be required reading for any uniform-wearing National Park Warden, Countryside Ranger, Conservation Volunteer manager, or Countryside Commission bureaucrat, states that:

"It is precisely the projection of cultural values upon the external world that determines the treatment meted out to it."

The catalyst to the intensification of this debate on mountain footpaths was the "treatment meted out" by the Snowdonia National Park Authority to the Pig Track on Snowdon.

The army were called in to blow up a bluff of rock; the Conservation Volunteers constructed a neat little border which could have come straight out of a suburban rockery; the gradients were levelled and sections of the 'road' were metalled. Elsewhere on the mountain, gabions propped up the thoroughfare against the possibility of collapse. On one level, this was an honourable and humane piece of *enabling*. In that environment it was mistaken and inapposite.

Why?

The argument goes on the one hand that the natural 'granny traps'—and I find that term offensively sexist and ageist, and am disquieted that our national representative body, the BMC, should stoop to its use in an official footpath repair policy document—by doing so it reveals its cultural values—should be left in place to stop our 'grannies' risking life and limb through being lured unwittingly into dangerous situations. That argument is transparent nonsense. Grannies, in my experience, are far too sensible and mindful of risk to be thus endangered.

The people who kill themselves on mountains are soldiers, public school masters and their charges, or advertising-space-salesmen from Basingstoke. People will go just as far as they desire to go, and difficulties which path-management-work can remove are not going to deter them. We should remember anyway that some of the best walking in Snowdonia is along tracks constructed to enable workmen easily to gain access to their places of employment.

The essence of the argument about enablement derives again from the symbolic dimension. It is that it is an attempt—albeit doomed to failure—to make the ascents of our mountains easier, and thus, subliminally, it is a devaluing of the symbol, which explains the inchoate response it arouses. I deplore the elitism and exclusivism implicit in that stance, but have some practical sympathy with it nonetheless.

The other side of the argument is the aesthetic one. These works of man are ugly. They do not fit. Frank Lloyd Wright would not have approved.

I agree with that entirely, don't question it for an instant. But who defines the parameters of aesthetic taste?

Which in this instance anyway are based on integration and therefore by definition are always relative, never absolute. That brings us up against a problem, and the problem is one of management again. It is one of where the power lies, and the powers-that-be in countryside management are The Countryside Commission, the National Park Authorities, local councils, The National Trust. The number of people in those august bodies whom I would trust with the responsible stewardship of the land is a fraction of one per cent, and most of that fraction are probably in this room. The key word should be devolution. The responsibility for footpath work must devolve upon the workers on the ground, it must not be dictated to them by higher and ever-farther-removed so-called authorities lacking acquaintance with the minuteness, particularity, uniqueness of each small landscape.

We began with allegories and images; let's return to

them. Not literary images this time but images from the landscape. I want you to *consider* the blasting of that bluff on the Pig Track, and the laying of duckboards on the path to Penyghent—probably by the 'tasteless tykes' to whom John Clare referred—consider them not as simple errors of aesthetic judgement but as attitudes imaged forth, each with their particular resonance.

They both have about them the echoes of war—the soldiers with their explosives, the duckboards across the mud.

Are we the invaders of our mountains, at war with them, aiming to conquer, alienated from their beauty? Or do we come as respectful, attentive pilgrims, nurturing and instructing our adult personalities on the way? Again, upon whom should their responsible care devolve?

Only upon those who can study, empathise, see.

The people who do not understand even the import

Ancient trackway above Dolwyddelan.

of the language they use, who reduce their arguments to numbered sequences of paragraphs, who think in meaningless newspeak terminology which stresses their status as its users and initiates rather than the necessity to communicate and reveal—these people have no useful part to play in the vital basis of conservation work, which is on the ground. That is the work of men and women who have acquired a sense of place, a responsive capacity to read the language of landscape, a delight in the handling of its natural materials.

Until we have learnt to mend our figurative ways of looking at everything to which we relate in the world, instead of accepting blandly and unquestioningly the strictures of power, authority and use, we should be allowed to play no serious part in mending the physical ways—falling yearly more critically into disrepair—which lead to the goals of our mountain pilgrimage. I want to show you some pictorial images now to demonstrate how indissociable it all is, how crucially it devolves upon our attitudes as human beings within a world we perhaps scarcely begin to understand. But before I do, let me end by quoting to you a passage from a wonderful book by Karl von Frisch entitled *Tanzsprache und Orientierung der Bienen*—dance-language and direction—information of bees:

"Once we can recognise and acknowledge how great and how wonderful the world is, of which we are a part and in which we take part, this leads to reverence before the unknown, and whoever gives such feelings a form on which he finds a firm footing for leading his life, he is on the right path."

The paths themselves, in the right hands, can be a firm footing and a proper expression of that philosophy.

Ecotopian Quarrypersons
Environment Now, 1987

It was outside an Egon Ronay and Michelin-recommended wholefood restaurant. I was sitting in the July sunshine, the air fragrant with roses and a cup of fine Darjeeling tea (World Development Movement-supplied) in front of me. Across the table was Bob Todd, acting Technical Director and a former lecturer in Control Engineering at Southampton University. T-shirted in the summer heat, we had been talking about solar energy, tidal power, water as a medium for heat storage.

Or rather, Bob had been talking about them, with great lucidity and humour, making technically complex topics with a popularly perceived aura of cranky modishness about them seem as accessible and reasonable as a scientific illiterate such as myself could wish. Just then, a practical problem intruded itself on what for me was becoming an exceedingly interesting seminar. The man from Reception came over:

"Bob, the drive-band on the Magic Roundabout's broken again—you wouldn't happen to have one of those big elastic bands on you, would you?"

Raised eyebrows. Grins, of the sort which say "Did you have to bring this up in front of a journalist?" The tacit question is answered by a remark vouchsafed me by the intruder on our conversation:

"They melt in the sun, you know."

A rubber band's produced from someone's pocket, fitted, and the Magic Roundabout rotates in response to the sunlight again. "Shade it from the sun and see it slow down," says the sign.

This is to trivialise, but it tells you something about the Centre for Alternative Technology, its atmosphere and its ethos. It is a sort of alternative university of earth science, which holds out an open invitation to view or participate in its work, takes that *work* very seriously indeed, but takes itself so hardly at all. There are displays which are delightfully tongue-in-cheek, are operated by the most makeshift contrivances, but which score significant points and root themselves in your consciousness. If the sun's rays and an elastic band can send the Magic Roundabout whizzing round, what about the whirligig on which we live?

The Centre for Alternative Technology, universally referred to amongst its habitues as "The Quarry", is located in a disused slate quarry just outside the Snowdonia National Park's southern boundary, and three miles to the north-east of the old market town of Machynlleth. It overlooks the Dulas Valley, which joins the Dyfi a couple of miles downstream. The whole area is green, sylvan and beautiful—the high hills of Cader and the Tarrens to the north, the high moorland of Plynlimon not far to the south, and rich, fertile, deeply incised valleys between. Alternative it certainly is, central it is not, and as for technology, it's hard to see how it affects an area like this. But let's accompany the originator, Gerard Morgan-Grenville, on his first visit to Llwyngwern Quarry at the outset of the CAT saga:

". . . the place was something of a jungle, scattered with ruinous buildings from which birch trees grew in profusion. The golden leaves were falling slowly in the still air and the sense of timelessness, with which I have always since associated this place, struck me forcibly. In such seclusion, so far from the pressures under which most people live, I had the feeling that something new, some fresh and saner way of living might be demonstrated. For some time I had felt convinced, along with many others, that unless the western world could pioneer for itself some way in which life could be lived without using up the resources of planet Earth, the collapse of civilisation was ultimately inevitable. From the outset the idea was to set up an exhibition whereby the 'environmental crisis' as it was then called, could be explained in quite simple terms to the visiting public."

This was in 1973. A lease was agreed at a peppercorn rent for the site in November of that year. Site clearance began in February 1974 and by the end of the year there was a permanent staff of five, renovation work on the houses had started, and Prince Philip had dropped in for a visit. (As the *Sunday Telegraph* put it, "On Wednesday the Duke of Edinburgh will visit a disused slate quarry near Machynlleth in Central Wales"). From 1975 onwards, development was rapid. It opened to the public and saw 15,000 visitors in the first year. Wates the builders contributed a low energy house; the first three windmills were installed; ten permanent staff on a subsistence wage were employed by December 1975; there were 35,000 visitors in 1976, 55,000 in 1977 and work had started on the central building complex of café, bookshop, accommodation and lecture hall. Prince Charles visited in 1978, the first residential courses were held in 1979, and there were 59,000 visitors in 1980. This, for an undercapitalised derelict quarry development in a distant area, and along lines which ran counter to the general trends of contemporary society, was a phenomenon. Why did it happen, and what did it provide which so attracted the people who came to view?

The latter question can be answered in part by telling what it does provide, for the casual visitors, say, who make up a large proportion of the tens of thousands who come each year.

You turn off the main road guided by the local landmark of a 15-kilowatt Polenko wind-generator on the hill above, pick your way tentatively along a quarter-mile of lane, and end up in the very large car park. (Invalids can drive up, dogs must stay in the car). A quarry track, a rather lovely avenue of ash, birch and alder with slate spoil covered by rhododendrons, leads steeply up to the centre, little notices allowing you

breathing space *en route*:

"We do not think your life-style is wrong . . ."

("If that were true," a *New Scientist* contributor tersely noted, "there would be no need to say it.")

You emerge at reception—log-cabin style with the aforementioned magic roundabout to hold the children's attention while you pay. The Swiss-style central building complex is off to your right, but you resist the temptation of tea for the present, carry on between the lecture hall and a bank of solar collectors to stop just short of a striking solar wall on one of the staff cottages. Simple and humorous display boards explain the principles to you. Bearing right round the back of the building complex you pass the Biofuels display and Llwyngwern Forge Limited—one of three separate initiatives within the organisation—to the Water Power display area. A turbine in a glass compartment reveals its innards to the public gaze, and also provides electricity for lighting the staff houses and other purposes, whilst a nearby overshot waterwheel gives a practical demonstration of the amount of power which can be produced by even quite a small head of water properly harnessed. The water from both drains away through a hydraulic ram to the fishpond and beyond that the smallholding. We pass on to the organic garden.

Our scatological instincts will find plenty to amuse us in this area, amongst the composts and manures and watering-cans marked "pee". (In the men's toilet there is, alongside more conventional urinals, a large water container with a funnel and a notice inviting you to pee in here—an invitation said to have been accepted by Prince Charles. In the same toilet there are also facilities for changing babies, which is a good introduction to the Centre's sexual politics.) Cloacal sniggers aside, the "Cycle of Life" display area is entrancing. You can almost see your fingers turning green. Reluctantly you leave it for the fishpond, smallholding and construction workshop area, where hens roost under miniature dolmens and cats, guiltily stalking ducklings, are driven away by goats. Next on the itinerary are Windpower and Solar Energy exhibitions, the latter with a kettle which boils on days of prolonged sunshine. There follow the energy-saving house, warm inside on the coldest days (but very stuffy), suburban and urban gardens, and the delightful maze (from which you only escape by making ideologically sound decisions). Passing the workshop of Dulas Engineering Ltd, of which more later, you finally arrive back at the restaurant/bookshop complex. Within or alongside this circuit there are staff greenhouses, staff houses, buildings under construction—all the parapher-

nalia of a busy and earth-orientated community.

Thus the groundplan. The amount of information, and beyond that inspiration, which it supplies is impressive. What is also very satisfying is the manner in which the information is conveyed. The constant points of reference are an awareness of whether fuel sources are exhaustible or renewable, whether effects on the environment are benign or prejudicial, but the point is generally implicit—it is not thrust down our throats. Quite the opposite, in fact. If there is a prevailing fault in the interpretative system, it is that an occasional lack of confidence, a defensive tone, creeps in. As an outsider, I don't see a need for it—the arguments put forward stand up to the closest scrutiny. Quiz their proponents and the responses are utterly convincing. But you can understand how the reaction evolved. Probably some of the initial displays were simplistic, and the philosophy homespun and apple-pie. There would have been (still is, in fact) a considerable amount of prejudice to be overcome: "Communists, that's what they are, and hippies, and Vegans, making a fortune from visitors, all on social security. Surprised the Government funds them, freelove, ban-the-bomb, bloody Reds, peaceniks . . ."

Prejudice and ignorance are always with us—what must have been harder to take were the dismissive attacks of the power-production mandarins, the Lords-Martial of the Nuclear Industry, who have never been slow to use attack as defence and sneer at less potentially harmful power sources. So the CAT interpretation boards are put on the back foot, but to my mind they still flick any ball that comes flying at their throats out of the ground.

This is partly to digress. We've skated across the surface of the CAT and fetched up by the restaurant at a table under the roses. Here we're joined by publicity officer Tim Brown, Bob Todd—whom we've met before, and Phil Revell, who is the Development Course Co-ordinator. It's time to look at the structure and philosophy in a little more depth.

I questioned Tim first. Like most of the people who work here he is highly intelligent, highly qualified (medical school and an Environmental Science degree before working for Friends of the Earth and then the CAT), and highly sceptical of some of the normative values of present society.

"Can you tell me simply how what looks to be a complex and various structure is organised and run, Tim?"

"The day-to-day decisions and budgets are decided by topic groups—gardening, buildings, restaurant and so on—which are each answerable to the whole centre at the fortnightly policy meetings. We try to ensure that we maintain a democratic and collective decision-making process amongst the thirty or so full-time staff."

"What would happen if a topic group made what the centre regarded as an ideologically unsound decision?"

"It would be discussed, and we would hope eventually to reach agreement."

"So if the gardeners were to order a barrel of Paraquat . . ."

". . . that wouldn't happen!"

". . . or a lorryload of muck from a local farmer, the whole centre would ultimately approve or reject the decision?"

"Yes, if need be."

"How much bigger can you get and still keep that collective decision-making structure?"

"I don't think the centre itself need grow much more, so that discounts that question. As to the allied enterprises, like Dulas Engineering, which is a separate electronics company specialising in instrumentation and control gear for renewable energy systems, they're really separate to the main structure of the centre, and we would hope they could grow into something more substantial. Then maybe they could help us financially!"

We were joined at this point by John Williams and Barry Wise, two luminaries of Dulas Engineering.

"How do you feel about becoming your ageing parent's means of support?"

Wry smiles bespoke economic stringencies. John replied:

"Strictly speaking we're functional, and not geared to high production runs. Also, like most other things round here we're under-capitalised so there's little chance of us getting into large profits, even if that were compatible with the spirit of what we do."

"What do you do?"

"We provide services like data-logging in the ongoing testing and development of windmills, circuit boards for rechargeable batteries, battery-powered instrumentation at remotely-sited windmills or water-power schemes. And there's the bugmeter . . .''

"What's that?"

"It's a device we've developed in association with Aberystwyth University which automatically makes adjustments in the brewing process."

". . . and presumably, judging by its name, has applications in the monitoring of Third World water supplies?"

"We hope so, eventually."

"Are there any areas of your work which you'd like to see develop, Barry?"

There appeared on his face the wistful engineer's expression which speaks of what's coming before the words arrive:

"Well, I wish we had more women coming into engineering. Even in the schools liaison and work experience projects we run, they're just not coming through."

"How do the sexual politics of the centre operate, Tim?"

"I think we've to a large extent broken down the traditional stereotyping. Cindy and Anne, for example, are the building topic group, and the restaurant topic group is mostly male."

I turned to Phil Revell at this point to ask him about the ten-or-twelve-day courses the centre runs for VSO or its Norwegian equivalent, Noraid. Phil is a trained engineer who spent three-and-a-half years in Zimbabwe before coming to CAT.

"Are you," I asked, "happy with the results of your work here?"

The response was very firm:

"When you're talking about the Third World, there is *no* room for any sort of complacency, the problems it faces are so massive. Development there can only take place when change occurs. Yet the net flow of money, for debt repayment, is *from* the Third World to the West, so the Third World is bound to remain impoverished. Things like VSO help, but the system has its shortcomings . . ."

Further probing was met with diplomacy—the centre walks a fine edge of solvency and VSO courses are an important factor in its continuing viability. Not wish-

. . . or wind-power, for that matter.

ing to tread on toes, I turned to Bob Todd, the acting technical director:

"Well, Dr Todd, here you are, a highly qualified former university lecturer, holed up in what many might term a hovel in the hills, and supporting a wife and family on less than £5000 a year. Can we read into that a rejection of the cash nexus and consumer society?"

"I certainly got out of university teaching in part because I was unhappy with consumerist aspects of the technological revolution. Also I was getting more desk-and-administration-bound and I wanted to *apply* my skills more usefully."

"You've been here almost from the outset. What was it like at the beginning?"

"Twelve years ago there was not much here other than ruined buildings and people sheltering under polythene in the rain. We probably underestimated initially the difficulties of capitalisation. We've always been under-capitalised. It was OK at first, but now, the level of awareness of the areas we're involved in having risen, it's even more difficult."

"You say the level of awareness has risen, but do you think that holds true for, say, government awareness and its reflection in official policy decisions?"

"We're still lacking an overall and coherent UK energy policy. The government says wave power isn't viable, for example, and won't fund research into it, but then the Norwegians prove it works. Our government still won't fund it, so you get the present anomalous situation of Japan funding UK wave research. And you get other anomalies. The Department of Energy has a definite energy conservation policy, and believes that it makes economic sense to use energy efficiently, but the supply side development is still based on past trends and an expansion of production to cope. In the USA the energy utilities actually pay consumers—indirectly—not to consume, and thus save themselves the investment in new plants. In Sweden economic growth and energy consumption are not parallel—there isn't, as we're told all too often in this country, particularly by the CEGB, an unbreakable relationship between the two. Here at CAT we've been involved with organisations like NATA (Network of Alternative Technology Associations), based at the Open University, and jointly with Harwell we've put forward a Low Energy Future scenario. It doesn't get publicised . . ."

"So if you had the £20 million of taxpayers' money which CEGB and BNFL are spending on PR in their current campaign, you would stand a chance of changing public awareness of energy needs and habits of use?"

"It's only the nuclear industry itself which shouts about that option—there's no clean bill of health for nuclear power."

"Are the renewables and alternative power sources viable in this country on a year-round basis, bearing in mind that you can't store solar energy—what little of it we get—and that the capital outlay is very high?"

"It's true that the economics of, say, solar collectors look better if the problems of storage can be solved. What seems to be emerging is a bigger-the-better principle. Sweden's way ahead on this. At Lamberhof, for example—a village of 60 houses—90 percent of space and water heating year-round is provided by a water-tank heat-store warmed by solar collectors."

"So it's the Gulf Stream principle?"

"Yeah—the important stage is the initial planning. Alternative energy sources work as part of a coherent strategy. They work less well in less integrated situations."

"How do you go on for research finance?"

Bob's normally cheerful and ingenuous expression crumpled into frowns and groans at this. He mulls it over.

"Pilkington's have been very generous on the solar projects . . ."

(A long silence.)

"We've had *very* little central government funding, no EEC money . . ."

"Would you have to compromise yourselves severely to gain those kinds of finance?"

(Chuckles. Sidelong glances.)

"We've been working on an inter-seasonal heat store. Hypothetically, it could work now, but we need money to take it that one stage further. Take the solar wall on the cottage . . ."

"Straight out of Mies van der Rohe!"

". . . that was developed from discussion over many years on how to adapt from clear sky, cold night conditions to those which occur in Britain. We concentrated on one wall and built it out of our own money. Now we're looking for enough to provide two years' salary and a minimum of equipment to carry on the research . . ."

"But that's peanuts!"

"Exactly!"

Go to the Centre for Alternative Technology. Go for a day. Go on a weekend or a week's course, in Self-build Techniques, Passive Solar Buildings, Wildlife Gardening, Blacksmithing, Windpower, Wholefoods, Environmental Education or one of a dozen other topics. Go and soak up the ambience of a lovely place. Go and acquaint yourself with a more-than-normally altruistic, intelligent and gentle community of people. Go and learn from them, their work, their exhibition and their example. Do all this and then ponder on the relative: a PR campaign *costing* us twenty millions of pounds to convince us of the value of something a majority of us fear and do not want; two years' subsistence salary *wanting* for a research worker in a friendly, green garden of an alternative university, an institution more true to the *idea* of a university than most that carry that name.

I walked away, past the roundabout which skips round on sunbeam power, melts rubber bands and charms, and on down the incline to the car, part-seething with thoughts like these, part at peace from contact with these calm, intelligent people. A noticeboard caught my eye:

"Alternative technology is a way of using technology so that it doesn't harm the environment or other people.

Electricity for example can be generated from wave or wind power rather than from coal or thermal nuclear power stations, which both use finite fuel resources and cause pollution. Food can be grown without the use of artificial chemicals which will ultimately poison the land, wildlife, and us . . ."

If you remotely need convincing of the truth of those arguments, get down to Machynlleth at once.

Edenic/Plutonic
Planet, 1988

In *The Cambrian News* there is a weekly column entitled "Weird Wonders of Wales". It reflects a tradition, a taste for the marvellous, a credulous appetite ever craving satisfaction, and there is no body more concerned to fulfil that basic human need than our dear old Central Electricity Generating Board, the activities of which in Wales and elsewhere all too frequently beggar belief.

The great strength of the CEGB is, of course, its public relations expertise. It has become so adept at this intriguing necessity of late-twentieth-century life that it can now happily twist conventions, manipulate argument and opinion, and even apparently convince *itself*—the monster of delusion having outgrown its masters—at will. Its frenetic activity has been frequently evident in Snowdonia this spring. There was the proposed experiment at Trawsfynydd Nuclear Power Station—the only inland nuclear power station in Britain—which was to have taken place in February. The cooling fans of one of the reactors were to be shut down to test if natural circulation of gases could supply the deficiency.

"All perfectly safe," the public was assured, and the *Cambrian News*, perhaps to reinforce that assurance or perhaps not, printed a front-page picture of CEGB chairman Lord Marshall shaking hands with Snowdonia National Park Officer Alan Jones—though to the eagle-eyed the handshake had all the appearance of being of the masonic variety. The public, however, was not assured. There was talk of a mass evacuation of the area, of the closure of schools. There were mass meetings and special sessions of the County Council. Lord Marshall promised to fly in to Trawsfynydd on the day of the test by helicopter. "And fly out again if it goes wrong," muttered the public, and still was not assured. The "test" was called off. Three months later, when the reactor on which it was to have been conducted was closed down for routine maintenance, irradiation was found to have

caused severe damage to welds and other components. It was not, on the whole, a public relations success for the CEGB.

Unabashed, they continued their activities, and another saga began. It concerned Snowdonia's most prominent eyesore, the pipeline from Llyn Llydaw down to Cwm Dyli Power Station. To approach the subject at a tangent, every National Park in the country is under a statutory requirement to produce a quinquennial National Park Policy Plan Review. No dereliction of duty on the part of the Snowdonia Park Authority is to be detected here. Its plan review was prepared, submitted to the Park Committee, approved last year, and is about to be published. It urges the removal of the Cwm Dyli pipeline at the earliest possible opportunity. But by one of those weird wonders of Wales we mentioned at the outset, when the CEGB put in a request for planning permission for the renewal of the pipeline, or rather its replacement with a larger diameter pipe resting on concrete plinths, it was approved virtually without discussion by the Park's Planning Department and Committee.

Even Lord Marshall had the good grace to be embarrassed by the backlash to this, er—shall we say discrepancy? Esme Kirby, the redoubtable septuagenarian who heads the Snowdonia National Park Society—the most effective, uncompromised, and independent conservational agency in Wales—was incandescent with fury: "This appalling and disgraceful Park Authority has behaved scandalously. If they allow this it will never be forgotten or forgiven."

"Why can't they bury the damned thing?" asked a few milder souls.

"Can't be done—costs too much!" said the CEGB.

"It'd cause greater ecological damage," added the increasingly lickspittle government quango, the Nature Conservancy Council—fixed, as research by Philip Lowe of University College, London, has revealed, by Mrs Thatcher's administration years ago and still a running dog for her policies.

For all the brusqueness of those dismissals, it's an issue which looks like having all the makings of a major row, and one which *should* spill over into the more serious debate fastening again on Trawsfynydd and all its works, where there are more plans afoot.

Being of the view that the perfect, prescient image of our technological age is Swift's Great Academy of Lagado, I find it difficult to take seriously what is being projected at Trawsfynydd, but let's try. The plan is for a Pressurised Water Reactor, the construction of which on an inland site will be some sort of triumph for British technology and a World first. It is intended to site it a little way west of the present Magnox station on the highly visible rock outcrop known as Craig Gyfynys. The CEGB has suggested that in order to render it less visible it will be sited mostly underground, but since this was also suggested and subsequently reneged upon in the plans thirty years ago for the Magnox reactors, we can safely discount it as a sincere proposal on the Board's part. The prospect of accident or explosion in an underground reactor is anyhow so dire that it truly brings us to "Edge of Darkness" terrain.

In order to cool this proposed PWR, two possibilities, each with very major environmental implications, are being canvassed. The first is for cooling towers to be built to a height, depending on your source, of 300 or 500ft. A report commissioned by the CEGB from the Institute of Terrestrial Ecology—a usually excellent body which was formerly a research wing of the NCC—and the Natural Environment Research Council, which is primarily a funding agency, comes down firmly in favour of this option:

"Even though the site is within a National Park, temporary damage to the visual amenity of the area is preferable to the destruction of valuable ecological features . . . the conservation of ecological features should have precedence over the more ephemeral effects on visual amenity".

It should be said that the Honest John who gave out this appalling hostage-to-fortune was simply a scientist working for one government department under the tight remit of another—jockeyed and blinkered, in other words, to allay his fear of the boundary rails. He wasn't to know that, a year after the completion of his work, the station manager of Trawsfynydd would categorically state that the present buildings, even when obsolete (which would be in two years according to original projections of useful and safe life), *would not be removed in our lifetime*. Yes, we are all temporary here, but how temporary is temporary, and what about the ancillary intrusions on visual amenity—pylons and the like?

And so to Plan B, which involves enlarging the area of the present Llyn Trawsfynydd by approximately five-and-a-half square kilometres, changing the whole drainage pattern of the area and sending the water off down the Afon Eden to the south. The ITE/NERC report is rightly shocked at the destruction of sites and ecosystems which this would entail. Water Authority engineers, however (whose sensitivity towards the environment was well demonstrated in recent years with the bulldozing of tracks up to Llyn Anafon and Llyn Bodlyn) and some power station personnel seem to prefer it. The delusional systems come into play as they talk about it—folk-tale motifs of inundations visited upon wicked inhabitants; the utterance of the name Eden, which imbues everything with innocence regained . . .

What the report's remit denies it from taking into account is that a third option exists, which is a concerted and massive public outcry resulting in early closure of the existing power station—the accident-and-emission record of which is second only to Windscale/Sellafield—and no possibility of the acceptance of a PWR here. Even the employment argument on which the CEGB invariably rests its case has been effectively rubbished (see *Nuclear Power and Jobs*: *The Trawsfynydd Experience* by Dr. Brian John, which analyses the social effects of the boom-and-crash economy created by power station construction).

Things are probably not quite that simple, though. The CEGB is cleverly hedging its bets. On the one hand, it has just announced a definite decision to build a PWR at Wylfa, and seems concerned to play the one site off against the other for the best advantage it can get—when things get too hot at Wylfa, it will probably use the diversionary tactic of announcing a new environmental atrocity at Trawsfynydd—a pattern of operation it has often employed in the past (consider, for example, the options canvassed before settling on Dinorwig/Marchlyn as suitable for a pumped storage scheme), and one which shouldn't blind us to the fact that Wylfa is itself an atrocity which has ruined and marginalised the most beautiful and wild stretch of coastline on Anglesey, and perhaps bears some responsibility for the abnormally high cancer statistics along the North Wales coast.

On the other hand, even before the granting of planning permission CEGB contractors have begun taking on labour for the construction of a new Trawsfynydd dam to be built at a cost of £8 millions, which will undoubtedly facilitate enlargement of the lake if that option is taken seriously—capital already invested being a powerful argument in favour of further development. And this, by a roundabout route, brings us to Ceunant Llenyrch, a National Nature Reserve and a Grade One (International Status) Site of Special Scientific Interest. Designations aside, this delightful gorge running down from Llyn Trawsfynydd to the Afon Dwyryd near

Ceunant Llenyrch as it was

Maentwrog is one of the most exquisitely beautiful intimate landscapes in the Snowdonia National Park. The same ITE/NERC ecologist who produced the report quoted above in its recommendations on cooling towers has also written one entitled "Maentwrog Dam Proposed Replacement: an ecological survey of the upper Ceunant Llenyrch Gorge and assessment of effects." His strictures on the latter point amount to little more than this one sentence:

"It is difficult to predict how severely this area will be affected but, with care, most features on the sides of the gorge could survive."

The author of this report may never have worked on a construction site. I have, and I would hasten to assure him that care for the environment is not prominent amongst the many admirable qualities of workers on such schemes. And just to highlight the sort of problems and perceptions with which we are dealing, let me tell him about one of the other uses to which this gorge is put. It is not only a very beautiful environment, it is also a rather dramatic one and as such appeals to adventure groups from outdoor centres, including army groups

in training from centres nearby. These latter groups are now forbidden use of the gorge because an army monitoring unit recently found levels of radioactivity in the gorge unacceptably high—the water from the lake which feeds it is used as coolant for the present Trawsfynydd Magnox reactors. If it is high now, what levels will it reach when *two* power stations pump their contaminants into it? If the army, which is not notable for the concern it evinces for the welfare of its men, reacts thus, what levels has it already reached? Why do parties of schoolchildren from Local Education Authority centres continue to use it in ignorance when grown men from the armed forces for their own safety are kept away?

There are questions to be asked in the coming months, and the CEGB, as a public utility, ought to stop trying to manipulate and mislead public opinion on matters vital to that public's wellbeing. It won't, of course, because there are matters which the government perceives as more important than the wellbeing of its electorate at stake. They are strictly commercial ones, and they form an alternative discourse to all the CEGB's pronouncements of recent months, which if it were overt might run like this:

Trawsfynydd's record of industrial safety is the worst of any British nuclear power station after Sellafield.

"We acknowledge that as a means of producing electricity nuclear power is hopelessly expensive and will never attain commercial viability. This is why we never release figures on the cost of energy production by nuclear fission. But this process has a most significant by-product, which is plutonium. When you take into consideration Britain's position as the third-ranking world power in the export of armaments, and the world's largest producer *and exporter* of plutonium for military purposes, then the rationale becomes much more clear. It is to do with safeguarding our ability to maintain an influence in world affairs . . ."

In that context epidemiological statistics on childhood leukaemias and other cancers, honest accounts of accidents or operating difficulties, local people's ambitions for materially comfortable lifestyles, the extraordinary meteorological anomaly which caused radioactive contamination from Chernobyl to be dumped 3,000 miles upwind, thus bringing about restrictions in the first

instances six miles downwind from the nuclear power stations at Sellafield and Trawsfynydd—these are all factors to be concealed, distorted, or manipulated at will. And in the case of Trawsfynydd, simple semantics have dealt the nuclear power industry an ace. But there is nothing Edenic about its designs on this Afon Eden, and the gods it serves are those Plutonic ones which the late James Cameron termed "these unthinkable and unspeakable instruments for genocide of which only a civilisation which had drifted utterly beyond the voice of conscience could conceive."

Ruth Pinner's Nature Column
Unpublished, 1988

The first time I saw him (for a him I'm sure he was by his very cocksureness upon the water) was in late December. He was feeding in one of the deep lagoons the tide leaves around Trwyn Penrhyn. Not that red-throated divers are all that uncommon on the North Wales estuaries and mudflats—most winters there are a few, down from Iceland or the Hebrides, to be seen at Traeth Lafan or on the Dyfi. But this was a magnificent specimen. The pearl braiding across his dark back glistened in the low winter sun, and despite this winter plumage he still had the rusty-red throat markings from which the name derives. I sat and watched him fishing, often as little as ten or twenty yards away. Occasionally, if he caught sight of me and became momentarily anxious, he would sink down in the water, head uptilted at a suspicious angle, and then, with an arched, serpentine spasm of neck and body, would disappear under the water for minutes at a time to re-surface forty or fifty yards away.

Frequently over the last few weeks I've seen him, up and down the estuary, never terribly cautious of my presence. It is, of course, a marvellous place at this time of year for birds. The curlews gather now in great flocks,

gliding down in wheeling formation on the sandbanks or in the coastal fields with the most graceful, droop-winged flight. At night they descant together in their bubbling, whistling, chuckling song until one soloist pitches up to the crescendo and every other bird's call then cascades after. It is the particular and identifying sound of the place.

But when the tide recedes, the curlews cease from song and play, and stalk stiff-legged and alert along the margins of the water, jabbing their long-curved beaks, coming up with ragworms which they toss wriggling along the length of their beak and swallow down with a little shake of the head.

Farther out, on the sands where the pilgrims needed guides to cross from Llanfihangel y Traethau above on their way by the Taith y Pererin to Ynys Enlli, the numbers of birds is at times spectacular. A flock of pintail, beautifully elegant and several thousand strong, occupies the whole of a heart-shaped sand-island. Each bird faces in the same direction, as though spectating at some great

"The place was empty, apart from a pair of red-breasted mergansers out by the point, which took to their wings the instant they saw me."

event. But they are only looking out over the huge expanses of sand and shallow water where the two estuaries meet, and where tide and river have sculpted the estuarine sand into a lyrical, bas-relief eroticism of texture and curve.

Here and there, standing amongst the creases and wrinkles, or bushing together like the bodily hair of this great tidal matrix, are groups of geese. One congregation of barnacle geese sets up a racket like angry Pekinese dogs as a pair of shelduck alight nearby and march stolidly across the perimeter of their territory. When the tide returns they'll take off and land upstream amongst the saltings to graze and to scold querulously at passing sheep.

Whilst all this communal activity is going on, the smaller birds are moving more or less quietly about their business. Here on the Dwyryd, oystercatcher and dunlin are always present, though seldom in the numbers to be found elsewhere. The latter stitch their patient trail hunch-shouldered along the tideline, whilst the oyster-catchers, with their dapper scurry and piping flight, race each other to the little draining eddies where handfuls of mussels are washed up.

In the empty middle of the estuary, where the geese squabble and preen, you have little time to stay and must time your visit cautiously. Slack water here turns with inexorable suddenness to rush up the network of channels and flood across the tidal flats. In a space of minutes you can be cut off, with no option but to swim. The sense of danger adds piquancy to the vast sense of space. From the oak-wooded banks, however, you can watch the whole drama enacted in perfect safety. There are abandoned slate-wharves here, now high and dry and scarcely distinguishable from the glacier-scoured ribs of rock which once marked their entrance.

Sit quietly on them and from every quarter come the seething territorial assertions of wren and shrew. So intense was this disputation yesterday that it devastated the peace of the place, so I continued on my way back to the car park at Abergafren.

On my way there I came across a dead bird, tossed aside from the path on the sheep-cropped turf. I picked it up. It was the diver, its neck broken, its red throat blasted half away by shotgun pellets. There had been a man shooting down there that morning, on his car the bird-brained dog-badge of the British Association for Shooting and Conservation! This diver, whose grace and primitive mystery were a benediction upon the place, would have offered no "sport", would have been a sitting target.

And when I walked along to the tidal lagoons at Trwyn Penrhyn today, there were no red-throated divers there. The place was empty, apart from a pair of red-breasted mergansers out by the point, which took to their wings the instant they saw me.

The Death of Reverence and the Birth of Despair: Reflections on the British Mountain Scene
Mountain, 1986

"I love this country passionately, expanding
To its wild immensity as a flower opens in the sunshine,
I am the last man in the world to hate these great places
And depend for my only comfort on the theatres and cafes . . .
I would not rather be sitting in the closed comfort of the Pullman,
A drink before me, surrounded by people I know,
And things I can understand."

The extract is from Hugh MacDiarmid's poem "The Wreck of the Swan", and though these are not specifically located by the passage, it describes his feelings for the wilder regions of his native Scotland. There is a stratagem in using it to preface this article. It is not put there merely for decoration. It is included to invite you to agree with the general sentiment it expresses, for without it the mountains are dead.

The topic with which this article deals—the desecration of British wild land—puts me in a rage, and though that response is too immediate for prior analysis, in retrospect it seems more appropriate than merely getting depressed. At least when you are in a rage you will fight anything and anyone, and fighting on behalf of our wild landscapes is what is needed—depression, to which one can all too readily accede, all too easily concedes defeat.

I want to start, because this is a mountaineering magazine (and an international one at that, so the peculiarly British slant may be of interest to those who enjoy the external view), by telling you something about cities. Like most people, I was born in one—Manchester, to be precise—in the years just after the Second World War, when there were ration books for everything, and orange juice for the children came in small bottles of

Climber "trespassing" at Pen y Holt Stack, Castlemartin Range West, Pembroke.

thick glass. My family lived in Hulme, down by the Pomona Docks, though what this part of the city ever had to do with the goddess of fruit trees it is hard to imagine. It was an area of narrow, cobbled streets between tight rows of dingy brick houses, raggedly punctuated by crofts where the bombs had fallen only a few years before, traversed by back-alleys full of dog-shit, rubbish and broken slates. In winter, the whole district often lay for weeks on end under a thick yellow industrial smog which you drew harsh and gasping into your lungs. I can remember the taste and the involuntary stutter of your breath against it to this day. In the summer, when the sun shone through the smoke haze, old people placed chairs outside their doors and sat there. Two old men, wounded in the Great War 30 years before, I particularly recall, because they both had parts of their face and head missing and dreadful raw flesh showing through, from the sight of which I shrank in horror as a child.

My grandfather lived in a slightly better neighbourhood a few blocks away to the south. He had fought in the Boer War—Bloemfontein, Ladysmith—he could tell me the stories. There was a park at the bottom of his street, and in his backyard, by the coalshed door, a chance small clump of brilliant green fern croziered out and fanned across the wall each year. I think if anyone had rooted it up, it would have broken his heart. He would touch it, softly and with an expression to which I could not have put words then but which I now know to have been reverence, for the mystery of the thing and the otherness of it in that place, which teased at his understanding. It taught me something instinctively which remains even after he, the fern, the cobbled streets and dingy brick, have all gone. The mistakes of the town-planners which succeeded them, the concrete towers and wall-encircled, ornamental planted trees, seem to have weighed against his reverence somewhere. And now schemes and attitudes like theirs spread abroad and the wild land, which rims the eastern skyline of Manchester and was my release from this background, suffers by them.

There is a vision in another city of which I am obscurely reminded when I let my mind dwell on this theme. I often re-visit it when I am in London, sit in front of it for half an hour or so and drink it in. Turner painted it and gave it the title of "The Fighting Temeraire tugged to her last berth to be broken up". It's not my favourite painting of Turner's—"Norham Castle at Sunrise" would be that (or in other moods "The Burning of the House of Lords and Commons"), but it does present an image which closes forcefully with my thoughts. The immediate focus of the canvas is on two foreground images—the thrusting, phallic steam-tug and the incubus-shape of a black buoy, born out of bloodied waters, for which the tug is making. Above the anti-sun of the buoy is the real sun, pale and setting. Behind the tug, the belching smoke from which is furling around her white spars, is the lovely sailing ship the Temeraire herself. The painting has extraordinary emotional force—the whole world of elemental grace and light is at the mercy of, drawn down by and into, these powerful dark images. In it Turner—who was a man who knew his mountains—gives us his image, rich with irony, of all the terrible birth and death which was the Industrial Revolution. A century and a half further on, we need a similar clarity of perception to understand what's happening to the lovely remnants of our mountain and hill landscape today. For vision is the precondition of action as surely as the mountains are still a source of spiritual refreshment.

It is a truism to say that these islands are small and overpopulated. South of the Scottish Border you're hard put to it to find yourself as much as five miles away from the nearest road. This is not to say that we don't *have* wild country, but rather to confess that, in comparison to America for example, it only exists on a small, and hence vulnerable, scale. "North of the Border it's different", people (and especially the Scots) will tell you, with more than a trace of the old, smug, it-couldn't-happen-hereness about their argument.

Let's test the truth of that assertion by taking a look at the fate of a place which has the grandest and most remote scenery in Britain, where the 1400ft sea-cliff of Conachair presents perhaps the biggest rock-climbing challenge still left in Europe, and which in a sense even witnessed the birth of the sport of rock-climbing—though it was never practiced as such, but rather as a means to a livelihood. I'm referring to St. Kilda, the group of islands 50 miles out into the Atlantic beyond the Outer Hebrides, which last had an indigenous population in 1930. It's now owned by the National Trust for Scotland, to which it was left in 1956 by the Marquis of Bute, "to be held in perpetuity for the benefit of the nation." It's a moot point how much benefit the nation might ever have derived from this last speck on its uttermost rim, but the good Marquis passed on his tradition of responsible stewardship to the NTS in the belief that they would conserve the natural beauty of the island for future generations.

The NTS was compromised from the outset. In 1956

the Government had decided to build a missile testing range on South Uist. Sixty miles away, out in the Atlantic, St. Kilda was held to be the perfect site for radar surveillance of missiles launched from the range. The NTS, accordingly, accepted the Marquis's gift and promptly leased it to a Government body, the Nature Conservancy Council, which in its turn designated the island a National Nature Reserve and sub-let part of it to the Ministry of Defence. The Marquis's intentions towards public amenity, which is the most plausible construction to be put on his phrase "for the benefit of the nation", were subverted at a stroke. If you were military personnel or a positively-vetted bird-watcher, your presence could be tolerated. If you were a celebrity climber on a media visit, you'd be hospitably entertained, the garrison finding irksome the loneliness of the place. But otherwise, you'd better have a good reason for wanting to go there other than just the appeal of being amongst its natural majesty.

Even these constraints might be thought acceptable if belief could be maintained that the principle of responsible stewardship which ought to be enshrined as the basic and underlying tenet of conservation was operative. But is it? Thirty years after the Marquis's will had been so liberally interpreted, the South Uist Range launches *Two-and-a-half-million-pounds-worth* of missile technology irrecoverably into the Atlantic *every day*, to keep the St Kilda garrison well occupied and justify its existence. But that garrison's treatment of the Island has betrayed the Marquis's trust. Here is a responsible contemporary report:

"The army has scarred the island with great ribbons of concrete, masses of gerry-built dwellings, and their space-invader domes and dishes on the summit of Mullach Geal. They seem to have little regard for ancient dwellings, especially on the west side in Gleana Bay, where their debris has rolled down the 1000ft slope and destroyed many of the 'horned dwellings', unique in the whole of the British Isles."

(*The Road Through the Isles*, John Sharkey & Keith Payne, Wildwood House 1986)

The example of St. Kilda is important to the British conservation movement for several reasons. It suggests what degree of trust can be vested even in those large and influential agencies which profess conservational concern and control a vast and increasing proportion of our shrinking hill-country. The records of the NTS and the National Trust in England are generally good, but not

Protection of the environment, MoD-style, South Pembroke.

unwaveringly so, as examples like St. Kilda, The Bradenham Bunker, the lack of concerted opposition to the Cowlyd-Ogwen Water Transfer scheme, clearly show. And *trust* is not a quality which can bear much qualification. The Nature Conservancy Council, though seemingly more educable in recent years, has not always been seen to pursue mutuality of interest with recreational bodies, and has at times been highly exclusive in its operations. The military, as its attitudes towards the St. Kilda environment clearly display, unless most carefully monitored appears not to give a damn. Those who destroy, or who are party to the destruction of, any of our beautiful landscapes, should not be entrusted with their care. Yet how much land lies under their stewardship?

Having wandered at some length from the mean streets and the marbled galleries out to the missile ranges and the most remote location, it's perhaps time to view the types of threats which erode the natural amenity of our limited British wilderness areas. They could be listed thus: industrial, civil engineering, agricultural, and silvicultural activity; military occupation where it involves exclusive use or destructive activity; visitor pressure; certain types of recreational usage or use for scientific study. These activities bring in their wake the associated problems of exclusion of access and alteration of the environment. There is not one area where an easy answer is available to the problems they pose or where a hard-and-fast rule can be laid down. In consequence, just as there is no single body to speak on its behalf, neither is there adequate legislation to safeguard wild landscape, and it would probably be against government's self-perceived interest to provide it. So the threats proliferate. Scan the newspapers any week and see the headlines recur: "National Park planners condemn water authority 'motorways,' ", "Scottish estate owner resists an army invasion", "Bird society joins moorland fight", "Dartmoor 'betrayal' condemned", "Low-flying exercises increase to 360 per day", "Trust in wrong to lease land", "Oilfield plan threatens award-winning coast", "Highlands to get 30-mile aerial for nuclear submarine control", "Army demand holds up Calke land deal", "Call for action to save uplands", "Paths on Snowdon reach 'motorway proportions' ", "Melchett backs direct action on landscape", "Park Chief clears way for PWR", "Range shooting fires safety fears". Look at the places threatened: Knoydart, the Cairngorms, the Monadhliath, Snowdonia, Dartmoor, Northumberland, Pembroke, the Peak District, the Lake District, Exmoor, Mid-Wales, Dorset, Skye.

"It doesn't bother me," retorts the climber, a true spirit of anarchy in his soul, "I really couldn't care less. Look, I come here to climb, right? I'm not interested in politics, I couldn't give a damn. I can go where I want and when I want—nobody stops me, nobody tells me what I can and can't do."

I wonder how many times, in arguing the case for conservation of the environment, people have received that response? It is quite difficult to counter. It's the old "sport-should-be-above-politics" red herring, which takes as its basic premise that "sport", for which those who propound the argument profess a quasi-religious fervour, exists on some higher plane, divorced from all other social realities. It does not, and cannot—the sportsman is as much a member of society as the bus-conductor, the stockbroker, the policeman or the tramp. The fact

that he displays an aggressive lack of interest in politics and puffs out his chest in a just-you-try-and-stop-me stance is neither here nor there, and no more or less than a sign of his lack of intelligent grasp of, and involvement in, human affairs. I would go so far with him as to agree that the issues of which we are talking here transcend to a certain extent party-political barriers, but politics (non-affiliated-and-with-a-small-p) mingle inextricably with human affairs: "the science dealing with the form, organization, and administration of a state or part of one, and with the regulation of its relations with other states". It just so happens that climbing, in relation to the other states jockeying for position in this wilderness province, is a particularly weak state, small in numbers and poor in wealth. Alright, so you don't care for politics, you loathe the committee and the minutely particularized formal deposition ("11.7. It is the view of this working party that on all future occasions where the necessity may arise, assurances should be obtained from appropriate official sources which will safeguard . . . etc. etc."). So do most reasonable people, but in some way, by some means (and puffing out your chest and saying 'just you try and stop me' will serve the purpose sometimes, though less and less frequently as the powers at the command of the opposition increase), you still have to make your voice heard, otherwise:

"Climbers fined for range trespass"; "Witches Quarry closed for climbing"; "Hay Tor ban proposed"; "Rights of way ploughed up for forestry plantation"; "Increased restrictions proposed for nesting season"; "Farmer bans climbers"; "Quarry extension threatens popular rocks"; "Shooting club buys climbing venue"; "Military to purchase Scottish peninsula".

None of them can stop you trying to get in, but you're more likely to get shot than have a medal pinned on that puffed-out chest of yours: ". . . an Army spokesman in Wales warned that there could be civilian deaths if people continued to wander on to the ranges, ignoring danger signs".

A curious change now occurs. Our anonymous climber—let's call him Wally Naff for convenience—starts to argue the case against his own interests: "The water-boards/estate owners/army/forestry look after the land better. They're true conservationists. We can always get in there discreetly when we feel like it, and the land under their care is so much better preserved."

"So much better preserved than what?" is the obvi-

ous rejoinder. There is no doubt that some landowners and farmers—probably even a majority amongst them—do take the responsibility of their stewardship very seriously indeed. There is also no doubt that many large private landowners, particularly in the Highlands, raise not the slightest objection throughout the greater part of the year to walkers and climbers enjoying the recreational amenity of their land. Of course, when desire to enjoy that amenity clashes with the economics of the deer-stalk or the grouse-shoot, then it is pretty obvious which interest will emerge victorious, and since those economics are the chief support of some rural populations, vested interest can adduce a populist argument in its own support which is difficult to counter. So the concession is made that we must live and let live (whatever our thoughts may be on killing for pleasure), and a slightly uneasy status quo prevails. When the Hooray Henries come up from the South and the high velocity rifles and individually-fitted shotguns by Purdey or Boss are taken out and oiled, then we keep off the Scottish mountains and Northern moors. The cash nexus and violence-to-life rule for a few weeks or months amongst the clean air, the midges and the rain, and then we're given back our qualified freedom to roam.

Most British mountaineers find this an acceptable-enough compromise. Threats to its stability emerge from our own ranks from time to time—a sponsored mass walk scheduled to take place in the middle of the deer-stalking season this August through the Great Wilderness, the Fisherfield Forest in Ross-shire, could not be better calculated to upset the apple-cart. A penny a mile and choose your charity! No doubt there are some who think it is time it was upset, and who are willing to brush aside the safety considerations which must weigh upon the venture. I suspect there are more important targets for their energies, and whatever we may or may not think socially and morally about the estate owners and their sporting activities, their stewardship of the land is generally less oppressive towards our sport than that of certain official bodies. It comes back to due respect for the land, and to the extremes represented by the Army's lack of regard for the natural beauty of St. Kilda and my grandfather's reverence for his fern. The landowner does care for his land. The government or quasi-governmental agency, be it Forestry Commission, Water Board or Ministry of Defence, cannot be relied on to do so. True, they plead their own cause as conservationists from time to time, but in doing so they remind me of Hazlitt's response to like arguments: "I see plainly enough that black is not white, that the grass is green,

that kings are not their subjects." On our area of concern, you could add a few phrases to that: "that those who shell archaeological remains do not seek to preserve them; that those who debar the public do not act in the public interest; that National Parks are merely notional parks; that the Countryside Commission is a running-dog of governmental exploitation (and fixed by the Government as such); that to offer no opposition is to admit defeat."

Before we stoop to castigate and abuse our opponents (if that is what they are, and I do not think that we should unswervingly identify the military, the forestry, the landowners or reservoir-builders thus) in the war which must be waged to conserve the natural mountain environment, we should consider whether our own house is in order. We daub and dust, carve, chip and gouge the rock-faces, decorate them even in the public's preferred beauty-spots ("So little courtesy from youths astride the path!" said the look on the woman rambler's face) with violent-coloured fronds of tape, leave our chalk-packets, squares of old carpet and other rubbish around their foot. It is climbers who do this. What right, then, to criticise the rusting tanks which the army leaves on the Castlemartin ranges (if anyone cares about them)? We break down walls and pass the farmer by in surly arrogance, so what belief has he when we politely come to negotiate for access, for a right-of-way? We agree with the Naturalists' Trust of this county or that to stay away from this cliff or the other during the nesting months, but we don't tell our own number of the ban and still they climb there. The birds go. There are thousands who like to see them, or in the abstract are offended at their departure. The action rebounds upon us. Fines and prison sentences come to enforce an avoidance we once volunteered—their lobby having more political clout than ours, for after all, what has politics to do with sport? On the mountains, the popular hills, the sparse vegetation is worn away and the thin soil is washed down the slopes and the scars of erosion spread. Workers labour to repair the damage, some for no reward other than the solace of knowing that they are helping something to be done. We curl our lip to decry and malign. "You are encouraging incompetents and fools up here," we say, "what right have they to be on our mountains? Leave the scars. Let them spread. They will keep people away." (That we, who all too often are excluded, should exclude!) What greater right have we, the initiates, to Snowdon, Scafell Pike, Ben Nevis, than those whose first challenge is this assault on their slopes? Thus the liberal dilemma? Come to that, what greater right have we, the climbers, than the gun-club members to exclusive use of Wilton or Duke's Quarry, Whatstandwell? What absolute assurance do we have that ours is the worthier claim? And despite the damage they do to the terrain, how can we deny the Army exclusive use of vast tracts of land in Dartmoor, Pembroke, Northumberland, when their training is so vital to "national security and the defence of the realm":

"A multi-national force of 70 aircraft will attack a mock Warsaw Pact airfield laid out at Otterburn in Northumberland today at the culmination of a Nato war game named the Tactical Fighter Meet 86."

Until we have found plausible, adequate and truthful answers to all these questions, we have no case, no precedence.

But if—our own house in order—we study the factors involved and seriously outline what opposition, if any, we have to them, we are on the road to preventing abuse of our wilderness amenity. Take the last quotation as an example. Despite the fact that Mrs Thatcher assures us that "the Russians are not our friends" and President Reagan regales us daily with his communistophobia, I am unconvinced that a *game* should be made out of bombing an imaginary airfield supposedly belonging to a nation with which we are not, nor are ever likely to be, at war. When I read further and am told that "Major Bob Hylton of the US Tactical Air Command will be in charge, shepherding 44 bombers, plus radar suppression aircraft and supporting fighters, through the electronic defences of Spadeadam in Cumbria", I have to say that I am mightily offended. If America wishes to act out her aggressions in this form of play, why can she not use her own vast country, where there is the space to do it? Why can she not bomb a few of her own irradiated rattlesnakes in the Nevada desert instead of denying me the recreational amenity of those lovely little Northumbrian sandstone outcrops? And should we take this sort of thing without protest when it is such a blatant affront to the international community of climbing? The Poles, the Russians, the Czechs, the East Germans, the Japanese, the Italians, even the Americans, as climbers are *all* our friends. The governments which tell us otherwise are the ones which most abuse our mountain land. For once I go along with the idea that sport is above Politics. My friends and family are the community of climbers, and I will hear nothing against them. I want no harm to befall them or their home, which is the world's hill and mountain

land.

Or at least, that's the ideal, but how does it work in a world, for example, where there are ten thousand Rambo-worshippers for every one who reads Buckminster Fuller? In a world, for example, where a National Park Officer can argue *for* the siting of a Pressurized Water Reactor in one of the most central and widely visible sites amongst the Welsh mountains, claiming that it will be a vital source of employment and a major tourist attraction? We have arrived at the Grand Academy of Lagado. There is no hope. Reason, compassion, logic, fellow-humanity are at an end. "Blessed are the powerful, for they shall inherit the earth"—and do with it as they wish. Did we think never to arrive at the place we were incessantly making for? We—our century—stepped over the corpses of those who fraternised between the lines on Christmas Day, 1914, and were ordered back on pain of being shot by their own officers into the trenches to take up their arms again. We read by the light of lampshades made from the tattooed skin of Jews. We marvelled at the mushrooms which sprouted and towered above Hiroshima and Bikini Atoll. At every step we lost something of our capacity for reverence, hope and love. Our fractured psyches carried on, and even the mountains, which once reigned supreme as symbols of order and beauty in creation, were trodden underfoot—conquered, as they would have it in the official media phrase . . .

Where there is little hope, few motives which demand respect, few actions undertaken for other than personal or national aggrandisement, there is little reverence or mystery. Only the hurt and the waste remain. Returning from evening climbing sessions I talk often at nights in a pub in Bakewell with a crony of twice my age—Jack Longland, who was on Everest in '33, and who came from a time before this unredeemable period of human history. There are times without number when I could recount his bafflement, anger and bewildered hurt at what goes on in our society, at what he cannot, for all the range of cultural reference at his command, begin to accept or understand. What is happening to our mountains is no more—and no less serious—than a function of all this. I think of my long-since-dead grandfather, his old veined hands cupped with reverence around a frond of fern, letting its delicacy rest lightly upon his skin, with the same magic and relief which our damaged, downtrodden hills have given, and still have the capacity to give—to me, his grandson, who came to them from the dirt and decay of a wasted city, and for tens of thousands of others like me. His basic attitude, held towards our mountains, is central. The mystery now is how to defend them against the ignorance and proliferation of threat which, unwittingly maybe, heedlessly, but inexorably, seek to destroy them, and the release, salvation and hope they can hold out for future generations.

Trees, Beauty and Truth
North Wales Lifestyle, 1989

The larch plantation which surrounds my house, and which has been bursting into vivid green life these last few days, is resonant with birdsong, and all the activity of spring. Goldfinch, siskin and chiff-chaff dip and scud about continually between its lacy, swaying latticework of branches and the apple-blossomed garden. I like living amongst the trees, feel almost generously at times towards the men who put them here. They did so, you see, with some sense of the form of the land, some feel for the hill-contour and the winding rhythms of the lichenous old boundary walls. And when I look out into the sunshine and the morning garden, and the teeming life which fills it from the trees, I can almost believe that here is an industry which has got its priorities right: "Respect the land you till, that it shall bring forth the good harvest!"

The pity is, that that injunction is scarcely ever observed, even in an area as lovely as North Wales. And silviculture is as guilty as any other form of land use in this respect.

Marion Shoard, in *This Land is Your Land*—her seminal treatise on the state of the British countryside —wrote that "Like modern agriculture, modern forestry takes little more account of the natural environment than does an engineering factory or an industrial estate." Given the contexts of forestry plantation in this country—the uplands, the wild places—that is a serious charge. When I first read it, I was inclined to dismiss it, to think that she was overstating her case and referring back to the bad old days of huge and heavy rectangular plantations of sitka spruce which blighted most of the mountain areas of this country in the immediate post-war years. Now I'm not so sure, and this is why.

Last year I had a commission to prepare a set of descriptions of walks in North Wales for inclusion in one of a popular series of tourist guides. The walks were for the most part to be original, or at least not the

habitual tourist-trods, and in checking them I frequently found myself amongst the forests. For someone who likes trees, it was a profoundly disheartening experience.

There was a day, for example, when my eight-year-old son and I tried to follow a public right-of-way from Pont y Pant in the Lledr Valley, over to Gwbrnant. It was clearly marked on the 1:25,000 Ordnance Survey map. We followed its line, checking carefully all the time that we were on route. But the path no longer existed. For half-a-mile, its line had been obscured by the felling of trees, and the difficulty of crossing terrain where that activity has taken place is indescribable. After a hundred yards or so—which took us twenty minutes—William turned to me and asked, "Daddy, are we ever going to get anywhere today?"

"Not if we keep on up this way," I answered, and we turned back to skirt round the edge of the plantation in the hope of picking up the line of the path on the moor above.

No such luck! Up there it had been planted, drained, fenced—and the Forestry Commission make good fences—sturdy, high, taut affairs with barbed wire on top. Though what they want to keep in or out is a mystery to me, because generally there's little that lives or grows amongst the conifers, however pleasing an exception the larches by my house may be. Walk through the sterile silence of a mature spruce plantation to test the truth of that assertion—the deadness underfoot, the straight dead trunks carrying the sap up to the dark foliage far above. There are no flowers, few mosses or lichens, little wildlife, none of the secondary growth of the deciduous forests—instead there is sombre, dark bareness.

The difficulties I've just described with this public right-of-way at Pont y Pant I've found replicated in dozens of places throughout Wales over the years: in Coed y Brenin, at Abergeirw, in Beddgelert Forest, at Llyn Glanmerin, all over the great wilderness between Tregaron and Abergwesyn. I'm sure the appropriate procedures were followed before blocking off or erasing these lines of communication which had been used since prehistory. But it seems to me a bad and an unsympathetic thing for the Forestry Commission to have done, and in a period when there has been a vast expansion of recreational interest in the outdoors (country walking is the most popular leisure pastime of the British people by far, according to a Countryside Commission study), any argument that these rights-of-way were defunct is surely fallacious. As a public relations exercise, their wholesale blocking-off by the Forestry Com-

Birnam Wood to high Dunsinane Hill hath come.

mission has been a disaster.

So much for the difficulties caused to public access by forestry plantation in Wales, but over the last year that's not the aspect of forestry practise which has disturbed me most. What causes me intense concern is the widespread clearcutting which has taken place, and the environmental effect of that. Take a drive, for example, up to Crafnant at the moment. You will surely know this popular and lovely valley above Trefriw. The hillside above the lake that was forested in the immediate post-war period is mature now. Wholesale felling is taking place there. It is a dreadful sight—one which I can scarcely comprehend being allowed to take place in a National Park.

Hundreds of yards of hillside have been cleared, and the effect of this felling is one of utter devastation. But even the aesthetic considerations—the effect which this has on the appearance of one of the most beautiful of Welsh valleys—pale into insignificance when the potential environmental considerations are also taken into account. Take a walk along the forestry track which runs on the north side of the lake and you'll see clearly what I mean.

Where the trees have been felled, the earth is bare—

soured by the needles which have fallen upon it for years, etiolated, deprived of the lifegiving power of the sun so its binding strength has gone and the rains now wash the meagre soil, the poor, thin tilth of the rocky hillside, down into the lake. Gullies are opening up everywhere, the bedrock is bared, the slope will never sustain the growth of trees again. That is bad ecology, bad industrial practise to deplete your most precious resource to exhaustion, bad humanity to be unaware, or worse still heedless, of consequence. And it is taking place throughout Snowdonia. The beauties of the landscape, affected often and obscured by the initial planting of the trees, are now being destroyed.

If there were no alternative method of forest management, there would be more excuse. But consider the example of the Swedish Forestry Act of 1979, which introduced regulations to forbid the felling of more than fifty per cent of timber stock in any one area at any one time. Far from ruining the Swedish timber industry, it has been both an economic success and a public relations triumph, revealing an industry which is concerned about the wise management of its resources. The legislation came about through public pressure; was a product of the Swedish principle of *allemansratt*—the right to roam freely over all open country. In Britain, public exclusion through blocking off rights-of-way sets the balance firmly against public awareness which can bring about wise regulation of activity. Democracy has many forms, and even more abuses! I could elaborate here on the financial aspects of timber-growing and the squalid chicanery of the removal of tax concessions on planting being balanced out by a trebling of grant aid from the public purse to private investors. But that's the sub-structure of an iniquitous area of industrial practise, and not the point immediately at issue. It ties in, of course. And the truth of the matter is that the beauty of the area—which is a matter, to my mind, of vital public interest—is being radically affected by the serious misconduct and mismanagement and deregulation of an industry which affects our countryside drastically, from which very few profit, and for which the rest of us pay.

The Clear Sight of Janet Haigh
Climber and Hillwalker, 1989

Mountains are no place, really, for memorials to Man, but there are one or two which are affecting enough in their way. I doubt if anybody, coming down off the Brecon Beacons in the twilight of a winter's day, could fail to be moved by the story behind the obelisk above Cwm Llwch to little Tommy Jones. And the great slab of slate with its simple inscription carved by Jonah Jones—Eric Gill's student—recently placed on a knoll amongst the tawny grasses of Bwlch Ehediad sets up a strange resonance between itself and the rather sinister pool with its single alder in the marsh below, from which for many years a DC3's tailplane protruded, and deep within which the bodies of those whom the stone commemorates still lie. But the memorial which has the greatest emotional force for me is that fragile, plain tablet of local slate which stands beside the old Harlech-to-London coach road where it climbs out of the Nant Ysgethin and on to the broad, grassy height of Llawlech. The words upon it run thus:

"Gogoniant i Dduw
To the enduring memory of
Janet Haigh
who even as late as
her eighty-fourth year
despite dim sight

and stiffened joints
still loved to walk this way
from Talybont to Penmaenpool."

I know nothing about Janet Haigh other than the above, and the two additional facts that she died in 1953, and that her son Melvyn was sometime Bishop of Winchester. But that is immaterial. What matters is the sense of due reverence which her stone imparts to this remarkable place. It is nothing to do with her spirit lingering here or any other such sentimentality. It may do so, but such a response is surely beside the point, which is this: stone, inscription and landscape together present an extraordinary and poignant specific expression of the great poetic commonplace which is the endurance of natural beauty by contrast with human life. That "dim sight", those "stiffened joints", labouring up this hill in their 84th year with the burden of mortality upon them are the fate we all share. Her capacity to delight in the glory of the place which the Welsh words suggest is not so general, though.

So let me describe for you the context of her stone. I may have misled you by that reference to the coach road, for it's almost incomprehensible that the London Stage, with or without its Pickwickian complement of jovial, be-toppered gents and genteel ladies, could ever have passed this way. It is an irretrievably ancient line of communication. The old green track eases its way through ice-scoured bluffs and over hillsides of bleached grass. It traverses a bare, wild valley stretching up into the innermost recesses of the Rhinogydd, which are the most rugged of Snowdonia hill-ranges. It bumps across the narrow, humped bridge of Pont Scethin and strains up the zig-zags on to the ridge of Llawlech at a height of 1840ft above sea-level, before edging gingerly down into the valley of the Mawddach below.

This is no ordinary "road", and the terrain through which it journeys is one of the most fragile and exquisite landscapes in the whole of Wales. Even the statutory bodies for the most part recognise that fragility (with one ignoble exception which we shall come to later). In 1979 a huge acreage with Pont Scethin at its centre was designated an "Ancient Landscape", with a strong consequent presumption against any form of disturbance within it. The lake of Bodlyn, a mile above Pont Scethin, is shortly to be accorded the status of a Site of Special Scientific Interest under the Wildlife and Countryside Act of 1981. A Management Agreement for 135 acres lower down the Afon Ysgethin is at present being negotiated under conditions laid down in the same

Act. The whole area, in the words of The Snowdonia National Park Authority's archaeologist Peter Crew, is "the most important archaeologically in Wales, and stands comparison with anything in Britain. The valley has an exceptional range of relict features, of which Pont Scethin is only the most obvious." Richard Kelly of the Gwynedd Archaeological Trust, with whom I visited it recently, adds that "What's important here is not just the number of scheduled monuments, but more particularly the context in which they're to be found, which shows with remarkable clarity the patterns of land usage and settlement over millennia. It's vital that nothing be allowed to affect any part of this whole landscape."

And of course it is also beautiful. From Janet Haigh's stone you can look out over that serpentine scar in the cerulean of Porthmadog Bay which is Sarn Badrig—St Patrick's Causeway. You can look across northwards to Snowdon: "Give me the stones of Snowdon/And the lamps of Heaven" wrote Kingsley, and from this angle you see the aptness of the collocation. The very end of the ridge you stand upon was the very first acquisition of The National Trust—Dinas Oleu—the citadel of light, and it is light which illuminates the divine and priceless manuscript laid out before you—hill-light, western light, that glowing, changing, suffusing light which floods into these western valleys beneath, around, through the clouds and makes them at times the most ethereally lovely places in God's creation.

I was talking recently with Fay Godwin about this unique and particular quality of light and Pont Scethin came into the conversation. She has a photograph of the place, the hills heavily black and clouded behind, middle distance a field of cloth-of-gold, and the elegance of the bridge, the exuberance of the foreground stream, picked out in a gleam of lichen on old stone, a crystal string of bubbles in peat-dark water.

"God forbid that anything should ever happen to that place!" was her instinctive response, the pain which is never far from her eyes focused on the thought.

Well, it has happened, and this is what it looks like now.

At the point where you cross the spur which ends in the Iron Age fort on Craig y Dinas and leave the harsh new track which the Welsh Water Authority, in its wisdom, has forced through to the high mountain lake of Bodlyn, there is a pile of alien aggregate dumped over the green moorgrass, dwarfing the standing stone which marks the old route. A few yards further and you look down the latter towards Pont Scethin, but its line is no longer to be seen. Instead, there is a scar, a dark slash,

a quagmire in places fifty yards wide. It ends a hundred yards beyond Pont Scethin. Walk along it and note the details. Those rocks breaking the surface of the moor, which the long-departed ice smoothed and ground to a fine sheen and in which the iron-hooped coach-wheels later wore their grooves—the caterpillar tracks of the JCB have crushed and shattered their way across them. More aggregate-from-God-knows-where is scattered about here and there to ease the juggernauts' progress. Almost certainly, archaeological remains have been affected, and the ancient trackway, which dates at least from the Bronze Age, has in places been erased. The sparse mountain vegetation will not recover in my lifetime. By the stone abutments of little Pont Scethin stand discarded drums of lubricant for the digging machines, and in the Afon Ysgethin likewise—in that pure, rapid stream, cast-off oil drums! On the greensward of Fay's photograph and across the first stones of the bridge concrete has been mixed, rubbish strewn, bottles smashed. Beneath it they have made a ford. On the other side, a hundred yards above, a great hole has been dug— quite possibly on the actual line of the old road, though it is now impossible to tell. The peat all around shimmers with the irridescence of spilt diesel fuel and stinks of the same and the monstrous machines which have made the mess stand idle nearby, claws stuck fast in the flesh of the moor. In the hole is a huge, shiny metal tank, a pipe, stop-cocks—all huge, huge—too huge ever to be fully concealed! It is to relieve pressure on the water mains, the pipework of which needs to be modernised and set in good order before being sold off. If it shows above ground when work is finished—as it clearly must—then planning permission will be needed, but this will be granted to the WWA retrospectively and automatically.

Is it the workmen's fault? It would be easy to point the finger at them, and some of their behaviour—if they were responsible—has certainly been remiss. But after the first rape, how easily does gang morality plunge. I talked to these men. They are sub-contractors, decent, tolerant, doing hard physical work often in bleak weather and under difficult conditions. Each one of them found it bewildering that they should have been ordered to put the tank here, that they should have been told to gain access by the route they did, that they should at no time have been overseen by WWA planners. But to question is to send tremors back along the chain of command, is to be difficult, and to be difficult is to be dismissed, which is a hard option in an area where there is no employment. In abjuring their responsibility to individual witness, undoubtedly they are culpable, But theirs is not the basic lack of perception towards that treasure of a landscape. They have worked in it, and their effect on it sits uneasily in their conscience as their consciousness of its worth grows. The real destructive arrogance has its root elsewhere.

The Welsh Water Authority, which is engaged in this work, has no need to gain planning approval for what it does to the landscapes through which it has rights of access and amongst which its interests lie. I remember the past atrocities it has perpetrated in the Welsh hills—the Bodlyn track, the tarmac road to Ffynnon Llugwy, the brutal destruction of archaeological remains in the bulldozing of improved access to Llyn Anafon. (After the furore caused by this latter, the WWA grudgingly acceded to the implementation of consultative procedures with the Gwynedd Archaeological Trust before future work at sensitive sites. At Pont Scethin, which of all sites is perhaps the most sensitive, these procedures were ignored.) The men who can countenance, condone and promote these actions are brutish. Invested with power, yet unaware of its effects and excused its responsibilities, their behaviour is an outrage. And these are the same people to whom the Government wishes to hand over private executive power!

Let's take this story as a metaphor. There is one image from this whole scene of physical and spiritual desolation which I cannot overstress—it is the mud, which is all-pervasive. The potency of that image haunts our dying century's consciousness. It transports us in an instant to the Somme and Passchendaele. The sepia images of nightmare flicker back at us—the slippery mud, the severed limbs, the putrescent flesh, the uniforms fouled, bloodied and torn. And the terrible antiphony of those names—what sleep here? What passion and suffering in this vale? Pro Deo, Rege, et Patria! Men doing their duty, acceding to force of circumstance, be it social, economic or whatever: "We shall miss you, we shall kiss you/But we think you ought to go . . .'

Let's keep the perspective, though—this is simply building-site mud, not that of a killing-field where 60,000 men—my paternal grandfather amongst them—will die in a day. And the jets which fill the shining chamber here will not hiss with Zyklon B, however much their technology repels. However close the crucial and underlying lack of life-reverence may be, there are no deaths involved here. Except, that is, for those insubstantial and unprofitable ones of beauty and hope.

Those are terms which Janet Haigh, whose dim sight surveyed the scene where this dereliction was to take place so many times from the hill above, would have recognised and understood. But we no longer live in her age, nor in that of her son.

We live in an age when public utilities such as water (the land for which was taken from people, for the most part by compulsion, for the greater good) must now be modernised and made efficient in order to be sold off for private profit. And when that has happened the land must be made to pay, so the public will be excluded.

We live in an age when so-called freedom fighters can explode bombs at Remembrance Day parades, can place explosives in the holds of aircraft so that the mutilated bodies of innocent victims are strewn by the hundred across just such bare hillsides as this, can commit rape, murder, infanticide, with American financial support and training and tacit British approval, against the free citizens of Nicaragua.

We live in an age when politicians, after a respectable gap of time, are rewarded with knighthoods for their serviceable lies; when politicians who have overthrown all parliamentary and environmental precedent in driving a new multiple-carriageway road through a National Park are rewarded for the same with the post of Secretary of State for the Environment; when political leaders in the West glorify, defend with sophistry, and allow to proliferate, weapons of genocide the use of which is totally against the words and spirit of the Geneva Convention; when our own political leader can lie about the details of an engagement which led to the deaths of 368 seamen of another nationality, and treat those deaths as a credit to her self-proclaimed martial spirit and beyond that an irrelevance—neither of which they can ever be.

You, if you have a trace of human fineness and sensitivity instead of the crudely corrupt self-interest, jingoistic blood-lust and philistinism which presently hold sway in our society, will know how long this bitter catalogue could stretch. So try to imagine something with me. This leader of whom I've been talking—I could almost envision taking her, for all that graceless and unnatural means of locomotion she has, up to Janet Haigh's stone, and pointing out this devastated scene to her: "If *you* seek a monument, look around!" I could *almost* imagine it, but not quite, for of course she has no place there, and that is the crucial point.

We are talking leaders, role-models, paradigms, examples. So how could this affected creature of the image-makers, with her deformed gait and undiscardable social armour, hope to reach even the modest heights which Janet Haigh, with her "dim sight and stiffened joints"

Oil drum, Afon Ysgethin.

regularly attained into extreme old age? Who, then—self-publicising stances aside—is the heroine? It would be impossible for Mrs Thatcher, in reflective solitude, to climb that hill. Which is, I think, cause for pity, because there is thus for her no hope of release from the artificiality, meanness, moral turpitude and narrowness of vision which her mode of life entails.

I never knew Janet Haigh. When she died I was a six-year-old slum-kid in Hulme—the seedier end of Manchester's Moss Side. When I was of an age to do so, I escaped its narrow, shabby streets to the hill-country of Derbyshire, then Wales, and the joy and the fulfilment their wildness brought me was liberating. I believe that you cannot go about *by yourself* amongst the hills without them having a beneficial, a salutary, an improving effect on your character. It is demonstrably so—take your arrogance, your self-conceit to the hills, and circumstances will soon conspire to make you lose them. How easy is it to stumble the wet miles down through the mist to shelter, lost and alone, with your self-congratulation intact? How ridiculous to retain the large sense of your own importance when you sit, dwarfed by your surroundings and silent and utterly stilled, in some mountain cwm?

I have no doubt whatsoever that Janet Haigh knew these things. (Yes, yes! Writers should not put thoughts into the minds of the dead, but will you, as readers, deny this?) But what of Mrs Thatcher? Where I cannot see her is climbing the hill of vision in penitence for the effect she has had upon it, learning her own inadequacies, seeing her mistakes, having imparted to her the humility and hence, perhaps, the magnanimity which can come from a simple-hearted response to natural beauty. The Nant Ysgethin provides one tiny example of what is happening throughout our hill-country. Elsewhere, the examples proliferate: forestry, farm-roads, second-home developments have all boomed in the last ten years, devastating the quiet places. And just as child-murder and child-abuse appear to have increased in our brutalised society under the Thatcher regimen, so too have activities like badger-digging in the countryside. Ten years ago I scarcely knew of one dug sett; nowadays the undug sett is an exception and the export trade to city dogpits flourishes.

Keith Thomas, in his monumental and masterful book *Man and the Natural World* (Allen Lane, 1983) writes that "nature parks and conservation areas serve a function not unlike that which toy animals have for children; they are fantasies which enshrine the values by which society as a whole cannot afford to live".

It is probably the most fatuous statement this excellent historian has ever made. Far from not being able to live by the values we enshrine within these places, it is vital to our continuing physical and spiritual health and even our existence that they are liberated and brought to play in society—the balance, the wisdom, the detachment, the quietude, the humility, the quiet courage as of a frail octogenarian labouring up a steep hill-slope, are as humanly indispensable as they seem—to our Government and its executives—unavailable.

Which is why, when I have sloughed through the mud which at present fouls Pont Scethin, I can arrive at Janet Haigh's stone and feel a profound sense of gratitude for her son's action in recording how, "even as late as her eighty-fourth year, despite dim sight and stiffened joints, [she] still loved to walk this way". For if ever an age needed that love of landscape expressing, and the human gifts such benediction brings, it is ours.

4: WORDS AND THINGS
— TEN BOOK REVIEWS

M. John Harrison climbing . . .

Climbers by M. John Harrison, Victor Gollancz £12.95
Unpublished, 1989

M. John Harrison.

The problem with the audience for climbing literature is that in large measure it is either unwilling or unable to read. I don't mean this in the literal sense, of course. Readers of climbing books are perfectly capable of scanning the simple text—as capable of that as they are of spelling out the big numbers with which the art of climbing is increasingly concerned these days: 7a; 6c red-pointed; Australian 33; French 8b; Stateside 5.14a. But my suspicion is that there are as few readers in this audience capable of de-coding a text whose argument is conducted in any but literal terms as there are climbers capable of assimilating the experience reductively denoted by those numbers.

In the last month or two this suspicion has been strengthened by the response accorded in some quarters of British climbing to the first "straight" novel by the established fantasy writer M. John Harrison. The editor of one of our domestic outdoor magazines, for example, dismissed it as "just journalism" and claimed to be able to identify himself in a character on the third page of the text. Such a reaction is asinine beyond belief, but the editor in question is not alone in his stupidity; a news writer for another magazine went into snarls of rage at what he saw as its pointless, depressing filth; yet another writer has indulged himself in the hoist-with-his-own-petard-cleverness of a poor parody (nothing so sad as

the unwitting parodist of parody!) Yet the text against which they froth, of which they make fun, or which they so idly dismiss is to my mind the finest piece of imaginative writing ever to have taken as its subject matter—on one level at least—the sport of rock-climbing. So where are they going wrong? And how fully achieved in absolute terms is climbing literature's best novel so far?

The focus, obviously, needs to fall more closely on what this novel is about, and the best way to start to clarify that is to say what it is not—title and appearances notwithstanding—about. It is not in any sense "about" climbing. It just happens to use as its framework the interweaving lives of a group of climbers from the grim valleys which run between West Yorkshire and Lancashire, and by peering at, pondering on, examining the quality of those lives, the nature of their worlds as they enmesh with each others' and with others' still in a wider spectrum of society, Harrison is attacking with a Lawrentian passion and moral energy what he sees—and yes, it is a vision which I happen to share, which predisposes me to like his book—as the abrogation of attentive, humane response to each other and to the nature of our surroundings.

Thus far, thus vague. It is a grand old theme, and the comparison with Lawrence is not at all gratuitous. *Lady Chatterley's Lover* — one of the great novels of the century and only cleared of obscenity in the famous trial of 1960—was written on much the same theme: the desiccation of human responsiveness, the loss of that "single, simple sensory organ we all used to have but now forget we possess". In *Climbers* Harrison repeats this last phrase twice, almost at either end of his book, and the space between is given over to rich improvisation and counterpoint around this refrain. Lawrence's novel's weakest sections are the preachiest ones—the theme has that danger. The first of his three drafts of *Lady Chatterley* is in some ways the most successful, because in that the narrative and its metaphors proceed unhindered. Harrison's post-structuralist fiction has virtually dispensed with narrative and the constant invitation it holds out to hector and harangue; instead it works through images which take new looks at a world gone stale, corrupt and seedy-sour, but which still holds out hope of redemption. His literary kinship in terms of method rather than theme is with J. G. Ballard and his drowned cities, lost aviators, concrete fortifications deserted amongst barren landscapes. *Climbers,* whilst forgoing the obvious disjunctions of Ballard's post-diluvian fantasies, expresses itself in a similarly quiet, wistful and acerbic tone. Its prose-rhythms are exquisitely modulated and impossible truthfully to parody. It takes an even more radical—because less distanced by depopulation— look than Ballard's at the grotesqueries of the everyday.

From the first chapter, entitled "Mirrors", Harrison is carefully distancing the reader from a simple, linear view of events. The first major gap between the reader and the old, unperceived reality is opened up by the brilliant device of a small boy's memory of an optical trick whereby people in a restaurant, reflected in a window, appear seated amongst the puddles of a car-park:

"They rubbed their hands and sat down to eat squares of dry battenburg cake and exclaim "Mm," how good it was. There they sat, out in the cold, and smiled at one another. They certainly were a lot more cheerful out there. The wind and rain had no power over them. A man on his own had a letter which he opened and began to read."

Already, Harrison's carefully regulated hatred of mindless enthusiasm for the unfruitful, tasteless commonplaces of modern living—relish the delicacy of that "dry"—is mingling with compassion for the solitariness and refusals in his characters' lives. As it proceeds, his text takes on the character of a powerful lament for the irrecoverable tactile, allied to an equally plangent threnody for the triviality and thinness of these characters' attempts at communication. In the rare moments when it becomes possible or vibrant, as with Sankey on the beach at Bamburgh just before his death, or in the Morecambe hotel room with Margaret offering herself dog-like, in pathetic mimesis of the sex magazines she and her husband Normal greedily devour, to the narrator ("It's best to get sex over with as quickly as possible in weather like this," she said. "Not that you don't enjoy it. But if you aren't quick you can get sticky."), the contact is broken as soon as established.

So what does climbing add to this scenario, that Harrison should seize on it as recurrent image?

"I had already seen that, to climbers, climbing was less a sport than an obsession. It was a metaphor by which they hoped to demonstrate something to themselves. And if this something was only the scale of their own emotional and social isolation, they needed—I believed then—nothing else."

Of Sankey again, the best, the one who has been climbing longest, amongst these climbers, "There was a kind of self-expatriation in the way he lived by himself in the cottage under the edge of the moor." After

his death, in a solitary, inexplicable fall, his friends can only find a single, polaroid photograph of him: "It was an eerie looking shot, its colours skewed by the fluorescent lighting, in which the climber could be seen suspended, not very high up, in a kind of threatening luminous greyness." Amongst his belongings, which two of them have to go through, everything is either depressingly ordinary or simply depressing—a small pile of worn records, a stack of magazines—aids to masturbation— under his bed.

Upon Sankey, the effects of the pornographies of eroticism and risk converge. His experience reduces to a soiled dimension of the tactile, a sad and further isolation, more divorced even from reality than the masturbatory fantasy one of the characters experiences of a girl on the motorway—the M5, of course, in the reductive coding given to these lines of communication— undressing in a moving caravan. Unshared, unfructifying, tactile and communicative potential decays and corrupts into a wasteland of exploitation, unreality and disregard. Climbing has resonances which these climbers barely hear; life has a richness of which those who move through it seem unaware, which they are unwilling to taste, from which they are as removed as if behind glass. There are depths of depressive insight here into the mean-spirited British society which Mrs Thatcher has encouraged, exploited and in large measure created, which will move the attentive reader to anger. *Climbers* is nothing if not a political, state-of-the-nation novel in the tradition of Dickens or the best of Mrs Gaskell.

But there are also, here and there amongst the intricacies of response between these men, women and children, patches of warmth, of rightness, of promise. Our lives may be spent driving along roads which are numbered A666 (the "Great Beast" resonance in this crucial juxtaposition is entirely relevant) instead of being called "Back Lorne Street"; we may be approaching "Earth, 1997," where "everyone lives under the ground and wears identical clothes. Something appalling has been done to their sexuality and they walk around staring directly ahead of themselves."; we may climb in places with names like "Running Hill Pits" or "Wilton Three", or worse, in filthy municipal dumps where tattered leaves from discarded wank-mags, cast-off children's clothing and used Durex spill and spew across the thrown-out, rotting vinyl furniture: but there are still redemptive moments like this:

"A waitress came over and said to his wife, 'I forgot to give you a spoon for your tart, love.' Gaz stared uncomprehendingly after her as she walked off."

There is still the astonishing, hopeful, Rousseauistic conceit of the Variety Club children left behind on the moors to grow wild. There is still the possibility of viewing even the unnatural, the artificial, the unappetising, with a clear, innocent eye again:

". . . little cakes iced in pastel colours—violet, yellow, and a strange, luminous green—and decorated with bits of crystallised peel."

Acts of attention like this become paradigmatic. "If only we could learn to look anew," they argue implicitly, "then we would revalue all that we do." As with what Gaz does at the butcher's: "Whatever he did at the butcher's was only tenable as a nightmare . . . With an unguarded comment he might show it up, to himself as much as anybody, as boredom and drudgery." As with Mick's job at the pipeworks: " 'I karate-kicked one of the cunts into six pieces.' He nodded. 'Six fucking pieces,' he repeated . . ."

The violence, the frustration, the vitiating obscenity of 'cunt' used in that context are not excused or approved, they are simply taken as feeding back into the image of a world where connection—between man and woman, between man and man, between adult and child—is consistently denied. The graphic, economical depiction of the attenuation of human sexual response is at the heart of this book. Harrison does not attempt to rescue—as Lawrence tries to do—'cunt' from its reductive usage. He enlists it as an index to the atrophying of perception, of understanding between the sexes. What hope in a world where the organs of most intimate and loving human connection are demeaned in the one gender to the most vitriolic term of abuse, in the other to the seediest exploitation, to being fed the tawdriest and most removed sensations, to being wanked off over servile, unreal images propagating the illusion of power—"double glossy pages of spread legs and splayed buttocks" in the porn-shop where the narrator works. "No room for anything else," the proprietor explains, "since Maggie got in!"

Perhaps the most striking image of all from this wasteland, this unreal city, comes from a child whose mother " . . . had got up, she told me, at five in the morning, to find that it had stuck elastoplast dressings on the limbs of its soft toys and immured them in the nine-inch gap between the double glazing panes. 'I don't know what he thought he was doing, do you?' She offered the child its drink, and it stared at her."

If the reader is to understand what the child is doing, or more properly what the image of the child's action is doing there in the text, then she or he must be prepared to read not just words but also the meaning of words, of images, must allow those to resonate back into the situations the novel presents for our understanding. (It seems to me no accident, incidentally, that the most intelligent and perceptive responses I've heard to this book have come from women. The misogynistic machismo which typifies so much of climbing culture— where the talk is all of conquest; where mountains are feminine and their peaks are to be "trodden"; where lists are substituted for the recall of experience, though "experience is not quantifiable in those terms: that much is evident"; where in their insistence on instant visual sensation rather than the holism created by accounts drawing on all aspects of the experience some of our sport's magazines come month by month more nearly to resemble pornography; where rock-climbs can be given names like "Cystitis by Proxy" or "Menopausal Discharge"—all this aligns itself all too nearly with this novel's social critique.)

There is nothing in Harrison's writing here which is mean or obscene other than the objects of his attack, and those who dismiss it as such miss the point entirely. On the contrary, *Climbers* has an urgent moral beauty and an extraordinary, inexhaustible richness of poetic texture. It grows better and better on re-reading. Its mirrors, memories and dreams reflect back in a way that only the most accomplished literature does into the nature of human life and contemporary society. Far from depressing me, it inspires that rich, hopeful anger which it is proper for good literature to arouse. The irony that a book not at all about climbing should have won the 1989 Boardman Tasker Award is too good to be missed. It should have won the Booker Prize as well. It's far better, more subtle and significant, than any of this year's contestants. But at least there's the consolation in that that climbing is not the only culture where literary judgement is sometimes at the mercy of an ignorant, inattentive and uncomprehending coterie.

Forbidden Land by Tom Stephenson, Edited by Ann Holt, Manchester University Press, £6.95
The Independent, 1989

In 1953 in Sussex two ramblers were shot in the face

Tom Stephenson.

by a spring gun. The gamekeeper responsible for setting the device was brought to trial on a charge of causing grievous bodily harm. His defence was that the apparatus—which a police witness told the court was correctly described as an alarm gun, and quite legal—had been mistakenly loaded with a twelve-bore instead of a blank cartridge. The keeper was acquitted.

This incident took place four years after the passage through Parliament of the National Parks and Access to the Countryside Act of 1949—a piece of legislation which Ann Holt, the exemplary editor of this, Tom Stephenson's last book, considers an opportunity lost, "even in the most favourable political climate for a root and branch change which had thus far come about", in the struggle to secure widespread public access to the mountain and moorland areas of this country. The shooting of the two ramblers illustrates in the most graphic and terrible manner the way in which recreational users of the countryside have become, in the demonology of the landowning interest, the equivalent of the poachers of previous centuries. The great work of Tom Stephenson's long life lay in poaching from that interest a bag not of concessions but of wholesale provisions for public access to our wild land.

At the time of his death, two years ago at the age of 94, Tom Stephenson left the manuscript of this book—which chronicles the continuing campaign to restore to the population of Britain the rights of access over uncultivated land which they had enjoyed before the Enclosure Acts—in a state nearing completion. His treatise has been admirably finished by Ms. Holt, and the volume rounded out to produce a tribute to a remarkable

character who is widely revered amongst the British outdoor movement.

Stephenson was the eldest of nine children of a Lancashire cotton operative. He left school at thirteen to work a 66-hour-week in a factory, took out a lending library subscription with his first week's wages, borrowed Darwin's *Origin of Species,* and ended up winning a scholarship to study geology at the Royal College of Science in London. As a conscientious objector in the Great War, he was sentenced to a total of three years' hard labour, two of which he served at Wormwood Scrubs before the general amnesty of 1919. Deprived thus of his scholarship he turned to politics, as an agent of the Labour Party, and then to journalism with the *Daily Herald* in its great days between the wars.

He was centrally involved in the tortuous political process which ultimately led to the 1949 Act and his account of it here—of the fudging and prevarication, the veiled initiatives of vested interest, the manipulations and machinations, the haplessness of men of principle when faced with parliamentary procedure—makes for a tale which is both essentially tragic and still very much of and for our time.

In the forty years since the National Parks and Access to the Countryside Act there have been two further major pieces of legislation in the same area of providing for the protection and public enjoyment of, and access to, open country. The first, the Countryside Act 1968, marked a slight advance over its predecessor. The second, the Wildlife and Countryside Act 1981, was a huge step backwards. There is now the threat of the Water Bill, which, if enacted and amongst its many other dangers, will have the gravest implications for continuing public access to parts of Derbyshire, Wales and the Lake District. And there is also the continuing problem of the political fixing of the Government's environmental quango, the Countryside Commission.

The value and strength of Stephenson's book is that it enables us to see these developments of the last forty years as the inevitable outcome of a historical process, and by doing so it gives us a clearer perspective on the motives and spheres of influence of those involved. It has to be said that here and there, particularly when dealing with the internecine strifes which vexed the outdoor world of the thirties and specifically on the subject of the 1932 Kinder Scout Mass Trespass, he can be tendentious. But generally, the clarity of argument and wealth of anecdotal material he adduces make it plain how weighty and committed a protagonist the outdoor movement lost with his death. Whilst the old *Herald* journalist will be writhing in his grave at the quality of proof-reading now allowed by a northern university press, the rest of us can permit ourselves the pleasure brought, as well as the concern aroused, by this fine old moral rambler's last bequest.

Fragile Edge by Maria Coffey, Chatto & Windus, £12.95
The Independent, 1989

Over the last few years there has grown up within the boundaries of mountaineering literature a sort of sub-genre—this may sound vaguely sexist but is intended as simply descriptive—written by women who either accompany men's Himalayan expeditions, or use them as a take-off point for their own trekking adventures. It has produced some remarkably good writing, far more precisely observant and empathic about, for example, native culture and European reactions to it in those regions than the general run of expedition literature, where flaccid and cliche-ridden gestures in this direction *en route* to the summits are the rule. The point at issue is probably that of direction of interest. The focus of books by writers like Linda Gill or Elaine Brook is not climbing—about which the amount that can be said is distinctly finite—but people, whether they be companions or those encountered along the way. That makes for a variousness which is not a characteristic feature of post-war mountain writing.

Maria Coffey's book adds an extraordinary new dimension to the genre, for its subject is the author's two-year love affair with the climber Joe Tasker, who disappeared with his partner Peter Boardman during an attempt on the North-east Ridge of Everest in 1982. If you were to judge this book by its jacket blurb, the direst potentialities would suggest themselves: "When Maria Coffey fell in love with Joe Tasker, she knew that he was already committed—to climbing the world's highest mountains . . . "etc, etc. Pure Mills-&-Boon-breathlessness, and it's a shame, because the book's far better than that. A writer of less delicate integrity than Coffey could have presented the story as one of a-man's-gotta-do-what-a-man's-gotta-do bloody-mindedness leading to a tragic-woman-nobly-grieving situation. She could probably have got away with that level of treatment too, given the inherent strength of the ingredients, and it's a mark of her achievement that she doesn't give in to the temptation.

Instead she gives us a real sense of a relationship which was never easy, where the balance was always tenuously held and where small infidelities were left undiscussed; where the context is as important as the internal dynamics; where the central subject's essential selfishness and apartness—not in a Lawrentian sense of detachment but in what seems at times a much more narcissistic concern with self-image—is accepted and observed with understanding and loving kindness. She presents us with a narrative where the mixture of tact and frankness is finely judged and the dangers of gushing are well avoided; and where all the temporary heroes of the mountain world are seen for the vulnerable, vivid, lively boys they were. And *were* is the operative word, because this is primarily a book about death, and about coming to terms with death.

Most of the male characters who stalk through its pages have gone—car-crashes, cancer, climbing—before the end of the period with which it deals, and several others have died since. It's a chronicle of deaths foretold, of lives lived on the brink, and of the difficulty of coming to terms with the waste of those outpourings of energy prematurely stilled. After Tasker's disappearance, Maria Coffey and Pete Boardman's widow Hilary made a pilgrimage to the base-camp on Everest from which the two climbers had set out on their fatal ascent:

"For many climbers I think Hilary and I represented a reality which they preferred to turn away from. They had spouses, lovers, families who would suffer if they died in the mountains . . . we were somehow stepping into their arena and bringing with us tangible proof of the pain they risked inflicting by indulging in such a dangerous sport."

Maria Coffey provides no answers to that implicit conundrum. But through her acceptance, and through a love which survived and transcended being in love, she offers a way out from the closed circle of opposition into which it could easily, and so often does, degenerate. Her book's written from the heart. That it is also enlivened by wise comprehension, perceptiveness and an earthy female humour (did you know that high altitude climbing has a deleterious effect on the libido of male mountaineers which often lasts for several weeks beyond return from expeditions?), is greatly to her credit. Her view of male ambition may not be as harshly mocking as the Wife of Bath's, or Dunbar's "tua mariit Wemen and the Wedo", but it's just as sound, and its humanity glows in your mind at the end.

The Mystery of Mallory and Irvine by Tom Holzel and Audrey Salkeld, Jonathan Cape, £12.50

The Independent, 1986

There is a school of writing which holds that assertion and its repetition will alone suffice to convince. Publishers love it. The more dillettantish the author and theme, the more outraged the informed reaction, the bigger the drum roll and consequent balance of profit will be. You only have to consider the phenomenal success of Erich von Daniken to realise how the principle operates. Take an author with a limited stock of arcane knowledge, add a fine, wild theme to which it can be applied, stir in the vital ingredient of a common man scoffing at the experts' lack of perspicacity, submerge all these in prose of unplumbable mid-Atlantic dullness, and see how it sells—*Chariots of the Gods, The Bermuda Triangle,* and now *The Mystery of Mallory and Irvine!*

At one point in this book the authors, with critical acumen notably lacking elsewhere in their text, exclaim that "if there is a puzzle about this, it is that there should be any puzzle at all." Their so-called "Mystery of Mallory and Irvine" has been going the rounds of mountaineering circles for over 60 years, since the disappearance of the two men at around the 28,000ft contour on the North Ridge of Mount Everest in 1924. The question—mystery is too grandiose a term for the kind of death which is one of the commonplaces of Himalayan climbing—is that of whether or not, at a date 29 years before its known first ascent, one or both of them reached the summit of Everest. Mr Holzel believes that Mallory did but Irvine did not, and proceeds to give us a quasi-factual account of the climb on page 289 of a 294-page narrative—a tactic entirely in keeping with the genre to which the book belongs:

"Splitting up at 1pm, Mallory quickly raced up the final pyramid of Everest's summit. Irvine returned past the First Step and started his descending traverse of the North Face slabs. At 2pm a snow squall started. It was not bitter enough to prevent Odell from clambering out on to the North Face for an hour in hope of aiding the climbers' return, but it dusted the down-sloping slabs with a slick surface that would prove fatal to Irvine . . .

Despite the manner of its presentation, this quotation contains not so much as a single unambiguous, incon-testable fact. It is conceived in the imagination of Mr Holzel and the balance of probability weighs heavily against it on almost every point. Conjecture of this nature is harmless enough—in a novel based on the story it would be entirely appropriate—and it will offer some solace to those who would like to believe that the sacrifice—as the generation to which Mallory and Irvine belonged would have had it—of these two brave men was not in vain. (In the correspondence columns of *The Times* recently the old controversy was aired again and one of the responses revealed a willingness on the part of Irvine's nephew to believe in just such a version.) It may even have happened—I would like to think it did—but there is not a shred of clear evidence to support it.

The likeliest interpretation, desire and other extraneous emotions put aside, is that the tired Mallory and inexperienced Irvine, their oxygen running out, perished as a result of the storm which closed around them and which would have been far more severe on their exposed ridge than at the tent in which Odell took shelter. Not themselves being mountaineers, this simple latter point seems to have evaded the authors of the book. Instead, they concern themselves with equations concerning speeds, times, rate of flow from oxygen equipment (which Irvine had modified on the mountain, in consequence of which the manufacturers disclaimed responsibility for it and considered that it would inevitably have leaked). It all puts me in mind of that grand old mountaineering chestnut, Naismith's Rule, which states that you must allow an hour for every two-and-a-half miles covered, and another for every 1,000ft of ascent. If mountaineering could only be reduced to such a formula, we could get our robots to do it for us!

Its one or two original, if inapposite, ideas apart, the book draws extensively on familiar material. There is an obsession with the minutiae of controversy tedious even at the time of its most active pursuit. The interminable library of Everest books is here allied to those even more prolix volumes on Bloomsbury and its fringe. The authors obviously have a subliminal list of all those who wanted to bugger, or be buggered by, George Mallory—who by all contemporary accounts was totally uninterested in this activity. But the preoccupation unpleasantly haunts the book, which drags in lengthy quotation from earlier and better books and remnants of biographical work on Mallory to stretch itself, regardless of narrative flow, to inordinate length. As is usual in these cases, a lengthy critical apparatus is included to give the appearance of academic respectability without any of its rigour. There is the odd Cartland-esque passage to ease it along here and there:

"They had fallen in love in springtime. Now, each year, as the air warmed and the first scented blossoms appeared, it seemed to George like a reaffirmation of their love and he needed her with him to relive some of the magic of their early romance."

There are excursions up every possible blind alley which will defer the vacuity of the conclusion for a few pages longer. But at the end the purpose of the whole book reveals itself in Holzel's mission, under the auspices of the "Atlantic Alpine Club" and various television companies, to search for the cameras of Mallory and Irvine, develop their film and prove his case, to be expounded at further length in this book's promised sequel, *The Search for Mallory and Irvine*. So we have a saga that could run and run. The specialist magazines should take its arguments apart piece by self-contradictory piece. There is scope for whole books to be written in rebuttal. It could signal a revival of the British publishing industry. But there is something in it which is death to the spirit of mountaineering and the dispassionate search for truth, on both of which subjects Mallory and Irvine might have had a great deal to say. To borrow one of the present authors' recurrent tactics and put thoughts in their heads, they would certainly have scorned this muddle-headed and fatuous piece of irresponsible Himalayan historiography.

Touching the Void by Joe Simpson, Jonathan Cape £10.95
The Independent, 1987

Why is writing—don't bestow upon it the accolade of "literature"—about sport generally so dull? Take cricket, which has, if reviewers of sporting books are to be believed, the best and most substantial body of writing of any sport. Its so-called classics, with very few exceptions (most notably CLR James's *Beyond a Boundary*), leave me quite cold, and the modern exponents feted by the reviewers as immensely talented or even great are invariably a disappointment. There was, for example, an extravagently praised volume by Peter Roebuck a couple of years ago with some limp title I now forget. I read it with high expectations. It put me in mind of Pope's strictures from *The Dunciad*:

"Here one poor word an hundred clenches makes,
And ductile dulness new meanders takes;
There motley Images her fancy strike,
Figures ill pair'd, and similies unlike.
She sees a Mob of Metaphors advance,
Pleas'd with the madness of the mazy dance:"

There's a school of mountain writing to which those lines apply equally well. The root problem, of course, in writers and reviewers alike, is a confusion of the factitious with the genuinely creative. We fail to temper our craving for novelty with a cool eye cast over the dimensions of human experience. The media demand image, image presupposes vanity, and vanity precludes wisdom. Our failure to recognise the essential insignificance of the sport itself results in gross distortions of language and perspective. Deploy the martial rhetoric as you will, the contexts remain trivial. These same truths are evident in books about mountaineering, writing about which actually has a better claim than cricket for pre-eminence amongst sporting "literatures".

But just occasionally, amongst the glib, smooth tales of "conquest" and success, something else gleams through—almost invariably as a result of the demands of harsh environments upon the human spirit and the latter's reaction to them. Perhaps disaster has become a prerequisite for the production of good mountaineering writing. Personal experience of disaster is the subject faced by Joe Simpson in *Touching the Void*—in doing so he has produced a book which is almost unbearable in its communication of the pain implicit in the necessity to endure, and told a story which, through fortitude and moral choice rather than posture, is perhaps even heroic.

The story is simple: in 1985 Simpson and Simon Yates set off to attempt the unclimbed West Face of the 21,000ft Siula Grande in the Peruvian Andes. Simpson's account of their ascent is succinct, exciting, and also remarkably fresh, unpresumptuous, aware of the nature of the activity in which they're engaged:

"If you succeed with one dream, you come back to square one and it's not long before you're conjuring up another, slightly harder, a bit more ambitious—a bit more dangerous. I didn't like the thought of where it might be leading me. As if, in some strange way, the very nature of the game was controlling me, taking me towards a logical but frightening conclusion . . .

The account lasts for barely twenty pages of exemplary,

tight-paced narrative. Thereafter, the excruciating detail of nightmare takes over. The descent from the summit is along a perilous ridge. In the course of it Simpson falls, shattering a leg at 19,000ft. The sequence of events which follows is told both in Simpson's words and in masterfully counterpointed versions of Yates's response—the latter written, in fact, by Simpson:

"He told me very calmly that he had broken his leg. He looked pathetic, and my immediate thought came without any emotion, You're fucked, matey. You're dead. . ."

Despite that knowledge, they carry on down, Simpson in agony, Yates hugely competent, supportive, but aloof, until, in the night and the howling storm, on one of the final lowers to the glacier Simpson goes over an ice-cliff and hangs helpless in space. Above him, his fragile steps in the snow collapsing and Simpson's whole weight on the rope, Yates is forced into accepting the sole and unthinkable course of action open to him. He cuts the rope.

"There had been nothing else left to me, and so I had gone ahead with it. I had done it, and done it well. Shit! That takes some doing! A lot of people would have died before getting it together to do that! I was still alive because I had held everything together right up to the last moment. It had been executed calmly. I had even carefully stopped to check that the rope wasn't going to tangle and pull me down. So that's why I feel so damned confused! I should feel guilty. I don't. I did right. But, what of Joe . . ."

Simpson plunges into a crevasse but lands, without further injury, on a snow bridge in its depths. When morning breaks, Yates searches for him, sees the apparently unplumbable crevasse, and concludes that Simpson is dead. Himself close to exhaustion, he returns to camp.

Meanwhile, by desperate expedients Simpson contrives to escape from the crevasse. For three days he crawls down the glacier, alone, dehydrated, racked by pain, snowblind, infection setting in, occasionally delirious, always with the choice confronting him of ceasing to struggle, of accepting the long sleep in the snow, but always holding to the harsher option:

"The game had taken over, and I could no longer choose to walk away from it."

As his ordeal nears its end and he weakens almost to immobility, the time-factor increases narrative tension. Yates and their camp-companion are preparing to leave for Lima. On the last night the reader, but not Simpson-as-victim, knows that if he sleeps he will die. He crawls on and, crying out to the night, is heard and brought to safety.

So much for bald narrative. Interwoven with it are strands of moral choice (but not judgement), intellectual honesty and rigour, precisely realised settings of vastly indifferent natural hostility and agonising presentations of states of human consciousness which most of us will be thankful never to have to experience, and which set this apart from other "sporting" books. It is certainly the finest piece of writing around the subject of greater-ranges mountaineering to have appeared since the last war, but it is rather more than that. On a technical level, it is a remarkably skilful piece of narrative art. On a human level, it is a book which searches the basic morality and lovingkindness of each individual reader. It seems to me on every level an outstanding literary achievement within its genre, and all the more distinguished for being the first book of a 26-year-old writer.

A Dream of White Horses by Edwin Drummond, Diadem £10.95
Climber and Hillwalker, 1988

Any consideration of climbing writing over the last twenty years has to take the contribution of Edwin Drummond into account. It is gratifying therefore that Ken Wilson at Diadem has gathered it into a single volume interlaced with new commentary material, and thrown it out into opinion's sea to discover on what shore it fetches up this time.

The climbate, as Drummond would have it, has grown more favourable to him these last few years. His former adversaries subside into the swell of memory, and his breakers surging against their codes are little lapping waves now too—*that* world's grown old.

There are problems, of course, with Drummond's writing. His insistent preoccupation with the agonistic engenders in many an irritation or even a dislike. Every page carries its overburden of the first person singular, like capitals for the deity in an illuminated manuscript. It is writing from the confessional, where pride and the priest battle for supremacy and even the language fractures, compresses and distorts—necessarily when it is the writer, bound to the rack of experience, who is setting on the inquisition of his art.

At times the effects have a fine, grim accuracy in communication; at other times they are—just effects. Come up against a compression like "warmoistasapie" and you shrug or even retch. Follow a narrative like "Great Wall" or "Mirror, Mirror" and the jewels drip through your fingers. He is everywhere his own man, yet compelled to perform, perhaps for us, and continually enraged by any affront or refusal to his skinless, naked sensitivity.

In these deconstructed essays, poems, letters and fragments there is a strong element of what Milan Kundera identifies as the "mania not to create a form but to impose one's self on others. The most grotesque version of the will to power." At the back of them somewhere lurks Celine, or Dostoevsky's underground man. His best writing is pathologically self-obsessed, the solipsist on the rock-face recording sensation in exquisitely remembered detail. This, given his main context, is as it should be. But when the externalities of human contact or diverse experience intrude, the fine intensity of that grip slackens. All manner of insecurity, animus, exploitation or desire for dominance then show through in "over-elaborated analyses" and wickedly-barbed sly diminutions of the character of others (especially women and those he might deem rivals). There are times when the book does not make pleasant reading, when the soft-spoken coercions of his polemic against normative behaviour display too livid an underbelly to our view. Or when it misses gear and reveals a slightly pathetic, self-justifying indignation: ". . . caught shoplifting three rurps, after having spent ninety dollars on gear for this climb."

The most anomalous essay here is the extended review of my book *Menlove,* originally set up by Ken Wilson for the *Alpine Journal* and rejected by that august periodical as being, in the words of its editor, "incomprehensible gibberish". The petty politics of our small world aside, it isn't that, and a short review here isn't the place to reply fully to it. But as a piece of critical writing it does have crippling deficiencies. Its thesis in part takes the hint from Eliot on Coleridge on Hamlet (Drummond is nothing if not an adept manipulator of sources). Its method is to misrepresent arguments and misquote texts to an extent which leaves me with serious doubts as to Drummond's capacity to ponder others' points of view:

". . . according to Perrin, a 'dirty puff of smoke' is flatulence".

I search my own text for any such fatuous suggestion and can find none. Almost every other quotation he uses is significantly inaccurate:

"Perhaps I have read into his book dangers that exist only in my own vision," he writes later. For 'dangers', substitute 'passages'! The essay is a startling and fascinating presentation of Edwin Drummond's world-view; it has very little to do with Menlove Edwards or my book about him.

For all the disagreements and criticisms this book will arouse—and you should feel no qualms about making them for it sets out those terms of reference for itself—it shouldn't be ignored. And for all the overwrought nature of its prose and the paradoxically thin poetic voice—Drummond's poems gain greatly from his performance of them (the agonistic element again) but shrink in the harsh noon light of the printed page—you should persevere with it. He is certainly unique, and that this book was not even shortlisted by the Boardman Tasker Prize judges last year was nothing short of scandalous. In terms of lasting quality, all irritations put aside, it was the only entry in the running. Perhaps it just insisted too loudly on its own superiority, causing those with the power to bestow instead to react and reject. If so, Edwin of all people should have appreciated the joke . . .

The Countryside We Want, edited by Charlie Pye-Smith and Chris Hall, with photographs by Fay Godwin. Green Books £6.50
The Independent, 1988

The manifesto is a sadly underrated and abused literary form. At its best, the necessary compression and commitment to perceived truths can produce work of extraordinary gnomic resonance. More usually it is harnessed to the sort of meretricious mendacities which have devalued British party politics over the last decade. The deciding factor is surely whether it is designed as an organ of electoral expedience, or as the expression of highly-charged belief. This slim volume, sub-titled "A Manifesto for the Year 2000", stands firmly within the

Chris Hall.

latter category. In a proper sense, it is millenarianist, looking forward to a period of benign management and control for our ravaged and vanishing countryside. But its writers are no hieratic apocalyptists—far from it, they are sane, sound and angry polemicists who have looked long and hard at the policies particularly of the last three Conservative administrations as they affect the environment, have liked very little of what they have seen, and have something substantial and considered to suggest in their place.

One of the most demeaning facets of late twentieth-century life is the exhaustion of the human capacity for moral outrage. Our empathic or subliminal guilt leaves us impotent of protest. A race that could visit on its fellow-members Auschwitz and Hiroshima can rely, by way of response to what it does to the natural environment, on the merest cynical shrug. We are wearied rather than appalled by atrocities.

In the scale of things it doesn't much matter that 95 per cent of flower-rich meadows have disappeared since the war, that hedgerows are grubbed out and wetlands drained, that acid rain continues to fall and that the government, unprecedentedly, stuffs its environmental quangoes with agricultural, silvicultural and landowning interest in order to stifle potential opposition to its designs upon the landscape. We are even, I suspect, wearied by those who take up the flag on our behalf. Environmentalism and conservation may be buzz words, but they're not for us, they're for sandalled and bearded

dullards throat-deep in statistics, or for squeaky young things in bright print dresses just down from Benenden to work in the voluntary sector for a year or two. It's nothing to do with us! Meanwhile, our country liberties erode.

What we could—and should—do about that is the subject of *The Countryside We Want,* expressed in a series of brilliant individual essays which seethe with furious insights into the effect of political shortsightedness and mismanagement on our countryside. Much of the specific and statistical material adduced is already well-known. A great deal of it came into the public domain four years ago when the Nature Conservancy Council for once broke free of its shackles and published the disturbing (and officially disregarded) report entitled *Nature Conservation in Great Britain.* Conscientious (or renegade) politicians—Sir Richard Body is a particularly good example—have brought other abuses, recently and notably in the matter of pesticides, to the fore. What is new about the stance of Chris Hall and Charlie Pye-Smith is its urgency and its appeal that the safeguarding of the land be referred as much to the domain of moral argument as to the ambiguous one of scientific analysis. The stratagem they repeatedly identify as a crucial weakness in the conservationists' tactics is a willingness to fight the oppressor on his own ground: to argue figures of which he is the master; to discuss economics where the real issue is danger to the population; to question industrial need when the crying demand is public amenity. In a country where almost all the senior conservational agencies have long been infiltrated and controlled by interests inimical to their proper operation, the point could not be more apposite:

". . . the freedom on which the countryside's present owners and managers insist is the freedom to deny us access to the land, to deprive us of the rich and variegated landscape we once enjoyed, to rear animals in conditions many of us find abhorrent, to douse the fields with chemicals that kill wildlife and pollute drinking-water. These are not freedoms we feel called upon to respect."

The arguments marshalled together here, with luck, attentiveness and widespread dissemination, will bring about an effective rather than tokenist revolution in our attitude—in the respect we show—towards the natural world. And as commentary on the vibrant words, there is a set of 24 black-and-white photographs by Fay Godwin—potent images of beauty and care resonating against others of degradation and offence, and capturing the whole tone of this marvellous, inspiring manifesto.

Native Stones by David Craig, Secker & Warburg, £10.95
The Independent, 1987

I started out by liking the flavour of this book and ended up with a severe case of indigestion, or that mixture of incredulity and dreadful glee which the boy feels at the end of "The Emperor's New Clothes", when the consciousness dawns of bare-arsed pretence. Wynford Vaughan Thomas, in his first radio broadcast, interviewed a gardener who gave the same response to every question: "It was the manure, Mr Thomas!" In this case the manure is David Craig's prose-style, self-consciously "poetic", with an insistent shrill energy and metricality which ultimately jars—at ten pages you marvel, after two hundred you fume. And it grows similes!

Similes in an appropriate context are all to the good, but let them proliferate and the clamour of the things becomes unbearable. They stud Craig's text like dead mosquitoes on a Greek hotel room wall. Scrutinize them and all the evidence is of imagination in an advanced state of dislocation or decay. Pulling on a fingerhold on a rock-climb has never felt to me "like swallowing a dram of Laphroaig" (nor even one of Bell's). The lichenous surfaces of stones do not to me "suggest the stomachs of very old Mediterranean tramps". Nor do climbers on a cliff-face seem "like parasites in the pelt of a bear". It is impressive enough as a performance to sustain that level of precisely-phrased invention through two hundred rambling pages, but it traduces imaginative integrity, is divorced from clear perception of object and theme, and ends up as little other than literary display—"creative writing", self-styled and so-called.

This "book about climbing" is essentially a book about David Craig, the Scottish Marxist critic and poet, who took up the activity in his forties and has progressed since then to the status of a "middling sort of club climber" and inveterate seeker-out of celebrities from past eras. His book is a discursive—deconstructed, if you like—patchwork of previously published pieces from poetry magazines, journals and climbing publications, stitched together with some new material and biographical anecdotes and poems. It is by turns fascinating,

infuriating, precious, pretentious, sycophantic, sneering, wise, ignorant, partisan, detached and profound. Its sense of the activity, and Craig's own time and place within it, is bizarre. If he truly climbed, for example, in the style of the 1960s—the lie to which claim is given by the picture opposite page 118, where the degree of protection is very definitely 1980s—then given the number of falls he appears to take he would by now be dead.

Likewise, Craig's judgements on mountaineering literature often blend eccentricity with a sycophantic arrogance. His jibe at W. H. Murray's attempts to describe mystical experiences—a term the import of which Craig, as an enthusiastic atheist, might well affect not to understand—runs thus: "lofty chimeras . . . Now we see them, now we don't". This is merely cheap, and unworthy of a supposedly serious critic. His remarks on Coleridge and Wordsworth are no more sound, and are based on very forced distinctions. The same vein of dismissive arrogance outcrops in his animadversions upon modern climbing controversies, the facile application to which of Yeats's Olympian sneer, "Great hatred, little room", denies the depths of affection and concern of which they are born and is as inapposite, as much of an ignorant pose, as was the charge in its original context.

The most interesting aspect of this book is its autobiographical content: Craig's injured daughter lying within lick of the tide; his possessive cry as his son climbs solo beyond his grasp; or his twenty-year-old self tongue-tied and aiming to deceive before the potent, bourgeois, Scottish father—all these are images of extreme horror which go some way towards explaining, and thus relieving, the artificial and unsympathetic tenor of much of his text. For all its oddities and self-indulgence, it sticks in the mind and, for me, recalls another writer from by the Mounth and the Mearns whose work is informed by the image of the hills—Lewis Grassic Gibbon and his great trilogy, *A Scots Quair*. If Craig could have acquired some of the rich aptness and integrity, rather than just the incantatory force, of Gibbon's prose; some of his magnanimity, clarity of vision and purpose; if he could have put aside the little, grudging self, the harsh moral judgements and the *ex cathedra* atheism, he might have written a very good book indeed. As it is, within its own idiom it stands as an interesting, irritating attempt around a grand theme, spoilt by the forced nature of its perceptions and a reach that too far exceeded its author's grasp.

Norman Collie: A Life in Two Worlds by Christine Mill, Aberdeen University Press £14.90

The Independent, 1987

Some books charm by their treatment of subject, others by the subject itself. The principle holds particularly true of life-writing. Hazlitt on Napoleon or Boswell on Johnson would score few marks for objectivity, but their artistry is immense (so, for that matter, are their subjects). They are very good examples of what Robert Gittings termed "impure" biography—a category to which most of the classic or classical biographies belong. For life-writing to be "pure", on the other hand, the special pleading must be put aside and a tone of affectionate neutrality allowed to preside. It is something which Christine Mill scrupulously maintains throughout her excellent life of Norman Collie.

Anyone who has heard of Norman Collie these days probably belongs to one of the two worlds—organic chemistry and mountain exploration—of this book's title. They may have wondered about Moss Ghyll's Collie Step, or know of the first ascent of Ben Nevis's Tower Ridge. Or they may have a dim recollection of an eerie little anecdote in Richard Hillary's poignant and humane war memoir, *The Last Enemy*. It tells of a visit to the Sligachan Inn in early March, 1940:

"We were alone in the inn save for one old man who had returned there to die. His hair was white, but his face and bearing were still those of a mountaineer, though he must have been a great age. He never spoke, but appeared regularly at meals to take his place at a table tight-pressed against the window, alone with his wine and his memories. We thought him rather fine."

After one escapade amongst the hills, Hillary and friend recounted it to the hotel landlord:

"His sole comment was 'Humph,' but the old man at the window turned and smiled at us. I think he approved."

He certainly would have approved, for Norman Collie, whom it was, is one of the great names in that Second Empire of mountain exploration which spanned the turn of the century. His journeys and discoveries, not only amongst his native hills of Scotland, Skye and Cumbria, but further afield in the Alps, the Himalayas, the Rockies and Arctic Norway, contributed greatly to the mapping and geographical understanding, and hence the further history, of those regions.

Curiously, the chapters which deal with this province of Collie's life are the dullest in the book. Ms Mill maintains her detachment towards her subject but gushes rather over his mountains. Her fascination with what is strange and entrancing about Collie is displaced by her enthusiasm for what may be more familiar to Christine Mill. But Collie's character in its other aspects quickly reasserts itself. From dull travel narrative we turn time and again as attention begins to wander to anecdotes of a scientific eccentric. There is the wonderful irony of this lifelong and reclusive bachelor starting a teaching career—which led to the first Chair of Organic Chemistry in University College, London—at Cheltenham Ladies' College. There is the collector of Chinese jade in his Gower Street rooms:

". . .everything was jumbled together. Books piled over the floors might rub shoulders with porcelain or bronze objects. Delicate jade bottles and jars peered out of old, and often dusty, cabinets. Yet everything was so placed as to pick up and repeat colour and lighting on a scheme designed for his own pleasure."

There is the scientific mind in its working environment, working with Nobel Prizewinner William Ramsay on the discovery of what are delightfully termed "the noble gases"—argon, helium, krypton, xenon and neon. Collie's scientific career in fact was most distinguished. Not only was he centrally involved in the work which led to the discovery of this group and its inclusion in The Periodic Table, he was also the first person practically to demonstrate the neon light and X-ray photography. The conditions under which the necessary experimentation takes place are a combination of Heath Robinsonism and great practical efficiency:

"It was to me a fascinating sight to see him . . . making the apparatus he used in studying the action of heat in the ammonium and phosphonium compounds in which he was interested at that time. He frequently asked me to watch him and I was very intrigued by the fact that he invariably did his glass-blowing with his lighted pipe in his mouth. He strongly advised me to take lessons in glass-blowing, saying that it was an invaluable accomplishment to a chemist."

This is the same man who proposed Aleister Crowley

for the Alpine Club, who lived on whisky and tobacco, whose friendships cut across the social barriers which bedevilled the society of his age and whose most constant companion (by whose side he lies buried in Struan Kirkyard on Skye) was a Highland peasant; who set sail for New Zealand in the 1930s taking only his pipe and the clothes he stood in; who met the Great Grey Men of Ben MacDhui, and believed in fairies and the Loch Ness monster; whose "unusual eyes with the iris both pale blue and sandy brown gave him an air of mystery and association"; who found the Cioch of Sron na Ciche and a cave on the coast of Donegal into which he persuaded his boatmen to take him after seals:

"For over 300 yards a tunnel stretched deep into the cliffs and the daylight slowly faded. The tunnel widened into a vast chamber from where other tunnels branched out into the bowels of the mountain . . . a thousand feet of rock lay between them and the sun."

I don't believe the latter exists. It, and perhaps also the Grey Man, were probably teases on Collie's part against his literal-minded and credulous friends. But with both tales you respond to the warm, strange ingenuity of Collie himself. And having done so, feel grateful to Christine Mill for introducing you into the company of this fascinating and near-forgotten man.

The Pure Land by John Beatty, Thames & Hudson, £12.95
The Independent, 1988

One of the main problems for those people whose outlook can broadly be categorised as environmentalist is that, because of the almost inevitable frequency of their complaining they are identified—and hence, perhaps, rather too easily dismissed—as a negative force. The capital which populist politicians can make of this is obvious, and yet the threats to our wild and beautiful environments so proliferate that there is no escape from the difficulty. The necessity is to strike the right balance between the critical and the celebratory, and that's far, far easier said than done. We can all respond positively to, say, an Ansel Adams photograph of the High Sierras. But is the assurance we thus gain of the existence of beauty counterpointed by an urgent desire to ensure its continuance? I'm not at all sure.

What I am convinced about is that when faced with a collection of photographs of the quality which the young wilderness photographer John Beatty has assembled in *The Pure Land* (the book is actually sub-titled "A Celebration of Wild Places"), a clear choice is posed. We can either see them as pretty pictures to flick through, criticise on the grounds of relative quality, and generally accept as aesthetically affirmative. Or we can take the pictures and the minimal text which accompanies them as being paradigmatic—the example they hold out to us being that of the active quest after the experience of natural beauty which implies a passionate desire for its preservation.

To take the first point—the "pretty pictures" slant—every member of that outdoor and mountaineering fraternity amongst which Beatty chiefly moves seems to possess a camera nowadays, and the technical expertise to turn out competent pictures (generally to accompany highly incompetent text). So these *aficionados*—as they have clamoured to do in the savagely incestuous review-columns of the outdoor press—will take Beatty's book to obvious task: the printing quality's not as good as Mondadori or Dai Nippon have produced for those extravagant Sierra Club volumes of the past; the short-comings of the 35mm format show through; they're snapshots; he's no Ansel Adams or Fay Godwin. So the complaints run on, and Beatty's publishers have not helped him to counter these charges. Too many of the compositions are ruined by being spread across the gutter, by awkward juxtaposition, cluttered layout and even, here and there, odd failures in the colour register. When I showed the book to Fay Godwin recently, her immediate response was: "I'd have been furious! Thames & Hudson have just not treated him as a serious photographer."

That's probably true, and it's an enormous pity, but don't get the idea that the book is wholly damned by it. The eye can be blinded by too critical an outlook. Beatty's photographs remain the most ambitious and serious attempt at pictorial representation of the beauty, value and spirit of the truly wild places to have been published in Britain for many years. His book is a considerable achievement, and what make it so are the energy, good fortune and ubiquitousness of his quest. The key to the real quality of his work as photographer and writer is that of *being there*. In even the simplest terms of geographical range, these photographs are extraordinary, travelling from the Derbyshire hills to the Alps, from Skye to Spitzbergen, Greenland to Connemara, Colonsay to California, South Georgia to the Staffordshire Roaches.

But they're not simply holiday snapshots taken in those places. One of their identifying characteristics is their expression of the natural cycles in all moods and adversities, and their precise location of man amongst them. In plate 43, the fragile spars of sledge-sails bend before the wind at sunrise on the Greenland ice-cap, spindrift snaking across the vast plain of snow. The two human figures are hunched and bowed against it, pointing up the indifferent ferocity of this natural splendour. In plates 54 and 55, by contrast, the photographer intrudes himself into the composition to focus attention on the falling water which he has rendered as brilliant, ethereal shafts of light. He uses stance as statement—watchful, reverential. It could have been appallingly gauche. It takes a huge risk and invites scoffing negativity. But through its absolute wholeheartedness it works, and creates a discourse beyond the simple image which is continued through the variety of involvements in landscape which Beatty portrays: mountaineers on sunset ridges; a figure traversing the recesses of a Colorado river-gorge; puffins coming in to land; a face reflected in driftwood firelight; a woodcutter solidly present in the grainy twilight of the forest. It's needless to look here for the compositional perfection, gravity and sustained effort of interpretation which mark out the traditionally great landscape photographers. In these moments and their cumulative wholeness of response to the wild places, in their fractured brilliance of realisation, there's a rare homage to the vital role the wilderness can play in our lives. They would calm even Swift's soul, and lead him out fearless and pure-sighted again on to the river-bank and under the wide skies.

Tribal Harrogate

Climber and Hillwalker, 1989

We're a migrant tribe, our village decamping and descending around a strict rota of venues throughout the year. There's Buxton every other March, Newstones on May evenings, August Chamonix, but none of these trips to the hallowed hunting grounds leads to a more bizarre or anomalous destination than the yearly November pilgrimage to Harrogate for the C.O.L.A. Trade Fair.

The initials are misleading. It's nothing to do with sticky American drinks in fertility-goddess bottles. This is the annual jamboree of the Camping and Outdoor Leisure Association, and for the last fifteen or so years that increasingly large sector of the climbing population which doesn't subscribe to Monday-to-Friday and nine-to-five has striven to subvert and re-direct what began as a thoroughly respectable and staid period of time allotted to the pursuit of mutually-favourable contracts and the display of new equipment, and has re-written the script so that it's now—beneath the continuing surface veneer of businesslike respectablity—the biggest thrash of them all, COLA! Your tongue thickens with the fur of a three-day-hangover almost before it's licked round the word. It's hospitality with a Capital 'H'; it's the climbing world's version of enterprise culture; it's the integration of those who make with those who do; it's booze, glitz, glamour and it all takes place in Harrogate as the November frosts spiral the sycamore keys down upon the verges of The Stray, the residents quit the benches of their Indian Summer for the softer seats of the hotel lounge, and the commissionaires huddle together behind doors amongst the palm trees in the controlled climate of the Royal Exhibition Halls.

Which is where the tribe congregates by day, and where the new arrivals head to bluff or demand or charm their way in, to be tagged and numbered, categorised and passed as welcome—be they press, exhibitor, visitor, or plain guest celebrity.

You know what climbers are like—you meet them on the crags or out on the hills, in cafes and bars, hair blown in the wind and their clothes ripped and stained. Every one of them you ever met or heard of is here, with the magic wand of commerce having waved transfiguration across them. Pat Littlejohn, massive forearms folded confidently across his chest, is talking rucksacks on the Karrimor stand; Lord Bonington de Caldbeck is posing as a pin-striped mannequin by the Berghaus bar, an outsize appendage like an AmEx gold card pinned to his tie and announcing him as this year's Guest of Honour. ("'Oo ees zees Chrees Bunnington?" asks a lovely Frenchwoman imported to draw attention to the Lyon Equipment display.) Ron Fawcett, meanwhile, is playing organ-grinder's monkey to the specially erected DR climbing wall, hovering there as though bound to it by an invisible rope; and Johnny Dawes has taken a flying leap on to the revolving Sympatex exhibition:

"The bloody thing turns round—only it stopped and everything fell over and so did I and all these people came round and were trying to pull me off it—it was so embarrassing!" he explains, after sneaking away from the ensuing hubbub back to the Berghaus Bar (and its famous Gaelic Coffee) whence he came.

"I'm stopping in the most amazing hotel—The Cairn Hotel—it's full of geriatrics—it's in a time-warp from about 50 years ago" is the drift of another conversation. Stephen Venables overhears it, and adds that he's supposed to be lecturing there tonight, the unconscious humour of his interjection not being lost on the listeners. And all across the warp of the climbers' talk is woven the weft of business deals, prices, discussions of contracts, this year's new lines, improvements, new looks, novelties—on the Millet stand Andy Bowman proudly holds up a small rucksack with a large plastic clock sewn in: "Just for fun, you understand, just for novelty, we're not saying the walker should be in a hurry". The voices around rise in hubbub: "So we've got a deal, then?"; "I sent it back with a letter to the maker . . ."; "I like sex, and sexual differences too . . ."; "Mine's a whisky and dry ginger". The clash of tone and idea blends with the clamour of visual sensation—bright lights, glinting metal, garish fabric, all in perpetual motion: "This year's thing", "This year's theme", "This year's style". It's the icing on the cake, it's the play of light on the hills, and underneath, underlying it, is the tribalism—the climbers who are making the *right* gear for the activities they pursue—the Lowes and the Carringtons, the Anthoines and Hamiltons, the Joseph Browns and Peter O'Donovans, pushing their stuff, telling the retailers, informing the trade about what it does, charming the gear-writers and handing out to the magazines for test and trial and report, being besieged for sponsorship and freebies by the Enterprise Allowance Professionals, the whole wonderful mad circus spinning on for three days in the great low fluorescent halls until time's called to the days and the nights begin—Venables at The Cairn—he forgets his slides but no matter—Roger Mear is dragged out of The George as a stand-in; Beatty at The

---

Facing page: *Jill Lawrence leading The Left Unconquerable, Stanage Edge.*

Majestic; the *Climber* pre-dinner party at The Old Swan; and all the time alcohol—that insistent grease of contract machinery—is lovingly, liberally, applied. In the restaurants and hotels the business interests collude and spar, hands are shaken, palms crossed, pints and drams passed freely around, gossip circulated, acquaintance made, intrigues buzzed aloud. There is huge energy, vitality, discourse at play, the whole event a marvel of integration, a necessity for the climbers who seek to regulate the commercial exploitation of the sport by involving themselves.

But let them not be deceived about their own power and stamina by the illusion of mutuality of interest. It stretches just so far, and in the long spaces of the night when the men and women of the outdoors have taken themselves to their own or each others' beds, in the echoing huge hotel bars from whence the tide of talk has drained and the empty strands of carpet are crossed and re-crossed by night porters, pockets heavy with tips, carrying tray upon tray of last wee drams, there rises from rock-like outcrops of sharp-suited sleeplessness the endless soft susurrus of small hours' business bonhomie. Just so! It is the richest of the hunting grounds, and in the end, in that small gap of minutes when the vast, exclusive hotels fall silent between the extinguishing of bar lights and the arrival of breakfast cooks, in the breathing darkness the presence and the totem is unmistakably money, and softly, like watchful parents as their children play, it has talked!

Necrophiliacs
High, 1986

A few years ago the prestigious German magazine Geo distributed, together with one issue, a separate supplement, wrapped and sealed in a plastic bag with the warning that its contents might be disturbing to some people of more tender and delicate disposition. What it turned out to be was a photographic feature on a Tibetan ritual—the so-called "Burial of the Air". In this, a priest dismembers a human corpse and chops it into small pieces, crushing the skull, smashing the larger bones, until the rock on which the ceremony is performed is covered with flesh. He then cries in the buzzards and vultures, the rock becomes a heaving mass of feathers, and within minutes is cleared and clean of all trace, the birds having feasted and flown away.

This is a Tibetan custom. The Tibetans would have their responses to our mode of burying our dead; we have ours on theirs. Except that ours are perhaps more prurient, more hypocritical, more salacious, and we package our reportage of theirs as we would pornography. In the last year, a British travel company which advertises package tours to Tibet has included as one of its enticements the possibility of viewing a "burial of the air". I have my own thoughts on the rights and wrongs of thus viewing the innocence and privacy of death . . .

Earlier this month there arrived in my post one morning an envelope containing an illustrated brochure describing the rationale and organisation of an expedition, leaving for the Himalayas in 1986, which is to operate under the acronym of MENFREE—not an all-woman expedition united by its sisterhood and love of mountaineering, this, but instead the Mount Everest North Face Research Expedition.

I must be careful what I say about it, because my thoughts are intemperate, and Americans—this is an American expedition—are notoriously litigious. But it disgusts me—and this is an entirely personal opinion—as nothing else in mountaineering history (with the possible exception of the actions of the pathetic and authentically mad Giveen) ever has done. Let me quote from the brochure:

"While a number of expeditions had started their climbs with expectations of perhaps conducting a search, none have had the resources to do anything other than struggle to reach the summit. MENFREE has been formed to carry out the search. It will be the first Everest expedition mounted whose primary mission is not to reach the summit, but to conduct a thorough search near the summit for the cameras, and other traces, of Mallory and Irvine."

The leader of this expedition is Tom Holzel, the American, who has previously put forward theories on the last hours of Mallory and Irvine in *Mountain* magazine—theories which involved the experienced Mallory sending the tiro Irvine back alone down the Second Step, having transferred to Mallory his oxygen, and then carrying on, solo, for the summit. Holzel was magisterially rebuked for this theory in the correspondence columns of the magazine and elsewhere. Walt Unsworth, in his authoritative history of the mountain (*Everest,* Oxford Illustrated Press 1989), notes that:

". . . it hardly squares with Mallory's character and upbringing. Even allowing for Mallory's fanatical determination to reach the summit, he would never have sent young Irvine down the ridge alone. Once above the Second Step they were committed together, and would have seen it through together, or perished in the attempt."

Walt Unsworth further notes that "some of Holzel's arguments and facts are questionable".

It might be argued that anyone who could propound such a theory can have no understanding of the *values* which prevailed in mountaineering at that time—of comradeship, reticence as to one's own claims on achievement, mutuality of support, and so on. Yet the man who has done so is the man who is leading this expedition.

No doubt Tom Holzel and his English co-researcher Audrey Salkeld are *bona fide* climbers, and no doubt Holzel's motives in organising this expedition are perfectly valid and sound. He admits that his stimulus has come from a reported sighting by the 1981 Japanese Expedition:

"The big break came in 1981. Japanese Everesters reported the sighting of an 'English dead' on the snow terrace at 8100m. This sighting made headlines around the world and revived the long smoldering debate . . . the news also set off something of an international race to reach and search the 8100m snow terrace, and so solve this mystery."

According to Jack Longland, who was on Everest in 1933, it is perfectly possible that a body could have remained on this snow terrace, perhaps even for the 62 years since Mallory and Irvine's disappearance. Perhaps the body *is* that of Mallory or Irvine? Perhaps "film frozen for a half-century [will] yield the Secret of Everest"? (The capital letter is the brochure's.) Perhaps photographs of whatever bones and rags may be found will be sealed in a plastic envelope and distributed with appropriate warnings in prestigious magazines (which will no doubt have paid enormous fees for them) throughout the globe.

It will be *news,* if it happens, and it will inevitably make its bearers very rich (though I am quite sure they are not undertaking their research with that aim in mind). But the bringing of this news is a venture with which I would be *ashamed* to be associated.

In the last week I have talked with several of the great pre-war British climbers about it, and their response is unequivocally one of unease, distaste, outrage. I share it.

If the bodies of George Leigh Mallory and Andrew Comyn Irvine, whose portraits appear oval-framed in tasteful sepia in the brochure, do still lie on Everest ("the finest cenotaph in the world to a couple of the best of men," according to that staunch old Quaker Howard Somervell), then I hope they remain there, unprobed, unphotographed, uncovered throughout time until the elements absorb them back, shred by shred, to their own, in the privacy and seclusion of their proper death. I do not ever want to hear Tom Holzel ("winner of a 1984 Rolex Award for Enterprise [Honorable Mention] for his 15-year research on the Mallory and Irvine disappearance") lecture, or read what he writes, on how they discovered the corpses which gave them a key to unlock the mystery. I do not want one scrap of their memory to become the property of this MENFREE expedition, for that memory properly and completely belongs with the mountain to the ascent of which they committed their will and, ultimately and tragically, their life. (In fifty years from now will we be looking for Mick Burke's—in sixty years Pete Boardman's and Joe Tasker's—"cameras, and other traces" in this fashion? Will they, in their turn, become the "Secret of Everest" which it is of such paramount importance to reveal?)

"Seek and ye shall find" is the expedition motto, and the conclusion to its brochure runs thus:

"Even if discovered to have been the first, Mallory and Irvine's achievement takes nothing away from the grand ascent of Hillary and Norgay.

"However, there are not many opportunities to be witness to such noble temerity, much less to hope to discover such a great secret. This Expedition is dedicated to honoring their bold spirit, a spirit that dwells in us all; a spirit we believe may have transformed Mallory and Irvine's brave defeat into lasting victory."

Read that! Read it carefully! Study its rhetoric: "a spirit that dwells in us all"! To be "honored" thus!

That is a temerity on which, in relation to this expedition, I need make no further comment. I may wish Tom Holzel many things, but I do not wish him luck. May the snow-plume be worn proudly from Everest's sacred summit in 1986. May the wind-priest pluck the slopes clean and offer up to frost and wicked storm the burial of the air! Chomolungma, Goddess-Mother of the World, pass judgment on such sacrilege!

Postscript 1990: The MENFREE expedition proved something of a fiasco, finding and proving nothing and engendering much rancour, even amongst its own members. See also the reviews section.

Confessions of an Unclubbable Man
High, 1985

With the leaves falling, and the year's aspirations realised or set aside, the season of club dinners and goodwill comes around. The calendar starts to fill up with Saturday nights of drunken congeniality at hotels in Snowdonia or the Lakes, and Sundays of massed penitential mountain walks in the mist and rain, to dispel the alcoholic fug from our abused bodies and reflect on the banter and good fellowship of the previous night.

It is a decidedly comforting concept, this one of the club, a perfect example of social man's imaginative life, which tends so strongly towards microcosmology. You can divide clubs into two broad categories—the club as gang and the club as family. Both types have definite and separate functions, and both are invaluable within climbing's scheme of things. If you accord to each type areas of significance, then you would have to say that the club-as-gang is the more historically, the club-as-family the more socially, important. Most of the great advances in climbing history were achieved by members of clubs-as-gangs. It's obvious why this should be so—young men competing against each other, displaying bravado, their time unallotted to pursuits or responsibilities other than that of climbing. So we have the Rock and Ice, the Creag Dhu and the Alpha, the Sheffield Climbing Club of the thirties, the Cambridge University Club of the twenties (all university clubs, of course, are clubs-as-gangs), and in their zestful, competitive and imaginative hands the levels of climbing achievement are pushed higher and ever higher. But at a cost, for what these clubs represent is, in some sense, an initiation into the traditional stereotypes of manhood, where physical toughness and hardihood, enterprise and endeavour are the qualities to be acquired and prized, and let the devil take the hindmost. If the participants in our sport were only grouped into clubs as gangs, invaluable though they are, then an unspeakably brash, aggressive, elitist lot we would be. Fortunately they're not, for the bedrock of the sport is the membership of the clubs-as-family, broad-church rather than dogmatic, where the spectrum of interest, personal situation and ability is much wider and the organisation and definition of responsibility that

much more precise.

There is an easy way of distinguishing between the two. The club-as-gang never has a club hut:

"Ah," you will retort, anxious to catch me in error, "but what about Jacksonville?"

(Well all that proves is that you've never seen Jacksonville.)

"But what about the university club huts?" you reply.

"What about them?" say I. "Aren't they the educational equivalent of Daddy giving Priscilla a Porsche for her 21st birthday?"

No, the truth is that no self-respecting club-as-gang would want a club hut, because it stands for what they're set against—social responsibility. And if they occasionally stoop to using them, then that's no more than the natural desire to go and hold a party in someone else's house.

Whereas the first impulse of the club-as-family is to set down its roots, to acquire property, and then to proceed to re-furbish it and raise it to the most palatial standards. My good friend Tony Shaw, of the Mynydd Climbing Club, told me the other day about an occasion when they let their hut, Blaen y Nant in Crafnant, for the weekend to another club which, for the sake of argument, we'll call the Lytham St Anne's Preparatory School Teachers' Mountaineering Association (if such a club really exists then I plead their hypothetical forgiveness). After the weekend was over they refused to pay their dues on the grounds that the decor left much to be desired. Forget the fact of its situation, at the head of one of the most wistfully beautiful Welsh valleys; forget its perfectly acceptable standards of comfort and amenity; let's just concentrate our minds on the decor and thus become the reductio ad absurdum of the club-as-family. It's the same attitude on display that you find in Swift's "Country Walk", which he couldn't enjoy for fear of what he might tread in. ("Cowpats? Human ordure? Good Lord, what's that compared to the decor?" snorts Claudia Percival-Fitzhugh, Ladies' Secretary of the Lytham St Anne's Preparatory . . . etc.)

In fact, the club-as-family is one of the most widespread and thoroughly admirable features of the British climbing scene. Its basic reason for existence is not the stimulus of competition, though in a modulated fashion it is wide enough to embrace that too, but mutuality of support. It is there to provide, and does so often in the most exemplary fashion: accommodation, transport, company and training—they're all freely available within the club-as-family. And if, along with all those benefits, you have occasionally to accept hierarchical structures, committee-diktat, other people's children, social friction and wife-swapping orgies, at least all that is microcosmologically sound—the great world is mirrored, but the moment still arrives when we can slip quietly out of the hut door on to the mountains and into their peacefully aloof existence.

The time for confession has arrived. In the wild years of my youth I was summarily ejected from a great number of clubs-as-families for most of the usual sins of adolescence: fighting, swearing, insubordination, drunkenness, instigating farting competitions, gluttonously consuming whatever food lay around with a fine disregard for the niceties of property—all the normal behavioural syndromes which characterise the club-as-family nuisance, and identify him as one who rightly belongs with the club-as-gang. So imagine my surprise, therefore, when a letter arrived in the late post the other day inviting me to speak at the dinner of one of these clubs with which I was briefly associated in my youth. Tolerance, I wondered? Forgetfulness? Or the prodigal's return?

"You will, I am sure, know many of our older members . . ."

I wrote back, gleefully accepting:

"Oh yes, I do—I have some very good friends in the --."

Ah, how the natural order re-asserts itself!

"I grow old . . . I grow old . . .
I shall wear the bottoms of my trousers rolled."

To be received back into the bosom of the family is, you see, such warm reassurance. You've been thrown out of the house, outgrown the club-as-gang (well, at least you're prepared to pretend, for the sake of appearances, that you have), and having pursued your Hegelian progress through action and reaction, you're ready for the synthesis, the real appreciation of what the clubs have meant and brought and tried to do, however much you kicked against them in the past. In retrospection, you excuse yourself, is the acquisition of wisdom. Your mind lingers on those training meets you attended so long ago, with their embargo on all climbs of more than Difficult standard, their heavily-learned treatises upon the Tarbuck knot and other such antiquities of safety, and their impalpable goodwill and good intent. I hope they still go on, somewhere. I hope that there still are sunny Sundays when implacably impatient fourteen-year-olds must sit on stances on the Gribin Facet, to be lectured on ropework by the benign elders of their club.

Club bouldering meet, Cricieth West Beach.

And I hope, too, that those same young persons will strain against the bonds of instruction, break away, form their own groups, and perhaps ultimately come to consider the process they have gone through, and the institutions which have assisted them in it. Between the two, there exists a balance and a tension which is one of the strengths of the British sport.

A True and Authentic History and Description of Fachwen
Climber and Hillwalker, 1989

The acid test for determining whether or not a person is a true climber is his or her devotion to the subtle arts of bouldering. I was talking to Rob Collister recently, just before he set off for Makalu, and the main thing on his mind was whether or not, in order to lighten his load, he could get away with taking a pair of rock slippers for the bouldering around base camp. That's the sign of a man who's got his priorities right.

My old friend Peter Crew, on the other hand, who always gave the impression that climbing was just a phase in his life to be hurried through on the way to the next (phase, that is, not life, though his style of climbing made that a fair likelihood at times), was without doubt the worst boulderer I have ever known. It wasn't a function of lack of ability, it was simply lack of interest. Pete was someone who climbed on momentum. He just accelerated away up routes until the holds ran out and gravity, in time-honoured phrase, supervened. He was like a climbing version of a Rolls Royce—no acceleration, no good on bumpy, intricate, winding narrow roads, but give it the long straight and you were into the *gran turismo*. Whereas Al Harris, who was the great boulderer of his generation, was a sort of climbing Kawasaki Z-1300: standstill to 6b in half a second.

It was on the back of Harris's bike that I was first introduced to Fachwen. It wasn't a Kawasaki, it was a Greaves scrambler, and Al loved to do wheelies on it in the field in front of his house. One day he took me for a ride over the back of Bigil. By the time I eventually parted company with his pillion there was enough adrenalin coursing round my veins to have kept San Francisco tripping for the whole of 1967, which was the year in question. So I wandered off, nursing all sorts of bruises, Harris's words about there being some bouldering thereabouts murmuring solace in my ears, and found myself on a beautiful hillside, looking out over Llyn Padarn with Snowdon opposite shining in the sun and Cloggy hulking in its shadow.

There were stands of Scots Pine and I saw a red squirrel. All around were suggestions of white rock gleaming out of the heather. I went and touched them. They were steep and clean. The sharp, sound little holds bit into my finger-ends and the sunlight flowed over and illuminated the whole intricate, lovely landscape. It was

coruscating visual and sensual delight to be there. I'd arrived in one of the primal places.

So this was twenty-two years ago and since then Fachwen has been one of my constant points of reference. I go there whenever I can. Things change. Holds snap off, companions disappear, groups make use and abuse, but the lyrical nature of the place is unchanging.

I don't know who first climbed at Fachwen. No true and authentic history attaches, just a matrix of anecdote and hearsay, memory and remembered desire. Some of the great problems have names bestowed, others retire shyly. The rowan branches grow across them over the years, they sink into a fading oral tradition and the moments of their discovery are all but forgotten, which is perhaps as it should be. But let me show you round, and gabble on a little about my own sense and recollections of the place as we go.

This is the how and why of getting there. You are sitting in Pete's Eats in Llanberis. It is late morning and late summer and you have worked your way through your sports plan for the year. Up the Pass, up on Cloggy, up on Cyrn Las, across on the slate, all the status routes are crawling with people busily ticking and collecting and adding to their personal lists. The whole scene gets you down (nothing new in this, it was always thus), for the moment you want no part in it, want something fresh. Someone mentions Fachwen, so off you go to look.

You drive a long mile up the Caernarfon road. If you're walking, there's a roadside boulder just beyond the Lake View Hotel to entertain you along the way—nothing too hard, but it stretches the muscles. At the end of the lake, where you get the famous view of Snowdon, turn right and right again. The old road goes straight ahead from here, closed off now, and above it is the Yellow Wall, which is extremely popular these days because you can drive virtually to its base. At one time, when the road beneath was in use, climbing here was deadly. Nowadays it's just deadly dull, quite the worst of the Fachwen buttresses. It's north-east facing, has been blasted, is smooth. The technical problems are on the left and involve cranking on tiny flat edges to reach a ledge system at 15ft, but the best problem is the tall, faint groove with the big jug on the right, where you get very high up very quickly, and are faced with some crucial and committing moves to finish 25ft above the tarmac.

I had a picture of young Andy Pollitt on this problem once. It was a beautiful picture—fine muscle definition, fascinating textures in the rock. A small gay painter from

Ginger Cain on the traverse of Electrocution Wall.

Bethesda, whom Andy and Johnny Redhead used to tease by going round to his studio in nothing but their floral Lycras with socks stuffed down the front, borrowed it from me to base a picture on once. I never saw it again. My stepdaughter moaned at me to get it back and have a print made for her for ages. The saga sums up Yellow Wall for me—good-looking, a bit of a tease, a bit of a disappointment. I don't go there much these days.

Electrocution Wall is quite different. You get to it by crossing the lake outflow, turning up the Fachwen road proper, and parking in the second layby. When Harris was alive, you risked your life climbing here. It's above the narrowest part of the road. He used to pass here at 60mph. Fall off and you'd have been wiped out. Nowadays no-one drives that fast down Fachwen*, though it's always possible that one day Johnny Dawes will discover the place. Electrocution Wall has a bold

easy classic at 5b—the mantelshelves. The crux comes right at the top, twenty feet up. Two feet behind your back as you grope insecurely upwards is the electricity cable which gives the wall its name. If you psyche out, it's grab for that or 20ft down to the tarmac—or a passing car bonnet.

There are three other problems worth mentioning. One is the traverse, which is good and balancey with the opportunity for some fancy footwork. There's a fine, steep wall problem going up from the resting place near the left end of the traverse to a notch. Pat Littlejohn did it first, in 1973. It used to depend on pinching a wobbly downward-pointing sliver. I've not been able to do it since that disappeared, but that's probably a reflection of my declining abilities rather than the route's increasing difficulty.

The problem to its right, going straight through the crux of the traverse, is the best on the wall. It involves

165

tenuous layaways to a point where you can tip two fingers into a nick to keep balance, then slap for a flat jug out right, mantel, and finish with some bold, easier moves direct. I did this once in 1981 when Stevie Haston failed on it. He called me a strong old bastard. I glowed with pleasure. It was definitely the proudest moment of my climbing career. Then I tried it again to show how easy it was and fell off, rolled backwards across the road and cracked my head open on the wall opposite. I've got the scar on my bald patch to this day. He told me it served me right for being so old and feeble. The young are so fickle. I still haven't worked out whether it was hubris or karma. So much for Electrocution Wall.

Above the small layby beyond Electrocution Wall are three or four problems which are usually avoided as not being on the main itinerary. This is because they are serious and frightening. Any true Fachwener will insist on at least one of them. There is firstly Harris's Mantelshelf, which is an innocuous little prow low down on the right, by the roadside. Harris was good at mantelshelves. To its left, slightly higher, is a square-cut, right-facing groove. It is hard to get into. Once you're in it, falling out of it does not appeal. By that time, however, holds have appeared. To its left, a thin crack soars up a tower of rock. This is the Layby Crack. It is 25ft long, the ground below is very steep, and the crux is at the top. It looks fearsome. Paul Williams and myself spent weeks eyeing it up in 1981. Paul said it was too high to be a proper problem, and that he was going to look at it on a rope first. I did it a few times to half-height, where you can step off left, looked down it from the top, then eventually lurched out into it one evening and thugged up to the top. It's about 5b. It is very frightening. There are good little holds for the top moves. They're not obvious.

These layby walls are at the foot of a steep gully with a right wall where there are any number of easy problems. Local centres have been so kind as to put protection pegs in some of them. One of the delights of Fachwen is that the range of standards available is very wide. There are things for everyone, from the most inept beginner to John Gill clones. I've even seen Ken Wilson get off the ground on a problem here. It was on "Brailsford's 6a", but we'll come to that.

If you head on up through the gully, in a hundred yards or so you come to Split Rocks, which is the best warm-up area. It's sheltered, attractive, interesting. There's a classic easy problem, stepping off a boulder into the obvious crack. This is Split Rock Crack. It rises out of a cave. If you sit in the cave with your feet off

the ground, what confronts you is the Fachwen Roof. Be prepared to leave some skin behind. The crack flares, and you have to jam hard. Some days it feels easy, on others desperate. It seems to depend on how much humidity is in the air. The arete on its right is about 5c, but very awkward and barndoorish at the start. I fell off it once from the top and landed between the boulders without a scratch. I don't know why I fell off it from there. It's easy by then. Anyway, they named it after me. Harris used to tell me that it was because it was two grades easier than his arete, which is a quarter-mile away, and that that was a fair reflection of our respective climbing abilities. I never saw him do my arete, though, but you could take an insult from Al. You had to—it was the substance of his conversation.

To the right of Split Rocks there's another cave roof. This is Shorter's Overhang. It's one of the great sitting problems. You start in the back of the cave, feet on the back wall, and crawl out horizontally. If you want to make Shorter's Overhang into a longer overhang, you can traverse along the lip. It's all quite exhausting. Nowadays the cave beneath is full of empty lager cans.

Round the back of the Split Rocks there are lots of little fingery things, all quite trivial and fun. One of them is a ten-foot wall on the north-west side, part of a great flake of rock. It used to have a blob of white paint marking it, because some misguided person had painted circuit-markings-à-la-Fontainebleau all around Fachwen. I'm not saying who it was, but I know. White was the 6a circuit. My old mate Barney Brailsford was immensely pleased because he could get up one of the problems on it. "Fifty years old," he used to gloat, "and I can still get up 6a!" It would be ungenerous of me to offer an opinion as to its real grade, so suffice it to say that "Brailsford's 6a" has passed into the book of great jokes, and as I said, I once saw Ken Wilson get off the ground on it. (In fact I think he finished it.)

After you leave Split Rocks, the serious stuff begins. Head north, cross a stile, descend round a corner and you come to the Swamp Walls, two of them, the Altar Wall and Far Swamp Wall. Altar Wall has two great problems, both on its right-hand section. Ken Tom's Crack is the slanting, energetic, difficult-to-start, often-wet little gem on the left at 5c. The wall on its right to the spiky little razor-jug in the middle is 6a. They're both 20ft high, and bold, but the landings are quite good out of bracken-season. They've been very neglected in recent years, and are almost as lichenous now as when we first found them in 1972. Far Swamp Wall has four problems in a logical progression left-to-right of 5a to

6a. The left arete is sharp and spectacular, the crack—Crew's Crack—demands a confident approach, and is the only Fachwen problem Pete ever did; the groove right again is awkward and delicate to start, but leads to some enjoyable swinging moves up on exquisite finger holds; the only thing exquisite about the right arete is the pain of pulling on scalpel-sharp tinies.

So much for the preliminaries. If you've got through the tour so far, you're ready for the upper circuits. Lion Rock's an obvious starting point from this end. It's the outcrop which looks down over the whole area. The slabs on the right are all easy and the habitual reserve of centre people, but the streaked wall of Gogarth-like quartzite on the left has a crack problem of Harris's where you'd leave the tips of your fingers behind in one place if your feet came off, and a ramp on the right which is indelicate and slippery. A fall from this could see you bouncing a long way down the hill.

Much safer are the conglomerate boulders. To reach these you wander off southwards through heather for what seems like miles until, quite close above the road and at the back of a boggy flat area, you find an incredible jumble of blocks with a strikingly beautiful little sharp arete on the left. This is Harris's Arete, it's 6b, and is reputed to date from the 1960's, though I have heard this disputed and I never saw it done then. It was Harris's party piece. You climb it direct, on pinches. Fall off and you'd only sprawl in a bog. I went there recently with Paul Trower. He floated up it. He's current King of Fachwen. I couldn't get off the ground. It's that sort of problem. Harris used to do it every time in a pair of floppy EB's wet from standing in the bog.

Well over to the left of here, over a little col and at the head of a small valley where there was once a dam is the Witch's Crag. I don't like the place at all. I saw a ghost here once, very angry, waving a stick at me. When I looked again she'd disappeared. It's a featureless place, the rock smooth, laminated and rather loose. Brian Molyneaux fell off one of the problems on the right and broke a leg. The two best routes are on the right, one by Rab Carrington, the other Henry Barber's. That gives you the measure of the place. You get more brownie points on the North Wales scene for having done a new problem on Fachwen than you would for a new route on Anglesey. And it's harder and more dangerous to do. But as I said, I don't like the Witch's Wall.

Ginger emerging from the Fachwen Roof.

Quite a lot of the upper circuit is of this character as well—bad landings, suspect rock, hidden away. But there is one gem amongst the hosts I'll leave you to rediscover. It's miles up near the top of the hill below the mast, and the best way to reach it is from the Bigil track. It's called Accommazzo's Wall, after an Italian-American from California who stayed with Harris for a time in the late seventies and was taken out to do his stuff on the Fachwen circuit. He flashed everything in sight, so Al took him to this wall, which Paul Trower had been working on for months. Paul was in the Alps. If he'd known what Al was up to, he'd have been back faster than the speed of sound.

But it was too late. Ricky Accommazzo sniffed it, felt it, and powered up to place his name amongst the neon legends of Fachwen. I've never been able to do it. Al took me there once. It was in 1981, the last time I was climbing well. He and I were very competitive with each other. It was a golden autumn day, and I was as fit as I'd ever been. I looked at it, flexed my fingers on the holds. It felt good, straightforward. Al gave me that big-toothed grin of his. I did it in one surge of movement, was so exhilarated that I reached wrong-handed for the top. Arms crossed, I couldn't mantelshelf.

"I'm jumping off!" I shouted to Al.

"I'll spot you!" he said.

"No, leave it, I'm going for the grass . . ."

There was a small patch of grass. I leapt for it. Al caught me and dragged me on to a boulder. My foot turned sideways, every ankle ligament torn. I lay in the grass and wept with pain. Toby, Al's son, helped me down to Bigil. Ice-cubes and boiling water. I had a week's guiding starting the next day with that strange Llanberis institution Roger Alton. Al just grinned, told me between those tombstone teeth of his that I could do it, and when I'd been paid could I lend him thirty quid for half an ounce of black?

A month later he was dead and the place has never seemed the same since. I still go there sometimes, with friends, hoping they'll appreciate it too. It's the great Welsh bouldering area. Even devotees of Almscliff or The Kebs would be pleased by it. Ah well, how does the line go? "In the dew of little things the heart finds its morning, and is refreshed."

*Not quite true! I was driving down Fachwen recently, when a beat-up Scirocco screamed round the bend in front of me, honked, skidded up on the bank, then gently toppled over on its roof onto my car. The passenger door prised open. Out of it, shrieking with laughter, burst Al's son Toby . . .

Gone West
Climber, 1987

Prelude

Need a break. Need a guru. Need to go West! Wet October night. Packed my sack, walked to the station in the rain, clacked along the diesel line for an hour, ran breathless across the city for the Liverpool train.

The bus from Lime Street takes you to the docks, down Dublin Street from *The Bull* to *The Palatine,* right into Great Howard Street and past *The Al at Lloyd's.* Here on the top deck, their bright signs flicker past the rain-flecked screen, evoking images from the cutting-room floor of life: carousing along these same bleak streets with Pete Minks and Billy McGrath 20 years ago; pub-meetings with Irishmen, whores and sailors; the fights: "So we want to play with bottles, do we, little boys . . .?" And the lonely times, the city streets at night, spaced lights gleaming on kerbstones and cobbles, walking, walking, singing Dylan love-songs as mantras to exorcise the desperate hours:

"There's no need for anger
There's no need for blame
There's nothing to prove
Ev'rything's still the same."

A relief to escape from these ghosts into the bustle of the Irish boat. The lock gates inch into their recess and a slick of muddy suspension creeps round into the black water. A gull flies through, assured as if the gates had opened for it alone. A discarded glove, rubbery fingers outstretched, bobs and floats until an oily ripple tips into it and consigns it, grasping and spiralling, to the depths. The engines thrum and heel us round into the river, mist and darkness lie ahead. I cocoon myself in a sleeping bag and settle down to eight hours on a slatted fore-deck bench. A young woman bestows on me a glance which mingles complicity and suspicion before she does the same, two benches away.

Dublin. Approaching the ferryport with a bright new morning dawning, and sea between me and the sun. I amble through customs and an arm fastens round my shoulder in a strong embrace. Unexpectedly, Dermot Somers has met me—fine mountaineer, writer of splendid fiction, first man from the Irish Free State to climb the North Wall of the Eiger and as good a friend as I've made these last ten years. We breakfast in Dublin and make plans. Soon enough, we're heading West to find the guru. He is a mapmaker, lives in Connemara, and it is part of the purpose of this visit to see him. But both he and the visit are more than that.

Maps! Do you remember how you used to pore over them? Perhaps still do? Treasure Island? "The National Bank at a profit sells road maps for the soul." "My soul, saith he, is but a map of shows." We didn't need a map just yet, though, for through the little towns of The Bog (we were caught up in a young girl's wedding at Hayden's Hotel in Ballynasloe, to which town Dermot had driven cattle as a young boy), through Galway and along by the Twelve Bens and the Maum Turks, Dermot knew the way.

We stopped in a Galway café. A man of sixty, small, with a presence upon him, great powerful hands clasped around the thick crockery and a sad, lined face above his dark clothes caught my eye:

"Chaucer's January brooding on his young wife?"

"No," scolded Dermot, "that's not common any more. In to see the bank manager about the mortgage on his farm, or his wife dying in the hospital of cancer, more like."

We drove on, to find the man for whom we were looking. Map-maker, artist, mathematician and writer, his name is Timothy Drever Robinson. We met him in a tiny Irish Development Association industrial estate by the small harbour of Roundstone, on an evening of cold crystal with a glint of gold and the Twelve Bens reflected in the water.

Instruction

He had been on the Island for ten years and now lives and works at mapping the shores of Connemara. There was a suggestion of ritual in the measured gait, of asceticism in the cropped hair and strong nose. He had the self-absorption of a man used to spending much time alone. Square-shouldered, there was a physical strength to match the mental power he expressed in gnomic, minimal utterances. His mapping, of the Island in particular but also of the limestone country down in Clare and latterly of the rough uplands and ragged coastline of Connemara, is almost less topographical depiction than the record of personal exploration—and *through* time, *into* pattern, *along* resonance, as much as *of* geography. The Island map shows ledges and cliff overhangs as well as monuments, points where fishermen had been swept to their deaths, or where a monk had planted hops before Cromwell's time:

"Each person entering the dark gallery finds a new surface, at first unintelligible, which is the record of his predecessors' explorations and will be recreated or annihilated by his own investigations."

This was written about a work of his art which went on show in London in the late 1960s. His attentiveness, watchfulness, enquiry, is exemplary. And draws people to him with gifts: "an old stone to show to the mapmaker from Roundstone." Within a generation or two all this would have gone. Scrupulously, therefore, he records, and explores, preserving both the history and his personal experience of a landscape, a loom of electrical connection, mathematical patterning woven through—the vision which refines and perfects rather than completes a task, and denotes mastery. It was the geometries of limestone which appealed to him, drew him West, where the influences are most slow, least strong, and once there he was led to commune with and conserve the experience of a people and enrich it with the uniqueness of his own attention:

"For an Islander to wander round the Island would be impossible."

I talked with him for an hour, so intensely as to set up a ringing ache inside our skulls, and the picture flashing in and out of that old Catholic priest of a quarter century before from whom I'd taken instruction towards a religious vocation in Manchester's Hidden Gem—the stuffiness, the heavy incense, the alcohol on his breath across the green baize cloth, the dark room into which I was led time and again by the intensity of his thought, the unplumbable beauty of mindlife and religious metaphor, before the agonies of questioning, guilt and ultimate rejection—Stanage rather than Mass on a Sunday. Yet here, in the country he had left behind, talking with the mapmaker, another exile in a light room at gleaming sunset, for all the aching effort in my head I could breathe, Lord.

And that night, in his house after food, there was *Sean-nos* singing, thrilling and captivating in its wildness of sound and sophistication of control, quartertones and scoops, resonances in all the cavities of the head—*Amhran Muighinnse* and *Currachai na Tra Baine*—Dermot singing them in an exquisitely musical and utterly strange voice which through the vibrancy of sound alone shakes you into consciousness of the great things—deaths and farewells and the elemental places— in a way that only the profoundest art can. After sleep, and a few mouthfuls of heavy, dry bread and water, we made our way to the Island.

"The more I see of humanity, the more I love Irish donkeys." (I said that.)

Pilgrimage

Why, you ask, do I not tell you where it is, this Island? And I cannot easily tell you why not. Except that it is partly out of politeness to Irish friends, who wish to preserve things popularity will kill more quickly than their present slow rates of death might allow. If it is true that "There is no love/Except in silence", then of what worth are my past protestations about landscapes? Or those of any of us writers on the outdoors? I had decided that I would not tell, but I can tell you what I saw: a captain in blue denims and cowboy boots who took us there; men on the quayside, beak-nosed and reticent, watching, clad in the baggy, dark Connemara tweeds; middle-aged men with tightened belts and corded forearms; grass a vivid, dark, polished green on the clifftops, like skeins of rich silk thread and on the cliffs themselves fifty-foot-long blubbers of dirty brown and green moss, tenacious, fed by springs issuing from between the

shale bands; crevices on the white surface rock spilling over with bloody cranesbill; men wheeling old bikes along the boreens, walking alongside you politely to talk; monuments by the roadside and even in schoolyards, in a place where the soil is too poor and precious for burial of the dead. (The environment is what we make of it? We are what the environment makes of us?); lazy beds picked out in the evening sun; a snatch of Dermot's conversation after enquiring in Gaelic of an old woman where we might get a cup of tea and following her directions: "It's the wrong way and we won't find a cup of tea up here, but I didn't like to offend her." And a solitary late-season American like some exotic, pulpy fruit cast aside on the quay, telling us that he had come "to get a little feel for the people".

We had come to climb. Once disembarked, we walked up to the cliff edge and found it facing into the Atlantic in frozen wave-posture for eight miles. Overhangs in which Kilnsey, Malham and Gordale placed end to end would be lost entirely, as would any climber who put himself in reach of the gently licking swell beneath. A zawnless rampart 300ft. high, dolomitic limestone, at wave-level a forty-foot surge up and down on a flat calm sea.

With our minimum of equipment, walking the length of the cliffs, we thought better of climbing here. At one point we descended a chimney to sea-level and saw the power there. It frightened us. Take the biggest cliff in Pembroke, double its height and stretch it out for mile after mile above a sea of terrifying, percussive unpredictability and you have this place. There are times, venues, in which the culture of climbing is an irrelevance and a trifle. We retreated to a bar in Fearann an Choirce, a modern bungalow with a Guinness sign outside, a girl behind the counter listening to some mid-Atlantic trash on the radio and mooning over a poster of Chris de Burgh. The only other customer, a gummy old sea-capped fellow guarding a glass of Guinness, engaged us with a rush of Gaelic-inflected English and a sceptical intelligence about Reagan and Gorbachev at the Reykjavik summit. The tension shrilled between himself and the girl as he praised Radio na Gaeltacht, talked of the loss of a traditional culture and railed against incipient colonialism. He told us of the egg and bird-collecting which had once taken place on the cliffs, men being let down on horsehair ropes to the midway ledge-systems to crawl about at night, 150ft above the water, sometimes being plucked off by one of the big waves, sometimes slipping to their deaths. He recounted the day "a few years ago" when there was a currach and three men wrecked who didn't know the waters—we pulled them out on a rope from the bottom of the cliffs."

We left him to go up to the fort.

I have a fondness for old monuments but this was a fearsome site. A wickedly-pointing thicket of a spiked limestone was the first line of defence, and three concentric solid stone ramparts twenty or more feet in height beyond that. Then came the inner semi-circle of flat grass whose other half was space. And on the very edge of the cliff, which cut away beneath in a great arc of yellow overhangs, was a platform, "Just a table standing empty/On the edge of the sea". What cloth could you spread on this table? What map could you draw here?

Skald's Death.

A reek and screaming echo of human sacrifice surged in at you as you stood on the brink and looked down a hundred yards straight into the sea. There are some cliffs, some planes, which invite you to climb upon them, like the one in Hugh MacDiarmid's poem "Skald's Death":

"I have known all the storms that roll.
I have been a singer after the fashion
Of my people—a poet of passion.
All that is past.
Quiet has come into my soul.
Life's tempest is done.
I lie at last
A bird cliff under the midnight sun."

A mile or two along this wave-roll of the vertiginous, we found such a place. And may go back to climb it, next year, next spring, when the waves and the fear have subsided and the longing for that simple conflict fills the mind. For the moment we came away fearful and empty-handed, but what of that? There was a sunset of extraordinary beauty, a glitter of moonlight afterwards on the sea, and by the time the leaping currach painted on the wall of Joe MacDonagh's bar was swaying into motion that night, our hearts were brave again, and uncowed, as might befit those who have been on a pilgrimage.

'Man Escapes from Jaws of Death after Conquering Killer Peak—Exclusive'
High, 1986

"What you need," bellowed the man with fuzzy lips, "is epics. Ya godda have epics." Flesh writhed and croziered around his teeth in some vain and anguished attempt to validate his argument, or to conceal the flaws in his reasoning and the self-importance of his stance. "The trouble with it is—" (he was consigning the greater part of mountaineering literature to oblivion) "—that it just doesn't have enough epics. Winthrop Young, Leslie Stephen, Mummery, Edwards—rubbish! No epics!"

I reached for the volume switch and turned it slowly down, playing for time, considering a response:

"Come now, Benito," I murmured, "there's surely more to it than epics, whatever you mean by that term."

"You know perfectly well what I mean," he exploded, in a welter of gesture and spray, "I mean people going

out and having epics—you know, epics, like, EPICS MAN!"

The last was delivered with clenched fists, eyeball to eyeball and at the top of his voice. Ten feet away, on the other side of the room, his young son looked up from his homework and protested:

"Daddy, you're covering me in spit."

I began to feel that the conversation was developing something of the quality he desired.

"Well, it can produce some interesting writing . . ."

"Interesting!" howled Benito. "Listen, if it doesn't have epics then it's *deeply* tedious. Do I have to spell it out for you? Epics are brilliant. Geddit? Geddit?"

Steam hissed from between his clenched teeth in a fair imitation of a pre-war Glasgow express breasting Beattock summit. I shrugged my shoulders and prowled off into the night to think about it.

What constitutes an epic? Doug Scott on the Ogre? Joe Simpson on Siula Grande? Shipton's and Tilman's descent from the Sunderdhunga Col? Shackleton on South Georgia? It doesn't strike me that any of the gentlemen involved in those adventures would in any way have relished the tag. So is "epic" a term for onlookers? "A Century of Great Adventure Stories"; "The Climb up to Hell"; "Snatched from the Jaws of Death—A Weekend Exclusive".

This last was a wonderful example of the genre. It was a re-telling, in a popular weekly, of a series of mishaps which befell Frank Cannings. Firstly he toppled down something or other on Lundy, then he was rescued, strapped into a stretcher, transferred to a helicopter, which promptly developed engine trouble and ditched in the Bristol Channel, leaving Frank, concussed and bleeding, to swim for his life under the handicap of a Thomas stretcher to which he was still tightly bound. The magazine made a meal of it:

"I thought my last moments had come," said red-haired hero, as his petite, attractive wife struggled to keep him afloat." etc., etc.

The effect on Frank was actually one of profound embarrassment, alleviated by wry humour—a good tale to be told against himself. One of the things I most like and respect about climbers is their refusal of all this inflationary guff. They like nothing better than to take the piss out of themselves, and if anyone else tries to jack them up to heroic status, like as not they'll take the piss out of him as well. Throw a hero at your average bunch of climbers, and it's like tossing a Christian to a bunch of well-fed lions on their day off. They'll play with him and knock him about a bit, but if he doesn't get too assertive the claws will be kept in.

On a false note, look at what happened to David Hempleman-Adams and his polar exploits. In a different key, consider the furore over the heroism award to Doug Scott after the Ogre. If you offer that sort of thing to a man with a perfectly commonsensical attitude towards what he's done, and then subject him to the sort of media-inflation which goes with it (noticed the number of media-connected people hanging around climbing these days?), you're surely heading for trouble. It's not a question of objecting to the stories involved, it's more one of looking carefully at the values implicit in how they're told. And the tellers must know the (particular and very moral) code. Anyone who's heard John Barry's bar-room tales, for example, will immediately recognise what he's up to—comic self-deflation, with everything leading up to the moment when the hero's foot inexorably descends towards the carefully-positioned banana-skin.

The unfortunate point about epics is that all too often they breed self-importance and punditry. Epic-identification is a spectator-sport, whereas the people involved in the process are too preoccupied with the simple business of getting on with the job in hand to allow their sense of the thing to get out of proportion. There is a sense in which epics are for people who've never had any. I have not an ounce of admiration for Doug Scott simply for having crawled on his knees down the Ogre, nor for Joe Simpson simply for having extricated himself broken-legged from the crevasse on Siula Grande, nor for any of the others I mentioned above. Because if they hadn't just got on with it they would have been dead, and if you know Doug Scott or Joe Simpson, you realise that they are too full of energy, of desire for life, for that ever to have been a realistic option with them. If the human machine cannot crawl on until it dies, it is running on the wrong spirit. Why praise a survivor when he's simply done what he had to do to stay alive? He might have a good story to tell, and I love hearing the stories, but at the root of the matter is the elementary and selfish fact that he's been involved in the business of saving his own skin. May all good luck befall him, but never call it heroism, resist the inflation to epic heights, put the trumpets away and save the ceremonial for those who are inadequate enough to desire it.

There was some poor squaddy on the radio the other week, who'd just been awarded a medal for the valour he'd displayed in sitting it out with a broken-legged captain by an Antarctic crevasse. He was being interviewed by one of those bits of Sloaney frippery in which the BBC specialises, who was obviously panting to touch a real-live hero. I've never heard a man reduced to such a cringing state of embarrassment, and all because of his consciousness of the disparity between what the Beeb and the Good-Old-Regiment-God-Damn-It were putting on him, and what he actually did:

"It must have been fantastically brave of you, lance-corporal, can you tell us exactly what it was you did?"

"Well, the captain fell down a crevasse—you know, a hole in the snow—so I stuck my ice-axe in and got him out."

"You actually fished him out of the hole?"

"Well, yes, with the rope . . ."

"And then you sat with him all night to keep him warm?"

"Yeah, we wrapped him up and got a tent over him.."

"And then you kept him warm! Well I can't imagine how frightfully brave you must have been to win this fantastic medal, lance-corporal . . ."

You could almost hear him shrieking at her with embarrassment and frustration:

"I didn't do it to win a medal, you imbecile—I did it because it had to be done!"

I used to go out looking for epics at one time. When the weather was bad, the snow coming down and a wind rattling the windows I'd thrust out of the door and set off into the Carneddau, seeking the white-out, the wind-howled slopes streamered with snow. I would brace my shoulders and pump fists and head pugilistic against the gusts until I was up there on the whale-roll of the great ridges with the snow-pall obliterating all stored sense of place. That circuit by Drosgl and Bera Bach and round to Foel Grach in the pelting sting of the easterlies, then with the gale at your back over Carnedd Llywelyn and down the long shoulder from Dafydd was a favourite.

Once, halting by a coronet of spiky rocks above the plunge of Ysgolion Duon, a figure resolved itself darkly from the snow-laden wind and drifted alongside to rest for a moment or two, squatted, loosened the drawcord of her hood. Hazel eyes shone out in a conspiracy of joy and she yelled, "lovely, lovely," at me in a breathy Welsh voice, drew the cord tight again and danced off into the gathering dusk on the arms of the wind. I felt a pang, but not the slightest qualm. There was nothing for me to do but descend homewards, chanting her gift . . .

Fictions
Climbers' Club Journal, 1981

My theme is the complex interdependence between the imaginary and the real. However much we may structure our approaches to experience, from individual to individual the approaches will vary. Likewise the moment when the apprehended is projected into reality will vary in the degree to which we commit ourselves as vehicles of its expression. There is a vital dimension of approach. St Augustine defines it thus:

"Who can deny that things to come are not yet? Yet already there is in the mind an expectation of things to come."

What happens within this dimension is unique in every person, though curious patterns will recur. Let me take one such pattern and ally it to my theme.

It is a matter for very considerable doubt whether Cesare Maestri and Toni Egger climbed Cerro Torre. There is scarcely any doubt that Keith McCallum did not climb many of the routes he reported in 1967. More recently, the account of the route Big Bug at Tremadog was almost certainly false. The people concerned have each been pilloried for their claims, but the issue at point is not so simple as that of telling lies. Each of these men researched their stories more or less exhaustively, studied their putative ascents from greater or lesser distances and, we must presume—otherwise it would be simple lying, believed more or less in their own accounts. In Maestri's case, the fiction was even re-written and physically enacted at a later date.

In all these instances, the primary stage of the ascent, the imaginative apprehension of the climb, was not at fault. Where the faults occurred, and faults they undoubtedly were, was in the dimension of approach. The 'expectation of things to come' worked upon their minds perhaps in such a way as to inhibit commitment to creating in actuality the ascents of their imagination. Their fictions thus did not through their own actions comprehend reality. In this they came quite close to the collective fictions of inadequacy which each generation of climbing creates in order to sustain the sport's momentum.

Clogwyn Du'r Arddu alone has seen at least three such: the Master's Wall was beyond the reach of Joe Brown, though he probed at it. Peter Crew, of the next generation, climbed it after the fashion of the times, and then created his own mischievous fiction of inadequacy in The Final Judgement, the name of which alone strives after apocalypse. Recently this has been climbed, as Psychokiller, by Ron Fawcett, and Fawcett's generation has its own fiction of inadequacy in the right-hand route on Great Wall attempted by John Redhead.*

*This line was climbed in 1985 by Johnny Dawes

Each of these in a sense is a measuring of ourselves against the 'expectation of things to come'. Each poses questions: can a climb exist, fictively, before it is co-erced into some kind of reality? Or indeed, can it ever exist in any sense beyond that of individual fictive consummation? St Augustine again:

"True then it is that man is purged by none but the 'beginning', but this 'beginning' is by them too variably taken."

The process is interesting. We are continually affronted by the exigence of reality. Against isolation, we set partnership; against time, regeneration; against our own inconsequentiality, we set the fiction of heroism. Fictive heroes each of us, asserting our adequacy, our consequence, in the face of loss and decay. Climbing provides an opportunity, a hollow marvel, for this. Let me take an example from my own experience; not a deeply significant or a traumatic one, but more in the way of everyday process.

When I first saw South Stack's Red Wall, in the mid-1960s, I did not think at first ever to climb upon it. It filled me with terror when I projected myself imaginatively upon it. But very soon, within weeks or months, I had created for myself the fiction of climbing it. This fiction was, more or less, my way of apprehending the contingencies of a sustained steepness, looseness, difficulty of access, intricacy and exposure beyond my experience in climbing at that time. As the mere fiction it was insufficient, its role being no more than one of imaginative acclimatization. But it was a transitional phase, a step leading across to its own transmutation into a moment of time—something close to Wallace Stevens's concept of a Supreme Fiction—something which I would call a consummate fiction. Which is what I want to consider—the climb as consummate fiction—a fiction made perfect by each one of us in its enactment. And a compulsion to experience, as I was compelled, within months of first seeing it, to climb on Red Wall.

Time is important in the argument that a climb cannot exist except as a type of fiction. The poetic metaphor's meaning expands in the resonance set up between object and context. For the climber, he makes himself the object, the climb is his context, and memory supplies the resonance. The perspective opens out, the contexts recede, memory drives the point home:

"Truly, though our element is time,
We are not suited to the long perspectives
Open at each instant of our lives.
They link us to our losses . . ."
(Philip Larkin)

This is to jump from prologue to conclusion. The fiction, the first stage, is so constructed as to apprehend experience and allow us to engage with it, the process of which engagement is 'too variably taken', or even not taken at all. With some of us, perhaps even the majority, the fictionalizing element continues beyond the moments of engagement. We conceptualize about the events which have taken place, we fine them down into more perfect versions than the records would allow. (The practice is widespread, and even where it is not blatantly pursued, we still create the conditions for our own fictions—we garden, rehearse, rig, bolt.)

And then, we climb. It is so brief, this experience of climbing. When we have primed ourselves with imagination, in which process our imagined ultimate victory is concomitant, when we have waited and plotted, created or happened upon the conditions for a successful engagement, when we have stalked through the dimension of approach and arrived at the central experience, then, in all probability, it distills down to a few crucial moves before the assurance of conquest.

And afterwards, what? Ecstasy? Increased self-assurance? Gratified desire? Or something more nearly allied to post-coital melancholy? Thus Tilman, on top of Nanda Devi:

"After the first joy in victory came a feeling of sadness that the mountain had succumbed, that the proud head of the goddess was bowed."

The proud head, of course, is not bowed. All that has happened is that, for once, imagination, action, and context have conjoined and we have nowhere left to go. So we start afresh, of necessity. We create new fictions, for their enactment, all too briefly, takes us out of time to fix us in time. Though they compel us, we are to some extent their masters. We sketch out their lineaments, we tailor them to our muscle, we abate their power as our own faculties fail. Ultimately, perhaps, we allow them to move completely beyond ourselves and bequeath

The author struggling to grasp the idea of a hold.

them, as fictions of inadequacy, to coming generations. To whom, also, the record of our consummate fictions is there to be read. Spots of time, peculiar to ourselves, yet catalogued, accessible to others' re-enactments. Climbs, stories, lies, aspirations, hallucinations, heroic acts:

"The generations of men run on in the tide of Time,
But leave their destin'd lineaments permanent for ever and ever."
(William Blake)

Out there, in the night, in the rain, the cliffs drip and lour. Their climbs are graffiti on the walls of our minds; attempts to apprehend, to define, to control, to bring solace. Shall the sun shine tomorrow, or shall it be colder? Shall I be strong tomorrow, or shall I be older? Fictions, friends, creations, transmutations—gold or base metal, let the experiences at least have been real, etched sharp in every detail, expected, created, lived through, and not forgotten. Each one of them an act of good faith, a memory, almost a prayer.

Trespassers
Climber and Hillwalker, 1988

Young Peter Wright is a friend of mine from the Lledr Valley. I knew his father, Brian Wright—one of the stalwarts of Welsh climbing, who was on the first ascents of classics like Bovine—from when I climbed with the Cromlech Club in the early sixties. Peter wasn't around then—hadn't been born—but here he is today, sprung fully rigged from his father's dreams, the eternal aspiring young rock star bullying and scathing at his elders to prove himself the better man—which of course he already is as they succumb to work, beer and responsibilities, and grow to Falstaffian proportions of gut and un-courage.

As for Peter, well, you've seen him around—he's the perpetual enthusiast whose name you find out when you've met him a time or two at Pen Trwyn or out on the slate. Like Dylan Thomas's park-keeper, "I know 'im," you can say, "I've known 'im by the thousand." And he's none the worse for that. If you want to find him when he's working, you'll have to go into *Climber and Rambler,* the Betws y Coed superstore which pinched our magazine's old name. You'll catch him there running the climbing department, where he'll tell you far more about the stuff he sells than I could ever do. It's the new expertise, and I was looking forward to seeing it in action. This is how it came about.

This anorexic young stalk of impudence has been on at me for months: "Why don't you make me famous instead of all these old farts you usually go out with. And anyway, can you still climb in the fat and senile state you're in?"

I just said "No." It seemed the best answer to both questions. Then, for variety, I said "Yes, where are we going?" His eyes lit up. They're bright anyway, and a nice hazelly colour, which is why my step-daughter fancies him. (She says she doesn't, but you can always tell in these things. It's the way she stamps her foot, tosses her hair, curls her lip and protests too much.) Maidenly protests aside, he plumped for the cliff of the maiden, Craig y Forwyn, and here's how he put it:

"We'll go to Craig y Forwyn, because if someone doesn't, they'll never allow climbing there again, and those idle buggers from the BMC aren't doing anything about it, are they."

"Oh, I think there's some backdoor diplomacy going on. I don't think they've abandoned hope of an agreement yet."

"Yeah?" he snarled. The cynicism of the young about the ability of anyone over the age of thirty to do anything other than make a fast buck and do down the rising generation is a marvel to behold.

"Yeah!" I mocked back at him, "Point taken!"

I picked him up from where he lives in Betws y Coed. He was sitting in front of the telly, ribs clacking together with the cold, scowling at Melvyn Bragg—a lean and hungry subversive watching askance the plump smugness of the articulate front man.

"Come on, Pete," I chivvied, "let's get on the road."

He was looking fragile. I asked him what he'd been doing. The previous night he'd been to see Hawkwind at the Working Men's Institute in Buckley—a hundred-mile round trip to see a band that'd been around when I'd been his age.

"That's right," he said, "the world's full of ageing thrash-bands," and he pulled on a peaked cap with Sons of Damnation or some such inscribed upon it.

So we drove to Craig y Forwyn. I didn't need to make any excuses because in his eyes I had the biggest excuse of them all—Old Mortality, one-foot-in-the-grave, being the wrong side of forty. But I was pleased to hear him indemnifying himself against the possibility of a lacklustre performance: "Hung over . . . haven't climbed for ages . . . Jeez, it's gonna be cold today"—just as I would've done in his position, at his age.

As you'll be aware, there was something provocative afoot. Climbing at Craig y Forwyn has been forbidden for over three years now. The owner of the cliff, John Webb, has consistently and vigorously enforced a total ban. We'd heard all manner of tales, no doubt amplified through the folklore, about what happened when you went to climb there, and we wanted to find out for ourselves. But it would be false to suppose that we weren't apprehensive. Sticks, dogs, vigilante squads of local farmers had all entered into the reported equation. So the one thing that Pete and I agreed on was a good Gandhian response to whatever happened. Even if mildness and amiability didn't win the day, at least they wouldn't prejudice any future progress against the restrictions.

It was a cold, grey day, and drizzling, so we went to the Castle Inn Quarry first to warm up. The sight of a smooth, 60ft buttress with unprotected E3s rising straight from the tarmac of a car-park chilled our blood, so we preferred the Castle Inn itself, and sat in front of the fire with our beer and steak-pie-and-chips:

"Give Pete a handicap," I thought, "He looks far too fit and athletic." I expounded the Redhead theory of overdosing on calories before you hit rock. He looked more interested in the barmaid than in climbing. I told him the beer was making him lecherous, and we set off into the dismal afternoon for our confrontation with Mr Webb.

Craig y Forwyn is the best, but by no means the only, outcrop of rock in the limestone country behind Llanddulas. It looks down over a tributary of the Dulas Brook, and across a landscape of green fields, fine old trees, white-painted houses and neat hedges. There is a legend about the devil, who lived in a cave on Cefn yr Ogof opposite and was vexatious to pregnant women, being frightened by the appearance of a pure and saintly virgin on Craig y Forwyn, and falling into a muddy pool in his own cave—which explains his black appearance, as well as the crag's name. Neither the legend nor the pure and saintly virgins have much currency hereabouts these days. The coastal caravan fungus has spread here and there up the valley, but only in isolated clusters. It's a quiet and appealing place.

Our plan was to park well away from Plas Newydd farm, which is beneath the rocks, so that no numbers or reprisals could be taken. We were expecting difficulties, but the first problem encountered was not quite the expected one. If it hadn't been likely to lay us open to the charge of being in possession of offensive weapons, we'd have gone back for our machetes. Three years is a long time in the growth of brambles and briars! Hooked and woody thorns clutched and slashed as we forced through. In no time at all our hands, faces and scalp —or at least my balding one—were streaming with blood. The old way in we'd chosen was not quite as it used to be. But we soon broke through on to a more recent one directly up to the crag.

It needs to be explained that Craig y Forwyn falls into two quite distinct sections. The right-hand one, above Mr Webb's house, is where the major routes lie. The left-hand crag is a series of short, steep buttresses on land belonging to another farmer—equally forbidden to climbers, but less visible and hence less strictly-keepered. It was under this that we were now making our way, and it was obvious from the fresh chalk marks that climbing still takes place here. It was obvious for another reason as well:

"Look at this!" Pete turned to me, a Coke tin in his hand. "And this, and this" he carried on, pointing to

Climbing on Craig y Forwyn—this is what our own irresponsibility has denied us.

chalk and cigarette packets strewn around. He didn't need to elaborate. The inference was obvious. Here, in as delicate and crucial a situation as you can find, climbers were coming and behaving as dirtily and unthinkingly as at the time of the worse complaints against them. I was incredulous at the evidence of their stupidity.

We crept along silently to Pete's chosen route—Mojo, an old artificial route which now goes free at E1, 5b, through a series of massive roofs up the front of the buttress left of The Great Wall. Underneath the line we geared up quietly and Pete set off. The start is technical, balancey and strenuous at the same time and leading to some vigorous stretches and pulls. Pete was huffing and puffing, complaining about his weight and lack of practice, climbing a bit jerkily at first but looking competent, organised and good. He scampered up to the first roof, traversed across and pulled round to beneath the second. Then we were spotted. A voice rang up at us, ordering us off. We grimaced at each other and kept quiet. I got my tape-recorder ready. Pete finished the pitch. By the time he was belayed, out on the lip of the roof 60ft directly above my head, there was a rustling in the undergrowth. I switched on the tape, its mike peeping out from under my jacket. Two large dogs, one of them a Rottweiler, appeared, followed by a solid, unsmiling man in red overalls and with long, sandy-coloured hair.

I knelt down and held the back of my hand out to the Rottweiler. It came lolloping over, wagging its stub of a tail, the other dog soon joining it in the quest for attention. Give me dogs any day as regards making friends. Mr Webb—for he it was—stood meanwhile with hands on hips watching this apostasy on the part of his animals, and then the conversation started:

"Off you get—this is for the birds, not for humans!"

"It's not as easy as that!" Peter shouted down from above.

"Well just bloody well get off—come on!"

"They seem to be shooting the birds from the number of cartridge cases lying about," I suggested.

"Is that right? It's probably other trespassers as well, isn't it? Now come on, old boy—off you get. There's a good lad."

"How're we going to do this, Jim?" queried Pete.

"Try jumping," Mr Webb replied, "You've got loads of bloody things hanging there."

"Can't you put the rope round the tree," I said, then noticed there was no tree, just a dog-rose growing out of the rock.

"I'm just wondering how we're going to get the gear

out," was Pete's response, so I turned to Mr Webb, who was watching, stony-faced.

"Would it really be a huge imposition if I were to go up there after him?" I inquired, keeping the ironic tone concealed.

"To the top?"

"Yes."

"Well, that's alright so long as you get off afterwards."

He was softening, facially, in his physical stance, in the pitch of his voice.

"We don't want to inconvenience you, but it would be easier for us that way."

"Alright," he agreed, "but please don't come again—this has been closed for three-and-a-half years." His voice was almost pleading.

"Has it?"

"Yes."

"Why's that?"

"Oh, I don't want to get into all that."

He backed away. I followed to keep him in range of the microphone.

"Oh, go on—what're your reasons?"

"Because I choose to have it that way—it's because of all the mess and shit—and I mean shit—and all the language that comes off here. I do not want to know!"

"But surely not everyone's like that?"

"No—but a fair proportion are, I can tell you."

"Well personally I'd be appalled if any of my fellow-climbers were to insult you or prejudice your livelihood, but . . ."

"Look—50% of climbers are great, and if it were just that 50% I wouldn't mind. But I tell you what—the other 50% are such a load of bloody rubbish that I don't want to know about it."

"I tend to agree with you," I said, realising he meant *High* readers, "but couldn't you . . ."

"No! I don't want the bother! All I want is my back garden, which this is—my house is there—I want my back garden kept clear, that's all. That's not much to ask, is it? There are loads of places you can climb in North Wales, aren't there?"

"True, but this is very useful because of the weather down here—that's the advantage of it."

"I hear this from all the climbers, and I understand the attractions of it. But you have to respect people's privacy, and that's the way it is."

"Yes, but if climbers did respect your privacy by courtesy and good behaviour, isn't it far enough away from your house and well enough hidden? Wouldn't it be reasonable then for you to allow them the use of it?"

"Yes, but you can't control the numbers, my friend!" he responded excitably, "There were 60 people up here one Sunday—and not one of them had asked permission. I had six notices down there requesting people not to climb without permission and they'd all been torn off the trees."

"But that's criminal damage. If you wanted to do something about it, why didn't you get the police in at the time and have the culprits dealt with?"

"Of course it's criminal damage, and I tell you what—it would be more than criminal if I could find them. And if my sons could find them, God help them, because those notices were engraved plastic, and quite a costly item, you know. And they were firmly fixed in place, so they must have taken a lot of trouble to get them down. And that's not all. I don't know—I've found blokes climbing with sticks on their backs ready to beat off the birds. I've found bird's nests all over the bloody floor here in the spring . . ."

"That sort of mindless vandalism is again actually criminal," I butted in. "You face very substantial fines, and rightly so, for that sort of thing. Surely, if you want to bring about a change in behaviour, you have a responsibility to bring those people to account."

"I know—but usually they've gone, they're half way to somewhere else by the time I've found out."

"Car numbers?"

"I've got other things to do—all I ask now is to be left alone."

"I'm sure you do, but in a sense it's unfortunate that you live underneath a natural amenity of which people would very much like to make use."

"Yes—and in the future I might let them hire it from me at a very substantial fee. And it would have to be substantial to make up for the disturbance. You don't know what it's like down there. It's quiet and peaceful and then suddenly you get 30 or 40 people up here shouting and calling instructions—the instructors are the worst—and this and that—and you may as well go and live on the A55."

"And you came here just for the quiet of the place?" I asked softly. I was beginning to sympathise.

"Yes—and it *was* quiet when I came. So—it's very difficult isn't it?"

"There's certainly no easy answer."

"No—and believe you me, if there was an easy answer, I would take it. But short of giving it to the RSPB—and if I did they've said they'd warden the place constantly . . ."

"What birds nest here?"

I rapped out the question knowing that his response one way or the other would prove his good or bad faith. When it came, it was as precise and honest as I could have wished.

"There's a colony of jackdaws which has unusual characteristics; there are sparrowhawks, kestrels, tawny and little owls. There are ravens, which are not common in this area . . ."

"It would be in your best interest, then, to get it listed as a protected site."

"It already is a Site of Special Scientific Interest."

"There are other SSSIs where people are allowed to climb."

"Not on this one they're not, because I've withdrawn any permission I gave previously. That's understood by the NCC, so again, you see, it's protected that way. If you saw the disregard that a lot of climbers have for the bird life, you'd understand my anger."

"I understand it anyway, and I certainly think it shameful the way some climbers do behave in that regard. But I think it's a *very* small minority . . ."

"No, it isn't I'm afraid—far from it—there's a sizeable proportion, a surprisingly sizeable proportion. I'd guess in excess of 20% of people who call themselves climbers—now there are climbers and climbers, aren't there?—misbehave like that. These fellows who strip off and go through the business of posing and so on—they don't come under the heading of climbers for me."

"Well, I'm not of that generation, as you can see!" I laughed, but I knew exactly what he meant. He went on:

"Another thing I'll tell you, when they used to park their cars on the road down there, we had four men urinating over the fence right in front of my kitchen window. And then, having parked their car on my land and pissed in my garden, told me to fuck off when I got up here, threatened me with violence."

"I can imagine local feeling does get incensed at that kind of behaviour."

"On another occasion the police came to my house and asked me to stop the climbing because they couldn't get emergency vehicles along this road. I couldn't get a trailer down it one Sunday, it was that bad, so you certainly couldn't have got a fire engine or an ambulance down it. So we're stuck with all sorts of problems, really."

"You seem very reasonable about it—most people subjected to those levels of abuse, would themselves become abusive."

"I'm ashamed of myself on occasions—I do get hot—

but there are other ways, and other attitudes from people."

"So if everyone were talking courteously as we're doing now, and were understanding of the other person's point of view, the problems wouldn't be there for you?"

"Quite—and eventually it may well open up, but only when I can see positive control. I can't say I'll give permission to 100 people to come here, because you'd then get 1000 people."

"And you'd have no checks and guards on who did come." I mused aloud.

"No—I *don't* know what the answer is, but at the moment I just want this cliff left alone, and its bird life left alone."

"It's a marvellous place and always has been—I first came here years ago and really liked it then."

"It's a special place, isn't it?" he agreed.

"The whole valley is, and it's an absolute tragedy that you get loutish behaviour in a place like this which then denies it to everyone."

Our conversation was petering out into platitudes. I was standing there in the wood at the bottom of the crag with a fundamentally decent and friendly man, wondering how I would feel if I looked through my kitchen window and saw four louts pissing over my garden wall, threatening me, telling me to fuck off from land which I sought to preserve in its natural splendour and then treating that same land with total disregard. It put it all into context for me—that, and the litter we'd seen, and his sense of place—expressed through the tone and inflection of his voice rather than his words. There was no doubt in my mind that the value he puts on the place is far more empathic and civilised than that of the climbers whose litter and painted route-names and graffiti and shit are scattered about for everyone to see, and which in his eyes, and mine also, defile the place.

I said goodbye to him, turned to the rock, and started to climb, stiff and cold and without much enthusiasm. Mojo is a brilliant, audacious climb, a little masterpiece, but I had no stomach for it. I felt saddened and angered. Just that morning I'd read some ungrammatical and ill-considered maunderings in another outdoor magazine about how everything's alright with climbing. When situations like this can come about and fester on over spans of years, it's plainly not. But what causes them? Is it that people no longer take the traditional approach to the sport as an extension of their initial love of the hills, and thus no longer learn the humility and respect which wild places engender? Is their irreverence for, their

brutalisation of, these special places the mirror-image of their own brutalisation by an uncaring and aggressive government which can coldly consign whole sectors of those under its governance to despair? Is it their own downwards-directed tyrannical reaction to the erosion of civil liberties? Is it the trickle-down effect from the amorality of those who rule? Can you imagine, say, people in Benny Rothman's day fighting for access to Kinder Scout and behaving towards that landscape in this way?

I fumbled Pete's karabiners out of the protection pegs on Mojo's last roof and swung out heavily to join him on the lip. We were both silent and chastened by the conversation to which Pete had been a bird's-eye witness. I led on through. The top wall is all overgrown now, dog-roses with their flaming hips wreathing the cracks, thyme sprouting golden-leaved and fragrant from the crevices. Do those who train on walls notice the absence of these things? When the regional competitions which commercial bodies are planning even now come in, will those who take part so much as feel the slightest sense of loss for them? Pete joined me on top. A rabbit darted away, stabbing at the gorse thicket, panicked by our presence. Two kestrels drifted past on shadowy, golden wings. We climbed down the gully, used by someone from the top here as a rubbish chute, in darkness. It is no use my preaching. As a climber, I am old, best days long gone, no hope of providing a role-model for younger generations. But someone like Pete, with years of improving ability ahead of him—where does he stand? With the louts and vandals? No!

"Perhaps we just deserve to lose this place! That bloke Webb—he wasn't bullshitting. He seems a good guy, and he's right to complain. He's right to do what he's doing . . ."

There will come a day when the hope and the decency and the reverence are restored, when the communications are re-opened, when the education into love of place flows freely and the faith in the restorative power of their beauty is widely shared again, when the Social Contract and the responsibilities that freedom entails are freely entered into through education and choice. It will take a massive social reaction against prevailing mores to bring it about. But it will come. And until it comes and despite my political beliefs, I cannot help but think that John Webb is right to stop and to check, even by an exclusion which rebounds on all of us, the destruction of a place that he, palpably, holds more dear than we do. Nor will it stop here, with John Webb and Craig y Forwyn. Last year Malham was nearly lost to us because of climbers' behaviour. Before that Chapel Head Scar, Cheddar—the list runs on. We only have a right to these places insofar as we accept our responsibility towards them—and instead we have traduced and betrayed it. "True liberty," Rousseau wrote in his *Letters from the Mountain,* "is never destructive of itself". If John Webb teaches us that—as I firmly believe he desires to do—then far from the villain he is so often portrayed as being, he may well turn out to be an example and a hero to us all.

Better Out Than In
High, 1986

For the last half-hour I have been lying on top of this rounded rock, this wind-sculpted orb of gritstone, watching the light drain out of Goldsitch Moss. When I first heaved myself on to it, after I had finished climbing for the night and was still shaky with adrenalin-release, the coverlet of heather and bilberry stretched across the pillowy backs of the buttresses was glowing with sunlight and looked soft and warm as a bed. Since I was in that psychochemically induced state of heightened perception so frequently consequent on having been a little frightened, it was also vibrantly bright, pulsating with colour and the extreme clarity which often comes after brief showers of rain. Whilst I watched, the peaks and waves of this spectrum slowly flattened into darkening monotones. As if to compensate, the whole turreted and pinnacled escarpment of Baldstones and Newstones was suddenly aflame—fiery coals, beacons studding the black moor. And now these too are fading and night is wiping the pastels from the western skyboard. Sitting up to catch the last of its splendour, my short day's activity over, the dramatic inevitability of it all has left me quite at peace with the world.

Scenes like this are, I would imagine, a commonplace within the lives of those who have devoted their free time or even their whole lives to the rocks and hills. It's possible that many amongst them would dismiss the attempt to describe, re-capture, re-create the experience as a vain and worthless exercise, mere literary pretension. After all, it's not an account of stirring deeds, it's not an entree to the company of heroes, and musing on times like these will never bring you admission to the in-crowd of the day. Nor, for that matter, does it encircle the heads of the literal-minded with the diadem of information, and a climber, as we all know, is a graduate of Coketown

Academy, "a man of realities, a man of facts and calculations, a man who proceeds upon the principle that two and two are four, and nothing over, and who is not to be talked into allowing for anything over."

Or is he?

I was talking the other day with someone who was convinced that the sport had no future and that it was about to die. "It was just something that lasted a hundred years and then fizzled out," he argued. "No more worthwhile new routes, you see—the only place left for it to go is into competition, and that's a dead end if you're in a sport which is coming up against the technical limits."

If you permit for a moment the idea that he might be right, then what you have is the vision of a sport whose *raison d'etre* lies in terms of objectively quantifiable performances. As the scale of achievement deals in ever-more-minute gradations, and the degree of media-inflation, hyperbole and acclaim is ever-more-exaggerated, a gap opens up and the realisation of absurdity breaks through to diminish the sport. How can we acknowledge greatness in a new route which merely occupies the space between this climb and that, the rules for which debar the use of holds on either? How can we find much to cheer about in the fact that Chrissie Gullsplatt got a clear round of 10s from the judges in the female freestyle (top-roped) section of the Ackers/Unibond ("Even Chrissie Gullsplatt can't glue herself to the rock as close as Tubagluc") British Climbing Championships? The contention that climbing is dead is pretty likely to come true if this *were* the way it's all going.

But is it?

I've always had a good deal of faith in the British climbing population at large. I reckon they're as gullible, as philistine, as narrow and prejudiced as any other sector of the populace. You can play on their feelings and flatter their egos and get away with it all—for a while! And then they'll turn round and they'll say, "Hang on a minute—what is all this? What's it got to do with what *we're* in climbing for? You won't catch me down the Ackers watching some charade of a climbing competition on a fine Sunday morning. I've got no wish to do the third ascent of Libidinous Librarian Meets the Meninblack (E8, 7b) on Squirt Buttress, Little Muddy Dale, even if I had the time to abseil down it, place all the gear, chalk the holds, give them the odd tap so that they fit the configuration of my fingers, then spend a week rehearsing the moves before ritually leading it. And for that matter, I've no particular wish to

John Beatty out at the Grinah Stones, Bleaklow.

kiss the bum of Chrissie Gullsplatt, even if I could be bothered waiting in the queue of others who are all too ready to do just that—and pay for it! Anyway, I gather she's already signed up with Andrea Smellmould to do a series of videos for Incubus Films, and Aleel O'Dono-thin of CBC has her on an exclusive contract for interviews—I read that in the magazines!''

The magazines! We have a lot to answer for, and it's about time we began to redress the balance. Climbing, as I understand it—and I've no doubt that understanding is partial and imperfect, but it is at least derived from 30 years in which I've spent the vast majority of my leisure time *out there* on the hills and mountains—is not about the great (great?) deeds of the particular in-group to which you belong, or desire to belong. It's not about worshipping some distant, lofty hero or writing your name in six-point print in the back of a guidebook or the new route section of a magazine. It's about friendship and comradeship and fair, impartial assessment, not in-group bitchiness and who frigged this, chipped that or dogged the other. It's about standing by your mates

and serving as best you can this community of interest to which you belong. It's about taking yourself out into wild or beautiful or taxing (or even at best all three together) environments and enjoying yourself amongst them, being exercised and thrilled and moved and perhaps brought to a state of peace by them. And the most satisfying achievements always lie within the bounds of your own consciousness.

You don't need me to tell you this. If you're a climber you already know it, and it's what brings you back to seek out the experience time and again. An hour ago I set off up the front face of Baldstones Pinnacle. I did that hard (hard?) little overhanging groove at the bottom without too much effort, felt good, and thought to continue up the slabby wall above to the top. Judging by the amount of granular lichen on the rounded breaks, it's not a very popular route. And it's also rather awkward and committing to start this upper section. But it looked as if it might get easier higher up, so I made the act of faith and on I went. You know the rule—a hard move at 20ft is harder than a similarly hard move at

10ft, and a hard move at 40ft is harder than either. Well the upshot of it was that at the top of Baldstones Pinnacle there is a distinctly difficult move. I know this to be subjectively true, because I rubbed my nose against it, I scrubbed the lichen off its bevelled edges with my fingers, and the distance above the rocky ground registered in my mind. I also knew that if I'd rehearsed it, or abseiled down it to look at the holds, or if I'd had a no.3 RP to put in a little ragged incipient crack at chest height, and a second holding the rope, any one of those would have halved the rate of my heart beat. What I got instead, as I anxiously scanned the top for likely holds, was a large drop of rain full in the face, then another and another—a downpour, in fact, and I could not have retreated down the moves I'd made if I'd tried. So I told myself that if I did not make the last moves impeccably and right away, then I was going to get hurt.

I made the moves.

Which is why I'm sitting on top of this rock, a bit smug maybe at having saved my skin yet again, quite alone, with the darkness falling now. It's getting a little cold and, as I said, I've finished climbing for the night. But I think I know something of what it's about and, thinking about what's *in* at the moment, it makes me pretty grateful to be *out* here, still experiencing, still enjoying and being thrilled and moved by it all . . .

October
The Book of the Climbing Year, 1987

It is the eighth month, the harvest month. Except that it is no longer the eighth month but the tenth, whatever it may have been to the ancient Romans (who had only ten months, of which this was the eighth). This is to play with number (Numa was the inventor of January and February), which they say holds sway over the flux. But count the days, count the lunar cycles as we will, we cannot allay loss of the green hours, or even divert the trickle of time. This is the red month, the year brittle with age and ready for the fire. The tendon snags in its sheath, the bone once broken nags its pain; but the days are so few now that we have to stumble on. The equinox is past; beyond the year's Rubicon, light gives way to the night.

You should start climbing in the spring of the year and the life—giving the impulse time to establish itself before the fingers chill and winter comes. Also, because you are set thus in the cycle your senses feel no dissonance between activity and age, attune more directly therefore to that which we should notice in the environments amongst which we move: the jackdaw chicks which hissed at our hand in that April crack; the hyacinth fragrance of bluebells beneath those boulders in May; or purple-veined Lloydia around us in all its delicate rarity as we lay on that Devil's Kitchen ledge the next day—all are chiming with our green age. Memories accumulate, to enrich in the long perspective the landscapes they inhabit. Come October, comes their synthesis, and the time to gather, revisit, re-live.

Let magic be encountered early. Do you know the painting by Turner, "Norham Castle at Sunrise"? It is all yellows, mauves, ochres and almost gentian-blue shadows, utterly saturated with colour yet delicate withal and unformed, the shapes unresolved, shimmering, optimistic. There is perhaps a valley, a castle, a cow, but as yet we cannot quite tell for behind the picture's gentian heart the sun's presence is veiled, not stated. It puts me in mind always of the October days in my first season's climbing. Do you remember what it was like to be awakened by daylight on your first outdoor mornings? You are in the Grand Hotel, say, as the carved name above Robin Hood's Balcony Cave at Stanage calls it. Your companions (having had a skinful of beer in The Scotsman's Pack last night which you, as a thirteen-year-old, could not afford and were not allowed) are still snoring. You slither, in your sleeping bag across the sandy floor, out of the entrance, over to the lip of the ledge and look out beyond. The cold air of morning on your bare shoulders causes you to shiver a little and shrink down in your cocoon. In front of you, from the pupa and chrysalis of the night, are being enacted the birth pangs of the butterfly day. There is a seawash and a swirl of white mist in the valley floor. It is all in motion, vaporous tongues licking at elephant peaks which laze on a white savannah: Win Hill, Lose Hill, Bleaklow. stretched out, with the sun not yet risen behind you so the colours are muted—but they will come, the bracken will crackle aflame amongst spectrums of heather, the mist will boil and distil, suggestion will resolve into form, it will all happen before your eyes on this autumn morning of your youth with much of your life before you and the whole day in which, perhaps, to climb.

Gritstone's the rock for autumn, the rowan fronds bright-berried across its grey-green walls, the leaves gathering to rot down in the dank undercliff, the fairy toadstools in the woods beneath. Its scale is all so appropriate. The day less expansive now, the intimacy of the crags keys in to the season as if the months' passage had shape-softened them into their blunt roundness of character. Every year, Indian summer! Or so it seemed in youth. It is not the great memories necessarily which remain. They have become too token, too oppressively of their stage of life, too often relived. It is the small glimpses come at by chance which retain their capacity for surprise. On a London train, during dull discussion at a committee, or sitting on your child's bed waiting to read him a story when he comes from cleaning his teeth, suddenly you're transported to *that* climb, *that* October day so very long gone. It is here now! There is no continuity. It is a single frame, a still from the life-film , a scene you'd always cut in the editing of your own story. Wait now—let me focus. There is a boy, slim and dark-haired, the rock and his clothes both drab against the autumn leaves. He is looking up, holding the rope, shouting encouragement. I turn to listen, half-irritated, testily ask to be allowed to concentrate. This is what I am concentrating on—a scoop just above knee-height in the surface of the rock, a ripple rubbed clean by the wear of feet, a rawness, pink flesh of sandgrains showing through. It glows in the afternoon sun. The rope runs down freely into his hands, no runners. He is thirty feet below and to one side. There are boulders beneath. Grains of sand, solidified, bite into the soles of my boots. I can feel them intensely, not in their individuality but in their effect. His voice comes up again, intrudes into my enjoyment of the feel of my body, its springy relaxedness on this sloping foothold, its caress of the round edge which I must somehow use to pivot around, to impel me upwards to that hold three feet out of reach above. The mind is at work, grappling with aesthetic conviction, calculating moment and force, and all of it instinctively done. My right fingertips, wrist cocked, squeeze the edge. I palm the rock with my left hand, leaning that way, curve out my knee and lift the rim of my right boot in total enjoyment of the precise, easy movement as it places itself just so in the scoop. And then—it is happening—the electric impulse from foot to hand to hip, and their suave hoist, reciprocity and interlock. Ah! I have made of those moves an elegance! I have done them well! There is happiness, smiles, relaxation. It will sustain me tomorrow in school as I stumble through the conjugation of irregular Latin verbs which I ought at this moment to be learning. It all fades. It is all gone. I am back on my son's bed with *The Magic Paintbrush* in my hand again and the first time I ever did Sunset Slab on Froggatt returns to the brain cell which holds it, to delight again, perhaps, at some future time, or to die in darkness.

The companionship, the friends you've made, figure large in these memories. Good days in good company have their own rich warmth and flavour to impart. Roll the years forward from that scene on Froggatt, and more than two decades later an October day in 1982 flickers on to the screen. Stanage again, but this time with Jill Lawrence. We drive down to it through all the furls and rolls of purple moorland by Langsett and Ladybower. If I had been taken out of time for those twenty years and were suddenly returned to the scene, the contrast would astonish. The crowds swarm, cars are parked on either side of the road in either direction for half a mile and more. The climbers themselves are so different. All the fawns and ragged greys, the tattered jumpers, the rusting krabs, the furry grey stiffness of nylon ropes and slings, have given way to bright multiplicity of colour and a purposeful adornment of equipmental intricacies. Yet the gaiety of outward show, the harlequin pants and jingle of Rock and Friend, is balanced by a seriousness of demeanour. These climbers are intent on acquisition, on attainment of objectives. Things will not just happen, they will be made to happen. It is not a world in which the friends with whom I grew up could easily have belonged. I try to imagine characters like Arthur Nirk and Pie-can and Brian Sullivan dressed up like this and behaving like this, and laugh aloud at how they would have relished the former, rejected and ruined the composure of the latter. But our old anarchic world of *outside* is subsumed now into convention and formality.

Still, we have arrived and parked at Stanage and if we look along the crag, there are great gaps in the crowds. It is only by the collectable routes that the people mill and gather. We walk up along the broadening track with the hillsides around not vibrant as they are in spring or in evening sunlight after rain, but pulsing with a soft resonance of light. It is easy at times to understand those old theories of the objects of vision transmitting not reflected but their own light to the eye. It is like the miracle of sitting by a fire of coal or wood on winter evenings and feeling in its heat and flame the release of energies born of ancient sunlight.

We arrived at the crag. Geraldine Taylor had just come down after a session working on The Dangler and that induced more positive thoughts. If ever a route had offered gender-stereotyping, even down to the matter of its name, it was The Dangler—the big, butch, macho crack up which real men with real muscles forced their

way, the whole scenario replete with images of sexual energy and violation. Yet I remember Barry Webb in drunken play swinging unroped across its roof on his way back from the pub. I remember the last time I did it, a year or two ago, cocksure, keyed in to memory bank with my imagination on other things, like a jaded lover going through the motions. But at the lip, my fingers on the edge, the programme went blank. I pulled up, people watching, the last runner too far back, arms weakening, unable to reach into the top crack, panic and impotence hovering, the memory-message insistently pleading the move's straightforwardness and ease and the body crying out that it was not so, this ridiculous conflict continuing until the logical mind stepped in: "Look, old chap, you just throw your right elbow over and get in an arm lock." Ah, so you do! Panic subsides, tension dissipates, laughter supervenes. "Just thought I'd do a few pull-ups for exercise, Pete," I call down, and afterwards expiate this arrogant irony by confessing to

him my panic and forgetfulness.

Jill and I talk with Geraldine. She is excited, fired by a desire, insistent, working logically on mistake and weakness, psyching up for the next attempt, at which she will get it right. It is good to watch someone in this honest and painful process. We move along the crag, take the traditional entry into a day by soloing the Rusty Wall routes—up Rugosity, with its skip-and-cling of a 5c first move, down Green Crack; up Rusty Wall of the pinch-and-lurch, down Via Media; up Via Dexter, cautiously, and down Oblique Crack. The feel of the rock, the sense of its friction, the tuning of the body-pitch, is achieved. We move on. It is to be a day on the classics. Harding's Super-direct finish to the Cave Innominate comes first, a wild, swinging one-armed jug-pull right at the top of the crag and surely one of the best 15–ft routes in Britain.

We pass on through the crowds and fetch up at Pedlar's Slab, snort with disgust at the chipped hold at its

Pedlar's Slab, Stanage. Photo John Beatty

ing and enables us both to move better and more rhythmically. It is the desire that the other should enjoy the routes that is coming out, and not that so-often-dreadful-in-its-effect game where the other must be outdone. On Pedlar's Rib—my own route and one of which I'm inordinately proud—I step up blind-footed and ask if my boot's on the hold before moving on. She guides it there. At her turn I stand beneath, confident and aware of what she can do and remind her of the hold not obvious from where she is. It is the brief gestures, the respectful minimalism of assistance, the arm slipped round a waist and then away again, not in sexual play but in friendship and support, which state the harmony, and thrill and thank. The day goes on: The Unconquerables, Goliath's Groove, Wall End Slab Direct, Tower Face Direct. There is a cool, gold wind blowing across the crag and a rhythm of chatter and silence between us. On Tower Face I watch her face on those creaking flakes which make the climb far harder than its given grade of HVS 5a and marvel at the honesty of emotion portrayed there: alertness, apprehension, the awareness of vulnerability. It is all so different to the non-expression of rock technocracy. And the bodily movements too have an effortless, rhythmical quality quite different to the thrusting economy of the best male climbers. Their characteristic is a lightness, a fluidity of movement centering around the pivot of the hips, an exquisite and almost formalised balance like that of Indian dance.

The crowds have drifted away as we work back—though work is the wrong word for this activity—along the crag. The light's going as we descend, and there are different points of the compass to which we must head. She goes north, my way's west. There is a spontaneous embrace by the cars at the recognition of how it was, a brief, warm, laughing, unerotic kiss—one of those moments of contact which make endurable the deserts of solitude—and all's then given over into October memories, harvested and stored away on the long drive west.

And West is the real October country. There is the low-angled light slanting into the hills and against the cliffs. There is the way the richness of texture in the rocks, the veins and foldings, the crystals and the ribs and the stippled lichens soak in the soft brilliance of the sun. There are the hillside woods like old tapestry or brocade, which seem to tell of stories set there. Wales—the text of its landscape is more resonant than that of any other country. And all the stories and histories have that autumn twilight quality, diffused and haunting and lingering down the sterile times of winter coming—for

base and work through its three-route repertoire—the slab, the arete, the rib, soloing again, building up an ease and support between us that relaxes into the climb-an industry, for a people, for a culture. They are so old, as old as the year in October. They rustle their suggestions amongst the quiet places of the hills, the soft clatter of their names like leaf-fall in a forest. In that oak-tree roosted the eagle from whose flesh the maggots fell. This split rock here was cleft by the flung spear. But it was so long ago. The barracks of the quarryman who came after that time, they are occupied now by the elder and the ash. Where the kettle hissed after the day's work, the leaf falls; where the fire flamed, the rowan flames. That wall blew down in the equinoctial gales, but who knows how long ago? It is gone, the memory, just as this year is going to join it, just as our years have added something before they rot, or are lost, or used up from the long store.

October, you are crowded with ghosts. Here, walking by my side over the road from Deiniolen with the morning sun in our faces, is John Brazinton. I am not even sure of the year—the autumn of 1969, perhaps, or 1970? We trek from Deiniolen to Llech Ddu, on foot, the wild ponies winter-coated now and watchful across the Afon Llafar, the grass bleached tawny summerlong by the sun and rain, the path squelchy with moisture. It is a return visit. Once before this same year I have come this way—to climb The Groove with Brian Fuller, that strange, sardonic, yet somehow likeable member of the Rock and Ice and Bradford Lads generation whose nickname was Fred the Ted. We had arrived beneath the great scar of rock up which The Groove cleaves its way, sat down to talk and gear up, and heard a whistling in the air above us. A sheep, fallen from a ledge 400ft up, landed 20ft away, spattering us with blood and intestine. We joked about it, wiped ourselves clean, took out sandwiches, and were disturbed by another whistling in the air. The same again, almost the identical place. We felt nauseated. Minutes passed. We roped up, studied the first groove. A shadow hung in the air above us, whooshed past, exploded by its two former companions, predeceased. We felt hunted, crept away to a quiet VS round the corner.

But this time, with John, the mood is lighter-hearted. He, at 19 or 20, is my apprentice and I, at 22 or 23, am supposed to be the young star and we want to do the route as near free as can be. Mo and Cam (neither of them ever known by anything other than these names), who did the first ascent four or five years beforehand, had given perhaps the only completely honest first ascent description written for a post-war route in Wales, mentioning every point of attachment used, whether for aid or gardening. Either through malice or uninformed

gossip, thereafter the climb had been looked on as over-aided, four or five aid-points in 400ft.

It is odd how fragmented your memories become over long periods of time. Three sections only of the route come back to me. There is a wet, loose, dripping bulge somewhere near the beginning—perhaps on the second pitch—where I had to layback on a downward spike which moved out towards me as if daring me to see what would happen if I pulled harder. There is a traverse left across a steep wall, with hard, blind moves into a shallow groove where a sidepull came off in my hand and I nearly swung off with it, and turned to swear at John for no better reason than that he was the only thing around who would take any notice. And finally, there is a stance in slings in the groove itself from which The Groove gets its name, and the near-disappointment of just pulling from hold to hold in an easy ecstasy of strength. I remember very little, then, about the route, nothing about getting back down to the foot of the crag, only vaguely recall the peaceful trudge out along Cwm Llafar towards the evening sun and the descent in darkness into Bethesda. But it's as clear as yesterday to me, the pleasure of going into the Douglas Arms and finding Keith Carr there in a corner of the front room.

Keith was a member of the Wallasey Mountaineering Club, which was one of the liveliest and most anarchic organisations ever to have graced the society of Welsh climbing. It had its heyday in the late fifties and early sixties, and was based at a club hut which was a converted barn set on a hillock right in the middle of Nant Gwynant, beneath Clogwyn y Wenallt. The club had close associations with Ogwen Cottage before that place became the staid outdoor centre of a local education authority. Its members were people like Mo Anthoine, Davey Jones, Ginger Cain, Terry Vasey, all of whom were climbing at the very top standards of the time, but it wasn't as a climbing ginger-group that the Wallasey was well-known. It was the originator of the tradition of the wild party which reached its climax in the Al Harris bacchanals of fifteen or twenty years later. The barn in the Gwynant was the perfect site—no fear of intrusion, objection or the giving of offence. The beer would be imported by the barrel, there would be none of the strobe-and-disco suppressions of the daemonic imagination on the crutches of which today's partygoers lean. Instead there were the evil geniuses, the out-drinking, out-phasing and out-grossing gamesmen (and women) and performers, all thrashing around in pursuit of the fiercest squeal of shock or outrage the evening could produce. Whose is that body the head belonging to which is under ---'s skirt? Why is Joe Brown helplessly giggling on the floor in a corner? What is the well-known warden of a mountain centre doing walking around dressed in nothing but his wife's underclothes? When will those three figures thrashing on the top bunk roll senseless to the floor? You shall see—the rhythm builds to a crescendo, noise and hilarity and confusion mount. The lords of misrule are gathering and this is of what their climax consists. A space clears round the stove in the centre of the barn. The men throw off their clothes and roll tightly a spill of newspaper—the older hands rolling it the more tightly for slower combustion. They light it at the stove, clench it between their buttocks and dance round in fiery, smokey display, the women cheering them on. Those who have not rolled the spill tightly enough soon shriek, clasp their posteriors and mingle back amongst the watchers. The cunning old foxes dance on, their wives and girlfriends re-lighting the brand when it smoulders out. Smoke coils into the rafters and the flames reflect on faces whose humours are worthy of Bruegel. The hilarity pitches higher and hysterically higher until the last dancer pirouettes incombustible and supreme. And then every man who has taken part ritually gathers round to piss on the stove. *Epater les Bourgeois*? It is the ultimate example, something of which even the Great Beast Aleister Crowley could have been proud, and it was enacted most weekends at these Wallasey parties under the legendary title, "dance of the flaming arsehole".

It was over times like these that Keith Carr, John Brazinton and myself squawked and joked this October evening in The Douglas, and continued late into the night back at his house in Mynydd Llandegai before John and myself walked back to Deiniolen over the moor in the moonlight, with the sea glinting down in Caernarfon Bay and the light on Llanddwyn Island flashing out to us. It sounds degenerate, yet was anarchically innocent and uninhibited and a part of what the climbing scene then was. You'd be arrested for it these days. *The Star* would do an exclusive on you. The December Day School of climbing writers would pen letters to the magazines proclaiming that your activities are frivolous, enforce sexual stereotypes and degrade the spectators. Perhaps they do, but I'd rather keep company with those who *played* thus than their puritan, prurient successors or the hard-faced mercenaries who now clamour to make a killing or a reputation from the sport. Then, it was fun, as naive and feckless as children's play. But the play's gone, the summer's over, the nights are drawing in. John and Keith, companions in

reminiscence those many years ago, are both dead: John killed by stonefall in the Chamonix Aiguilles the season after we did our route together, having volunteered typically to go back up to the foot of a route to collect his and his partner's sack. And Keith, in his forties, of cancer or another such gratuitous disease. All along your path you lose the friends you make and only your memory keeps their names alive: John, with whom I enjoyed a single day's climbing of a quality I've not often known; Keith, in whose warmth and wit I've basked and revelled many times in the pubs and convivialities of the climbing world. The months, the years draw on. The leaves fall.

Let me go to the sea to rid myself of this despondent mood! One seaside weekend of October springs to mind. It is 1972. I'm living in London at Ken Wilson's flat but he, arch-enemy and sometime friend that he is and has always been, is not coming on this trip. We are going to Pembroke, which is unfashionable—so much so that Colin Mortlock, myself and a very few others are the only ones to have climbed down there. "We" are John Kingston, Rob Ford and myself, and on the Friday we set off in John's Sunbeam Rapier down the M4, which ends at Cardiff and we bear on down through Morriston and Pontardawe, Carmarthen and St Clear's, rattling on all the while in one of those wonderful London weekend protracted arguments which passes away the long driving hours and covers every topic from politics and the Stock Exchange to sexual anthropology and the invertebrate life of Hemel Hempstead before bringing us after midnight to the deserted and derelict cottages (National Trust holiday lets now) at Stackpole Quay, where we creep upstairs, spread out our sleeping bags on the dusty floor, and rap out our concluding comments before sleep rules all further discussion out of order.

The next morning we breakfast on cream cakes in Pembroke and walk across the untrodden, clean-washed beach of Barafundle to Mowing Word. All those miles of coast along to Stack Rocks from St Govan's, where new routes were done in their hundreds in later years, we ignore. We're not here to pioneer, don't feel like the mental strain involved in that. All we want to do is disport ourselves a little on known rock in the late-season sun. We solo down Square Chimney, always a good little testpiece to see how the nerves will cope with the day's climbing. On the wave-platform beneath we skip across the razor-edged scallopings and walk to the tip of the promontory. The sea's in a lovely green calm, with waving fronds of weed clearly visible deep down in the water. I point out the routes. We traverse round beneath

Jill Lawrence on Tower Face, Stanage.

the south-west face, the sharp rock nicking and grazing at our hands, and gather beneath Cormorant Flake, with the water idly trickling into the little coral pools. I've been thinking that a combination of the first pitch of Heart of Darkness and the top pitch of New Morning would be a perfect combination, so talk John, who's enjoying the rock and the scenery into leading off. I psyche him up for it: "Once you're round that arete, John, it's a hundred feet across an overhanging wall into a bottomless corner, and then forty feet out to a hanging stance!" What I'm omitting to tell him is that huge holds, good jams, ease the strain of the hugely impressive situation. He launches out, disappears round the corner, and is soon chortling with glee. Rob follows, and at John's insistence, to reverse the joke takes all the runners out. The ropes swing across a void. I reach the corner and gulp down my anxiety: "You bastards" I shout across. "V Diff!" John retorts. I know it's not that, and scuttle across before my arms tire. We move on up to a higher stance and I hustle for the top pitch:

"It's all jamming, this, John—you'd better let me lead!"

He does. I exult in it, a perfect thin crack running up an otherwise blank head wall for 70ft, the rock a gorgeous bright orange colour from the sunlit lichen. The jamming's a joy—there's surely no more satisfying technique of climbing, nor any which is more elegant or relaxed. You stretch, place the jam, arch your back, run up your feet, jab in a toe, lock in one-handed, stretch and arch again in a smooth, unhurried flow. It is sensuality in movement. You ration runners to keep the aesthetic line of that rope running down, to conserve strength and maintain the thrill—one good one every 20ft will do! Rob and John run up and rave. We slither down Square Chimney again for another route or two, then give best to the incoming tide and repair to the pub. The next day we go to Mother Carey's Kitchen (which sounds like a local name but isn't), do a few routes, recover a sling left behind a month or two before, already bleached white by the sea, and as the tide comes in again we pack up and drive vociferously back home. Weekends away! What a habit and a delight they once were! But the month's ending. November looms. The clock, which goes always forwards, has gone back. Hallowe'en, All Soul's Night, Samhain, all the pagan festivals of fire and darkness concentrate in the mind.

And at this time of year always there comes back the memory of one particular friend who represented much of what I loved about the world of climbing, with whom I had many of my best times on rock—Al Harris. He died in a car crash on the way to a party in Chester in the late October of 1981.

Either the cars or the parties were bound to have got him in the end. There was the party of the JCB Joust, when two of those machines had been left in a field by his house and Harris's idea was that the perfect game would be a wrestling match between them. So the whole of Bryn Bigil resounded nightlong to the sound of heavy rock music, screeching metal and roaring diesel engines as the mechanical monsters wrestled each other to the ground. Or there were the chicken matches at what's now Dinorwig's Bus Stop Quarry, when Harris had laid in a stock of scrap cars and we took them up there, unhooked the gap in the wire netting specially cut for the purpose, and sent them screaming over one by one into the dark water, their doors taken off first so that we could jump out the more easily at the last minute— Al, Tim Lewis, Nick Estcourt—all the lovely boys whose smiles are dust, all gone before, all burnt in the fire, and the last leaves hang grimly, limp and tired on the trees. I must walk out on the hills. It depresses me too much to think of what has been, of all the dead playboy friends of this western world.

I drive to Cwm Ystradllyn near my home, walk up to the shoulder of Moel Hebog by way of the old, hidden and deserted quarryman's village that has no name beneath Braich y Gornel. The mist circles the hill at the level of the shoulder. It is full of presences, my mind peoples it with memory, projection and desire. With shortening breath I pant on up the slope. A stonechat chips away at silence from a rock. Where the steepness begins to relent, the cloud thins and soon blue sky's above, and a cold wind chills across my face. I wipe the drop from my nose and leave its stain on the light green of my sleeve. Obdurately the body paces itself to the summit cairn, the rough brown rock around it solid, solid, solid to the touch.

Beneath me now Nant Gwynant is fading into shadow, the brilliant golds and ochres, the yellow and orange of the trees mutely retreating out of the light, the lakes lying leadenly amongst them, the knoll where Menlove's ashes were scattered standing out like a peacock's crown in a twilight garden. Behind me, the sun is setting out at the point of the Lleyn. Ynys Enlli, the Isle of the Currents, of the Saints, hides its western Avalon or Eden behind the hump of a hill. I know about Saints, have known some in my time, of all shades from self-abnegation and denial to voluptuousness. Sainthood is the perfect expression of reverence for creation, and Dostoievsky's underground man will tell you, even if by

Stone circle, Rhinogydd.

default, as much about that as the theologians can. It is getting dark now. The slope steepens in the descent. Only Bryn Banog lies before me to complete the circuit, and Moel Ddu, the black hill, which I must cross before I reach home.

6: NOTES ON THE ARTICLES

Keeping Company
Page 15

The pieces in this section are all taken from my regular monthly column "On the Rock", which appears in Climber & Hillwalker *magazine. Looking through the pieces from this series of which I'm most fond, the absence of "famous" names intrigues me. I suspect that the desire for fame is often just another manifestation of the will to power, and both are qualities to which I would not willingly pander. "That which is popular cannot be good"? I'm not sure how far I could go along with Johnson's maxim—at times it strikes me as appalling. But whatever the reason, the everyday, ordinary experiences which these essays describe, the enthusiasms, the diversity of companions, conversations, environments, for me are somewhere near the centre of the outdoor experience.*

No Pain, No Gain: Ron Fawcett
Page 59

Written as an introduction to the instruction manual, Fawcett on Rock, *this seems to have been the right opportunity to assess Fawcett's contribution to climbing. A new marriage, new interests and a new baby have taken him away from the competitive aspects of the sport in recent years. I interviewed him for* Climber & Hillwalker *this year and asked him about his current involvement with the outdoors: "Running round Bleaklow or Win Hill . . . flying and climbing on Stanage. That's what I enjoy doing and what I hope I will always do. My roots are stuck in the climbing community, but for me it's the fun which counts. Working on routes just makes climbing like a job, boring as hell . . ."*

The Character, Life and Times of H. W. Tilman
Page 65

An invitation to lecture on Tilman at the Royal Geographical Society gave me the opportunity to look back on the life of a man I am profoundly grateful to have known. This was the seventh piece I had written about him, and remains my favourite.

Benny Rothman: The Making of a Rebel
Page 73

Whenever I hear comments about the "evil of communism" fall disparagingly from the lips of Mammon- and Lucifer-worshipping conservative politicians, I think about the integrity and human qualities of this man whose worn and peat-stained size five boots few of them are worthy even to lick. But perhaps this is to air a prejudice.

Exploring Eric Shipton
Page 80

For those interested in the life of Shipton, the biography which I've been working on and pondering over for some years and towards which this essay might be considered as work-in-progress, is to be published by Hodder & Stoughton.

The Essential Jack Longland
Page 85

The only time I ever tried to tape-record an interview with Jack Longland, the machine ceased to function after five minutes' conversation. I don't know how valid it is to construct a composite interview in this fashion. As a single conversation, obviously it never took place, but if Landor could indulge himself in wholly imaginary conversations, perhaps there won't be too much objection to this piece's taking a few liberties with chronology in order to synthesize some remarkable memories. The anecdote about Sir Percy Wyn Harris—later an ambassador—and "the fucking soldiery" still makes me chuckle.

Three Obituaries
Page 91

When the Sunday Correspondent *magazine ran a feature on the new style of obituary writing in the quality papers, it singled out that of Len Chadwick, quoting it at length and remarking that it was "memorable, verging on parody". That seemed to sum Len up. He was a huge influence on my early life. An affectionate but not practising homosexual, he used to take me when I was twelve or thirteen to Esperanto discussion groups in a coffee bar at the end of Deansgate in Manchester. I learnt more from them than from any lessons at school. The only things about my association with Len which used to bother my father were his appearance—he used to refer to him dismissively as "That tramp!" and snub him brutally— and the socialist arguments I picked up from the Tuesday evening discussions, with which I used to attack his working-class Toryism. In retrospect, the freedom he allowed me in spending time with Len seems to me— particularly now my own eldest son is the age I was then—both liberal and bravely trusting. But we live, thirty years on, in a changed world. I loved the irony and contrast of this obituary's appearing in the* Telegraph *between those for Brigadier-general Sir Timothy Fenton-Wright and Professor Mallender St. John Smythe.*

Brenda Chamberlain: The Artist Islanded
Page 99

I was living in Bangor at the time of Brenda Chamberlain's death and saw the effect it had on the artistic community there. After this article came out in The Guardian *a correspondent, brandishing many of the tenets of the separatist sorority, wrote in a furious tirade which appeared to centre on how dare a mere man ever presume to write about women. Whilst appreciating the historical and cultural reasons which could lead to the adoption of that stance, it seems to me a mistaken, absurd, and potentially malignant position to hold. As someone who endeavours, no doubt with only varying levels of success, to live by pro-feminist ideals, I put my faith in empathy and the dialectical, and abjure the exclusivist in whatever form it might take. This may be hopelessly simplistic, but it seems to me the only way through to a humane synthesis and balance. Arguments about language, the power-nexus, condescension and paternalism taken as proven, the capacity of oppressed minorities to guilt-trip potential allies in the liberal and ameliorist conscience through unconscionable outbursts of spleen is*

itself an oppression, an egotism and a waste. That resistant energy would be far better employed in being directed against the real aggressors and wielders of power, instead of attacking the fellow-workers towards their demise.

Trust is Just a Five-letter Word
Page 109

This is a slightly revised version of an article which appeared, despite strenuous efforts on the part of the Masonic network which has infiltrated many of this country's senior conservation agencies to suppress it, in Rural Wales/Cymru Wledig, *the magazine of the Council for the Protection of Rural Wales of which I was then editor. These efforts were only defeated by the staunch and vigorous advocacy of Baroness White, Socialist peeress and then-President of the CPRW. Shortly after its publication—which released a flood of rebuttal and abuse in the national press from the National Trust—my position as editor was made untenable and I felt it proper to resign. Within a few weeks of this—perhaps unconnectedly—I became the object of an Inland Revenue tax enquiry. Three years later, the Aberporth expansion saga rumbles on, its proposed effects now spreading even to that holy landscape at the western end of the Lleyn Peninsula. Finally, as a comment on contemporary journalistic ethics, the environment correspondent of a reputable and liberal Sunday newspaper to whom the article had been circulated reproduced its content and even much of its phrasing under his own name and without any acknowledgement of source.*

Mending Your Ways
Page 114

In a context where it is generally alien, to introduce a parabolic dimension can be helpful and enhancing to the debate. And for me, the opportunity to read Bunyan as he should be read—out loud—was pure regression.

Ruth Pinner's Nature Column
Page 126

Bryn Havord, friend and fellow-subversive, asked me to write a nature column under a pseudonym for the pilot of a project he had in mind. The project never got off the ground, but I liked the idea of working towards a female authorial persona, and the memories held here are, in the main, good ones from a generally bad period of my life. my thoughts on the shootists are unprintable, apart from the reflection that no organisation could have a more appropriate logo than the fatuously-titled British Association for Shooting and Conservation, with its bird-brained cur.

The Clear Sight of Janet Haigh
Page 137

As I write this note, in the morning's paper is the report of a speech given by Mrs Thatcher to the Conference of Conservative Women, in which she talked of how, once you have climbed your hill, in front of you still lie further and further summits. Perhaps she should rock back on her heels once in a while and ponder the view. Or perhaps the heels are the problem. This article was sent after publication— along with a detailed picture-file—to the Chairman of the Welsh Water Authority. To his personal credit, the people responsible for the atrocities at Pont Sce-thin were disciplined and a concerted attempt was made at reparation of the landscape.

Native Stones by David Craig, Secker & Warburg, £10.95
Page 154

In an ill-considered moment and at the behest of a charming and importunate young woman from the publishing company's publicity department, I read a few pages of this book's proofs and wrote a "puff" for its jacket. When Sebastian Faulks of The Independent *rang me up to ask me to review it, I pointed out that I'd "puffed" it and that if, on a careful and critical reading, I found myself in dis-agreement with the earlier, less considered opinion, it would be very embarrassing for me. He told me not to worry, and even if I did find that I'd revized my* opinion, just to go ahead and write what I thought. Look-ing back, it was, I think, the right thing to have done, but I am very careful about "puffs" these days.*

Necrophiliacs
Page 160

Gloating is not an admirable trait, but I found myself close to it when the MENFREE expedition turned out to be a fiasco, finding and proving nothing and returning to Britain to a saga of ego-rivalries, money-grubbing and acrimony. The whole story, to me, seemed to resolve into a morality play, like a twentieth-century update of "The Pardoner's Tale". I hope someone writes a novel.

Fictions
Page 174

The only pre-1985 piece in this collection, it was left out of my last collection of essays because of too strong a thematic alliance with the story "Fiction Heroes", which was included and on which it acts as a gloss. As a rearguard statement of belief, it seems to me more important now than it was first written.

Trespassers
Page 176

Time has passed on and Craig y Forwyn still remains closed to climbers. At times, I find myself hoping that it will remain so for years to come, as a reminder of how much we stand to lose if we allow our standards of consideration for others and for the environments in which our activities take place to fall.

Better Out Than In
Page 181

This was more or less the last of my columns written for High *magazine, with which I had been closely associated for five years, and implicit within it are many of the reasons for my leaving. There were grave differences of opinion between myself and Geoffrey*

Birtles, practically over his treatment of the magazine's contributors and ideologically in the matter of editorial direction. I wanted to move further in the expression of "green" responsibility by the outdoor community, in the promotion of young and new writers, and in the celebration of adventurous rather than competitive activity. *I was fortunate, after leaving* High, *to be given the opportunity to do all those things under Cameron MacNeish's supportive and enlightened editorship at* Climber.

7: Envoy

P.S. The hare won . . . Photo John Beatty